Recreational Sports Programming

Recreational Sports Programming

Kathryn G. Bayless, M.S.
Richard F. Mull, M.S.
Craig M. Ross, Re.D.

The Athletic Institute

Copyright © 1983 by The Athletic Institute
ISBN 0-8767-093-8
Printed in the United States of America

Published by:

The Athletic Institute
200 Castlewood Drive
North Palm Beach, FL 33408

Library of Congress catalog number 83-072429

J I H G F E D C B A

TABLE OF CONTENTS

PREFACE

As seemingly insatiable interest for active participation in sport and fitness during the last decade has reached unprecedented proportions, a cultural change has occurred not only in the United States but also in many corners of the world. Sport opportunities for the non-athlete has come of age. The management of recreational sport has reached such significance that its seemingly unlimited potential for growth presents quite a challenge to those responsible for its interpretation and application.

This challenge is met by satisfying the proliferations of participant needs and interests in sport. Regardless of the setting—community, military, commercial, educational, or industrial—the public is not indifferent toward recreational sport, but seeks and expects quality from the providers of recreational services. The attitude and statement, "programming just happens" is a misconception. Quality sports programming is "MADE" to happen by knowledgeable and skilled programmers.

This manual is designed to ensure that the philosophy and programming body of knowledge specific to recreational sport is properly understood and applied. We have developed content for all recreational settings and operations, which should be valuable to all those carrying recreational sport responsibilities.

Our recreational sport programming material represents a "hybrid" concept since it combines theories and practices from both parent fields of Physical Education and Recreation. Consequently, it is relevant to practitioners as well as the undergraduate student studying either discipline. All content matter is practical by design, applicable to the entry-level professional, as well as the highly-sophisticated sports management administrator. We attempt to provide a perspective on current recreational sport programming that may be used to better serve the sport interests of any group.

We have organized our content into three sections: Foundations, Programming Operations, and General Operations. Section I, 'Foundations', provides an introduction to the practical and theoretical bases for sport within the recreative process. This content is presented in answer to basic questions about recreational sport: what, when, why, where, how, and to what extent? This section also focuses on the concept of 'Participant Development', as an underlying purpose and function of recreational sport. Content is presented to increase understanding of how to design programming that will enhance the physical, social, and psychological growth and development of participants. Section II, 'Programming Operations', covers the techniques and methods of recreational sports programming so that any programmer responsible for informal, intramural, extramural or club sport may act with greater confidence. The final portion, Section III, attends to 'General Operations' and incorporates administrative duties with which the programmer may come in contact. The topics covered include personnel, program control, finance, facilities, equipment, safety, planning and evaluation, promotion/publicity and recognition.

While our work treats each topic from the programmer's perspective, subsequent writings will focus on these same topics from an administrative viewpoint. Additional information will cover computer application, office and personnel management, group dynamics, coping skills, professional preparation, legal concerns, staff development, professional service and creative activity, case studies and future trends.

We have developed our material from years of practical experience, contemplation, research, and professional interaction. We trust our treatment of this information will provide to be logical, realistic, and productive enough to be of service to any person with a responsibility for recreational sport programming.

ACKNOWLEDGEMENT

We now have a clear understanding for why authors recognize the contributions made by those people closest to them in the completion of their efforts — without such support most manuscripts would not become books. We certainly feel very fortunate and privileged to have enjoyed strong support from many sources throughout the duration of this project including direct or indirect contributions from our students, student leaders, interns, alumni and colleagues.

We feel particularly indebted to The Lilly Endowment, Inc. for their insight, commitment and financial support in this project as well as The Athletic Institute for their patience and guidance in what we considered to be a pioneering venture for each of us.

We also wish to express special gratitude to our families and our current staff, for they have provided significant moral support and day-to-day assistance required to maintain perspective, crystalize our thinking, and manage responsibilities. The challenges inherent within such an undertaking has reinforced our awareness and appreciation for the spirit within that makes all things possible.

CHAPTER 1

FOUNDATIONS

When studying any subject, it is valuable to have insight and a fundamental understanding of its theoretical basis. Sport within our society reflects a complex, multi-faceted, socio-economic system. It also represents a tremendous diversity in participation from a child's frolic, to unstructured and random play within the home, to the fulfillment of a dream in winning a tournament championship, to the pursuit of a healthy lifestyle through regular sport participation.

The role of sport in this country, as well as all over the world, has been shaped by tradition, popularity, and potential for profit. This situation has resulted in prosperity and growth for some areas of sport while others remain neglected and ill-attended. One area of sport that has suffered most from this predicament is recreational sport. Its true potential as a positive contribution to society has been neither documented nor articulated professionally. A fundamental presentation articulating the existing knowledge about recreational sport follows which can help illuminate this important aspect of sport. We have selected a simple but comprehensive approach to facilitate understanding by answering the following questions about recreational sport: what, when, why, how, where and to what extent?

WHAT

The initial question to be answered is: what is it? Accuracy of identity and consistency in communicating basic information about recreational sport is essential, not only for serving the participant, but also to facilitate communication among professionals. Unfortunately, confusion in interpreting recreational sport among educators, participants, and others associated with athletics has stifled this process.

Traditionally, recreational sport has been described in many ways, including: intramural sport, recreational programming, physical recreation, physical activity, or fitness programming. These terms, however, do not encompass or reflect what is actually taking place. In most settings, the content within a recreational sport program is similar, but the titles lack consistency and accuracy. The following terms and descriptions should help identify the meaning of recreational sport and support its use as the appropriate title for this aspect of sport.

Leisure. This is a concept subject to many interpretations. The word leisure is derived from the Latin word *licere* which means to be free, and is closely related to the French word *loisir,* to be permitted. The essence of leisure appears to be freedom—freedom in terms of time. Leisure is a time in an individual's life apart from earning a living or biological self-maintenance. Leisure, then, is a time span in which there is freedom of choice and lack of compulsion.

Recreation. Recreation is often defined as a diversion from work, a retooling of energy for work, or as positive and socially acceptable leisure activity. We support the view of recreation as a leisure time experience where the choices and expected outcomes of participation are left to individual choice. The goal in recreational programming is to provide everyone with an opportunity to select from a wide variety of satisfying activities.

Recreation is a broad and encompassing term. For our purpose in identifying recreational sport, a closer look at definitions for the major areas of recreation programming is needed. This examination will include a more explicit identification of sport as part of leisure time pursuits.

Social Programming. This is recreational activity that fosters congenial, cooperative, non-competitive participation in a common interest. It emphasizes human interaction and often takes the form of banquets, parties, dances, dining, or other social activities.

Cultural Programming. This is an area of recreation that provides opportunities for individuality, creativity and self-expression in the following areas:

Art and Craft. Activities which focus on creating personally aesthetic objects. (Examples: painting, woodwork or macrame)

Dance. Activities focusing on rhythmic movement patterns. (Examples: folk, square or ballet)

Drama. Activities focusing on theatrical communication expressions. (Examples: story telling, skits, theater or plays)

Literary, Mental and Linguistic. Activities focusing on mental challenge. (Examples: reading, puzzles or writing)

Music. Activities focusing on vocal and instrumental expression. (Examples: informal singing, concerts, choirs or bands)

Special Events Programming. A catch-all area of activities providing a change of pace in a unique or non-traditional format. (Examples: pageants, parades or festivals)

Sport Programming. Although there have been many attempts to define sport, an acceptable definition could not be found. Subsequently, the authors suggest that sport be defined as: playing cooperative/competitive activity in the game form. This definition liberates sport from a traditional, restrictive mold which fails to recognize the diversity that exists within sport: namely; instructional sport, recreational sport, athletic sport, and professional sport.

Careful consideration of this definition involves breaking the word down into its major parts. The first part "playing" describes the expectation that evolves out of human action in sport. "Playing" is a broad, encompassing word used to represent the state of mind or feelings that evolve from participation. These feelings are often described as challenge, risk and chance. The varying degrees of this state is often interpreted as fun or stress. Challenge incorporates the excitement of the contest and the struggle toward satisfaction. Risk is the element that stirs the mind toward failure and hazard. Chance represents the unpredictable or unknown element in sport. Play has been normally used in association with sport in phrases such as playing cards, playing little league, or playing professional football.

"Cooperative/competitive activity" represents the manner or style of action in sport. The use of the words cooperative and competitive reflects the basic behavior which occurs

SPORT CONTINUUM

SPORT

Peace ◄────── Cooperation   Competition ────► War

within any form of human interaction. Both are part of every sport experience, although one may predominate at a given time. By placing the words within two extremes on a horizontal continuum, their interrelated existence within sport may be better understood. The left side of the continuum represents harmony, coordination and collaboration while the right side represents rivalry, struggle and conflict. The fact that cooperative and competitive behavior are blended within sport reflects the degree of intensity that exists, and accommodates different interests and abilities of participants.

The final part of the definition "in the game form" describes the design, structure, and format within which sport occurs. The structural component of sport incorporates such characteristics as: rules and regulations, strategies, facilities and equipment. The rules and regulations of sports establish the procedures for playing and the boundaries that control and direct the action. Strategy represents the planning, thinking, and situation judgement exercised by the participant(s) that affect the outcome of participation along with physical and mental abilities. Facilities and equipment are those structures, objects, or props that are necessary to the sport in order that the process may take place.

The game form is the factor which separates sport from such other forms of cooperative/competitive activity as dance, music, art, and drama. These activities could be considered sport, in its broadest sense, if conducted in the game form. For example, auditions for musical or theatrical productions could incorporate characteristics of the game form as do art contests that are designed to rank order the artwork of contestants according to pre-determined criteria. Such an interpretation is an extreme view of sport, and is mentioned only to appreciate the recreational approach to sport. In keeping with the practical focus of this material, we present examples of sport in Figure 1-1 at the end of this section to indicate the diversity.

A complete definition of sport as playing cooperative/competitive activity in the game form also encompasses the following broad areas of sport: instructional sport, recreational sport, athletic sport, and professional sport.

Instructional Sport: Teaching sport skills, strategies, appreciation, rules and regulations for the purpose of educating the participant and improving performance. Instructional sport incorporates teaching on an individual or group basis through methods such as clinics, short courses and lessons. Usually there are three levels of instruction: beginner, intermediate, and advanced.

Recreational Sport: Programming sport activity for the sake of participation and fun. It is a diverse area that incorporates four separate program divisions: Informal Sport, Intramural Sport, Extramural Sport and Club Sport. Each of these four divisions represent varying levels of ability and diverse interests in cooperative/competitive activity in the game form.

Athletic Sport: Directing individuals in sport toward the margin of excellence or success in performance which can be identified as winning. The participant receives specialized external leadership with an emphasis on excellence in performance. Athletic sport usually carries organizational sponsorship through two levels: junior varsity and varsity programming.

Professional Sport: Marketing sport events places emphasis on entertainment and a financial remuneration to highly skilled participants. Participation occurs between representatives of corporate sponsors. Spectator income is a major factor in professional sport since income affects the perpetuation or demise of the business. Professional sport is organized, then, to employ the premier sport participants who will attract spectator and financial support.

Proceeding from a general description of the major areas within sport to a singular focus on recreational sport is necessary to futher identify its scope. The four program divisions within recreational sport are informal sport, intramural sport, extramural sport, and club sport.

Informal Sport. Informal sport involves a process of self-directed participation. An individualized approach to sport, this program area acknowledges the desire to participate in sport for fitness and fun, often with no pre-determined goals except that of participation. Informal sport requires minimal administrative or programming attention other than making sports facilities available for utilization based on the individual's schedule, interests and resources.

Intramural Sport. Intramural sport structured contests, tournaments, leagues or other events where participation is limited to the setting within which the total recreational sport system is located. Only those individuals within the setting (school, business, community or military base) may participate. Eligibility restrictions usually are placed on participation. These restrictions may be mandated by the participants themselves through boards, committees, or councils. Most activities are structured into programs for men, women, and mixed participants often with varying levels of ability taken into consideration.

Extramural Sport. Extramural sport is structured participation between settings. An extension of the intramural sport program, this programming area is primarily designed to utilize intramural champions. Extramural sport can also incorporate sports extravaganzas, play days, or festivals which may involve participation of many representatives from many different settings.

Club Sport. Club sport is undertaken by interest groups organized because of a common interest in a sport. Clubs vary in focus and programming since the membership manages the operation. For example, membership interests may focus upon teaching, team sponsorship, socialization or a combination of the three.

Spectator and participant interest in sport has served as the catalyst for the development of numerous traditional and non-traditional recreational sport activities. These activities may be found within informal, intramural, extramural, or club sport program divisions.

An exhaustive classification of recreational sport activities is not necessary at this time. We present a partial listing of traditional and non-traditional recreational sport activities in Figure 1-1, including examples of events that are customarily associated with a sport and some of the events that have been developed from a sport by making rule modifications. The reader can choose how to classify the listing into the categories of team sport—participation by one or more distinct groups of individuals; meet sport—participation by individuals or teams in a specific number of events within a sport; dual sport—participation by one or two sets of participants; individual sport—participation on an individual basis; or special event sport—participation on an individual, partner and/or team basis in an unusual, novel, or creative event. Examples of sports recognized as fitting within these categories include:

Team Sport—basketball, volleyball, soccer, field hockey, lacrosse, rugby

Meet Sport—wrestling, track, field, swimming, diving, gymnastics, weightlifting

Dual Sport—racquetball, squash, tennis, badminton, table tennis, handball

Individual Sport—archery, skiing, scuba diving, swimming, judo, fencing, bowling, golf, target shooting

Special Event Sport—new games, sport festival, superstar competition

WHEN

To describe **when** recreational sport occurs, we need to take another look into the concept of leisure. Leisure can be categorized qualitatively or quantitatively. Qualitative concepts of leisure, exemplified by the early writings of Aristotle on the Greek upper class, perceive leisure as a way to express superior and spiritual activities of the mind and body. This school of thought subscribes to the theory that leisure is a state of being

RECREATIONAL SPORTS ACTIVITIES

Aikido
Kata
Mini Dori
Randori Kyoghi
Tanto Randori

Archery
Archery Bowling
Archery Golf
Archery Horseback
Archery Skiing
Bow Birds
Bow Fishing
Clout Shoot
Crossbow Competition
Field Shooting
Flight Shooting
Free Style Barebow
Hunting
Target Shooting
Wand Shot
Wheelchair

Badminton
3-Man

Backpacking

Ballooning

Baseball
Cork Ball
Grounders
Hit-Pin
Kick-Pin
Left Field Ball
Pepper
Pitch, Hit and Run Contest
Rounders
Stickball
T-Ball

Basketball
Basketball Golf
5'9"
Free-Throw
Horse
Nine-Court
One-on-One
Roller
Scooter
Sideline
Slow-Break
Twenty-One
Two-on-Two

Billiard
American Snooker
Bumper Pool
Carom
Eight-Ball
14-1 Continuous Call Shot
Line-Up
Pool
Rotation
Three Rail

Boating
Canoe Sailing
Canoeing
Sprint
Slalom
Wild Water
Kayaking
Offshore Racing
Paddle
Power Boat Racing
Regatta
Roller Sailing
Rowing
Sailing
Sand Sailing
Yacht Racing

Bobsledding

Boccie Ball

Bowling
Bowling on the Green
Gym Bowling
Progressive
Skittle
Table
10-Pin Bowling
3-Pin Bowling
Triangle

Camping
Miss and Out Race
Pursuit Racing
Time Trials
Touring
Track Racing

Conditioning Sports
Aerobic Dance
Calisthenics
Cross Country Skiing
Cycling
Jazzercise
Jogging
Rope Jumping
Swimming
Walking
Weight Lifting

Cribbage

Croquet

Cross Country
Fun Run
Marathon
Race Walk
Steeplechase
10 K
Turkey Race

Cycling
Cyclo-Cross Racing
"Grand Prix"
"Little 500"

Darts
Aerial
Around the Clock
Closing
Fives
Killer
Lawn
Metal
Scram
Shanghai

Decathlon
Discus
400 Meter Dash
High Jump
100 Meter Dash
110 Meter High Hurdle
Pole Vault
Running Long Jump
Shot Put
1600 Meter Run
Triple Jump

Diving
Highboard
Meet
Back
Forward
Inward
Reverse
Twist
Scuba
Skin
Snorkel

Equestrian
Hunting
Jumping
Racing
Trail Riding

Fencing
Epee
Foil
Sabre

Fishing
Angling
Bait Casting
Casting
Fishing Derby
Fly Casting
Accuracy Fly
Long Distance Fly
Skish
Surf Casting

Football
Flag
Flickerball
Indoor Pass
Powder Puff

Punt, Pass and Kick
  Contest
Six-Man
Tackle
Touch

Frisbee
Bicycle
Free Style
Frisbee Golf
Guts
Lacrosbee

Golf
Clock
Driving Range
Hole-In-One Contest
Match Play
Miniature
Mulligan
Par 3
Putting Contests

Gymnastics
Balance Beam
Floor Exercise
Horizontal Bar
Parallel Bars
Rings
Side Horse
Trampoline
Tumbling
Uneven Parallel Bars
Vaulting

Handball
Chinese
Cut-Throat
Four Wall
One Wall
Rotation
Three Wall

Hiking

Hockey
Bandy
Box
Broomball
Field
Floor
Hurling
Ice
Roller Skate
Target

Horseshoes
Horseshoe Golf
21

Hunting
Bow
Deer
Duck

Judo

Karate

Kendo

Lacrosse

Luge Tobogganing

Mountain Climbing

Orienteering

Polo
Bicycle
Innertube
Water

Racing (Animals)
Dog-Sled
Greyhound
Harness Horse
Horse
Horseback
Pigeon

Racing (Motor)
Bicycling
Circuit
Dirt Bike
Drag
Go-Cart
Grand Prix
Ice
Indy 500
Moto-Cross
Motorcycle
Soap Box Derby
Speedway
Sports Car

Sprint
Stock Car

Racquetball
Jai Alai
Paddleball

Rodeo

Rugby

Shooting
Air Rifle 10m
Bigbore Free 300m
Clay Pigeon
Down-the-Line
Olympic Trench
Skeet
Pistol
  Free Pistol
  Rapid Fire
  Target Pistol
Rifle
  Air Rifle
  Bigbore
  Smallbore
  Smallbore 50m
  Smallbore Free

Shuffleboard
Curling

Skating
Dance
Distance

Distance Glide
Figure Skating
Ice Dancing
Pair
Singles
Ice
Roller
Roller Derby
Roller Disco
Skater in a Cage
Speed
Sprint

Skiing
Alpine
Barefoot
Biathlon
Bobsleigh Racing
Grass
Nordic
  Cross Country
Ski Jumping
Skibob Racing
Snow
Snow Shoeing
Water
  Ski-Jumping
  Slalom
  Trick

Soccer
Crab
Gator Ball
Indoor
Korfball

Line
Netball
Speedball
Target

Softball
Batball
Cricket
Fast Pitch
Kickball
Long Base
Medium Pitch
One-Pitch
16"
Slow-Pitch
Three-Pitch
12"
Wiffleball

Squash

Surfing
Board
Body
Wind

Swimming
Backstroke
Breaststroke
Butterfly
50, 100, 200 Meter
  Races
400, 1500 Meter Races
Freestyle Relay
Innertube

Medley Relay
Relays - Tee Shirt
Swimnastics
Synchronized

Table Sports
Backgammon
Battleship
Card Games
Bridge
Canasta
Euchre
Hearts
Pinochle
Rook
Rummy
Yatzee
Chess
Checkers

Chinese Checkers
Dice
Dominoes
Foosball
Jacks
Mah-Jongg
Marbles
Monopoly
Othello
Pacman
Pinball
Scrabble

Tennis
Aerial
Deck
Floor
Hand
Lawn

Paddle
Racquet

Track and Field
Discus
400, 800 Meter Run
Hammer
High Jump
Hurdles
Javelin
Jogging
Long Jump
Medley Relay
Mile Run
100, 200 Meter Dash
Pole Vaulting
Shot Put
Springs
Steeplechase

Triple Jump
Two-Mile Run

Tug-of-War

Video Sports
Asteroids
Pacman
Space Invaders

Volleyball
Beachball
Bonus
Cageball
Keep-It-Up
Mini
Newcomb
Power
Push Ball

Sitting
Spike-It
Tetherball
Volley-Bounce
Volley-Tennis

Weight Lifting
Body Builders
One Hand Clear & Jerk
One Hand Snatch
Power Lifting
Two Hand Clear & Jerk
Two Hand Press
Two Hand Snatch

Whitewater Sports
River Rafting
Slalom
Tubing

Whitewater Racing
Wildwater Racing

Wrestling
Arm
Free Style
Greco-Roman
Leg
Mud
Thumb
Wrist

Figure 1-1. Recreational sports activities.

or state of mind in which man is free from any biological or work constraints. The mind is focused upon contemplation and reflection, activities which were usually reserved for highly educated or upper class individuals. Since education is no longer restricted to an elite class and available to the masses, less emphasis is being placed on leisure as a "state of being."

A quantitative school of thought exists which views leisure as "discretionary time", "free time" or any block of time which may be used as an individual chooses. This time span is usually measured in such quantitative terms as days or hours of leisure. We function in life within a time system where there are three general blocks of time: personal care, work and leisure. *Personal care* needs are associated with eating, sleeping, or attending to individual maintenance and bodily functions. *Work* incorporates both the process of preparing for a vocation (training) and the participation in gainful employment. *Leisure* is time not devoted to work or personal care functions. It is the time when recreational sport participation occurs.

In accepting leisure as the "time frame" in which recreational sport exists, one may take a more in-depth look into leisure. Although leisure is broadly interpreted, there are two types of leisure patterns pertinent to recreational sport participation. The first is the potential of negative use. Not all of one's use of time outside of work or personal care is positive. Many times individuals do unhealthy or socially unacceptable things, such as excessive drinking, utilization of dangerous drugs, excessive smoking, excessive inactivity, and reckless driving. A person's moral or value system and peer group are key factors which influence how leisure time is used. The courts of law ultimately determine when an act is so unacceptable that corrective legal action results.

The positive use of leisure time is self-directed and may include social, cultural, or sport activities. Examples of positive leisure time activities include parties, dances, concerts, ballgames, swimming, movies, reading, cards, tourism, jogging and other activities not related to work and personal care.

Public attitude toward leisure has undergone many changes in current years, including a view of leisure as either something to be earned after hard work, an opportunity improperly used by the masses, a luxury basically reserved for the privileged, or a legitimate pursuit by all segments of society. The leisure movement has had a tremendous economic impact on society. Current data indicates that it is the number one industry as measured by consumer expenditures. Figure 1-2 illustrates recent leisure spending and projects the growth expected in the 1980's.

If leisure is discretionary or unobligated time, then the positive utilization of that time is recreation. As described, recreation incorporates a number of programming areas, one of which is sport.

WHY

Why people involve themselves in recreational sport involves more of a theoretical explanation than a factual one. The programmer, however, should understand why people participate

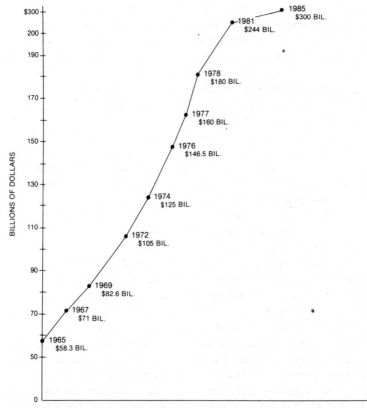

Figure 1-2. Growth patterns of leisure spending. Source: "Challenge of the 80's", *U.S. News and World Report.* May 23, 1977, p. 62; August 10, 1981, p. 62.

in recreational sport in order to provide relevant programs. Two categories to explore in addressing the question of "why" are: personal and professional.

Personal (Avocation). People participate in recreational sport during their leisure time for enjoyment and satisfaction. However, participation that is enjoyable and satisfying for one person may not produce the same results for another person.

One popular motivation for participation is the development or maintenance of fitness in mind and body. There is sufficient research to support participation in sport as a contributor to one's overall well being and life expectancy. Personal sport and fitness programs have acquired elevated social status and meaning as a result.

Other people are attracted to recreational sport participation because it affords opportunity for social interaction. Sport participation rarely occurs on an individual basis. There is characteristically a direct or indirect involvement with others. The sport environment offers a means to: relate to others, observe the effect of cooperative, competitive, and conflicting behaviors upon social relationships, develop communication skills and broaden one's viewpoint. For others, sport participation is enjoyable because it affords a change of pace, release from tension, physical exhilaration, goal attainment, or ego gratification. Regardless of the specific motivation, well-managed recreational sport systems are satisfying these and other desires.

Professional (Vocation). Recreational sport is a specialization or field within Recreation or Physical Education. The specialist in recreational sport pursues three basic objectives that help explain 'why' the specialist is necessary: service, development and relations.

Service. The primary purpose for the professional in recreational sport is to provide the highest quality program within the setting in which he or she is employed. The types of programs and the degree to which they are applied in a quality way is a direct result of the commitment and philosophy of the setting. The service process encompasses the actual delivery of sport through a combination of activities, facilities, and personnel with participant interest and satisfaction foremost in mind.

There are two reasons why recreational sport services are provided. The first is encouragement of participation. The professional is motivated by knowledge that the participant derives valuable benefits from involvement. Programs are supported by state and/or federal funds to provide individuals with an equal opportunity to participate to the fullest extent. Settings which observed this approach include education, municipal and military systems.

Services may be designed and delivered for profit-making purposes. Fees and charges are assessed for the services rendered and careful consideration is given to the marketing and quality of the service in order to sustain and expand participant involvement. Settings which observe an income or profit motive include YMCA's and YWCA's, resorts, bowling leagues, country and racquet clubs.

The two approaches are not mutually exclusive. Many settings benefit from a combination of tax support and service revenues. They are interested in providing a quality service maximizing enjoyment and profit. Such combinations are becoming a standard practice rather than an exception.

Development. Involvement in sport holds developmental experiences for participants. These experiences are judged to develop social, mental, and physical awareness of self. The ability to control and guide participant experiences to be developmental adds value and meaning to the professional's role in society.

Social awareness results from interaction with others through sport. Discovering and understanding the consequences of cooperation, competition, and communication among people is critical to success in both life and sport. Mental awareness is enhanced through sport because experiences can reveal an ability to control emotions, improve memory, interpret situations, and make appropriate adjustments. Physical awareness is often the most recognized value of sport. Through regular participation, benefits to the cardiovascular, neurological, and muscular systems are attained. A body that engages in regular exercise is a more sound body and one that functions more efficiently.

Relations. A quality delivery service of recreational sport coupled with a developmental approach in programming, contributes to public relations. Benefits derived from sport participation often exceed those of other life experiences and, when properly designed, our programs contribute significantly to the appeal and desirability of a setting for inhabitants.

Recreational sport programmers play a major role in shaping positive public relations through competent efforts.

HOW

Describing **how** individuals participate in recreational sport is a complex area because values, standards, interests, and abilities are so varied. An individual's decision to participate in an activity involves a complex interaction of both internal and external motivations. Therefore, in reviewing how people participate in recreational sport, one should remember that there are varying degrees of involvement. Involvement may be interpreted as intensity, arousal, or activation. For recreational sport, a decision regarding how to participate is a matter of individual choice. The individual chooses when, where, and why and then sets goals on what he or she hopes to accomplish in terms of personal satisfaction and enjoyment.

There are two basic classifications which can be used to demonstrate how people participate. One is termed *passive* and represents the spectator aspect in sport. The other is termed *active* and represents actual participation in a particular sport.

Passive (spectation). Watching sport is part of the recreational sport domain. Anything an individual witnesses for enjoyment, whether it be on television or in person, qualifies as recreation. Spectation suggests watching athletic or professional sport, but it may include watching intramural sport, extramural sport, or club sport. People find pleasure in observation because of an appreciation for the skill or performance of the participant, or because they may be a participant in that particular sport and identify with the athlete or professional they are watching.

Spectation, or passive participation, is important to athletic and professional sport. The enthusiasm and support of spectators often affects the outcome of an event. The enthusiasm of fans may spur the active participant to levels of performance that otherwise might not occur. So the spectator, as a recreational participant, is important and should be understood, appreciated, and provided for.

The reasons motivating spectator behavior may be obscure, but spectators become involved in the sport mentally and emotionally. Helping people find a greater appreciation for sport as spectators is a worthwhile goal for the recreational sport programmer. Enhancing the knowledge base for a spectator in sport can increase their enjoyment and satisfaction.

Active (Participation). Choosing and accomplishing active participation in sport is our next focal point. Recreational sport represents the sport segment with the greatest variety and diversity of involvement. None of the programming divisions are considered more important, worthwhile, or valuable than another. A key principle within recreation is the individual's choice of activity. No value judgment should be placed on an individual's interest or skill level in active participation. For some people, participation may entail little organization and commitment. Others may prefer activities involving extensive organization and commitment. The following figure indicates the varying degrees and diversity of involvement from which an individual may select.

As one considers the spectra of sport, each may be applied to two forms of active participation: structured and self-directed.

BROAD SPECTRA OF PARTICIPATION

Informal ———————— Organizational Design ———————— Formal

Simple ———————— Rules and Regulations ———————— Complex

Low ———————— Skill Performance ———————— High

Minimum ———————— Physical Exertion ———————— Maximum

Relaxed ———————— Mental Concentration ———————— Intense

Low ———————— Risk ———————— High

Few ———————— Rule Modification ———————— Numerous

Low ———————— Emphasis on Winning ———————— High

Structured participation represents the intramural, extramural and club sport program divisions since each requires external leadership to facilitate participation. The informal sport participant requires little leadership since choices regarding when, where, and to what degree are made by the individual and the activity is conducted on a self-directed basis.

Another factor that may influence how a person chooses to participate is the individual's skill level and performance level. These levels may affect the satisfaction derived from participation. A sense of success and accomplishment following participation is important to most people. Individual performance then is dependent upon the participant's own agility, strength, endurance, timing, and coordination, regardless of the programming area or specific sport.

External factors also affect participation in sport and whether one becomes involved in a passive or active way.

Geographic location and climate. The availability of many recreational sport activities depends upon terrain and climate. Skiing is more feasible in mountainous areas and accessibility to water encourages development of aquatic sport activities. Certain locations foster sporting traditions resulting from the ethnic or cultural heritage of the local population. Field hockey and lacrosse are sports closely associated with the northeastern part of the United States where native Indians influenced the early sport activities of European settlers.

Socialization. Social environment plays an important role in how one chooses to participate in recreational sport. Parental and peer group attitudes toward sport have a tremendous impact on decision-making, as do the actual participation patterns of family members and friends. In general, people tend to reflect the participation patterns and attitudes of their families, peer groups, and other role models especially through the adolescent years.

In addition, participation choices are shaped by previous experiences. If participation is pleasant and satisfying, it usually continues, but if unpleasant, it usually ceases. Our efforts must be geared to designing programs and experiences that will result in positive outcomes and will encourage participants to try new activities.

Availability and accessibility. It is unlikely that people will engage in recreational sport pursuits unless opportunities are available and accessible. Program offerings should be diverse to accommodate different interests and abilities. Programmers should make services attractive to the consumer in terms of location, cost, and time.

WHERE

Where recreational sport may be offered has involved some confusion and inconsistency. Although educators and philosophers have differed over the classification process, we may conclude that there are two broad locations where recreational sport is programmed: indoor and outdoor.

Indoor. Indoor recreational sport refers to participation within a structure that is partially or completely enclosed. A variety of sports are found indoors, ranging from bowling, swimming, and racquetball to those traditionally thought of as taking place outdoors but brought indoors for year-round participation. Factors that influence the recreational sport programming of indoor facilities include cost of operation, construction, maintenance, and the needs and interests of the participants. The degree to which individuals seek participation plays a major role in the development of indoor facilities. Sports often played indoors include: basketball, volleyball, racquetball, tennis, badminton, swimming, jogging, weight-training and conditioning, ice skating, gymnastics, wrestling, archery, riflery, and martial arts.

Outdoor. One consideration in outdoor programming emphasizes the traditional sports where participation occurs outdoors. Some sports engaged in outdoors include: football, tennis, swimming, rugby, soccer, golf, softball, and lacrosse. A second consideration in outdoor programming emphasizes the environment. Satisfaction and enjoyment is derived from interaction with natural elements such as air, trees, water, grass, and terrain. Such sports as white-water canoeing, hiking, fishing, skiing, hunting, mountain climbing, and spelunking are included as a part of this interpretation.

A combination of both emphases in outdoor programming may occur. Historically, however, professional preparation curricula have placed traditional outdoor sports within Physical Education and sport activities focusing more on the natural elements within Recreation. Unfortunately, inadequate preparation of the recreational sport programmer who oversees both areas of outdoor programming has resulted.

Among the variety of ways to provide recreational sport, the approach taken is influenced by the agency's philosophy and the nature of the setting where the program exists. Consequently, we present a look into some of the settings where recreational sport programs can be found. "Settings" incorporates both the administration and programming of Recreation, a major portion of which is sport-related.

City/Community. This setting consists of family units, employment structures, government and school systems, all of which have an impact on the lifestyle of people within the community. The city or municipal governmental structure provides funds, facilities, and leadership for recreation in the form of a tax-based program which may be supplemented with fees and charges. The recreational sport programs in this setting are available to all residents.

Educational. Among our many systems of education are public schools, private schools, and institutions of higher education. Each of these educational settings has goals which tend to focus upon student academic development or satisfaction. Sport, whether it be instructional, recreational, or athletic, is considered part of the learning process within these settings.

Military. The military is organized into four branches: Army, Navy, Air Force and Marines. Since military personnel and families tend to be more confined within their settings, recreational programs become a major part of their daily life. Sports programming receives high priority as an avenue for positive utilization of leisure.

Correctional. This setting is a mechanism designed for dealing with persons who have demonstrated socially unacceptable behavior and the need for detention. When people are confined to this setting, the only "benefit" they may have is their recreational pursuits. Sport is popular and may be used in rehabilitative efforts through both structured and self-directed participation in correctional settings.

Private Clubs. Clubs provide a variety of recreational sports for their membership. Private clubs may limit their membership based on facility capacity or social status. An example is a country club that offers swimming, tennis and golf along with dining facilities for the pleasure of its members. Usually, the sports facilities are the primary attraction and yield much of the income necessary for maintaining the operation through dues and supplemental user fees.

YMCA/YWCA. Historically, YMCA's provided housing facilities in cities for individuals visiting on a short-term basis. With the need for more services, gymnasiums, pools, and other facilities were built. In recent years Y's have changed their philosophy of operation, placing a significant emphasis upon sport and fitness programming for its members while de-emphasizing the lodging aspect.

Commercial. Because of the popularity of such sports as handball, racquetball, squash, tennis, swimming, bowling, boating, and fishing, many commercial ventures have appeared. Profit is absolutely necessary for keeping these operations functioning. Commercial recreational sport management has grown greatly in the last decade and adds a whole new dimension to the field.

Industrial/Business. In the interest of maintaining good employee health and morale, management has ceated recreational opportunities for employees. The idea of increasing production by satisfying employee recreational interests has received strong support within industry. Large companies often have specialized recreational sport programs for employees and their families.

WHO

When examining **who** participates in recreational sport, we are referring to the participant. An insight into the people we serve enables the programmer to meet their needs and interests while taking appropriate precautions for their safety.

Recreational sport is intended for the enjoyment of all ages with no limitation due to shape, size, skill level or interest. Recent development of recreational sport programs for the mentally and physically disabled has facilitated their inclusion into the mainstream of society. Currently, recreational sport constitutes an important part of day-to-day existence for many people. The following age categories include a brief description of participation within recreational sport characteristic of the particular age group.

Children. The child from newborn to age five participates in activity centered in the home. Little formal participation in a cooperative/competitive activity in the game form occurs among children at this age. Activity is in the form of frolic with minimal structure.

As a pre-school youngster has little organizational ability, most everything he or she does requires limited physical and mental concentration. External leadership has little effect upon actions which are exploratory and self-directed. Often parents and other adults influence early sport skill development, contributing to the child's performance ability later in life. Little emphasis is placed upon winning and high achievement.

Youth. Between age 6 and 12, many young people learn about the world of structured sport. Participation often revolves around the school or community in the form of "youth sports." Youth sports have grown tremendously in the past decade. They begin athletic sport careers for some, while for others, they are simply recreation. This dichotomy involves conflicts in philosophy, but, under proper leadership, a healthy, meaningful and balanced experience may be provided.

Leadership, a key to youth sports, emphasizes teaching fundamental skills, strategies, rules, and maintaining health and well-being. Various training programs for parents, coaches, and officials involved in youth sports have surfaced in recent years that have had a positive effect. Some of the principal settings that sponsor programs include the YMCA, YWCA, Boys' Club, Girls' Club, schools, and community or municipal recreation departments.

Adolescent. The individual between the ages of 13 and 19 years of age experiences a complex period of development leading to maturation. Involvement in sport may or may not have a positive influence on this process. At this age level, athletic sport receives its greatest emphasis, primarily in school settings. Unfortunately, recreational sport opportunities for the non-athlete barely exist. Adolescents unable to make an athletic team usually find themselves with few opportunities to participate in sport. These so-called non-athletes are discriminated against because of their limited mental and physical abilities or lack of interest in athletic sport.

Some programs for adolescents are found in other settings—primarily in the community or city recreation department or other service agencies. Unfortunately, the voluntary leadership support available to youth sports is not carried to the adolescent level. Emphasis on youth sports hampers the availability of facilities and resources for the adolescent level of recreational sport. We hope to see more positive sport opportunities for the adolescent in the future.

One may conclude that adolescents not involved in structured sport participate in recreation on an individual, peer group or family basis. Since sport may not have a high priority for some, it is their responsibility to determine their own recreative needs and preferred interests.

Adult. After 18 years of age, sport interests are generally well established. Other than those involved in an athletic or professional sport career, adults participate only in recreational sport programming areas, centered through the setting in which they live or work. Although totally dependent upon the programmers' decision of what can be provided, adults have the most flexibility in making choices as well as evaluating their recreational sport experience. The degree of involvement is up to them. When the opportunity for involvement does not exist, they may often influence its development. Such alternatives as structured tournaments, self-directed activities or club leadership positions are all opportunities available to adults in almost any setting.

Seniors. One of the most rapidly growing areas in the entire process of recreation is that of providing opportunities for participation by the elderly. More and more elderly people find enjoyment, satisfaction and exercise through recreational sport participation. Their degree of involvement is totally dependent upon individual enthusiasm and physical and mental limitations for that involvement. While age may limit the degree of involvement, it does not prevent interest or enthusiasm for participation.

Retirees have more leisure time once they have left the work force. Recreational sport can now play a major part in their lifestyle, and becomes a most important outlet for many.

A summary review of this section can be found in Figure 1-3. It provides an overview of the types of involvement in sport that are most common within a specific age group.

TO WHAT EXTENT

Recreational sport participation in our society is reaching unprecedented levels. Almost everyone finds some form of recreational sport expression whether it be through personal fitness programs, organized sports competition, family sport outings, spectating, or playing video and other electronic sports.

A review of the historical evolution of the recreational sport process within this country, and other cultures of the world, is a task that has resulted in the development of complete texts on the subject of sports history. Much documentation comes from teachers (Physical Education) or coaches (Athletics). Consequently, much emphasis is placed on success through winning or on skill development.

Although instructional sport, athletic sport and professional sport are important historically, the recreational aspect of sport also has a place of importance in history. The following summaries present a glimpse into the past and present of recreational sport, as well as a forecast for the future.

Past. Attempting to summarize all factors in the past that have affeced recreational sport would be unproductive. Much of the available documentation is not directly related to the recreative process of sport due to the emphasis on athletic and professional sport. Yet, recreational sport, in one form or another, has been in existence since the beginning of time. In its most fundamental form, human existence was based on an ability to survive in nature. The process of practicing or training for survival took on game form. Whether mock hand-to hand combat or wrestling within a cave, these activities resembled a primitive form of recreational sport. As pleasure and enjoyment flowed from these challenges of prowess and ability, greater design and direction to the activity occured.

Survival and Pre-Christian Civilizations

The sporting habits of prehistoric man during the Paleolithic and Neolithic periods reflected a struggle to survive. Unlike

PARTICIPANT GROUP	AGE	INSTRUCTIONAL	INFORMAL	INTRAMURAL	EXTRAMURAL	CLUB	ATHLETIC JUNIOR VARSITY	ATHLETIC VARSITY	PROFESSIONAL MINOR	PROFESSIONAL MAJOR
Children	1 - 5	X	X							
Youth	6 - 8	X	X	X						
	9 - 11	X	X	X						
	12 - 14	X	X	X	X	X	X	X		
Adolescent	15 - 16	X	X	X	X	X	X	X		
	17 - 18	X	X	X	X	X	X	X		
	19 - 20	X	X	X	X	X	X	X	X	
Adult	21 - 25	X	X	X	X	X	X	X	X	X
	26 - 50	X	X	X	X	X			X	X
	51 - 65	X	X	X	X	X				
	66 - 70	X	X	X	X	X				
Senior	71 - 80	X	X	X						
	81 - ?	X	X							

Figure 1-3.   Sport participation by age.

modern society, primitive man did not divide time into work, personal care, or leisure. There was no routine for establishing the patterns of activities for the day. Work was done when it had to be done. Early recreational activities often had their origin as preparation for warfare or as part of religious festivals and celebrations. Primitive sports arose out of man's quest to overcome the challenges he faced. Skills were passed on from generation to generation.

As primitive societies began to stabilize and increase in size, they began to specialize the functions necessary to maintain the society. As certain tasks were divided by function of labor, divisions in classes began to appear. Once permanent villages and cities were established, the upper classes began to enjoy increased wealth, power, and leisure while lower classes maintained the lands. From 3000 to 1500 B.C., a leisure class had its first beginning in the Middle East.

The upper classes in Egypt participated in various sports and exercise as a part of military training and as a form of enjoyment. Dance activities were prominent as a major religious activity. The two nations of Assyria and Babylon did not emphasize sport as much as the Egyptians, but did view sport contests as a means of military training much as dancing and music were tied to religious practice.

The city-states of Greece, and particularly Athens, gave great attention to the arts, education, and sport. Although these pursuits were largely restricted to the upper classes (who had full citizenry), they were introduced during early childhood and regarded as an obligation to the state. Leisure was an opportunity for intellectual cultivation while sport was a utilitarian avenue for enhancing and demonstrating strength, fitness, and courage. Organized sport, through the Olympic games and other sports festivals, began as religious and cultural functions. Gradually, by the second century B.C. these events were weakened by athletic specialization, commercialism and corruption.

The early Roman republic was characterized by an interest in military conquest. Unlike Greece, Rome focused upon the physical vigor of its citizenry and demonstrated less concern for intellectual pursuits, or physical training for grace, beauty, and symmetry. The Romans held numerous sport events in connections with the worship of gods and held in highest esteem those which celebrated military triumphs. Sport was valued primarily for its practical benefits to military purposes. During the first two centuries after the death of Christ, sport in Rome was commercialized and debased as emperors attempted to placate the bored masses by sponsoring parades, feasts and sport contests.

The Dark and Middle Ages

The Teutonic invasions of the Roman Empire began what historians term the Dark Ages because of the resulting curtailment of literature and educational attainment. The rise of Christianity coincided with the declining years of pagan Rome. Revolting social mores and persecution gave rise to early Christian doctrine that worldly and material things were not of God. More concern rested with the soul than the body. Rather than sport or other forms of physical enjoyment, manual labor was regarded as the appropriate means for disciplining the flesh to escape the evils of idleness. During this time, monasteries became centers of education and industry. Feudalism provided the social, economic, military, and political system for medieval society. Despite church disapproval, some sport existed among the knights, nobleman, and peasantry. As living conditions improved, medieval tournaments, which had once served as a serious form of training for warfare and self-preservation, became a pastime for recreational sport and amusement.

The Renaissance

The period from 1350 A.D. to the early 1500's marked a transition between the medieval world and modern times, and saw a rebirth of interest in classic philosophy, arts, and literature present in ancient Greece and Rome. The religious emphasis of the Middle Ages shifted to a worldly view, examining man rather than God as the object of philosophy. Renewed interest in exploration, science, and education marked this period. Unity of mind, body, and spirit was considered and values of physical exercise, hygiene, and sport participation became important aspects of education.

The Protestant Reformation

During the Renaissance, sport still suffered religious disapproval. The Protestant Reformation during the fifteenth through eighteenth centuries represented the challenge of a growing middle class to the position of the Catholic Church. This period also saw attempts to repress interest in sport. Subsequently, Protestant schools taught reading, writing, and religion while discouraging any form of sport or public amusement. The only valid form of sport activity to receive consideration was gymnastics because it was a way to preserve health and divert people from gambling, reveling, and intemperance.

The New World

The first settlers to colonize the new world came from diverse national origins. While they brought the different customs and pastimes of their homelands, they were bound together by a common desire for freedom and a common struggle for survival. The development of sport in America was influenced not only by these settlers but also by native American Indians and by the African slaves. Although early religious restrictions and work demands necessary for survival allowed little opportunity for recreation, the settlers' strong tradition for sports survived and developed into a major element of American culture by the nineteenth century. After towns and cities became well-established, Americans adopted some native Indian sports along with some African dance styles.

A major legacy of the colonial period was an interest in a common education for all children. Early elementary education emphasized reading, writing, arithmetic, spelling, and Bible study. Secondary education was rarely offered to girls and was considered a means for preparing young men for the ministry, law, or medicine. The subjects most frequently offered included Latin, Greek, elocution, and rhetoric. Prior to the Revolutionary War, school sessions were so long that there was little time for involvement in sports. Once academies and colleges appeared after the War, some time for sports and physical exercise was permitted.

The National Period

The first sixty years in United States history was characterized by tremendous diversity in social customs and the beginning of urban living environments. Americans began to have more leisure time once their homes, farms, and cities became more established. Although there were a few commercial and social centers along the eastern part of the country, most of the land was rural.

Sporting interests continued to be influenced by the heritage of the people within each particular region as well as the extent to which the region was developed. In the East, club sports began to appear among the upper class, while others enjoyed recreational sports activities in a family or neighborhood context. The pursuit of regular physical exercise for the sake of fitness also began in Eastern cities. In the rural and frontier West, sport served the people's need for social interaction. Sporting activities were primarily informal, spontaneous, and physically vigorous, a reflection of daily life.

American education focused upon conservative curriculum geared to prepare students for social and economic roles, showing little concern for their health and recreational needs. Once reformers demonstrated the benefits of exercise and sport activities, administrators began to include them in the school programs. Although organized sport was not common, it was becoming a part of the American culture.

The Nineteenth Century

Tremendous social change occurred due to the impact of the Industrial Revolution and the influx of immigrants from Europe. Advancements in transportation and communication facilitated a significant shift in population from rural areas to urban centers—a factor which eventually precipitated the development of the recreation movement.

As workers began to have more free time and money, recreational sport interests became popular from both a spectator and participant standpoint. Once mass production allowed standardization of sporting equipment, it became less expensive and more readily available to the American public.

Similarly, industry and technology provided an impetus for the development of organized and professional sport. Sports such as baseball, rowing, yachting, archery, track and field represent examples of activities that began as informal pastimes, became organized clubs and by the latter part of the century became national sport associations. The associations began to standardize rules, promote their sport, and sponsor national championships.

Public and private organizations reflected public concern for the health of American citizens. A number of societies and associations, such as the YMCA and YWCA, developed and provided facilities for conducting gymnastic and sport activities.

Public education became established and the option of coeducation was accepted. Early efforts to establish instruction in physical education was resisted by faculties who felt exercise and sport should occur after school. By the middle of the century, the same concern for the health of Americans that prompted the development of non-school recreational sport also influenced the establishment of formal physical education in public schools. Although the first programs emphasized gymnastics and exercise, they began to reflect popular desire for organized recreational sport and athletic sport. By the end of the century, teacher training in physical education had begun, the American Association for the Advancement of Physical Education (known today as American Alliance for Health, Physical Education, Recreation and Dance) was founded, and club, intramural, and athletic sport programs appeared on college campuses.

Another development of major significance, spurred by an increasing concern for wholesome use of leisure, was the recreation movement. This movement represented the provision of organized, leisure-time activity by various agencies. At first, the focus was upon children in urban settings, but by the end of the century, public recreation for all began.

The Twentieth Century

After the turn of the century, technological advances continued rapidly. Prior to World War I, local volunteer agencies, industry, churches, or municipalities provided recreational sport on a more structured basis. The Boys Club of America, Boy Scouts of America, Girl Scouts of America and the Playground Association of America (known today as the National Recreation and Parks Association) all had their beginnings. Sport was more accepted as a legitimate part of the school program, especially at the collegiate level. The popularity of sport required educators to design intramural sport programs for all. Men continued to pursue their sport interests while unfavorable public sentiment discouraged women from athletics.

After World War I, recreational sport and physical education received strong public backing due to overwhelming concern over the poor physical condition of American soldiers. Although school athletic sport and physical education, along with municipal recreation, experienced some curtailments during the depression, the Federal government instituted a number of emergency work programs related to recreation and sport. As a result, recreation training, facilities, and programs expanded significantly. The depression spawned a consciousness that recreation was a vital part of life for all ages. The physical education programs at schools and colleges were often viewed as places where the necessary skills could be developed, and the growing school, college and community recreational sport programs were considered laboratories for participation.

During World War II, sport participation patterns, particularly in intercollegiate athletics and professional sport, varied as resources were redistributed to serve the armed forces and defense plants. Opportunities for recreational sport participation were not eliminated. They were provided at home and abroad by special services divisions of the armed forces, the Red Cross, the United Services Organization, and industrial recreation programs. In addition, the Federal Security Agency established a Recreation Division to assist community programs, many of which were continued after the war as tax supported programs.

Another Federal government program, the Works Projects Administration, stimulated the construction of sporting facilities between 1935 and 1941. An estimated $1.5 billion was spent on recreational facilities, and sport benefited from close to half of the amount (Betts, 1974, p. 287). Once the war ended in 1945, returning servicemen and women, accustomed to recreational sport services, continued to support their provision.

Sport was now an integral part of American life in terms of recreation and was becoming a part of education. Physical education programs within colleges and schools replaced the traditional gymnastic-based program with sport and a focus upon physical fitness—spurred once again by the poor test results found by selective service examinations and the Kraus-Weber tests of the early '50's.

Demand for trained personnel has not been restricted to the educational setting but has included community, commercial, industrial, correctional, and military settings. A struggle within the fields of physical education, health education, and recreation for control of professional preparation has resulted. This conflict, in addition to a new orientation towards parks management, disrupted the close cooperation between recreation and physical education that charcterized earlier periods of history. Physical education focused more and more upon teacher and athletic coach preparation and skills instruction while recreation focused upon the preparation of programming and management practitioners for non-school settings. Unfortunately, the separation left recreational sports an unattended area until the 1950's when the National Intramural Association formed. The NIA initially focused upon intramural sports programming on college campuses, but has expanded to include all aspects of recreational sports programming with an interest in non-educational settings. In 1975, the membership voted to adopt a new name to represent the transition and is now known as the National Intramural-Recreational Sport Association (NIRSA).

The rise of professional sport after World War II derived from the tastes of a technological society. By the 1970's, the American public was enjoying diverse pleasures in numerous sports such as baseball, boxing, automobile racing, football, basketball, golf, tennis, racquetball, soccer, volleyball, ice hockey, and bowling. Growth in athletic sport, which now boasts regional, national, and world championships in numerous disciplines, has been no exception. One of the more distinctive features of both professional and athletic sport has been the tremendous increase in active participation by women. Until the 1950's, women were limited to intramural sport participation. The civil rights and feminist movements of the 1960's and '70s fostered an expansion.

Although the tremendous popularity of professional and athletic sports as a form of entertainment prompted concern that the American public would prefer observation to active participation, this speculation has not been borne out of fact.

Participation in recreational sport has grown and diversified in conjuction with spectator interests.

A remarkable growth in organized recreation services and sports programs has been a part of America's seemingly insatiable interest in sport. During the past twenty years, sport and fitness programs have been implemented which respond to the specialized needs and interests of women, youth, elderly, minorities, and handicapped. This period is also characterized by expansion of commercial sponsorship for recreational sport facilities and programs.

KEY EVENTS IN RECREATIONAL SPORTS EVOLUTION

1734 —Charleston Jockey Club, Virginia, formed

1790 —Formation of community cricket clubs

1795 —Savannah, Georgia, Golf Club established

1802 —Opening of National Race Course (Horses), Washington D. C.

1814 —Georgetown University permits students to play handball, swim, box, and fence.

1817 —Military Gymnasium established at U. S. Military Academy of West Point

1820's—Formation of community club sports in boating, archery, and angling

—Sponsorship of community walking races began

1821 —First track trotting race (on Union Course, New York)

1823 —Round Hill School, Northhampton, Massachusetts founded; curriculum included program of sport and gymnastic exercises

1825 —First swimming school, Boston, Massachusetts, established by Frances Lieber

1837 —Mont Holyoke Seminary for women opened with exercise required

1839 —Detroit Boat Club formed

1843 —First Collegiate Rowing Club, Yale

1844 —First Steeple Chase in the USA at Hoboken, New Jersey

1845 —Knickerbocker Baseball Club of New York City developed written set of rules which became the basis for modern baseball

1849 —Philadelphia, South Carolina, first ice skating club
in USA
1851 —Young Men's Christian Association (YMCA)
founded, Boston, Massachusetts
1852 —First intercollegiate sport contest, rowing, Yale vs.
Harvard
1853 —Caledonia Club Games, Boston, Massachusetts,
prompted growth of Track & Field in U.S.
1854 —First national provision for recreation in an industry
by the Peacedale Manufacturing Company, R.I.
1859 —First national billiards match, Detroit, Michigan
—First intercollegiate baseball match between Amherst
and Williams
1860 —Olympic Country Club founded, California (possibly
the oldest athletic club in the world)
1861 —First college men's physical education program,
Amherst College
1865 —First college women's physical education program,
Vassar College
1866 —First state physical education legislation, California
—First municipal swimming pool—"floating bath,"
Boston
—Young Women's Christian Association (YWCA)
founded, Boston
1868 —New York Athletic Club founded and sponsored
track & field meets open to male amateur participants
from all parts of the country
1869 —First professional baseball team, Cincinnati Red
Stockings
1871 —National Rifle Association founded
—American National Rifle Association founded
1875 —The National Bowling League founded (today's
American Bowling Congress)
1876 .—National League of Professional Baseball Clubs
founded
—Polo introduced by James Gordon Bennett
1877 —First championship swimming races sponsored by
New York Athletic Club
1879 —Madison Square Park renamed Madison Square
Garden and taken over by P.T. Barnum
—The National Association of Amateur Athletes of
America (NAAA) founded (today's AAU)

1880 —First national lawn tennis tournament sponsored
by the Staten Island Cricket and Baseball Club
—The American Canoe Association founded
1881 —American National Red Cross founded
1882 —Handball brought to U.S. from Ireland
1883 —First authentic rodeo, July 4th, Pecos, Texas
1885 —American Association for the Advancement of
Physical Education founded (today's AAHPERD)
1886 —USA Figure-Skating Association founded
1887 —Softball invented at the Farragut Club, Chicago,
Illinois
1888 —Development of the "safety" bicycle promoted
widespread interest in cycling
—Formation of the Amateur Athletic Union from the
NAAA
1889 —Establishment of two playgrounds in New York
City
1891 —Game of basketball invented by James Naismith
1894 —Amateur Golf Association of the United States
founded (today's United States Golf Association—
U.S.G.A.)
1895 —Volleyball introduced at YMCA sports conference
at Springfield College
—American Bowling Congress founded
—U.S. Amateur Hockey League founded
1896 —First State Federation of High School Athletic
Associations established, Wisconsin
—Modern Olympic games inaugurated
1897 —Military Athletic League organized
1900 —Davis Cup tennis competition inaugurated
—American League of Professional Baseball Clubs
founded
—Tug-of-war, Rugby football and clay-pigeon shooting
included in Olympic Games
1902 —Judo taught at West Point Military Academy
—First Americans fought in the Amateur Boxing
Association Championships
—Beginnings of motorcycle speedway
1903 —First baseball "World Series" played
—Public School Athletic League of New York City
organized to foster intramural sports (followed by a
girls' branch in 1905

1904 —Cornell University coaching staff gave instruction
        in their specialties to students not on intercollegiate
        teams. Considered one of the first departments to
        give attention to intramural sports
        —Boxing introduced in the modern Olympic Games
        —United States National Ski Association founded

1905 —Intercollegiate Athletic Association (ICAA) of the
        United States founded (today's NCAA)

1906 —Playground Association of America founded
        (today's NRPA)
        —National Association of Boy's Club founded

1908 —Hockey, polo, race-walking and throwing the javelin
        included in Olympic Games
        —Figure ice-skating first winter sport to be included
        in Olympic Games

1909 —YMCA initiated national program for teaching
        swimming and diving

1910 —ICAA changed its name to the National Collegiate
        Athletic Association
        —The Boy Scouts of America and Camp Fire Girls
        founded

1911 —Playground Association of America adds Recreation
        to its name—PRAA
        —Indianapolis 500 established

1912 —The Girl Scouts of America founded
        —University of Chicago physical education staff
        member given responsibility to program intramural
        sport
        —Modern pentathlon included in Olympic Games
        —First women's swimming events included in Olympic
        Games

1913 —The University of Michigan and The Ohio State
        University inaugurated departments of intramural
        sport under the direction of a faculty member
        —The U.S. Football (Soccer) Association formed
        —Shuffleborad introduced in Florida

1914 —Red Cross initiated its Lifesaving Service
        —Harley Davidson Racing Department (motorcycles)
        established

1917 —National Hockey League formed, northeastern
        United States and Canada
        —Committee on Intramural Sports of the Athletic

Research Society recommended a comprehensive classification of playing units in its annual report
—The American Physical Education Association established a Committee on Women's Athletics to standardize women's athletic programs
—The National Athletic Conference of American College Women met—Opposition was expressed against athletic sport in favor of intramural sport

1919   —National Boxing Association formed
—International Greyhound racing Association formed in Tulsa, Oklahoma

1920   —Intramural directors of Western Intercollegiate Athletic Conference began holding annual meetings (Today's Big Ten Recreational Sports Directors Conference)

1920's—State Leagues of Girl's Athletic Associations begin to form and focus on intramural sport versus athletic sport

1920-5—Stock-car racing originated

1922   —National Federal of High School Athletic Associations founded   .
—First Women's Olympic Games in Paris sponsored by the Federation Sportive Feminine International (FSFI)
—National Amateur Athletic Federation founded
—Women's Amateur Athletic Association founded

1923   —National Conference on Women's Sport leading to a women's division of the National Amateur Federation
— Support expressed for sport by all, rather than the few highly skilled

1924   —Amateur Trapshooting Association of America founded
—Boston Bruins ice hockey club became first professional NHL team in USA

1925   —Elmer D. Mitchell, referred to as the father of intramurals in America, authored first book on intramurals titled "Intramural Athletics"
—Contract bridge invented by Harold Vanderbilt
—First water-ski jump, Ralph Samuelson, USA
—The American Judo Club established in New York City

1926   —Parachuting competitions begin
1928   —Women's events formally accepted as a part of the

Modern Olympic Games
First collegiate intramural sport building in
America constructed at the University of Michigan
1929 —First weightlifting National Championships sponsored
by the A.A.U.
1930 —Catholic Youth Organization founded
—Playground and Recreation Association of America
changed its name to the National Recreation Association (NRA)
—First challenge match in contract bridge between
USA and Britain
1931 —The Women's Division of the National Amateur
Athletic Federation affiliated with the American
Physical Education Association
1932 —Amateur Softball Association founded
1933 —The College Physical Education provided a section
for the discussion of intramural sports at its annual
meetings
1934 —Men's Collegiate basketball tournament, Madison
Square Garden
—U.S. Platform Tennis Association founded
1934-5—New Deal serves as impetus to the building of
recreational facilities. In 1934, 1036 cities reported
organized recreation programs and by 1935, 2190
cities offered organized programs
1935 —Works Progress Administration formed—facilitated
construction of sports facilities, trained persons to
perform recreational sport programming and organized
community recreation programs that included sport
1936 —First graduate recreation courses, New York
—American Badminton Association founded
—Trampoline developed
—Basketball first included in Olympic Games
1937 —American Physical Education Association added
health to its name and affiliated with the National
Education Association (AAHPE)
1938 —AAHPE added recreation to its scope and became
the American Association for Health, Physical Education, and Recreation—under its Division of Men's
Athletics, a section on intramural athletics was
established
1939 —The Women's Division of the National Amateur

Athletic Federation merged with the National Section
on Women's Athletics
—Little League started
1940's—Growth of Pop Warner football, Biddy Basketball,
Pee Wee and Midget Hockey, AAU age group swimming and track
1941   —National Industrial Recreation Association founded
to assist programming in war plants
—Federal Security Agency's Office of Community
War Services established a Recreation Division to
assist programs on community level
1943   —All-American Girls Baseball League formed
1945   —First State recreation commission organized, North
Carolina
1946   —MV Augusta motorcycle manufacturers established
1947   —National Association for Stock Car Racing formed
(NASCAR)
1948   —Olympics of the Paralyzed first held
1949   —Ladies Professional Golf Association formed
—National Basketball Association formed
1950   —The National Intramural Association founded by
Dr. William Wasson of Dillard University, New Orleans
1951   —The U.S. Handball Association formed
1952   —Karate introduced by Matsutasu Oyama
—National Paddleball Association founded
1953   —National Section on Women's Athletics changed its
name to National Section for Girls and Women's
Sports (NSGWS)
—First ascent of Everest, May 29
—National Darts Association founded
1954   —Roger Bannister breaks 4 minutes for the mile (May 6)
—National Open championship in squash rackets
1955   —The College Physical Education Association, the
American Association for Health, Physical Education,
and Recreation and the National Association of
Physical Education for College Women jointly spon-
sored an intramural conference in Washington, D.C.
1956   —The American Association for Health, Physical
Education, and Recreation sponsored a national conference on fitness in Washington D.C.
—President's Council on Youth Fitness established

by President Eisenhower

1959 —The National Intramural Association became an affiliate of the American Association for Health, Physical Education and Recreation (AAHPER)

1960 —White House Conference on Children and Youth inaugurated

—International Soccer League began play at the New York polo grounds

—American Football League (AFL) founded

—Biathlon included in winter Olympic Games

—Skateboarding begins in California

1961 —The National Intramural Association rejected an offer to merge with AAHPER

—First White House Conference on Aging

1962 —Bureau of Outdoor Recreation created

1963 —President Kennedy renames the President's Council on Youth Fitness to the President's Council on Physical Fitness

1964 —National Wilderness Recreation System Act signed into law

—Judo included in Olympic Games for first time

1965 —Older Americans Act signed into law

—The National Recreation Association changed its name to the National Recreation and Park Association (NRPA)

—Houston "Astrodome" opened

1966 —The National Intramural Sports Council (NISC) was formed as a joint project of the Division of Men's Athletics and Division for Girl's and Women's Sports of AAHPER

—Football's first "Superbowl"

1967 —New Jersey first to approve state certification for recreation personnel

1968 —President's Council on Physical Fitness renamed by President Johnson to President's Council on Physical Fitness and Sports

—A National Conference on College University Recreation, sponsored by AAHPER, was held in Washington, D.C. to discuss campus-wide recreation

—Present structure of Madison Square Garden, New York, opened

—The North American Soccer League formed
—First U.S. Orienteering championships held, Southern
  Illinois University

1969 —Diane Crump first women jockey to ride at a major
  horse track
—Racquetball selected as name for modified paddleball
  and the International Racquetball Association formed

1971 —United States Orienteering Federation formed
—Second White House Conference on Aging held
—ACTION — CAP programs started
—The National Intramural Association admitted
  female members
—Association for Intercollegiate Athletics for Women
  established (AIAW)

1972 —Bobby Fisher won a much celebrated world
  championship chess competition from Boris Sparsky
—The Education Amendment Act enacted—it included
  Title IX which banned discrimination based on sex
  and provided women with equal opportunities to participate in sports

1973 —Billie Jean King defeated Bobby Riggs in a tennis
  match

1974 —Council on Recreation Education Accreditation formed
—AAHPER reorganized and changed its name to the
  American Alliance for Health, Physical Education, and
  Recreation

1975 —The National Intramural Association membership
  voted to change its name to the National Intramural-
  Recreational Sports Association (NIRSA)
—First National Leisure Educational Conference held

1976 —The National Intramural Recreational Sport
  Association formed on ad hoc committee on Professional Preparation

1977 —White House Conference on Handicapped held

1979 —American Alliance for Health, Physical Education, .
  and Recreation added Dance to its name (AAHPERD)

Present and Future

The decade of the 80's continues to reveal that recreational
sport is a major component of American lifestyles. The follow-

ing points illustrate the major trends expected to endure through the decade.

1. Participant interest has increased in martial arts; high-risk, adventure sports such as hand gliding, wind surfing, sky diving, sky diving, mountain climbing, white water rafting, orienteering and outdoor recreational sports such as canoeing, snow skiing, sailing, and bicycling.

2. There has been a growing interest in non-traditional sports activities which emphasize self-testing and cooperative behaviors such as the "new games" approach and "stress-challenge" activities.

3. Physical fitness programs continue to gain in popularity amoung all age groups. The most popular fitness-related activities include jogging, swimming, bicycling, racquetball, aerobic dancing, and "jazzercise." Closely associated with the physical fitness craze is the interest in wellness which emphasizes prevention of illness. More Americans have become interested in stress testing and activity programs tailor-made for their own level of fitness and wellness.

4. The 70's gave birth to an electronic sports age reflecting the proliferation of computer, arcade, and home video sports games that have stormed the market.

5. A tremendous influx of women into sport at all levels has been accepted as a pattern for the 80's.

6. Greater attention has focused on problems associated with providing programs for our youth, disabled, and aged.

7. Concern for the energy shortages and environmental protection are curbing long distance travel and tourism.

Actions taken today by recreational sports programmers will determine the direction of programs and the construction of facilities for the future. How well we provide services to satisfy the needs of tomorrow depends on our understanding of the impact current conditions, issues, and trends have upon the future. A look at a few critical items affecting recreational sports services and participation is useful, although it is not within the scope of this section to engage in detailed interpretation. The reader is encouraged to consider carefully the information, keep abreast of changes, and pursue an understanding of the implications. (Mobley and Fairey, 1980)

Population and Age Groups: The population in the United States in 1980 reached approximately 222 million and is expected to increase to 260 million by the year 2000. A redistribution of age group proportions, as illustrated in Figure 1-4, is occurring which will affect recreational sport services. By 1990, people under the age of 20 will represent just 30 percent of the population, persons 20 to 64 years will account for 58 percent and persons 65 and over will reach 12 percent— almost 30 million citizens!

Composition Shift: Central cities will continue to lose residents, declining from 27 percent of total population to 22.9 percent, with an accompanying shift in the composition of residents. (USN & WR, 1979, p. 49) More young, affluent professionals are returning to the city while the middle class and many blue collar workers leave for the suburbs, resulting in an unusual mix of classes in an urban environment.

The geographic location of the population changes as the move to the sunbelt and other southern and western states continues. The changes are expedited by the recent shift of industry to rural areas.

The average family size has shown a continual decline from 3.3 members in 1960 to 2.7 in 1980 and a projected reduction to 2.5 members in 1990. There are more women heading households than ever before. Single parent families have increased 76 percent between 1970 and 1978. Double parent families have decreased by 3 percent. (*Statistical Abstract of the U.S.*, U.S. Govt. Printing Office, Wash., D.C., 1980, p. 47)

Education and Schools: The increasing education level of the total population is reflected in Figure 1-5.

More people are pursuing some form of higher education. This increase in educational attainment suggests a greater potential for leisure education.

Population shifts, shown in Figure 1-6, affecting the number of school age individuals will result in an imbalance in education systems in the upcoming years. More elementary schools will be needed as the number of births increase. College population will decline while including a greater proportion of older working students and retirees.

Work Force and Patterns: Changes in composition of the work force affect the way in which individuals choose recreational sport experiences. A heavy influx of women and nonwhites into the labor force continues as does a trend toward

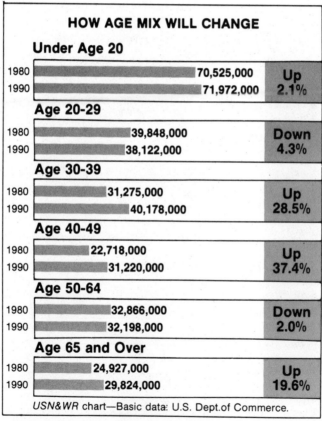

Figure 1-4. Projected change in age distribution.
Source: "Challenge of the 80's", *U.S. News and World Report*, October 15, 1979, p. 48.

Reprinted from "U.S. News & World Report"
Copyright, 1979, U.S. News & World Report, Inc.

two-income families. The unemployment rate is expected to reach 8.2 percent before falling to 5 percent in 1990, while the median income rises from $22,000 to around $46,000. (*Statistical Abstract of the U.S.*, U.S. Govt. Printing Office, Wash., D.C., 1980, p. 57) Although the work week has decreased since 1850 from 69.7 hours to 35.9 hours in 1978, it has stabilized at around 40 hours. The structure of the work

EDUCATIONAL ATTAINMENT

Percent of Adults Who Have Completed Four
Years of High School or more: 1950 to 1977

Percent of Persons 25 Years Old and Over

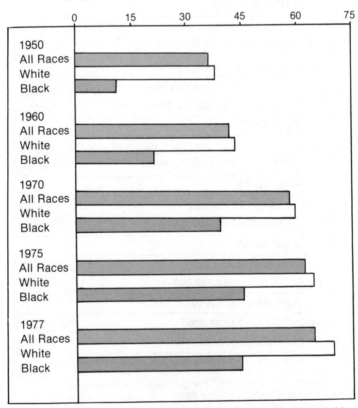

Figure 1-5. Educational attainment; percent of adults 25 years or older, who have completed four years of high school or more: 1950-1977. Source: U.S. Bureau of Census.

week has undergone major changes with four-day work weeks, "flex-time," and job sharing—which leaves larger blocks of time for potential use for recreational sport pursuits.

Economy: Inflation is expected to decrease while personal income by 1990 will increase to 40 percent compared to a 35 percent average in the '70s. (Statistical Abstract, p. 58) Indications suggest that much of the American public's disposable income will continue to be spent on leisure-related goods and services despite inflation. While $58 billion was devoted to leisure time spending in 1965, the figure rose to $244 billion by 1981—an increase of 47 percent adjusting for inflation. (USNWR, Aug., 1981, pp. 61-63) By 1985, leisure spending will reach $300 billion—almost a six time increase in 20 years.

Implications: Recreational sport programmers will experience different working conditions: changes in normal popula-

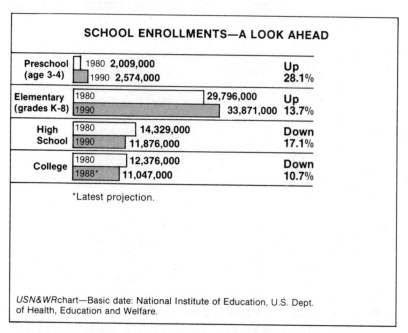

SCHOOL ENROLLMENTS—A LOOK AHEAD

Preschool (age 3-4)	1980 2,009,000	Up 28.1%
	1990 2,574,000	
Elementary (grades K-8)	1980 29,796,000	Up 13.7%
	1990 33,871,000	
High School	1980 14,329,000	Down 17.1%
	1990 11,876,000	
College	1980 12,376,000	Down 10.7%
	1988* 11,047,000	

*Latest projection.

USN&WRchart—Basic date: National Institute of Education, U.S. Dept. of Health, Education and Welfare.

Figure 1-6. School enrollments predictions, 1980-1990. Source: "Challenge of the 80's", *U. S. News and World Report,* October 15, 1979, p. 74.
Reprinted from "U.S. News & World Report"
Copyright, 1979, U.S. News & World Report, Inc.

tion and employment patterns combined with the realities of limits—shrinking financial resources, natural resources, and fuel supplies. Emphasis will focus upon accountability, better business management, cost effectiveness, and increased operations efficiency. We must pursue alternative funding sources. Most practitioners anticipate utilization of user fees and charges for funding as state and federal governments tax support decreases.

Each of these considerations, and others will necessitate long-range planning. Although historical perspective informs the programmer about the major events which have shaped recreational sport, it will be virtually impossible to make an important contribution to the improvement of the quality of life for the American citizen unless a concerted effort is made to plan for the future.

REFERENCES—FOUNDATIONS

Betts, J.R. *American Sporting Heritage.* 1850–1950. Reading, Massachusetts: Addison-Wesley Publishing Co., 1974.

Carlson, R.E., MacLean, J.R., Deppe, T.R., and Peterson, J.A. *Recreation and Leisure: The Changing Scene,* 3rd edition. Belmont, California: Wadsworth Publishing Co., Inc., 1979.

"Challenge of the '80s," *U. S. News and World Report.* October 15, 1979, pp. 45-80.

Clarke, J.S. *Challenge and Change: A History of the Development of the National Intramural-Recreational Sports Association, 1950–1976.* West Point, N.Y.: Leisure Press, 1978.

Chubb, M. and Chubb, H.R. *One Third Our Time? An Introduction to Recreation Behavior and Resources.* New York: John Wiley and Sons, Inc., 1981.

Cuddon, J.A. *The International Dictionary of Sports and Games.* New York: Schocker Books, 1979.

Epperson, A.F. *Private and Commercial Recreation: A Text and Reference.* New York: John Wiley and Sons, Inc., 1977.

Frost, R.B. and Cureton, T.K. (eds.). *Encyclopedia of Physical Education, Fitness, and Sports: Sports, Dance and Related Activities.* Reading, Massachusetts: Addison-Wesley Publishing Co., 1977.

Horowitz, A. *The World Chess Championship—A History.* New York: The MacMillan Company, 1973.

Kraus, R. *Recreational Leisure in Modern Society.* Englewood Cliffs, N.J.: Prentice-Hall, Inc., 1971.

Malo, J. *Malo's Complete Guide to Canoeing and Canoe Camping.* New York: The New York Times Book Company, 1974.

Mobley, T. and Fairey, K. Social Indicators and Leisure. Bloomington:Indiana University, unpublished paper, 1980.

Mueller, P. and Reznik, J.W. *Intramural-Recreational Sports: Programming and Administration.* New York: John Wiley and Sons, 1979.

"Our Endless Pursuit of Happiness," *U. S. News and World Report.* August 10, 1981, pp. 58-67.

Oxford, J. *The Oxford Companion to Sports and Games.* London: Oxford University Press, 1975.

The National Industrial Recreation Association, 203 N. Wabash Avenue, Chicago, Illinois.

Rice, E.A., Huthcinson, J.L. and Lee, M. *A Brief History of Physical Education.* New York: The Ronald Press Co., 1969.

Schroeder, C.R. *Karate.* Reading, Massachusetts: Addison-Wesley Publishing Company, 1976.

Spears, B. and Swanson, R.A. *History of Sport and Physical Education in the United States.* Dubuque, Iowa: William C. Brown Co., 1978.

Statistical Abstract of the U. S. Washington, D. C.: U. S. Government Printing Office, 1980.

Zeigler, E.F. *A History of Physical Education and Sport in the United States and Canada.* Champaign, Illinois: Stipes Publishing Co., 1975.

CHAPTER 2

PARTICIPANT DEVELOPMENT

A programmer may become so preoccupied with the tasks and procedures involved in program delivery that he or she neglects program impact upon participants and leadership personnel. Programmers need to understand and evaluate the degree a program meets peoples' needs and contributes to their growth and development. In this context, growth refers to the physical and physiological changes that occur throughout life, while development refers to such functional changes as language skills, emotional control, interpersonal skills, identity, competence and autonomy.

While the tasks involved in program delivery are initially challenging, they often become routine. A commitment to participant development adds meaning and direction and continuity to the programmer's efforts. Procedural knowledge alone—how to set up tournaments, run a club, design and

operate a facility, schedule personnel, or publicize a program—does not guarantee program quality. Such expertise
does not contribute to development unless founded upon insight into the characteristics and needs of participants. By
understanding how program design and delivery satisfy needs,
we may influence participant development.

For perspective on participant development, we need to
examine the human growth and development process. Miller
and Prince (1977, p. 5) describe human development as a continuous and cumulative process of change in physical,
psychological and social function which may be divided into
an orderly series of life stages. Each of these life stages is
characterized by specific developmental tasks that require a
person to alter present behavior and master new learning. In
addition:

—Development is most likely to occur in an environment
that anticipates change, where people feel it is safe to
explore and are encouraged and reassured during the
process. Additional ways to facilitate development include opportunities to reveal thoughts and feelings, to
receive feedback, to seek and receive information, and
to experiment with and practice new ways of thinking
and acting.
—A systematic integration of mental, emotional, social,
and physical experiences produces the most effective
development.
—An individual's development may be advanced by exposure to an organized problem-solving process that
enables him or her to attempt and complete increasingly
complex developmental tasks. (Ibid., pp. 5, 6, 15)

Our knowledge of the nature and process of human development is incomplete. Among the principles receiving wide
acceptance, the following may help the programmer understand participant development. The first principle concerns
the concept of life stages.

.   A life stage is a period of time that establishes numerous
developmental characteristics common among human beings.
Human growth and development proceeds through successive
life stages. It involves a progression from simpler to more complex tasks and activities, occurring wtih some degree of con-

tinuity and cumulativeness from stage to stage. As one faces challenges, one draws on previous experiences and learning. Since a life stage is an arbitrary category and individuals progress from stage to stage at their own pace, it serves as a framework for program planning and operations (Ibid, pp. 6, 7).

The second principle involves developmental tasks comprising a particular life stage. Each life stage requires the acquisition of particular skills, attitudes, knowledge, or functions to meet challenges. The extent to which an individual succeeds in completing these tasks is determined by heredity, environment and individual attributes, although the tasks encountered within each stage are relatively uniform. For example, some of the developmental tasks associated with adolescence include achieving an appropriate balance between dependence and independence, learning a social role, accepting one's body, selecting and preparing for an occupation, developing a value system and learning to give and receive affection (Ibid, pp. 9, 10).

From the standpoint of a recreational sport programmer, we need this insight because the more we learn about the specific occurrences within each life stage, the better we may design programs and experiences that fit a particular life stage and enhance development.

The notion of a developmental approach to recreational sport programming is not new. Since the beginning of organized physical education, recreation and intramural sport programs, practitioners and educators have claimed that participation in sport contributes to the emotional, social, mental and physical development. These claims were largely based upon theory, observation and speculation rather than upon research.

Since the 1960's, participant development has emerged as a major focus for physical education, recreation and recreational sport practitioners. A major impetus has been the increased pressure on all sport programs to demonstrate accountability to taxpayers. Recession in the American economy necessitated cutbacks or elimination of those sport programs not making significant contributions to the goals of the setting, or those unable to support themselves financially. In response, educators and practitioners sought to prove (through research) what contributions sport makes to physical, mental, personality and social development. Although most inquiry has focused on interscholastic, intercollegiate, or professional sport, some studies apply to recreational sport.

PROGRAM DESIGN AND DELIVERY

Before presenting a synopsis of information on participant characteristics for each life stage, we will review the program design and delivery factors having a developmental impact upon participants. These factors include staff, program content, rules and regulations, governance, personnel and recognition. Due to the diversity of variables (life stages, settings, and program divisions—informal, intramural, club), it is not possible to address each factor in detail. Rather, we provide a general indication of how these factors impact upon human development.

Staff. Staff members can have a positive impact upon development when they have insight into the human growth and development process and competence in providing quality programs based upon needs and interests of participants. However, knowledge and competence are not enough. Staff should develop positive relationships with participants by being accessible and possessing communication skills. Consequently, the recreational sport programmer should design opportunities to increase contact with participants by having an "open door" policy for communication and by providing leadership positions (team captain, unit manager, advisory, or governing committee member, official, supervisor, lifeguard) that include them in the operational aspects of the program.

Participants are encouraged to display acceptable behavior and explore their potential when staff members are competent role models. The programmer will be called upon to assume several interrelated functions in this regard, including instructor, trainer, consultant, advisor, and evaluator. He or she should know the appropriate time for assuming each role.

Program. One of the concerns most commonly voiced by recreational sport specialists is the need for suitable, well-balanced programs. The type and number of sport activities we provide are important. Since people have diverse interests and skill levels, programmers should provide variety in the sports, program types (informal, intramural, club) and skill classifications offered.

Sports vary in the way they impact upon development. For example, table tennis offered as an intramural single elimination tournament provides distinct developmental opportunities in comparison with table tennis offered on a club sport basis. In addition, differences exist among and between team sports, dual sports and individual sports.

The types of classification systems used within sport programs also affect development. Co-intramural sport participation may provide opportunities for males and females to appreciate differences and similarities in skills, interests and limitations. Classification systems which allow for variations in ability or levels of intensity may contribute to autonomy, competence, and interpersonal relations skills. These systems structure opportunities to experience success and gratification, outcomes that usually encourage continued participation.

Finally, the social interaction and challenge resulting from sport participation, regardless of the sport, skill level or program format contributes to the development of physical and mental abilities, emotional control, autonomy, self-esteem, interpersonal skills, integrity, identity, and health.

Rules and Regulations. Rules and regulations that are selected or designed to facilitate equity and safety among participants contribute to development. When rules enhance the perception that one can achieve some degree of success and satisfaction, they encourage continued involvement. For example, most programs use eligibility statements to counter unfair distinctions between participants. One of the most common eligibility requirements in recreational sport programs restricts or eliminates the athletic or professional sport participant in a specific or related sport. This restriction, based on skill transfer research, indicates that domination by athletic and professional sport participants minimizes the chance for equitable participation by the player-participant in recreational sport. A different approach to controlling unbalanced competition exists in some youth sport programs where all members of a team are guaranteed an opportunity to participate regardless of skill level. Each person has the chance to benefit in terms of self-esteem, acceptance, recognition, identity, emotional management, responsibility, interpersonal skills and competence. Such rules recognize that development is contingent upon participation.

Rules and regulations provide explicit directions for behavior. When a rule is enforced, individuals learn to alter their thoughts and actions to comply with the rules or they suffer the consequences.

Governance. A governance board, committee, or council is a vehicle for involving participants in leadership capacities. Membership in these groups permits more frequent contact with staff and other role models. Involvement helps the player-participant and leader-participant develop and refine decision-making skills, benefit from mistakes, interact with others, listen effectively, and consider the needs, concerns, and motives of others. As part of a governing body, participants learn responsibility, strengthen their identities through the varied roles and experiences they encounter, and develop consistency between their values and their behavior in decision-making situations.

Guidance, not domination, is key to objectivity in the governance process. The amount of responsibility granted participants making governance decisions depends on their age, experience, and maturity. Decisions made by a governing body should not be over-ruled without just cause. Otherwise, the value of the experience may be minimized.

Personnel. Other positions of responsibility within the recreational sport program that have a developmental impact upon participants include: team captain, unit manager, coach, committee member, club or committee officer, official, lifeguard, supervisor, and activity leader. Such roles contribute to autonomy, integrity, emotional control, competency, identity, and interpersonal skills.

The level of maturity required to assume one of these positions increases from team captain to coach, unit manager, official, supervisor, and governing committee. The programmer places persons in positions commensurate with their abilities while allowing them room to develop.

Recognition. The public relations and recognition aspects of the program promote development by encouraging participation. Aspects of recognition and public relations having particular impact are point systems, awards, and public relations personnel.

From a developmental standpoint, point systems have positive and negative aspects. A point system or similar recognition system has a negative effect when people become discouraged and lose interest because a goal is unattainable. Point systems designed to regard achievement in participation and sportsmanship provide alternatives to winning as a prime objective.

Another form of recognition uses awards, whether they be certificates, medallions, trophies, apparel or other tangible objects. They may discourage participation when directed exclusively to winners or best performers. By honoring accomplishments in leadership, sportsmanship or service, awards reinforce appropriate behavior and encourage participation.

Finally, the public relations and recognition tasks of a program may be incorporated into a leadership position to afford opportunity for development. Participants can improve their sense of purpose by experiencing practical vocational situations, promote self-reliance by completing specified tasks on their own, and feel competent by practicing of art, journalism, photography, telecommmunications, and marketing skills.

PARTICIPANT CHARACTERISTICS

We have illustrated some of the ways that program factors impact upon development. Our contributions to development will be minimal unless decisions regarding program design and delivery are based upon an understanding of participant characteristics. Consequently, we will discuss general characteristics for established life stages—middle childhood or youth (6–12 or 14 years), adolescence (13–19 years), early adulthood (20–39 years), middle adulthood (40–65 years), and later adulthood. Each set of characteristics, describing the growth, development and behavior of an average American, involve physical, mental, personality, and social parameters. Included within the characteristics are some of the major developmental tasks associated with each life stage. A section on implications demonstrates how knowledge about participant characteristics may be applied to program design and delivery for player-participants and those involved in leadership or administration (for instance, team captain, coach, officer, committee member, official, supervisor). This material, while not exhaustive or conclusive, is representative of current knowledge regarding participant characteristics and the implications for programming based on recent research, a review of the literature and professional experience.

Although some agency-sponsored programs in such sports as swimming, ice hockey, and gymnastics are offered for children (newborn–5 years), their primary recreational sport involvement is organized and provided by the family on a casual basis with an emphasis on instruction and lead-up games. Since structured programs for children are not widespread or prevalent in sport literature we will not include material on this life stage at this point.

Middle Childhood (6–12 years)

Middle childhood (youth) is an era of new experiences and challenges. Youth, no longer confined to the family, home or neighborhood, begin to act on their own in new settings. How they adjust to a school environment, new peer contacts, and involvement in group activities influences self-image, self-esteem, sex-role identification, emotional maturity, and social relationships. Opportunity for recreational sport participation on an organized basis typically exists through community-sponsored youth sport programs. Physical and psychological development is crucial at this age, so the programmer should plan appropriate sport activities and select qualified leaders for this group.

Physical Characteristics:

1. Height ranges from 44 to 62 inches and weight ranges from 44 to 100 pounds. On the average, boys are slightly taller and heavier than girls. (Gallahue, 1982, p. 130) (Turner & Helms, 1979, p. 193)

2. Body growth progresses at a slower, steadier rate in comparison with preschool years.

3. Muscles develop in size and strength but are still immature in function compared with those of an adolescent. Boys tend to have more muscle and fatty tissue than girls.

4. The skeleton reaches maturity as bone replaces cartilage.

5. The heart grows at a slow rate and is smaller in proportion to body size than at any other time in life. (Turner & Helms, 1979, p. 196)

While boys and girls at this age are full of energy, they often possess a low endurance level, tire easily, and need periods of rest. Since their muscles and skeleton are prone to

strain during vigorous or sustained physical activity or continual pressure, avoid activities which involve running on hard,
unyielding surfaces, pitching, throwing or rough bodily contact. Concentrate on lead-up activities and games to facilitate
the transition from fundamental motor skills to sport skills. As
growing awareness of physical self occurs, attitudes toward
the body often reflect self-concept. The acquisition of fundamental motor skills helps children develop a positive body
concept. Once interest in sport begins, opportunities to participate in a variety of sports aids development of all motor
skills.

Mental Characteristics:

1. Attention span lengthens. As adolescence approaches,
   an individual can spend hours concentrating on an activity.

2. Youth exhibit an improved ability for reflective thinking
   and can handle more than one perception at a time.

3. Abstract thought processes become evident at the end
   of this life stage. Youth begin to think and reason
   logically. They can think through actions that previously
   had to be carried out in actuality. (Turner and Helms,
   1979, p. 205)

4. A growing mastery of the concept of numbers, clock
   time, calendar time, and spatial relationships occurs.

5. Vocabulary, as opposed to physical gesture, dominates
   as a vehicle of expression. Social interactions are
   crucial to language development.

6. Youth know rules which specify right and wrong
   behavior but may not understand the reasons behind
   them.

Recreational sport activities can be more firmly structured
by rules because they are more readily understood by participants. Youth at this stage are capable of learning more
complex sport skills. Facilitate learning and retention through
teaching by the part-whole method and providing time for
"mental rehearsal" of sport activity. Since improvement in proficiency requires knowledge of results, provide feedback on
performance and encourage children to analyze their own

actions. Since youth also learn skills and behavior patterns through observation, furnish appropriate role-models and reinforce desirable behavior.

Participation in sport affords opportunity for cognitive learning through exposure to rules, regulations, strategy and decision-making. Although attention span has increased and cognitive processes have developed, youth can not be expected to act in a safe manner without frequent reminders about taking precautions.

Personality Characteristics:

1. Interactions with adults and peers serve as the basis from which self-concept and identity begin to crystalize.

2. Youth demonstrate a growing concern for competence, achievement, and approval from others.

3. A desire for achievement for its own sake occurs more in boys. Girls tend to be more interested in seeking approval and affection. The differences are closely related to sex-role development. (Smart & Smart, 1972, p. 422)

4. Youth exhibit a preference for separation into sexually segregated groups.

5. Fears or anxiety about personal safety and animals decline as concerns related to school, social relationships and economic difficulties increase. (Turner & Helms, 1979, p. 246)

6. Expression of physical aggression diminishes, although boys demonstrate more aggressive behavior than girls. (Turner & Helms, 1979, p. 247)

Since youth are curious and enjoy the adventure and challenge sport provides, assist them in establishing realistic expectations and levels of aspiration. Offer sport activities that provide ample opportunity to experience success and approval, as failure may discourage involvement. Keep activities compatible with abilities and allow for individual differences. Diversity in sport activity intensity and ability allows youth an opportunity to participate at a level compatible with their maturity and demonstrates acceptance of differences.

When classifying youth for participation, consider variations in ability. Otherwise, the late maturers and the lesser skilled may experience ridicule and dissatisfaction. Such negative reinforcement may lead to rejection of future sport participation and contribute to poor self-concept. Since youth often make unrealistic comparisons of themselves with others, encourage them to focus on their own previous performances as the basis for improvement. As they experience achievement and recognition, their motivation and self-confidence are likely to improve.

Help youth realize that winning and losing are not a reflection of self worth. Give them encouragement and recognize their accomplishments, especially upon the occasion of a poor performance or a loss of a game. Criticism, ridicule or sarcasm diminishes confidence and provokes unfavorable emotional responses.

Youth need to feel that they are involved in decision-making. They should have an opportunity to share their ideas and opinions, while realizing that their every wish will not be granted. Such involvement fosters a sense of independence, identity and personal worth.

Social Characteristics:

1. Youth compare their ideas, beliefs and interpretations with those held by others. When discrepancies occur, they may modify their own thoughts, seek to modify those of others, or justify their thinking to those who disagree.

2. Youth begin to internalize the cultural rules which govern behavior. They exhibit growing respect for authority and wish to please others. This is a stage characterized by conformity.

3. Youth become aware of other peoples' intentions and demonstrate concern over the way inappropriate actions or responses affect relationships.

4. Youth's attitudes toward other ethnic groups are related to those of their parents. (Smart and Smart, 1972, p. 455)

5. Social values and behavior are transmitted to children through child-rearing practices and vary from class to class. (Smart and Smart, 1972, p. 456, 457)

6. Peer groups exert a compelling pressure on youth to accept their values in order to become a member. Conflicting pressures between adults and peer groups influence the development of autonomy in making decisions. (Smart and Smart, 1972, p. 444)

7. Peer group acceptance or rejection greatly influences self-concept. Some proficiency in physical activities contributes to popularity. (Smart and Smart, 1972, p. 468)

Adolescence (13–19 years)

Adolescence is critical to human development in making the individual's search for identity. It begins with the biological onset of puberty and ends with an imprecise entrance into adulthood. Experiences affecting one's sense of competency—intellectual, social, moral—take place that shape one's sense of self. This age is one of introspection, a search for autonomy and selfhood—a self that is acceptable to society: family, friends, teachers, employers and sweethearts. Of special interest to the recreational sport programmer is the differentiation that occurs between adolescent boys and girls. Social roles and sexual factors accentuate physical, psychological, and personality differences.

Physical Characteristics:

1. The period preceding puberty is characterized by rapid growth, occurring for girls between the ages of 10 and 12 and for boys between 10 and 16. Growth seems disproportionate, primarily because the trunk grows at a slower rate than the legs, while the hands and feet develop more rapidly. A sense of awkwardness accompanies these changes. (Turner and Helms, 1979, p. 258)

2. Marked muscular growth leads to an increase in strength in boys. With larger hearts and lungs, they

have a greater capacity for oxygenating the blood. (Schiamberg and Smith, 1982, p. 453)

3. Since weight gain is proportionately greater than gain in height, the adolescent gains a stockier appearance. (Turner and Helms, 1979, p. 260)

4. The heart, digestive and circulatory systems undergo more rapid growth than do veins and arteries. Capacity of the lungs also increases rapidly. (Turner and Helms, 1979, pp. 260, 261)

5. Maturation of the primary and secondary sex characteristics signifies the onset of sexual maturity. The adolescent experiences heightened sexual feeling and desire, boys more so than girls. (Turner and Helms, 1979, p. 261)

6. Sebaceous gland activity often causes acne and other skin problems.

7. Maturation results in vocal changes. For boys, the change in pitch is usually greater and is often associated with a period of lost voice control.

8. Adolescents continue to improve in strength, reaction, and coordination abilities, although boys surpass girls in overall motor-skill development. Physical characteristics, personal motivation, social approval, and opportunity to participate may account for this advantage. (Turner and Helms, 1979, p. 266, 268)

After puberty, physiological differences between boys and girls suggest separate sport programs are appropriate for equity and safety unless rule modifications are made. The increase in muscle strength by boys results in better performance in strength-related activities while the lower center of gravity of girls leads to better performance in balance-related activities. Diverse levels of development require programs to promote comfortable alternatives for participation in light of the awkwardness that often accompanies adolescence. Although endurance activities may help control weight and reduce body fat, they are more appropriate for older adolescents whose heart and lung capacity have increased.

Offer weight training programs that avoid routines placing excessive stress upon joints.

Mental Characteristics:

1. The adolescent is capable of mental perspectives regarding the past, present and future.

2. Qualitative mental changes that occur include the ability to think about things as they are and as they could be, the ability to work with symbols (metaphors and algebra), and the ability to systematically coordinate a number of factors in problem solving. (Schiamberg, and Smith, 1982, p. 460)

3. Adolescents have the capacity to think about the meaning of words and in terms of ideals and absolutes. This type of thinking permits planning for the future. (Smart and Smart, 1972, p. 535)

4. Inductive and deductive reasoning occur.

5. While youth are capable of describing situations or phenomena, adolescents are capable of explaining them. (Smart and Smart, 1972, p. 534)

6. The adolescent begins to reflect about his own thinking and that of others. Until adolescents see themselves and others more realistically, they tend to regard themselves as unique. (Smart and Smart, 1972, p. 538)

7. Youth are concerned with being industrious, achieving a sense of duty and accomplishment, and dealing with reality while the adolescent experiences a resurgence of imaginative thinking and creativity. (Smart and Smart, 1972, p. 543)

8. In a quest for identity and direction, the adolescent begins to contemplate the meaning of life through religious and philosophical perspectives. (Schiamberg and Smith, 1982, p. 475)

New qualitative cognitive skills enable adolescents to grasp the significance of values and standards. Consequently, they can understand sport rules, regulations, etiquette and the reasoning behind their development and application. A tendency to question relevancy and the status quo accompanies their outlook. Involvement in making decisions about participation, program development and standards contributes to development of cognitive skills and enhances acceptance of program standards and rules.

Although adolescents can anticipate the consequences of inappropriate behavior and exhibit greater control over emotions, there is no guarantee that they will act accordingly. However, they are capable of responding to reason and need to be held accountable to assist development of proper social behavior.

While the adolescent has improved analytical abilities, transfer of knowledge is not automatic, particularly when it concerns values and behavior. The development of acceptable values and behavior and their transfer from sport to life situations involves a number of variables. Illustrate the relationship or parallel between sport and life experiences. Since shaping or modifying values and behavior requires time, provide an attractive role model who has sufficient contact with participants and who demonstrates a consistent value system. Focus these efforts within the club sport and instructional sport programs where opportunity exists for contact with participants over an extended period of time.

Sport contributes to mental development in the sense that sport participation involves employing strategy and reasoning. Further contributions are possible when adolescents are placed in such leadership positions as team captain, official, supervisor or assistant coach.

Personality Characteristics:

1. Adolescents reexamine old values and attitudes as they experiment with new ones.

2. The adolescent strives toward a stable self concept as it relates to vocational, sexual and moral identity. (Schiamberg and Smith, 1982, p. 480)

3. Changing sex roles have resulted in an increasing flexibility in general behavior but may lead to confusion in self-concept, particularly in regard to career and family orientation. (Schiamberg and Smith, 1982, pp. 467–469)

4. The adolescent determines what is right or moral independent of the expectations of others although

parents, peers, adults, school and the media continue to influence moral development. (Schiamberg and Smith, 1982, p. 475)

5. The anxiety produced by a search for identity often results in a premature acceptance and integration of the values of society—an outcome which may damage personal integrity. (Schiamberg and Smith, 1982, p. 421)

6. The adolescent strives to achieve emotional independence from parents and other adults. This desire for autonomy produces a dilemma: the adolescent can no longer be treated as a child, but he or she is not yet considered adult. (Turner and Helms, 1979, p. 292)

Feelings of self-consciousness due to body changes and body concept are common, particularly among late maturers. Those who suffer from poor self-concept and those who exhibit extreme concern for social acceptance need diverse opportunities for comfortable, satisfying sport experiences. Adolescents need to feel good about physical activity to promote lifetime participation habits. Programs offered on the basis of chronological age alone may accentuate physiological changes rather than help the adolescent cope with them.

While the adolescent is interested in self-testing activities that sport can provide, he or she is not interested in having failures or poor performances unduly noticed. Program designs which accommodate different ability levels provide adolescents opportunities to develop skills and to follow interests in a non-threatening way. Avoid sheltering adolescents from discovering their limitations but keep self-testing activities commensurate with potential abilities. The adolescent should perceive that success is achievable whether it is actually realized or not. A program that makes these distinctions contributes to self-esteem and reinforces autonomy.

The search for identity thrusts an adolescent into decisions about acceptable or unacceptable behavior. The challenge and social interaction in sport affords numerous opportunities for making choices. Unless the adolescent learns the value of cooperation and develops a sensitivity to the needs of others, he or she will have difficulties that can result in negative behavior.

Pressure to conform to cultural stereotypes of masculinity and femininity and concern for self and peer acceptance produce anxiety and tension. Non-threatening sport opportunities provide constructive outlets for reducing these anxieties. Although mixed-sex sport activities facilitate social interaction, self-consciousness and poor body concept can lead to non-participation. Consequently, participation in mixed-sex sport activities should be voluntary.

Since adolescents need to express their ideas, place them in leadership positions to provide practical experience in adult roles. Experiences that require new skills and abilities also foster independence, autonomy and a realistic outlook.

Social Characteristics:

1. The peer group is a prominent source of influence in early adolescence. Self-evaluation is furthered by school and peer group experiences. (Schiamberg and Smith, 1982, p. 417)

2. The peer group affords an opportunity to develop social relationships with both sexes.

3. Same-sex peer relationships help the individual discover intimacy and norms for male or female behavior. (Schiamberg and Smith, 1982, p. 421)

4. The adolescent uses the peer group as a testing ground for emotions, abilities, values and lifestyles. Feedback shapes self-concept and behavior. Affiliation challenges the development of self-confidence in the face of pressures for conformity.

5. Sharing of thoughts and feelings, in addition to more superficial types of sharing experiences (time, things, or activities,) occurs with friends. During this period of self-testing and evaluation, the adolescent needs the support these friendships provide. (Schiamberg and Smith, 1982, p. 438)

6. Since popularity has such a premium importance, it may require the compromise of personal values. Feelings of inadequacy and inferiority plague adolescents who do not feel popular, while those who significantly

compromise their values to attain popularity may experience guilt. (Smart and Smart, 1972, p. 576, 57; Atwater, 1983, pp. 168–176)

7. Although the adolescents still respond to parental influence, they often look to other adults—teacher, recreation worker, or employer—for role models.

The main socializing agents affecting adolescent attitudes toward sport (participation and spectatorship) include parents, family, peers and "significant other" adults. Since recreational sport is not as popular as athletic or professional sport, many do not include it in their daily lives. Leisure education and specialized programming may mitigate this situation.

Sport takes place in a social context, serving as a practical laboratory for social skill development. Team and club sport experiences expose the adolescent to the effect of competitive, cooperative or conflict behaviors upon group goals and morale, the effect of self-centeredness upon group functions and peer acceptance and the effect of irresponsible behavior on performance.

Sport participation also affords opportunities for improving interpersonal relations skills. As participants share time and common interests, they learn about such requirements for successful relationships as commitment, trust, respect, unselfishness, and affection.

Appreciation of sport from a spectator perspective may also serve as an enjoyable medium of social interaction. Sport continues to be of significant interest to adolescent boys, while girls need to learn more about it to facilitate interaction by sharing common interests. When we help adolescents acquire an appreciation of sport, they are better equipped to make better use of leisure time.

Leadership positions provide adolescents with practical experience in adult roles, career situations and work environments. The practical experience of leadership broadens perspective and contributes to an understanding of others.

Early Adulthood (20–39 years)

The entry of the adolescent into adulthood signals the potential for such experiences as beginning a career, marriage, and parenthood. While abundance of literature exists concerning the changes that occur from birth to entrance into adulthood, there are few studies covering the twenties to sixties. These years are the "prime of life," a time of maximum opportunity for fulfillment. Persons entering adulthood already possess an accumulation of distinctive life experiences, that have resulted in a unique set of abilities, skills, attitudes, strengths and weaknesses. While adolescence was a period for crystalizing identity, early adulthood signals a move toward self-actualization.

Physical Characteristics:

1. Males do not reach full height until age twenty-one. (Schiamberg and Smith, 1982, p. 528)

2. Peak muscular strength occurs between twenty-five and thirty years of age. (Schiamberg and Smith, 1982, p. 528)

3. Vision and visual adaptation functions begin to decline. Nearsightedness and farsightedness increase, and more contrast is required to distinguish an object from its background. The cumulative effect of visual deterioration is noticeable to most adults around the age of forty. (Schiamberg and Smith, 1982, p. 529)

4. During this period, reaction time remains stable. (Schiamberg and Smith, 1982, p. 530)

5. The body reaches its maximum physical potential in terms of muscles and internal organs between the ages of nineteen and twenty-six. (Turner and Helms, 1979, p. 333)

6. Settling of the vertebrae and spinal disks results in a slight height decrease. (Turner and Helms, 1979, p. 333)

7. Brain weight reaches a maximum between the ages of twenty and thirty. (Turner and Helms, 1979, p. 334)

8. Aging is not uniform in terms of mental ability, physical condition and other functions. (Schiamberg and Smith, 1982, p. 496)

Adults should undergo medical screening and fitness testing to determine what sports are compatible with their health and fitness level. Testing provides the adult with information needed to accomplish specific fitness goals. Regular participation in sport and exercise decreases the chances of injury and sickness. Programs should accommodate different abilities and fitness levels through special rule modifications.

Mental Characteristics:

1. Stability in intellectual skills occurs between twenty and fifty years of age. (Schiamberg and Smith, 1982, p. 536)

2. The ability to form concepts, use abstract reasoning, and perceive complex relationships (fluid intelligence) declines gradually during adulthood. (Schiamberg and Smith, 1982, p. 535)

3. Formal reasoning, abstraction, and perception of complex relations to learned tasks (crystallized intelligence) improves gradually during adulthood. This type of intelligence, more dependent upon education and experience, compensates for loss in fluid intelligence. (Schiamberg and Smith, 1982, p. 535, p. 536)

Young adults are capable of pursuing self-directed activities. Satisfy these interests through ladder and challenge tournaments, club sport, informal sport, and personalized fitness programs. Since participants of this age are expected to respect their own safety and that of others, many recreational sport programs apply the principle of voluntary assumption of risk.

Young adults possess a broad base knowledge and experience that facilitates their involvement in program leadership roles. They have a more secure sense of independence and autonomy and a greater insight into the relevance of rules, regulations, standards and justice. Although preoccupation with career and family may not permit individuals time for service functions until they are well into their 30's, leadership experiences provide the challenges needed for their continued intellectual growth.

Personality Characteristics:

1. Identity becomes more defined or modified through experiences involving the family, work and the community. Early adulthood involves a challenge to maximize skills and abilities. (Schiamberg and Smith, 1982, p. 536)

2. A more secure concept of self permits the early adult to better cope with problems and demonstrate greater

emotional stability. Conflicts still arise from obstacles to self-fulfillment and inability to reorient goals. (Turner and Helms, 1979, pp. 340–345)

3. The young adult demonstrates the ability to become absorbed in interests and pursue them over extended periods of time.

4. Experience with adult roles and responsibilities helps the young adult develop a more realistic perspective of self and the world. (Schiamberg and Smith, 1982, p. 498, p. 537)

5. Sex roles affect how men and women demonstrate competence. Traditional sex roles tend to label female behavior as passive and irrational, while male behavior is expected to reflect a rugged, dominant personality. A mixture of traits are currently acceptable for both males and females: caring, self-confident, warm and intelligent. (Schiamberg and Smith, 1982, p. 537)

6. Early adulthood involves the integration of self with roles and responsibilities within society. Adults are interested in realizing their aspirations, achieving specific and definite life goals. (Turner and Helms, 1979, p. 344)

Greater emotional stability, coupled with mature intellectual skills, enables the adult to pursue self-directed activities with greater satisfaction. However, the tendency to engage in less physically vigorous activities results in body composition changes (more fat, less muscle) and declining physical abilities that may negatively affect self-concept. Consequently, promote sport as a means for weight control, fitness, and an overall sense of well-being. Provide adults with convenient opportunities to pursue sport through different program formats to foster lifetime participation habits. If sport is still unappealing to some, identify and minimize deterrents. Among the reasons given for avoiding sport are the fear of failure, fear of injury, social isolation, inadequate reward, absence of enjoyable or perferred activities, cost, inconvenience, poor health and inaccessibility.

New responsibilities, experiences, and challenges inherent in adult lifestyles require adequate coping mechanisms. When goals are thwarted or pressures become too intense, a person may exhibit anti-social behavior. Minimize frustration by using competent personnel, providing well-maintained facilities, focusing on competency improvement and utilizing an objective governance system.

Social Characteristics:

1. Early adults relate to people in a more open and honest way than adolescents do. Their friendships are characterized by greater intimacy.

2. Early adults are less self-centered than adolescents. They develop an appreciation and understanding of the perspectives of others. (Schiamberg and Smith, 1982, p. 537)

3. Early adults are occupied with a career, a family, and community involvement.

4. Early adults expand their social relationships through new contacts within the occupational and community-neighborhood settings.

The peer group for the early adult expands to include more variety in terms of age, gender, interests and abilities. Since it includes all segments of society, sport participation provides an opportunity to meet a greater cross-section in terms of race, ethnicality and cultural background than possible in church, work or other social settings. For those adults who lack meaningful socialization within a small group, sport, particularly through team and club sport activities, may help satisfy them. Specialized sport programming can facilitate social interaction among target groups by designing activity among such classifications as pregnant women, families, church, age groups, singles, parents, industrial workers and housewives. When group participation is impractical, individual and dual sports still afford opportunities for socialization.

Since young adults have acquired additional experiences in mixed social situations and exposure to more flexible sex role expectations, provide more opportunities for gender integration within sport programs and leadership positions. Maintain segregated sport programs while also providing specialized programming where men and women are partners or team members.

A keener interest in activities of one's children and a sense of social duty is often translated into a desire for volunteer work. Volunteers may exist within the program as coaches, officials, concession stand workers, ticket takers, program assistants, and tournament coordinators. Volunteers often experience an increased understanding of others and an improvement in the interpersonal relations skills necessary for service on committees, councils and boards. Since family attitudes strongly influence a child's desire to participate in sport, involve parents as volunteers as well as active participants and spectators.

Middle Adulthood (40–65 years)

"Middle age" is a paradox. To some it is the prime of life, while to others it marks the beginning of the end. Middle age symbolizes regulated lifestyle, introspection and concern for the future. In contrast to other life stages, middle age lacks such biological or social landmarks as school, puberty, career, marriage, or retirement. In comparison with the child, youth and senior, the middle aged person is ignored. Yet this life stage encompasses peak levels of social, personal and economic activity. Many of the implications noted for young adults apply to this life stage.

Physical Characteristics:

1. Aging is manifested by greying and thinning hair, receding hairline, wrinkles around the eyes, mouth, and forehead, and loss of skin elasticity.

2. The tendency to gain weight is characteristic of middle age. The fat composition of the body, about 10 percent during adolescence, climbs to about 20 percent by middle adulthood, marked by increases in the abdomen and hips and decreases in bust and chest. (Schiamberg and Smith, 1982, p. 568)

3. Recovery from glare and adaptation to darkness take longer. Close to fifty percent of adults require corrective lenses before the age of sixty-five. (Turner and Helms, 1979, p. 379) (Schiamberg and Smith, 1982, p. 569)

4. Auditory loss occurs after forty, particularly at high frequencies. This occurrence is more marked among men. (Schiamberg and Smith, 1982, p. 569)

5. Gradual changes in sensory functions occur. After age fifty, taste buds begin to atrophy. By sixty, one experiences difficulty identifying faint aromas. Sensitivity to pain increases around forty-five years of age. (Schiamberg and Smith, 1982, p. 569)

6. Movement function declines. As reaction time increases, greater performance losses occur in more complex tasks. Sustaining a long series of complex movements becomes more difficult. (Schiamberg and Smith, 1982, p. 570)

7. Menopause, experienced by women in their late forties or early fifties, may be associated with hot flashes, irritability, fatigue, anxiety and difficulty in breathing. While men experience a gradual lessening of fertility, their reproductive functions do not cease. (Turner and Helms, 1979, p. 380, 381)

8. Chronic illnesses, which increase as individuals reach the age of forty-five, include diabetes, arthritis, coronary heart disease, arteriosclerosis, hypertension, cancer, and emphysema. (Turner and Helms, 1979, p. 384)

The middle adulthood years are associated with a gradual decline in physical abilities and noticeable changes in appearance. Those who have neglected regular participation in sport and exercise experience a decrease in strength, reaction time, stamina, and skill performance. Programmers should accommodate differences and minimize health risks by using classification systems according to age and ability level.

Another consequence of inactivity, obesity, poses a serious threat to health during this life stage. It increases one's chances for hypertension, diabetes, digestive system disorders and cardiovascular disease. Programs which contribute to physical fitness, especially cardiovascular endurance, become increasingly important. Some middle adults become so preoccupied with appearance and the physical signs of aging that they over-exert themselves during participation. Regular medical check-ups, fitness testing, exercise prescription, nutrition and diet should be essential considerations for this group.

Mental Characteristics:

1. There is no evidence of physiological changes in the brain. The middle aged person may be slower than the young adult in grasping and solving a problem, but he or she can call upon a wider range of experience. (Turner and Helms, 1979, p. 386)

2. A majority of people reach their peak productive and creative capacities between the ages of thirty and forty-five or even fifty. Creativity shows no apparent decline. (Turner and Helms, 1979, p. 386)

3. Intelligence and cognitive skills remain stable, while reasoning and verbal skills may improve. (Schiamberg and Smith, 1982, p. 579)

While the young adult refines decision-making and problem-solving skills, the middle adult applies the required skills for making significant decisions, planning for the future and anticipating the needs of others. Their ability to comprehend, their flexibility in thinking and their creativity are excellent reasons to recruit them for leadership positions, particularly as organizers, directors or advisors. These qualities, however, may be counterproductive to your efforts when the individual does not hold the same philosophy or objectives as those of the agency.

Personality Characteristics:

1. The middle adult strives for a stable self-concept through integration of such roles as worker, parent, spouse and community member. (Schiamberg and Smith, 1982, p. 582)

2. Many adults experience a renewed self-awareness and introspection that prompts evaluation of accomplishments and concern about the future. (Turner and Helms, 1979, p. 389)

3. The middle adult may experience psychological conflict during such adjustments as divorce, career change,

loss (money, spouse, friend, family members, job, possessions), health problems, children leaving home and change in residence.

4. Middle adulthood marks an opportunity for an individual to focus on ego maturity and self-actualization—the fulfillment of potential. (Turner and Helms, 1979, p. 393)

Signs of aging spur thoughts and worries about growing old. Such self-consciousness prompts introspection that escalates during later adulthood. Adults who feel a sense of accomplishment and fulfillment show an interest in social and civic service. Those who are dissatisfied or feel a sense of failure often become stagnant and self-centered. If our programs require volunteer assistance, we should seek to involve those eager to serve as well as those who need to engage in meaningful service as a way to bolster self-esteem and use time more constructively. People who experience the loss of others or who must give up specific pursuits also need to find new objects of focus and fulfillment. We can help satisfy these needs through programs and experience that increase social contact with peer or special interest groups such as parents without partners. We must also provide leisure education to familiarize adults with opportunities and counter any previously acquired negative images about sport participation. Otherwise, middle adults who have spent a large part of their time at work or devoted to family may have difficulties preparing for increased free time in later adulthood.

Social Characteristics:

1. Middle adulthood represents the peak time for involvement in social and civic activities. (Schiamberg and Smith, 1982, p. 562)

2. Middle adults customarily move into positions of leadership and prominence in their work. The quest for career satisfaction may involve career change.

3. Middle adults may face a responsibility for supporting both their adolescent children (financially or psychologically) and their aging parents.

4. Adults need to restructure their time and interests once children leave the home. This new development may result in reevaluation of the marriage. (Turner and Helms, 1979, p. 401)

5. Middle adulthood represents the time when many adults become grandparents.

Since many people in this stage have managed to pursue a career, establish a household, and begin a family, they are able to redirect their time and creative energy to involvement in service activities. Most adults approach such functions as an opportunity to influence the quality of life for themselves and others. Consequently, middle adults are frequently recruited as leaders in administrative functions and as role models in youth sport programs. As you work with middle adults in service responsibilities, respect their backgrounds and permit them flexibility in decision-making and problem-solving unless their ideas conflict with agency ideals.

Family relationships vary depending upon the age of children. Couples with school-age children tend to be very involved in their extra-curricular activities. Since recreational sport is popular with most children, we should provide programs where children and parents participate in enjoyable activities together. Parents with teenagers often face challenges developing common interests, yet sport, as a vehicle to facilitate interaction and sharing, may bridge the so-called "generation-gap". Once all the children in the family have grown up and left home, the middle-age couple must reallocate time to other activities. Encourage their interest in recreational sport by extending opportunities for volunteerism as well as providing for new social contacts. Many programs report success through club sports, mixed doubles tournaments and special event programming for couples.

Late Adulthood (over 65 years)

New medical discoveries and improved health care delivery systems have helped extend an average life span from forty-seven years at the turn of the century to seventy-two years today. Our elderly, who comprise the fastest growing segment of the population, require new social and recreational services to meet their needs and interests. While sixty-five is an arbitrary landmark for determining retirement age or the age when some social benefits become available, it is not useful to describe limits of adult functioning. Variations in biological and behavioral function among older adults are greater than among early and middle-aged adults. Despite the perception that they are ready to withdraw from responsibility, the elderly desire an active, meaningful life.

Physical Characteristics:

1. Health statistics indicate an increased risk of heart disease and hypertension. (Schiamberg and Smith, 1982, p. 619)

2. Decline in perception of one's position in space may affect balance and coordination. (Schiamberg and Smith, 1982, p. 619)

3. Conditions affecting visual acuity include difficulty seeing objects close at hand due to loss of lens elasticity, continual loss in the ability to adjust to changes in light, and reduction of peripheral vision. (Schiamberg and Smith, 1982, p. 620)

4. Hearing loss in the higher frequencies increases. (Schiamberg and Smith, 1982, p. 621)

5. Approximately half of all sixty-five year olds have lost their teeth. (Schiamberg and Smith, 1982, p. 619)

6. Internal organs operate less efficiently. For example, resting cardiac output for an average older adult is seventy percent that of a thirty year old. (Turner and Helms, p. 422)

7. Superficial signs of aging are most noticeable in terms of wrinkles, greying hair, loss of hair, and weight gain.

8. Among the factors contributing to reduced motor performance are: increased reaction time, changes in bone mineralization, calcification in cartilage and ligaments, degeneration of joints, decline in muscle size and strength, and changes in the properties of nerve cells and fibers. (Schiamberg and Smith, 1982, pp. 622, 623)

The variance that the effect of aging has upon physical performance and health requires supervised activities that provide appropriate degrees of participation. Complete medical screening and fitness testing should precede activity. Since the elderly are less homogeneous than other age groups, provide programs that are tailor-made. When programs are planned on a progressive basis, regular participation avoids health and injury-related problems while contributing to fitness. Those older adults who have maintained a reasonable level of fitness throughout their life may participate in active sports without modifications. Most can participate in and enjoy a wide variety of modified sports that do not require a great degree of hand-eye coordination, speed, or strength. Those unable to manage physical activity may participate in table sports. Physically active older adults report greater vitality, mental capacity, and desire for socialization than their sedentary counterparts.

Mental Characteristics:

1. Abilities that require speed, endurance or short-term memory decline faster than those that are untimed and depend upon experience. Well-educated and mentally-active individuals do not encounter the same memory decline as peers lacking similar opportunities for using mental skills.

2. Many retain and even improve verbal skills.

3. The time required for memory recall increases.

Older adults have the capacity to learn new skills, although they will have difficulty mastering *perceptual* motor skills. They will also experience difficulty learning complex rules and regulations if they cannot recall new information quickly. Consequently, permit them to make their own decisions about participation while also encouraging activity in mentally stimulating sports. Always instill in older adults a concern for safety.

Personality Characteristics:

1. The personality types that describe older adults include: "mature" (possessing a sense of integration and satisfaction), "rocking-chair" (looking forward to retirement and freedom from responsibility), "armored"

(afraid of growing old and in control of showing emotions), "angry" (unable to reconcile themselves to growing old), and "self-hater" (upset about growing old and a tendency to blame oneself for current problems). (Moran, 1979, p. 42)

2. Self-concept tends to be more dependent upon internal thoughts and feelings than such external factors as the opinions of others. Older adults tend to see themselves as they have always been, rather than encountering dramatic self-concept changes. When self-evaluation occurs, it may lead to feelings of greater self-reliance or a sense of inadequacy and depression. (Schiamberg and Smith, 1982, p. 630)

3. Men tend to move from active involvement in the world to a more passive, self-centered situation while women tend to become more active and open. (Schiamberg and Smith, 1982, p. 630)

4. An important dimension of self-esteem for the older adult is a sense of competence and control over one's life. (Schiamberg and Smith, 1982, p. 631)

5. Older adults need to establish a sense of self-worth beyond previous work roles, social relationships, and body concept.

6. After retirement, traditional sex roles may reverse, as the female becomes more assertive and the male more passive and nurturing. (Aiken, 1978, p. 81)

Sport activities should emphasize strengths and capabilities of the individual or group and provide for liberal recognition of accomplishments. Encourage spectators to join in the organizational tasks. Whenever possible, provide the older adult leadership responsibilities, not only among their peer group, but also among young children. The interaction promotes and enriches both young and old by reducing the psychological distance between them. Structure such opportunities on a regular basis to facilitate adjustment and develop rapport. Older adults often prove to be most dependable workers due to their previous experience and the satisfaction they derive from being needed.

Self concept in old age, as in any other time, is critical to happiness. Organize activities so that a person experiences competence and receives respect from others. Restructuring of time can be a frustrating, demeaning experience involving frivolous activity. Anticipate this potential problem by helping the older adult prepare for creative, fulfilling use of leisure time through sport. If limitations exist in physical mobility, finances or energy, make participation as accessible as possible and familiarize older adults with activities conducted on a self-directed or partner basis.

Social Characteristics:

1. Retirement may reduce the means but not the interest for social interaction. A significant restructuring in the use of time is necessary.

2. A higher death and remarriage rate among men leaves many single women among the elderly. (Schiamberg and Smith, 1982, p. 604)

3. Most older people prefer living as independently as possible. (Schiamberg and Smith, 1982, p. 599)

4. The proportion of older parents who help support their adult children is larger than the proportion of adult children who help their parents. (Schiamberg and Smith, 1982, p. 599)

5. The opportunity for marriage partners to spend time together increases due to retirement and the absence of children in the home.

6. Remarriage is hindered by limitations in physical mobility, finances, energy and opportunities for social interaction.

7. The impact of the death of a spouse affects both social group and family relationships. Women are more likely than men to seek a confidant to share the problems of widowhood. Widows tend to grow emotionally closer to their daughters while they look to their sons for assistance with tasks. (Schiamberg and Smith, 1982, p. 604)

8. As the scope of social life decreases, self-directed activities increase. Forms of social interactions that develop involve helpfulness, advice and consolation.

9. Kinship relations for most retired couples focus on their children and grandchildren. Many prefer living near, but not with, their children. (Turner and Helms, 1979, p. 446)

10. Sexual interest declines slightly with age. (Turner and Helms, 1979, p. 442)

The recreational sport program for older adults should continue to focus on opportunities for positive interpersonal relationships. Team, group, and club sport activities may furnish a social group to replace lost co-workers or companions. Specialized target group programs may also increase social contacts for singles, grandparents and retirees and help married couples adjust to increased time together. Since older adults may hesitate to pursue physical activity when relocated, provide programs at neighborhood sites and arrange transportation. Each effort made to involve them in activities with peer or other age groups may stimulate a desire to keep in touch with the world.

CONCLUSION

Sport is a "mini-society" because it holds opportunities for individual growth and development that parallel those found outside the sport environment. Throughout one's life, benefits occur through active participation in sport and exercise. The recreational sport programmer has both an opportunity and a responsibility to enhance the development and the quality of life for persons of all ages, interests and abilities. A commitment to participant development is central to the attainment of this goal.

REFERENCES

Aiken, L. *Later Life.* Philadelphia: W. B. Saunders Company, 1978.

Atwater, E. *Adolescence.* Englewood Cliffs, New Jersey: Prentice-Hall, Inc., 1983.

Cratty, B. J. *Social Dimensions of Physical Activity.* Englewood Cliffs, New Jersey: Prentice-Hall, Inc., 1967.

Gallahue, D. L. *Understanding Motor Development In Children.* New York: John Wiley and Sons, 1982.

Geller, W. W. *Student Development In Intramural Sports.* Unpublished doctoral dissertation, Bloomington: Indiana University, 1976.

Hellison, D. R. *Humanistic Physical Education.* Englewood Cliffs, New Jersey: Prentice-Hall, Inc., 1973.

Humphrey, J. H. *Child Development Through Physical Education.* Springfield, Illinois: Charles C. Thomas, 1980.

Miller, T. K. and Prince, J. S. *The Future of Student Affairs.* San Francisco: Jossey-Bass, Inc., Publishers, 1977.

Moran, J. M. *Leisure Activities for the Mature Adult.* Minneapolis: Burgess Publishing Company, 1979.

Schiamberg, L. B. and Smith, K. U. *Human Development.* New York: Macmillan Publishing Co., Inc., 1982.

Smart, M. S.; and, Smart, R. C. *Children Development and Relationships,* 2nd edition. New York: Macmillan Publishing Co., Inc., 1972.

Thomas, J. R. (ed.). *Youth Sports Guide for Coaches and Parents.* Washington: AAHPER Publications, 1977.

Turner, J. S. and Helms, D. B. *Life Span Development.* Philadelphia: W. B. Saunders Company, 1979.

Vanderzwaag, H. H. *Toward A Philosophy of Sport.* Reading, Massachusetts: Addison-Wesley Publishing Company, 1972.

CHAPTER 3

INFORMAL SPORT

We define informal sport as self-directed participation in competitive/cooperative activity in the game form. Informal sport programming involves the provision of indoor and outdoor sport facilities that are not scheduled for short-term events or on-going structured programs. While some seek an avenue for leisure time enjoyment in structured sport programs, others prefer access to facilities without imposed design or direction.

Informal sport, in the broadest context, encompasses traditional and nontraditional activities and settings. A backyard volleyball game, a card game, a weekend skiing trip, an evening bike ride, a roller skating party, target shooting at cans, windsurfing, figure skating, an early bird swim at the local YMCA—all these are examples of informal sport. Participants determine the type of sport and facility site for participation, as well as the length of their involvement.

We may regard informal sport as an experiment in which participants practice or prepare for involvement in the structure of instructional, intramural, extramural, club, athletic, and professional sport. Consider intramural team members who arrange to meet at the gymnasium to play a pick-up basketball game, the beginning tennis player who practices strokes before a lesson rallying with a friend, the karate club member who finds an open spot in the gym to practice her moves, the varsity football player who runs track to improve his endurance, or the Olympic hopeful who needs access to a weightroom to work out for powerlifting competition. Each needs access to a facility free from structured events and ongoing programs.

Informal sport has not received recognition as a specific program area that requires planning to meet an important need. Its identity has developed through renewed interest in personal fitness and increasing public enthusiasm for recreational sport participation. Self-directed sport activity has been one of the growth activities that has carried over from the seventies. Its popularity is evidenced by the current proliferation of commercial and private sport facilities. Informal sport now involves the largest number of participants active within recreational sport.

Whenever sport facilities exist, whether it be a commercial, military, correctional, industrial, community or educational setting, an informal sport program is possible. This program area requires as much planning consideration as do structured sport programs to allow adequate time and space for the participant who prefers self-directed sport activity.

Effective management of an informal sport program requires an understanding of the factors that affect participation and a system to conduct daily operations.

PARTICIPATION FACTORS

When planning an informal sport program, a programmer should concentrate on techniques to facilitate participation. Our highest programming priority is the creation of a positive, satisfying experience—an elusive goal since the "quality" of the experience is a matter of personal interpretation. Although program design for attaining this goal varies from setting to setting, some participation factors have universal relevance.

Facility availability/accessibility. A quality informal sport program recognizes the diversity in participant interest and abilities by providing an adequate number and variety of sport facilities for the largest number of potential users. This process is initiated through an analysis of the participants and promoted by the philosophy of the setting toward facility utilization. For instance, a commercial skiing developer would carefully scrutinize such factors as terrain, weather, transportation, economy, and participant interest before committing resources to the construction and operation of a ski lodge. His or her primary goal would be to provide a quality service at a profit. In a military setting, facilities reflect two primary objectives: training and fitness of military personnel and recreational opportunities for their families. Construction of supplemental facilities or access to facilities within the surrounding community enhance opportunities for informal sport in this case.

Informal sport facilities should serve all age groups. When possible to do so, locate them close to residential areas to facilitate accessibility for children, the disabled, the elderly, and others with transportation problems. Schedule facility availability to coincide with the free time of various target groups. Examine design problems which pose obstacles for persons with disabilities and recommend the necessary renovations.

Seasonal factors. Many recreational sport activities—basketball, water skiing, soccer, snowmobiling, softball, cross country, tennis and volleyball—are associated with a season of the year. Anticipate increased participation in sports that are "in season" and keep facility availability for them at a maximum.

Scheduling. Since the whole concept of informal sport participation involves convenience, facility scheduling is critical. Scheduling should take into account such factors as participant age, the time required for participation, the needs of other programs using the same facilities, budget constraints, and the popularity of particular activities. An effective communication plan should inform participants about the location of all facilities and the times they are available for use. In addition to a printed schedule for mass distribution, a daily notice posted at each facility site, communicating any temporary changes, is a minimum requirement.

One of the most difficult problems in facility scheduling for informal sport is balancing utilization. Consistency is difficult to achieve since structured programs which use the same facilities affect the time available for informal sport use. Although scheduling specific percentages of time for informal sport use has not been common, this policy could become more popular with increasing demand.

Other techniques for facility use include short-term reservations and specified times for such target groups as children, women, senior citizens, faculty or officers. Monitor all scheduling practices to assure that the schedule does not become structured to the point that opportunities for self-directed use are compromised.

Conveniences. Persons interested in using a facility for informal sport are attracted to conveniences that add to the enjoyment of their recreational experience. Availability of equipment is a bonus to the individual interested in trying a new sport who does not own the proper equipment. Others who own equipment often do not have a convenient way to transport or store it.

Another convenience promoting participation is the availability of locker rooms. The size of the area, number of showers and such amenities as sauna and steam rooms reflect participant demand and available finances. Most participants appreciate the convenience of storing their sports clothing and equipment at the sport site and the luxury of showering after an activity. When participants live close to the facilities, as in a collegiate, military, or correctional setting, this service is often unnecessary.

Additional conveniences attracting participants to indoor facility sites are: adequate parking, restrooms, seating, food and vending services, "pro" shops, lounge areas, video games area, and a conditioning area. Conveniences increasing outdoor facility appeal include restrooms, concessions, seating, parking, shelters, telephones, water fountains, and lighting.

Cleanliness. Clean and attractive facilities for participants have a positive impact on the public image of any program. Although a facility may not be extensive or modern, participants appreciate good maintenance and attractiveness. If resources are unavailable to fund major facility repairs and renovations, attention to such details as picking up trash, maintaining attractive bulletin boards and outdoor signs, cleaning rest rooms, sweeping and mopping floors, keeping lights functional, replacing broken or bent basketball rims, using nets without holes, keeping water fountains clean and unobstructed, and mowing the grass preserves participant confidence in the integrity of your program.

Personnel. Even the most attractive, well-maintained, and complete recreational sport facility may not attain the greatest use or provide maximum participant enjoyment if the supervising personnel do not act in an appropriate manner. Not only should informal sport personnel be congenial, helpful, and knowledgeable about facility uses, but they must also be capable of controlling safety hazards, facility misuse and disciplinary problems. Personnel must employ effective communication and conflict resolution skills with maturity and tact.

Another factor affecting participation is reliability of information provided to participants. It is vital that all personnel be current on schedules, policies, and procedures that affect participants, and communicate the correct information to avoid inconveniencing participants.

Cost. The charging of fees that characterize commercial sport facility operation has become a factor affecting participation. Commercial sport facilities which provide racquetball, ice skating, tennis, swimming, skiing, and bowling rely heavily upon individuals pursuing informal sport opportunities. Non-commercial settings dependent upon local, state, or federal funding to support facility operations are experiencing cutbacks and have turned to the use of fees and charges to help offset operating costs. Such revenue may also assist in expanding services and facilities, fund specialized informal sport opportunities, and help control facility use.

The cost of informal sport facility use affects the extent of facility use. Fees and charges common to informal sport include:

Annual User or Membership Fees—Fees charged for unlimited access to sport facilities. There may be instances, particularly in commercial settings, where an additional user fee is charged for a specific activity. For example, most racquetball clubs charge an annual fee for membership plus a daily fee for court time.

Daily User Fees—Fees charged for facility use during a given day. Examples include a greens fee, a swimming pool daily pass, a snow ski lift ticket, an ice rink admission, and a tennis court reservation. The daily user fee may be used for accommodating guests or as a back-up mechanism for persons who can not provide the proper identification showing they are eligible users.

Rental Fees—Payment guaranteeing exclusive use of a facility or equipment. The patron may enjoy all the advantages of use as long as property is not destroyed, damaged, or lost. A rental fee is usually applied when facilities or equipment are available during "low use" times of the day, week, or month.

License and Permit Fees—Charges for the right to participate in government monitored activities such as hunting or fishing.

Policies and procedures. Policy statements outline the conditions for participation while procedures direct the manner in which these policies are enforced. The objective is to explain the "ground rules" for informal sport participation. The creation of policy and procedure statements for informal sport programs involve the following topics, written often as a "participants' manual."

Eligibility.
1. Eligibility statements specify who is permitted to use the sport facilities most often in terms of individual or group eligibility: student, faculty, staff, alumni; public employee, executive; non-commissioned officer, commissioned officer; inmate, guard; resident, non-resident; and member, guest. Group eligibility statements may specify age levels (children, teens, adults, senior citizens), social or civic groups (Lions Club, Girl Scouts, Boy Scouts), living units (dormitory, fraternity, sorority, married housing) or affiliation with the agency or setting (residents, non-residents; university, public; member, guests).

Settings may prohibit certain categories of individuals from facility access altogether, while under other circumstances their access may be restricted to specific days, times, or activities: private swimming club may limit guest pool use to certain hours during the week; a university may prohibit non-affiliates from facility access; a military base may confine the dependents of active duty personnel to facility access during the evenings and weekends; a corporation may designate in an industrial plant special hours for executive staff access to a weightroom.

Eligibility statements describe the intended user of a program. As eligibility requirements become more stringent a monitoring system is needed to discourage ineligible participation.

The development of eligibility statements involves the following considerations:

—What kinds of people are we serving?
—What can our facilities handle?
—Are there certain facilities or times when use must be restricted?
—What personnel are available or necessary to monitor facility use?
—What financial resources are available to support monitoring and control systems?
—What effect will eligibility statements have upon public relations?
—Are there any legal considerations that affect eligiblity?
—How will participants prove they are legitimate users of the facility site?

2. Fees and charges. The charging of fees requires the development of a sound collection and security system. It may involve an identification system which enables the user to verify payment for facility use. Procedures for fee collection and identification systems should be determined well in advance. Are adjusted fees available for low income participants? Can fees be prorated? Are credit cards or money orders acceptable? Are charge accounts available? Is there a penalty for bad checks or delinquent accounts?

3. Facility Reservations. The priorities for facility use largely determine the amount of time available for informal sports. Once these priorities are finalized in policy form, participants will know how to take advantage of opportunities to reserve facilities for informal sport participation.

The most prevalent reservation technique used within informal sport is the court or field reservation. This technique is needed to accommodate a large number of participants and is useful for handball, racquetball, squash, tennis, basketball and softball facilities. Most common reservation policies make several of the following stipulations:

a. Reservations must be made in person.
b. One in-person reservation will be accepted, then one phone-in reservation.
c. A valid identification card or user pass is required to make a reservation.
d. Only one reservation per day is permitted.
e. Reservations may be made only for same day use.
f. Reservations may be made a number of days in advance.
g. Cancellations must be made in person with proper identification.
h. Cancellations must be made 24 hours in advance or a no show penalty will be imposed.
i. Persons absent 10 minutes past the reserved playing time forfeit all rights to the facility.

Programs that prohibit phone-in reservations or cancellations either have no way to verify user eligibility, require a user fee, or rely on the phone for other uses. Programs that accept phone-ins check eligibility at the facility site when fees are collected. The major advantage of accepting phone calls is to accommodate participants having legitimate scheduling conflicts. A disadvantage regarding phone-in cancellations is the potential for tampering with reservations.

While variations exist, reservations reflect demand, use patterns of clientele, and staff availability. Publicize your policy in writing and include information on eligibility, reservation procedures, court availability, and fee requirements.

4. General Sport Facility Use Policies. These policies present information pertinent to all eligible users of facilities regardless of their specific sport interest.

INFORMAL SPORTS RESERVATIONS

Handball-Racquetball-Squash Courts

DAY _____ DATE _____

	4:00 pm	5:00 pm	6:00 pm	7:00 pm	8:00 pm	9:00 pm	10:00 pm
Court 1							
Court 2							
Court 3							
Court 4							
Court 5							
Court 6							
Court 7							
Court 8							
Court 9							
Court 10							
Court 11							
Court 12							

NOTE: A valid ID must be shown when making reservations. Only one court time per/day, per/ID will be allowed.

Figure 3-1. Informal sports court reservation form.

Since participation is self-directed, participants must understand these policies in the interest of their safety and enjoyment.

a. Accident Prevention and Reporting—The risk of injury and accident constitutes a major concern of all informal sport programmers. In order to protect participants and staff personnel and minimize the potential for legal action stemming from injury, develop a comprehensive plan for accident prevention, first aid, and reporting. Efforts should focus upon facility and equipment inspection, hazard control, risk management, staff training, accident prevention, emergency medical procedures, and participant awareness.

Policies for informal sport facility use must convey information to participants regarding safety awareness and specific procedures for handling accident situations. Printed statements, supported by notices at activity sites and staff supervision help ensure proper facility use and participant behavior.

All policy and procedure statements should describe how and where to obtain assistance at the facility site in the event of an accident or injury.

Participants must be aware of their responsibility to provide the necessary information for accident reports. Accurate and complete forms are essential for hazard and injury analysis, for insurance claims, and for possible legal action. Accident reporting begins at the scene as soon as it is possible to communicate with the victim. Unnecessary delays may result in incomplete or inaccurate information.

Finally, policy statements should inform participants whether the facility carries insurance to cover injuries sustained at the site. If the facility requires outside insurance or a medical examination prior to participation, the informal sport staff may bear responsibility for assuring participant compliance.

b. Emergency Procedures—Risks apart from the potential for personal accidents merit our attention. A fire, tornado, electrical failure, chemical leak, avalanche, explosion, or bomb threat necessitate an emergency plan, despite the unlikelihood of their occurrence. Such a plan includes provisions for training personnel and informing the public in emergency procedures. Specific evacuation plans, procedures, and safety codes should be prominently posted at facility sites. In the event of an emergency, informal sport staff should be ready to take charge.

c. Children—The presence of children and young adults often requires the development of specific policies governing their participation. This group lacks the maturity, safety consciousness and awareness of other participants. Rules used to structure informal sport participation by children and young adults include:

—Requiring that children be under the direct supervision of a parent or adult.
—Providing specialized supervision for children.
—Designating special times for children to use facilities.
—Requiring parents or guardians to sign statements acknowledging potential risks of youth activities and their awareness of user policies and procedures.

While these strategies cannot eliminate problems or the potential of an injury, they represent our best effort to minimize risk for all informal sport participants.

d. Participant Conduct—Policies in this area are designed to encourage appropriate participant conduct and courtesy. Such policies involve:

Litter   —where it should be
                         disposed
Smoking   —where permitted

Food and Beverages	—where items may be purchased and consumed
Spitting	—where recepticals and fountains are located
Dress	—recommended or required clothing and footwear
Pets	—restrictions mandated by state health and safety regulations
Sportsmanship	—expectation for fair play, positive social interaction and proper conflict resolution behavior
Lost and Found	—procedures for submitting or claiming items

5. Individual Facility Policies. Most settings establish specialized policies peculiar to each individual facility. Statements illustrating areas of policy development for selected sites follow.

Racquetball, handball and squash courts
—Ball required that avoids marking court surface
—Eye guard required
—Challenge court rules

Swimming pool and diving well
—No street shoes on the pool deck
—Shower required before entering the water
—No diving from 10 meter platform
—No starting block

Weightroom and conditioning area
—Shirts required
—Equipment returned to proper location when workout completed
—No shoes on exercise mat
—Spotters required

Gymnasium
—No dunking of basketballs
—No street shoes on the court
—Half-court rules
—Shooter's court rules
—Equipment set-up by authorized employees

Outdoor field
—Use of lights authorized by informal sport staff
—No authorized vehicles on the fields
—Cancellations of activity due to inclement weather
  determined by on-duty employee

Ice skating rink
—No street shoes on the ice
—Established directional pattern for skating
—No "horseplay" on the ice

Water slide
—One person on the course until past the half-way mark
—One person per mat—no tandem riding
—No riding the course in a backwards position

Ski slope
—No swinging in the chairs
—No "bushwacking"—leaving established paths
—Keep the chairlift bar in position

Public lake
—No motor boats
—Swimming permitted when a guard is on duty
—No pets in the water
—No fishing from docks or bulkheads

Tennis court
—Do not cross the court while a game is in progress
—Do not throw racquets
—No roller skates permitted

Park
—No bicycle or motorcycle riding off pathways
—Fires restricted to grills
—No firearms or horses

Softball diamond
—Spectators are restricted to specified bleacher
  areas

—Watch for wildly thrown or batted balls
—Masks recommended for catcher

Snowmobile trail
—State registration required for all vehicles
—Headlights and taillights required after dark
—Stay clear of roads, parking lots, and landscaped areas

Drag strip
—Safety inspection required
—One person per car
—Approved safety belts and helmets required while on the course

The key to public acceptance of policy statements is the justification for their existence, consistent enforcement, and a sensitivity for public relations. If personnel are brash, aggressive and impertinent in policy interpretation or enforcement, they provoke negative participant reaction.

Participant acceptance of facility utilization policy requires their involvement in the decision-making process. The programmer may accomplish this through informal conversations or through more structured channels as evaluation sessions and advisory councils.

6. Governance. Personnel need preparation to handle situations involving participant abuse to facilities, employees, and others. Each occurrence requires a documentation for objective review and possible disciplinary action. When a problem arises, determine whether currrent program practices contributed to it.

    We suggest these guidelines to help minimize problems:

—Provide attractive, well-lighted and well-maintained facilities.
—Facilitate participant access to facilities and services by minimizing red tape.
—Utilize committed, conscientious, and diplomatic personnel.
—Replace or repair vandalized equipment.
—Provide adequate supervisory or security personnel

for monitoring participation and identifying maintenance needs.
—Enforce consistent policies.

Effective governance involves keeping participants and staff informed about expectations governing conduct, including an explanation on the consequences of policy violation and the procedure used for resolving problems. In practice, policy statements need written administrative approval before implementation. Otherwise, the programmer may be thrust into an embarrassing situation when his or her decision is overruled or disregarded.

To assure fair and thorough governance, we recommend that the following principles be followed. (For more detailed treatment of this subject, consult the Program Control chapter.)

—Record the situation as soon as possible. Obtain statements from the party involved, employees, and witnesses.
—Conduct an investigation and review the facts with all involved parties.
—Establish a ruling based on severity of the incident and precedent.
—Provide an appeals process.

7. Participant's Manual. When informal sport is recognized as a distinctive program, it is possible to plan, deliver and evaluate services more effectively so that activities are attractive to participants and effective in meeting their interests. A manual for informal sports is an excellent means to help employees and participants understand the program and follow proper policies and procedures. We present a suggested format for such a manual in Figure 3-2, listing topics most frequently covered in an informal sport program.

OPERATIONS

The primary functions performed by informal sport personnel are grouped into three categories: safety, security, and public

---

INFORMAL SPORT PARTICIPANT MANUAL

TABLE OF CONTENTS

Figure 3-2. Sample table of contents indicating suggested topics for an informal sports participants manual.

relations. The programmer must anticipate problems in these areas, have procedures for reporting problems, and plan to resolving them.

Personnel Considerations. Informal sport activities typically require the services of door checkers, cashiers, equipment room and locker room attendants, supervisors, lifeguards, facility managers, and custodians. The programmer should determine what jobs are necessry for program delivery and proper supervision of facilities and participants, taking care that job descriptions specify the tasks personnel are expected to perform. Even though a written description spells out performance expectations, use an oral presentation and discussion to specify general areas of responsibilities common to all types of jobs, and the tasks peculiar to each job.

A more effective tool to inform personnel of their responsibilities and conditions of employment is an employee manual. This manual discusses: job descriptions, program philosophy and purpose, organizational structure and flow chart, employment application and payroll procedures, benefits, performance expectations, dress code, reasons for termination, concern for liability, financial accountability, grievance procedures, program policies, and facility maps and diagrams.

Due to the minimal involvement by personnel in informal sport, interaction with participants is sporadic and tasks often become routine and unchallenging. To avoid apathy, inconsistent job performance, and resentment that may result, we suggest that a programmer:

a. Develop a regular system for monitoring performance and conducting evaluations.
b. Keep work shifts short, especially for less desirable tasks.
c. Know the personalities of your personnel and match them up with the demands of the job.
d. Use a sequential pay rate scale that increases with the demands of each job type.
e. Develop a job classification system which provides for upward mobility.
f. Seek recommendations from personnel for improving job conditions.
g. Take disciplinary action as warranted.
h. Recognize and reward quality job performance.

All informal sport personnel should have a clear understanding that they are expected to project a positive, capable
image in appearance, attitude, and actions— regardless of the
pressures of the job.

Reporting considerations. The programmer has the
responsibility for recognizing, reporting, and reviewing operational concerns within the informal sport environment. This
responsibility may be facilitated by a communications network
including on-site supervisors and participants who are familiar
with the reporting process.

One of the primary reasons for establishing a reporting
system using both personnel and participants is the im-
possibility of having professional staff at each facility site
during all hours of operation. Using volunteers, employees or
participants already on-site increases the likelihood that items
of importance will be reported since everyone has a stake in
making improvements, and adds new perspectives to situations where staff may have developed blind spots.

Although we discuss the principal areas of reporting in
the Personnel chapter, those which have particular relevance
for the informal sport program are facility usage reports and
financial summary reports.

1. Facility usage. Profit and non-profit informal sport programs can obtain useful information through facility
   usage reports. Regular monitoring reveals user trends
   in terms of increased or decreased participation,
   popularity of facilities and activities, and peak or low
   time periods for use. Further analysis specifies the
   type or age group of users—male, female, youth, senior
   citizens, students, residents, officer, or executive.

   Facility usage reports aid in the planning and
   evaluation of informal sport participation. Data can
   suggest a demand for additional facilities, a change in
   the number of supervisors needed for certain facilities,
   alternatives for the number of hours a facility is
   available for use, strategies for improving utilization of
   certain facilities, and cost-efficient methods of
   operating them.

2. Financial summaries. Financial transactions require
   the keeping of records to satisfy legal requirements,

INFORMAL SPORTS PARTICIPATION COUNT

Tennis Courts

DAY _____ DATE _____

TIME	SOUTH BATTERY	NORTH BATTERY	WAITING TO PLAY	TOTAL	INITIAL
12:15 pm					
12:45 pm					
1:15 pm					
1:45 pm					
2:15 pm					
2:45 pm					
3:15 pm					
3:45 pm					
4:15 pm					
4:45 pm					
5:15 pm					
5:45 pm					
6:15 pm					
6:45 pm					
7:15 pm					
7:45 pm					
8:15 pm					
8:45 pm					
9:15 pm					
9:45 pm					
TOTAL					

Count everyone using and waiting to use the facility for informal tennis. Do not count spectators, classes, intramurals, club sports, athletics, or reserved time.

Supervisor taking count should add the row total and then initial it.

After final count, supervisors should add the columns.

Figure 3-3. Informal sports participation count form.

safeguard assets, and control operations. Transactions that commonly involve informal sport personnel include: sale of membership and user passes, equipment rentals, concession sales, clothing or equipment sales, and locker and towel rentals.

While we cover accounting procedures in greater detail in the Finance chapter, we offer several guidelines regarding transactions handled by informal sport facility personnel:

a. Provide each person responsible for cash with a separate and fixed change fund and a safe depository.

b. When cashiers share the same cash drawer, have the incoming replacement verify the amount left prior to shift exchange. Record discrepancies and include the signature of each party.

c. Use written receipts for all income.

d. Keep a daily record of revenue and deposits.

e. Conduct a regular check comparing sales to an inventory or merchandise.

CONCLUSION

Unlike structured sport programs, the informal sport program involves a greater emphasis upon facility management and supervision than upon activity design and supervision. While the informal sport participant determines an activity and format for involvement, he or she depends upon the programmer to expedite access to the necessary facilities and services. When one considers the tremendous variety of participant interests that require facility access, the programmer faces a major challenge to provide sufficient and diverse facilities to meet these interests.

The programmer has a further responsibility for making the facilities and participation opportunities as attractive and appealing as possible. A quality informal sport program involves more than constructing a sufficient quantity of facilities and making them available for self-directed use. It entails a commitment to establishing effective operating policies, providing capable supervision, responding to participant feedback and maintaining facilities properly to increase their usefulness.

FITNESS PROGRAMMING AS INFORMAL SPORT

An additional way to provide meaningful service through the informal sport program is to emphasize the relationship between self-directed participation and fitness. The programmer stresses the concept of fitness awareness and how persons of all ages may attain fitness by participating in self-directed sport and exercise. Because of its ease of implementation in all settings, fitness programming enhances the informal sport concept.

Historically, educators and practitioners have taken different approaches to fitness. Some programs in the public and private sector emphasize it from the perspective of health and safety, while others view it from the standpoint of physical education and exercise.

More recently, fitness programming has included an emphasis on the benefits occurring from regular participation in recreational sport activities. New discoveries in exercise and sport have contributed to understanding how one can improve the quality of life.

Today, persons of all ages, body types, and sport activity preferences are demonstrating interest in the elements of an active, healthy lifestyle. An awareness of the benefits derived from regular participation in exercise and sport does not guarantee actual participation. People need encouragement to make time available for regular involvement.

If improvements are going to take place in general fitness levels, programmers need to take specific steps to counter the sedentary patterns perpetuated by the rise of technology. We must provide a means for programming exercise and sport into present day lifestyles as well as for encouraging participation as a life-time pursuit.

Physical Fitness

When we think of the word "fitness" we often envision its physical aspect. Although physical fitness is but one dimension of a discipline that includes mental, social, spiritual and emotional components, a focus on the physical aspects of fitness through regular participation in sport and exercise contributes to positive physical and mental health. Some of the health benefits resulting from regular participation in sport and exercise are listed in Figures 3-4 and 3-5.

Physical fitness involves health-related and performance-related aspects. Components of health-related physical fitness contribute to well-being by reducing the risk of degenerative diseases, increasing work efficiency, and eliminating muscle

THE PHYSICAL HEALTH BENEFITS OF SPORT AND EXERCISE

Major Benefit	Related Benefits
Improved cardiovascular fitness	Stronger heart muscle Lower heart rate Possible reduction in blood pressure Reduced blood fat Possible resistance to artherosclerosis Possible improved peripheral circulation Improved coronary circulation Resistance to "emotional storm" Less chance of heart attack Greater chance of surviving a heart attack
Greater lean body mass and lesser body fat	Greater work efficiency Less susceptibility to disease Improved appearance Less incidence of self-concept problems related to obesity
Improved strength and muscular endurance	Greater work efficiency Less chance of muscle injury Decreased chance of low back problems Improved performance in sports Improved ability to meet emergencies
Improved flexibility	Greater work efficiency Less chance of muscle injury Less chance of joint injury Decreased chance of low back problems Improved sports performance

Other health benefits of exercise and physical fitness	Increased ability to use oxygen
	Quicker recovery after hard work
	Delay in the aging process
	Greater respiratory efficiency
	Possible increase in efficiency of the
	    vital organs other than the heart
	    and muscles
	Decreased muscle tension

Figure 3-4. Major and related physical health benefits of sport and exercise. Source: Corbin, C. B. et al. *Concepts in Physical Education* (4th ed.). Dubuque: W. C. Brown, 1981, p. 9.

soreness. These components include cardiovascular and muscular endurance, strength, flexibility and body composition. Performance-related components relate to the skills considered important for enjoyable participation in recreational sport activities. These components involve speed, reaction time, power, agility, balance, and coordination. (Corbin, Dowell, Lindsey and Tolson, 1981, p. 8.)

Cardiovascular endurance refers to the capacity of the heart, lungs, and blood vessels to function efficiently during

THE MENTAL HEALTH BENEFITS OF SPORT AND EXERCISE

Major Benefit	Related Benefits
Reduction in mental tension	Relief of depression Fewer stress symptoms Ability to enjoy leisure Possible work improvement
Opportunity for social interactions	Improved quality of life
Resistance to fatigue	Ability to enjoy leisure Improved quality of life Improved ability to meet some stressors
Opportunity for successful experience	Improved self-concept Opportunity to recognize and accept personal limitations
Improved physical fitness	Improved sense of well-being Improved self-concept Improved appearance

Figure 3-5. Major and related mental health benefits of sport and exercise. Source: Corbin, C. B. et al. *Concepts in Physical Education* (4th ed.). Dubuque: W. C. Brown, 1981, p. 10.

periods of vigorous muscular activity over time. Unless the heart, circulatory, and respiratory systems function efficiently, insufficient oxygen supply impairs activity.

Muscular strength refers to the maximum amount of force a muscle or group of muscles can exert against resistance. Strength has been a traditional symbol of fitness for many years. Although the development and maintenance of muscular strength leads to a more attractive physique, its major important fitness benefits are the protection of the joints and injury prevention during participation.

Muscular endurance is the capacity of a muscle or group of muscles to apply and sustain force over a period of time. Muscle endurance aids maintenance of good posture and resistance to fatigue.

Flexibility refers to the capability of the joints to enjoy a full range of movement. When the joints are not exercised often enough through a full range of motion, the surrounding connective tissues are not able to retain their normal length and flexibility. Lower back pain, postural misalignment, and crowding of internal organs are symptomatic of inflexibility. Having experienced a decreased range of motion in a joint, a person cannot benefit from the full strength of the muscles positioned around it. A reduced range of motion often involves a compensation from the proper mechanical principles in the execution of a movement that lowers the level of performance, and may result in injury.

Only recently has *body composition* received recognition as an important component of fitness. Most people tend to equate total body weight as the indicator of fitness rather than the relationship between fat and lean body mass. Since muscle is more dense that fat, body weight is a deceptive measure.

While concern with weight is understandable, it is the ratio of body fat to weight that reflects optimal fitness. Obese individuals strain their cardiovascular systems during any form of activity. They are prone to hypertension, diabetes mellitus, gallbladder disease, degenerative arthritis, digestive diseases, respiratory infections, kidney disease and posture dysfunction.

Balance involves an ability to maintain body position. Static balance is the ability to maintain equilibrium while in a standing position. Dynamic balance is the ability to maintain equilibrium while moving or performing some task. Three major principles affecting balance are:

1. Center of gravity—the lower the center of gravity, the greater the balance and stability.

2. Base of support—the larger the base of support, the greater the balance and stability.

3. Relationship between center of gravity and base of support—when the center of gravity is closest to the center of the base of support, the greater the balance and stability.

Agility refers to an ability to change the direction of the body or body parts rapidly. This involves speed, accuracy and control in making quick starts and stops; rapid changes of direction; and efficient footwork. Influenced by heredity, agility improves through practice, training and instruction involving such other aspects of skill-related fitness as reaction time, strength, and coordination of the large muscle groups.

Power is defined as the ability to transfer energy into a fast rate of speed. (Corbin et al., 1981, p. 7) Participants capable of combining strength with speed of movement are considered to be powerful. Power is exhibited in such activities as putting the shot, rowing, pitching and punting.

Coordination is the harmonious integration of muscular movements necessary to execute a task smoothly. Heredity tends to affect coordination. While it is possible to improve coordination through practice and experience, progress is often specific to the task or skill performed so the programmer should offer the choice of a wide range of recreational sport activities.

Speed is the rate at which a person moves his or her body or body parts from one point to another. Speed of movement is exemplified in running, boxing, swimming, skating, fencing and lacrosse.

Reaction time involves the amount of time required to initiate a response to a particular stimulus. Individuals considered to have quick reaction times make fast starts in football, swimming or running events, react quickly to a moving baseball or basketball, and move rapidly to dodge or defend against such attacks as occur in fencing or martial arts.

Contributions of Sport and Exercise to Fitness

In order to maximize the benefits from health and skill-related fitness, we should help individuals learn which sport and exercise activities contribute specifically to each aspect of physical fitness.

Figure 3-6 demonstrates health-related benefits of familiar sports. Each sport is rated according to its contribution to health-related fitness.

Benefits to health from sport participation depends upon the frequency, intensity and duration of participation. The ratings depicted here require that the sport be performed on a regular basis. Determining the relationship of sport or exercise to health-related fitness requires an understanding of the following:

1. Fitness target zone—One identifies a range of participation from the minimum necessary to bring about improvement in fitness to a maximum amount, beyond which activity may be counterproductive. This continuum constitutes the fitness target zone.

2. Overload principle—To improve an aspect of health-related fitness, one engages in more than normal (overload) participation.

Sport or Activity	Develops Cardiovasc. Fitness	Develops Strength	Develops Muscular Endurance	Develops Flexibility	Helps Control Fatness	Lifetime Sport or Activity
Archery	Poor	Fair	Poor	Poor	Poor	x
Backpacking	Good	Good	Excellent	Fair	Good	x
Badminton	Good	Poor	Fair	Fair	Good	x
Baseball	Poor	Poor	Poor	Poor	Fair	
Basketball	Excellent	Poor	Fair	Poor	Good	
Bowling	Poor	Poor	Poor	Poor	Poor	x
Canoeing	Fair	Poor	Fair	Poor	Fair	x
Dance, Ballet	Good	Good	Good	Excellent	Fair	
Dance, Disco	Good	Poor	Good	Fair	Good	x
Dance, Modern	Good	Fair	Good	Excellent	Good	
Dance, Social	Fair	Poor	Fair	Poor	Fair	x
Fencing	Fair	Fair	Good	Fair	Fair	
Football	Fair	Good	Fair	Poor	Fair	
Golf (walking)	Fair	Poor	Poor	Fair	Fair	x
Gymnastics	Fair	Excellent	Excellent	Excellent	Fair	
Handball	Good	Poor	Good	Poor	Good	x
Hiking	Good	Fair	Excellent	Fair	Good	x
Horseback Riding	Poor	Poor	Poor	Poor	Poor	x
Judo	Poor	Fair	Fair	Fair	Poor	x
Karate	Poor	Fair	Fair	Fair	Poor	x
Mountain Climb.	Good	Good	Good	Poor	Fair	x
Pool; Billiards	Poor	Poor	Poor	Poor	Poor	x
Racquetball; Paddleball	Good	Poor	Good	Poor	Good	x
Rowing, Crew	Excellent	Fair	Excellent	Poor	Excellent	
Sailing	Poor	Poor	Poor	Poor	Poor	x
Skating, Ice	Good	Poor	Good	Poor	Fair	x
Skating, Roller	Fair	Poor	Fair	Poor	Fair	x
Skiing, Cross-country	Excellent	Fair	Good	Poor	Excellent	x
Skiing, Downhill	Poor	Fair	Fair	Poor	Poor	x
Soccer	Excellent	Fair	Good	Fair	Good	
Softball (fast)	Poor	Poor	Poor	Poor	Fair	
Softball (slow)	Poor	Poor	Poor	Poor	Fair	x
Surfing	Fair	Poor	Good	Fair	Fair	
Table Tennis	Poor	Poor	Poor	Poor	Poor	x
Tennis	Fair	Poor	Fair	Poor	Fair	x
Volleyball	Fair	Fair	Poor	Poor	Poor	x
Waterskiing	Fair	Fair	Fair	Poor	Poor	

Figure 3-6. Health related benefits of sports and other activities. From FITNESS FOR LIFE by Charles B. Corbin and Ruth Lindsey. Copyright © 1979 Scott, Foresman and Company, p. 169. Reprinted by permission.

3. Threshold of training—One identifies the minimum amount of participation which will produce improvements in each aspect of health-related fitness.

Just as there are sports and exercises which contribute more to health-related abilities, Figure 3-7 demonstrates which aspects of skill-related fitness are required in various sports. The ratings have been based on recreational level participation. A **Poor** rating means no skill is needed, **Fair** means that little skill is needed, **Good** means that some skill is needed, and **Excellent** means that much skill is required for that particular sport.

Physical fitness requires regular exercise. The recreational sport programmer contributes to fitness of participants by providing and promoting exercise opportunities rather than by leaving participation to chance alone.

Sport and exercise are the primary techniques of fitness programming. Exercise, as a fitness activity, involves reasonable vigorous or continuous physical activity. Sport, on the other hand, encompasses a broad category of non-work activity that may or may not involve exercise. One may engage in exercise without participating in a sport (Johnson, Updyke, Schaefer and Stolberg, 1975, p. 2). Most persons engage in an exercise program in the interest of attaining some specific fitness outcome. Those who engage in sport may do so as a form of diversion, fun and socialization with little or no regard for fitness.

The level of skill, frequency, intensity, and duration of participation all affect fitness benefits derived from sport participation. While most sports require basic conditioning to attain a high level of health-related fitness and experience significant improvements in skill-related performance, one does not have to be fit or skillful to still enjoy participation.

Due to differences in participant preference for, and fitness benefits from, sport activity, an informal sport program should provide a wide variety of activities from which to make choices. Programmers should facilitate accessibility to facilities, equipment and playing partners. Otherwise, any inconvenience involved in making these arrangements becomes a deterrent to participation.

Fitness programs emphasizing exercise must recognize that results are affected by the intensity, frequency, and duration of the workout. Calisthenics and weight training do not necessarily contribute to cardiorespiratory endurance and often require supplemental activity that stimulates use of the heart and lungs. A sound exercise program offers variety. Since people vary greatly in level of fitness, body structure, motivation, and fitness needs, we recommend an individual instead of a group approach to exercise.

Activity	Balance	Coordination	Reaction Time	Agility	Power	Speed
Archery	Good	Excellent	Poor	Poor	Poor	Poor
Backpacking	Fair	Fair	Poor	Fair	Fair	Poor
Badminton	Fair	Excellent	Good	Good	Fair	Good
Baseball	Good	Excellent	Excellent	Good	Excellent	Good
Basketball	Good	Excellent	Excellent	Excellent	Excellent	Good
Bicycling	Excellent	Fair	Fair	Poor	Poor	Fair
Bowling	Good	Excellent	Poor	Fair	Fair	Fair
Canoeing	Good	Good	Fair	Poor	Good	Poor
Circuit Training	Fair	Fair	Poor	Fair	Good	Fair
Dance, Aerobic	Fair	Good	Fair	Good	Poor	Poor
Dance, Ballet	Excellent	Excellent	Fair	Excellent	Good	Poor
Dance, Disco	Fair	Good	Fair	Excellent	Poor	Fair
Dance, Modern	Excellent	Excellent	Fair	Excellent	Good	Poor
Dance, Social	Fair	Good	Fair	Good	Poor	Fair
Fencing	Good	Excellent	Excellent	Good	Good	Excellent
Fitness Calisthenics	Fair	Fair	Poor	Fair	Fair	Poor
Football	Good	Good	Excellent	Excellent	Excellent	Excellent
Golf (walking)	Fair	Excellent	Poor	Fair	Good	Poor
Gymnastics	Excellent	Excellent	Good	Excellent	Excellent	Fair
Handball	Fair	Excellent	Good	Good	Good	Good
Hiking	Fair	Fair	Poor	Fair	Fair	Poor
Horseback Riding	Good	Good	Fair	Good	Poor	Poor
Interval Training	Fair	Fair	Poor	Poor	Poor	Fair
Jogging	Fair	Fair	Poor	Poor	Poor	Poor
Judo	Good	Excellent	Excellent	Excellent	Excellent	Excellent
Karate	Good	Excellent	Excellent	Excellent	Excellent	Excellent
Mountain Climbing	Excellent	Excellent	Fair	Good	Good	Poor
Pool; Billiards	Fair	Good	Poor	Fair	Fair	Poor
Racquetball; Paddleball	Fair	Excellent	Good	Good	Fair	Good
Rope Jumping	Fair	Good	Fair	Good	Fair	Poor
Rowing, Crew	Fair	Excellent	Poor	Good	Excellent	Fair
Sailing	Good	Good	Good	Good	Fair	Poor
Skating, Ice	Excellent	Good	Fair	Good	Fair	Good
Skating, Roller	Excellent	Good	Poor	Good	Fair	Good
Skiing, Cross-Country	Fair	Excellent	Poor	Good	Excellent	Fair
Skiing, Downhill	Excellent	Excellent	Good	Excellent	Good	Poor
Soccer	Fair	Excellent	Good	Excellent	Good	Good
Softball (fast)	Fair	Excellent	Excellent	Good	Good	Good
Softball (slow)	Fair	Excellent	Good	Fair	Good	Good
Surfing	Excellent	Excellent	Good	Excellent	Good	Poor
Swimming (laps)	Fair	Good	Poor	Good	Fair	Poor
Table Tennis	Fair	Good	Good	Fair	Fair	Fair
Tennis	Fair	Excellent	Good	Good	Good	Good
Volleyball	Fair	Excellent	Good	Good	Fair	Fair
Walking	Fair	Fair	Poor	Poor	Poor	Poor
Waterskiing	Good	Good	Poor	Good	Fair	Poor
Weight Training	Fair	Fair	Poor	Poor	Fair	Poor

Figure 3-7. Skill related benefits of sports and other activities. From FITNESS FOR LIFE by Charles B. Corbin and Ruth Lindsey. Copyright © 1979 Scott, Foresman and Company, p. 129. Reprinted by permission.

Fitness Delivery

Fitness programming may be offered to participants in three stages: awareness, testing, and participation.

Fitness Awareness. In situations where resources limit provision of fitness testing or special activity and event programs, a program may be limited to educational functions. Common approaches that can be taken to better educate participants include the following:

Clinics and workshops are helpful when information is too difficult or lengthy to explain in printed materials; when the information requires demonstration; when it will receive better attention if there is an opportunity to answer questions "on the spot"; and when it may require participant involvement to try out an activity.

These may be scheduled as needed or they may be set up and promoted on a regular basis. The time span for these events customarily range from one hour to two days.

In contrast to clinics and workshops, a **lecture series** is not designed for participant involvement and interaction, other than a question and answer period. A speaker simply addresses an audience on a fitness or health-related topic. The format may offer different views on the same topic, involve a number of different speakers, involve one speaker on a number of related topics, or provide a more in-depth view of a topic over a number of lecture sessions. Events may be scheduled successively on the same day, during a weekend, or over a number of weeks. Generally this format should not exceed 1½ hours per topic.

In instances where knowledgeable, credible and effective speakers are unavailable, use **films and slide-tape presentations.** This is an expensive approach when rental fees are involved but most professional A/V pieces are effective attention-getters. Always preview your material for appropriateness and accuracy before use.

Pamphlets and brochures addressing a wide variety of topics and may be obtained through local, state or national health organizations, medical and professional associations, often free of charge. Simple distribution of printed materials alone precludes an opportunity to rectify misconceptions, emphasize important points, and secure feedback.

A **newsletter** is a useful communication medium for a specific readership. It may include announcements, fitness and safety tips, articles, a fitness "hot-line" for questions and answers, surveys, program reminders, recommended reading lists, and addresses for obtaining outside materials.

TV and Radio are valuable tools for increasing fitness awareness. Success requires familiarity with available options and wisdom in selecting qualified spokespersons. The main types of public service broadcasts include full-length specials, panel discussions, and interviews, and shorter segments— news stories, announcements, and editorials. Some stations program regular spots for fitness tips. Since competition for public service air time is intense, effective preparation and presentation are essential for obtaining continued access.

The posting of attractive and informative materials about fitness and related topics on **bulletin boards and displays** is underestimated as an effective mechanism to promote awareness. Such materials are inexpensive and reusable. Most public and private buildings and sport facilities have bulletin boards or display cases, so your sole expenditures may be for materials and artwork. Change your materials frequently (every 2 to 4 weeks) to maintain viewer interest.

A **sport and fitness planning center** can help participants assess their knowledge and interests regarding sport and fitness and familiarize them with existing opportunities for participation. A center serves as an assessment, planning, referral system and clearing house for those interested in discovering their current fitness level, modifying detrimental habits, and deciding future sport and fitness endeavors.

Fitness Testing. A second tool for fitness delivery is the provision of fitness testing and appraisal services. First, decide the purpose for which you will use the results. Testing provides a physician, program coordinator, or exercise leader with sufficient information upon which to plan appropriate and safe participant activity. Test results help a participant assess current fitness level and monitor changes occuring over time. In any case, encourage participants to have a physical examination prior to starting any sport or exercise program.

Some form of medical screening and fitness evaluation is required by settings that prescribe individual fitness programs. The procedure may include a complete medical history and physical exam and a resting and exercise ECG (electrocardiogram) prior to evaluation. Some flexibility exists in these re-

FITNESS RELATED IDEAS

Aging and Exercise

Alcohol, Drugs, Smoking and
Exercise

Body Awareness

Cardiovascular System

Cardiac Rehabilitation

Clothing and Footwear

Conditioning
Specificity
Overload
Frequency, Intensity, Duration
Warm-up
Cool Down

Exercise
Intensity
Duration
Frequency
Target Heart Rate
Exercise Prescription
Medical Screening

Flexibility
Ballistic Stretch
Static Stretch
Stretch Reflex
Specificity

Heart Disease

Injury Prevention
Blisters
Muscle Soreness
"Runner's Knee"
Achilles Tendonitis
Shinsplints
Stress Fractures
Stone Bruises
Dehydration
Heat Stroke
Heat Exhaustion

Nutrition
Adequate Diet
Fats
Carbohydrates
Protein
Minerals
Vitamins
Fiber
Water
Cholesterol
Triglyceride Level
Salt
Sugar
Fast Foods
Food Preparation

Posture and Body Mechanics

Pregnancy

Relaxation

Risk Factors
Age, Sex, Family History
High Blood Pressure
Diet
Cigarette Smoking
Heart Disease
Stress
Glucose Intolerance
Inactivity

Sport
Endurance
Muscular Strength
Flexibility
Agility
Coordination
Reaction Time
Balance
Power

Strength Development
Isometric
Isotonic
Isokinetic

Stress Management
Alarm, Resistance, Exhaustive
Stages
Body Responses to Stress
Stress Related Problems
Role of Exercise

Test for Fitness
Cardiovascular
Muscle Strength
Muscle Endurance
Flexibility
Body Composition
Balance
Agility
Power
Reaction Time
Speed
Coordination

Training Programs
Continuous Exercise
Internal Training
Circuit Training
Strength Training
Mode of Training

Weight Control
Overweight, Underweight, or Obese
Calorie Needs
Exercise
Diet and Nutrition

Figure 3-8. Fitness related topics for lectures, workshops, and clinics.

quirements, depending upon the participant's age, health, family history, and present level of fitness.

If a person is under 35 and considered a low risk for coronary heart disease, the screening and testing requirements may be less stringent. Major risks associated with coronary heart disease are listed in Figure 3-9. Although they should not be considered conclusive, Pollock, Wilmore, and Fox (1978, p. 77) report the presence of two or less symptoms places one in a low-risk category, three to four symptoms represent moderate risk, while five and above represent a high-risk category.

Risk Factor	Relative Level of Risk				
	Very Low	Low	Moderate	High	Very High
Blood pressure (mmHg)					
Systolic	110	120	130-140	150-160	170
Diastolic	70	76	82-88	94-100	106
Cigarettes (per day)	Never None in 1 yr.	5	10-20	30-40	50
Cholesterol (mm/100cc)	180	200	220-240	260-280	300
Triglycerides (mm/100cc)	80	100	150	200	300
Glucose (mg. 100cc)	80	90	100-110	120-130	140
Body fat (%)					
Men	12	16	22	25	30
Women	15	20	25	33	40
Stress-Tension	Almost never	Occasional	Frequent	Nearly constant	
Physical activity minutes above 6 Cal/min (5 METS) [a] per week	240	180-120	100	80-60	30
ECG stress test abnormality (ST depression-mm) [b]	0	0	0.5	1	2
Family history of premature heart attack [c] (blood relative)	0	1	2	3	4
Age	30	35	40	50	60

[a] A MET is equal to the oxygen cost at rest. One MET is generally equal to 3.5 milliliters per kilogram of body weight per minute of oxygen uptake or 1.2 calories per minute.
[b] Other ECG abnormalities are also potentially dangerous and are not listed here.
[c] Premature heart attack refers to 60 years of age.

Figure 3-9. Risk of developing coronary heart disease. Source: Pollock, M.L., Wilmore, J. H., and Fox, S. M. *Health and Fitness Through Physical Activity.* New York: John Wiley and Sons, 1978, pp. 78, 79.

Medical screening and fitness evaluation prior to sport and exercise participation may be required in settings that do not offer individualized exercise programs but have the necessary access to qualified personnel and equipment— through a cooperative arrangement with a local hospital, physician, or a college or university medical, health, or exercise physiology program.

When resources are limited, a fitness program may focus upon self-directed participation, dispensing with medical screening and fitness evaluations.

Examples of representative tests used to assess health-related fitness follow. This section groups some of the options in sequential order beginning with those which are basic and inexpensive to those which are more complex, technical, and expensive.

Health-Related Fitness

Option #1:

An inexpensive basic test involving:

1. Heart rate and blood pressure

2. Body composition with a skinfold caliper and girth height and weight measurements

3. Flexibility by evaluating trunk extension and flexion through the sit and reach method

4. Strength by using a hand grip dynamometer

5. Muscle endurance by use of rapid pushups and bent leg sit ups for one minute

Personnel: Least demanding in terms of personnel expertise and training, Option #1 requires properly trained persons to make blood pressure readings who understand when to refer a participant to a physician. Testing staff should know the purpose and procedures for use of skinfold calipers and the dynamometer, for girth, height, and weight measuring, and for flexibility testing.

Comments: This system does not require certified/

licensed personnel or an exercise physiologist present on the testing staff. Staff should not issue opinions about test results nor make recommendations on the type of activity program a person should pursue based on results. The participant may compare results with accepted norms and standard scores and keep an on-going chart for recording them.

Option #2:

Another basic test that can be performed outside of a laboratory setting measures:

1. Heart rate and blood pressure readings, in conjunction with step tests or the 12-minute field test, provide indicators of cardiorespiratory fitness

2. Body fat composition with skinfold calipers along with girth, height, and weight measurements

3. Flexibility by self-testing on a the normal range of motion, in degrees, for various joints on a "pass-fail" basis

4. Muscle strength through a series of specified one-repetition exercises

5. Muscle endurance through such exercises as bent knee sit-ups, pull-ups (or modified pull-ups), and dips on the parallel bars.

Personnel: Once testing involves more activity on the part of the participant, additional monitoring skills are necessary. Use of such step-tests as the—Tecumseh Submaximal Exercise Test, Michael-Adams 1-minute Step Test, and the Modified Step Test—requires the ability to determine resting heart rate and heart rate recovery from exercise. Staff must know how to administer these tests and detect when a test should be stopped. Most programs require a medical check-up and clearance prior to administration of the 12 minute field test to participants. Personnel must be able to detect potential problems and stop the test if necessary. Testing staff should know the purpose of exercises used to test muscle strength and endurance, and the procedure for measuring results.

Comments: Testing staff need not be certified or licensed nor hold a degree in the areas of physical education or exercise physiology, but they should have a sound knowledge about the specific safety hazards and precautions involved with cardiorespiratory function and muscle strength and endurance testing. We also suggest that a medical clearance for participants who engage in this or any similar testing format.

Option #3:

A test requiring specialized equipment and laboratory work to determine:

1. Cardiorespiratory function using a resting and stress ECG on a motorized treadmill, and pulmonary function using a computer analysis

2. Body fat composition using a water emersion tank

3. Joint flexibility involving mechanical means for measuring joint extension, flexion, or rotation

4. Muscular strength and endurance for various muscle groups using barbells or specially adapted weight training machines.

Personnel: This procedure requires trained medical personnel, exercise physiologists, or persons having a degree from an accredited college or university in fitness or sports medicine. We recommend that a physician oversee the ECG testing.

Comments: This approach provides the most expensive and comprehensive test of fitness, requiring a high degree of expertise.

Skill-Related Fitness

Skill-related fitness tests help reveal a person's strengths and weaknesses, and help him or her select suitable recreational sport activities. Since aspects of skill-related fitness are specific to the part of the body and type of task involved, we do not present testing options in the same manner we did for health-related fitness. Instead, we list examples of tests commonly used for each aspect of skill-related fitness accompanied by comments about testing.

Balance (Static)
    Stork Stand
    Bass Stick Test (Crosswise and Lengthwise)
    Progressive Inverted Test
    —Tripod
    —Tip-up
    —Head
    —Head and forearm
    —Handstand
Balance (Dynamic)
    Bass Test
    Positional Balance
    Modified Sideward Legs
    Nelson Balance Test
Comments: Balance tests are practical to administer in terms of time, space requirement, equipment, and cost. The Bass test of dynamic balance is better suited for use with high school and college age groups. Some of the limitations associated with balance testing include the effect of strength or fatigue on test results, the number of trails needed to achieve the exact positioning required, and the lack of test norms for participants other than the college age level.
Agility
    Burpee Test (Squat Thrust)
    Side Step Test
    Shuttle Run
    SEMO Agility Test
    Quadrant Jump
    Illinois Agility Run
    LSU Agility Obstacle Course
Comments: These tests are more practical to administer in terms of time, equipment and cost. Each of the tests listed is suitable for use with either sex and may be initiated with the middle high school age group. Problems or limitations associated with agility tests include: variance in footwear and surface conditions, and overemphasis upon running ability. Agility, like balance, is specific to the body part being tested.
Power
    Vertical Jumps (Sargent Chalk Jump)
    Standing Broad Jump
    Vertical Arm Pull (Distance)
    Medicine Ball Put

Vertical Arm Pull (Work)
Vertical Power Jump (Work)
Margaira Anaerobic Power Test
Comments: Of these tests, the vertical arm pulls for distance and work are only suitable for males. Many power tests focus on measuring the distance attained upon release of maximum force. A more accurate assessment of power includes measurements for the amount of time required and the amount of force involved (or weight) to complete the performance. When administering tests of power minimize the effect of fatigue on tests involving jumping performance, and the influence of extraneous movements upon a "pure" reading.

Coordination
Hand Eye:
Stick Test of Coordination
One half flip
Full flip
Alternate Hand-Wall Toss
Softball Repeated Throws
Whole Body:
Edgren Side Step
Right-Boomerang Run
AAHPER Shuttle Run
Auto-tire test
Dodging Run
Eye Foot:
Soccer Wall Volley
Soccer Dribble Test

Comments: Coordination, like agility, is rarely manifested in isolation but often is an interrelated, simultaneous movement involving balance, agility, flexibility, and endurance. The tests apply for males and females for the middle school age group up. The laboratory tests and instruments that measure fine motor coordination are not practical to administer in the recreational sport environment. The following tests are reliable indicators of coordination in terms of hand-eye, foot-eye, and whole body coordination:

Speed and Reaction Time
Nelson Hand Reaction Test
Nelson Foot Reaction Test

Nelson Speed of Movement Test
Four Second Dash
Six Second Dash
Fifty Yard Dash
Nelson Choice—Response Movement Test

Comments: These tests are suitable for use with both sexes although age group suitability varies. Practical to administer, they do not require sophisticated timing instruments. The measurement of reaction time is influenced by the sense organ involved, intensity of the stimulus, the preparatory set, general muscular tension, motivation, practice, the response required, fatigue, and health status. Consequently, plan the testing situation carefully to produce optimal performance. If speed of movement and reaction time are measured separately, take care that the tests selected are specific and related to the movement involved in the task.

Our discussion should give you an adequate perspective on possible fitness testing designs. When you put together a testing program tailored for your finances and participant needs, follow these general principles:

1. Control hazards.

2. Select testing methods commensurate with personnel skills and credentials.

3. Follow standard practices and procedures.

4. Offer testing on a regular basis.

Fitness Programs. The final consideration in fitness delivery is the provision of sport and exercise programs and events. As individuals become more aware of the benefits resulting from fitness, they are prime prospects to participate in the following ways: on a participant-directed basis, a staff-directed basis, or a combination of the two.

Self-directed. When resources for structured fitness activity programs are limited, encourage the participants to direct their own patterns of sport and exercise based upon their particular needs and interests. We can aid this process by: promoting information regarding facility and equipment availability during informal sport times; providing opportunities for participation in other programs within recreational sport such as intramural and club sports; maintaining personal fitness profile cards on participants and encouraging continued participation through the use of incentives.

Keep in mind that a self-directed program does not involve setting up specific activities or events, but helps people understand more about the advantages and disadvantages that their current sport and exercise patterns offer and provides incentives for fitness improvement. Participants need fitness testing so that they may maintain a record of the results and monitor their own progress on a regular basis. Provide a log for those interested in monitoring how their participation contributes to fitness. A typical log is shown in Figure 3-10.

DAILY FITNESS LOG

Date: _____

Sleep: _____

Weight: _____

Aerobic Workout: _____

Total Aerobic Time or Mileage: _____

Training Area: _____

Anaerobic Workout: _____

Training Area: _____

Calorie Consumption

Breakfast _____

Lunch _____

Dinner _____

Total _____

Physical Attitude: _____

Mental Attitude: _____

Personal Comments & Observations: _____

Figure 3-10. Sample daily fitness log.

To further motivate participation, use an award points system based on the intensity and duration of sport/exercise participation. The aerobics point system is based on research which indicates that this form of exercise is the most beneficial to cardiovascular conditioning. (Cooper, 1977) From his data, Cooper has developed a point system which quantifies aerobic activities and provides the format for determining the number of points necessary (how much exercise) to achieve predetermined fitness goals. He suggests that record keeping of personal progress is a great motivational tool. An example of such a chart is provided in Figure 3-11.

WEEKLY PROGRESS CHART

Date	Activity	Distance	Duration	Points	Total

Figure 3-11. Sample of weekly progress chart.

An additional technique to motivate some is recognizing those who achieve their established goal. In addition to such familiar forms as certificates and trophies, other effective incentives are to: recognize participants in the newspaper, establish 25, 50, 100-mile clubs with presentations of t-shirts or other clothing items, give coupons that provide a discount on items at sporting goods stores, implement the Presidential Physical Fitness Award and Sports Programs, or give discount prices for enrollment in other sport programs.

A fitness trail often stimulates people to participate in self-directed exercise on a regular basis by providing a fun activity which may be enjoyed alone or with others. Such trails vary in cost depending upon the number of stations, materials used in construction, and the expense involved in purchasing or clearing land for its installation. Most trails have low construction and maintenance costs compared to those for other sport facilities. A resource guide describing fitness trail options and marketing information is available through the National Parks and Recreation Association.

The informal sport approach to fitness programming appeals mostly to persons who are highly motivated, self-disciplined, or those already engaged in physical activity on a regular basis. The programmer must use other techniques to involve the marginal participant.

Staff directed. An alternative approach involves staff-directed, structured activities and events to motivate and satisfy participant interests. Some of the most popular activities offered in recent years include aerobic dancing, jazzercise, aquathentics (exercise to music while in a swimming pool), aerobic exercise (usually set to music), trimnastics, postcardiac fitness, stretching, sport skills instruction, weight training and conditioning instruction. These activities are scheduled to occur several times a week and involve a program leader or instructor.

As in the case of fitness testing, the leaders or instructors must have the training necessary to conduct the activity properly. They should not ask a person to continue an activity when discomfort occurs, and they should know how to manage accident and emergency situations. Scheduled group activities enjoy greater popularity when the leader or instructor has a congenial personality, supports individual effort, understands individual needs and establishes a non-threatening environment that decreases participant self-consciousness. Structured activity programs are easily modified for such target groups as youth, the elderly, pregnant women, post-cardiac patients, and persons with disabilities.

Another popular programming approach that is staff-directed involves prescribing an individualized sport and exercise program for participants based upon such factors as medical and fitness testing results, participant interests, and, availability of facilities, finances and equipment. This concept may be the one most appealing to participants, but it also requires some involvement by trained and certified technicians, medical or exercise physiology personnel to implement it as a service. In fact, if other program staff who are involved with fitness testing or who serve as program leader/instructors engage in interpreting results or prescribing the type, duration, or intensity of sport/exercise to participants without authorization and supervision from qualified personnel, legal problems may arise. The guidelines that follow may help persons interested in the exercise prescription approach. (Pollock, Wilmore, and Fox, p. 118).

Preliminary Suggestions

1. Have adequate medical information available to properly assess health status: medical history, physical examination, risk factor, and laboratory evaluations.

2. Know physical fitness, sport and exercise habits.

3. Know the individual's needs, interests, and objectives for the exercise or sport program.

4. Set realistic short-term and long-term goals.

5. Give advice on proper attire and equipment.

Suggestions for Initial Phases of an Exercise Program

1. Educate the participant in the principles of exercise, exercise prescription, and methods of monitoring and recording exercise and sport experiences.

2. Give adequate leadership and direction in the early stages of the program to assure proper implementation and progress.

3. Remember that education, motivation, and leadership are the keys to a successful program.

Long-Term Suggestions

1. Re-evaluate the program to reassess individual status, functional physical fitness, and exercise/sport prescription.

2. Re-evaluate as a means to educate and motivate.

Special events may also enhance fitness activity programming. Because of their flexibility, special events take place as interests, needs, and resources permit.

Fitness Awareness Week. This event emphasizes the sport activities and programs presently offered through the department, agency or institution, and offers clinics, fitness assessment, films, demonstrations, and displays that represent fitness-related organizations and services. An official proclamation from the mayor or other administrative figure proclaiming a Physical Fitness and Sports Week can help promote the concept.

Distance and Fun Runs. Runs have become very popular across the country, particularly in local communities where they receive sponsorship through the Parks and Recreation Department or a YMCA/YWCA. Flexibility in distance, eligibility and number of entries receiving recognition furthers participation. Guidelines on race organization are available from the National Jogging Association (see Bibliography).

Jog and Walk Day. These events emphasize the involvement of as many people as possible in jogging or walking set distances. Provide group recognition by keeping track of the number of persons representing organizations (Lions Club, Sorority, Squadron, Industry) and individual recognition by determining the greatest distance accumulated by a participant in a specified amount of time. Both races and jog or walk days may include presentations and demonstrations concerning proper running, jogging, and walking techniques, injury prevention, and proper clothing and footwear.

Marathons. Marathons involve continuous physical activity over a specified period of time, rewarding those who can continue the longest or accumulate the greatest distance. Interest may focus on individual or group activities in dancing, skating, cycling, swimming, jump-roping, running, tennis, basketball, racquetball, etc. Although marathons attract spectators and media, few participate due to the strenuous demands upon the body.

Presidential Sports Award Program. Designed for persons who are at least 15 years of age, this program consists of 43 different sports, each with specific qualifying standards established to encourage sustained participation. The program may be organized by scheduling opportunities for participation or by encouraging participation on a self-directed basis. Upon qualification, the participant receives a personalized Presidential Certificate of Achievement, an embroidered emblem, and a lapel pin.

Presidential Physical Fitness Award Program. To be eligible for this program, participants must be between 10 and 17 years of age and must have scored at or above the 85th percentile for his or her respective age group on all six items of the AAHPER Youth Fitness Test. Winners of the award receive a certificate suitable for framing and an emblem designed to wear on sweaters, jackets, or blazers.

CONCLUSION

Fitness programming will continue to grow as a part of the total recreational sport service, especially since the public's interest in sport and exercise has spawned a "fitness renaissance". Consequently, the programmer has the responsibility to undertake efforts, singularly or cooperatively with other professional practitioners and educators, that will help people make their own decisions about fitness, sport, and exercise in a responsible manner. While there are many types of fitness programs from which to choose, our approach described the programming of fitness as a part of the informal sport program. Although an individual may select an activity according to personal interest, the decision will be affected to a large degree by the participation factors outlined in the informal sport segment.

BIBLIOGRAPHY

Books

Allsen, P. *Fitness for Life.* Dubuque, Iowa: William C. Brown Company Publishers, 1980.

Anderson, R. *Stretching.* Bolinas, California: Shettel Publications, 1980.

Ardell, D. *High Level Wellness.* Emmaus, Pennsylvania: Rodale Press, 1977.

Beaulieu, J. *Stretching for All Sports.* Pasadena: Athletic Press, 1980.

Buxbaum, R. and Micheli L. *Sports For Life: Fitness Training, Nutrition and Injury Prevention.* Boston: Beacon Press, 1979.

Cooper, K. H. *The Aerobics Way.* New York: M. Evans and Company, Inc., 1977.

Corbin, C. B. and Lindsey, R. *Fitness For Life.* Glenview, Illinois: Scott, Foresman and Company, 1979.

Corbin, C. B., Dowell, L. J., Lindsey, R. and Tolson, H. *Concepts in Physical Education.* Dubuque, Iowa: William C. Brown Company Publishers, 1981.

Cureton, T., Jr. *Physical Fitness Workbook For Adults.* Champaign, Illinois: Stipes Publishing Co., 1975.

deVries, H. A. *Physiology of Exercise.* Dubuque, Iowa: William C. Brown Company Publishers, 1980.

Falls, H., Baylor, A. M. and Dishman, R. K. *Essentials of Fitness.* Philadelphia: Saunders College, 1980.

Fisher, G. A. *The Complete Book of Physical Fitness.* Provo, Utah: Brigham Young University Press, 1979.

Forbes, E. and Fitzsimmons, V. *The Older Adult: A Process for Wellness.* St. Louis: C. V. Mosby Co., 1981.

Getchel, B. *Physical Fitness, A Way of Life.* New York: John Wiley and Sons, Inc., 1979.

Hockey, R. V. *Physical Fitness—The Pathway to Healthful Living* 4th edition. St. Louis: C. V. Mosby Company, 1981.

Johnson, B.L., and Nelson, J.K. *Practical Measurements for Evaluation in Physical Education* 3rd edition. Minneapolis: Burgess Publishing Company, 1979.

Johnson, P. B., Updyke, W. F., Schaefer, M., and Stolberg, D. C. *Sport, Exercise, and You.* New York: Holt, Rinehart, and Winston, 1975.

Kerns, G. *Aquarobics.* Bellevue, Washington: Aquanastica, 1980.

Kirkendall, D.R., Gruber, J.J., and Johnson, R.E. *Measurement and Evaluation for Physical Educators.* Dubuque, Iowa: William C. Brown Company Publishers, 1980.

Miller, D. and Allen, T. E. *Fitness: A Lifetime Commitment.* Minneapolis: Burgess Publishing Company, 1979.

Mirkin, G. and Hoffman, M. *The Sportsmedicine Book.* Boston: Little, Brown, and Company, 1978.

O'Neill, F. *Sports Conditioning.* Garden City, New York: Doubleday, 1979.

Polley, M. *Dance Aerobics.* Mountainview, California: Anderson and World, 1981.

Pollock, J. L., Wilmore, J. H., and Fox, S. M. *Health and Fitness Through Physical Activity.* New York: John Wiley and Sons, 1978.

Sheehan, G. *Running and Being: The Total Experience.* New York: Simon and Schuster, 1978.

Smith, E. *Exercise and Aging: The Scientific Basis.* Hillside, New Jersey: Enslow Publishers, 1981.

Sorenson, J. *Aerobic Dancing.* New York: Rawson, Wade Publishers, 1979.

Publications

The Athletic Institute. Publishes and distributes over 300 books on fitness, sports, physical education, nutrition and

health. Write 200 Castlewood Drive, North Palm Beach, Florida
33408 (305-842-3600) for free catalog.

The following publications are available from private or public
sources as indicated.

Building A Healthier Company, Blue Cross/Blue Shield, President's Council on Physical Fitness and Sports. Single
copies free from local Blue Cross Association. Designed to
assist in setting up a corporate physical fitness program.

Exercise and Weight Control, The President's Council on
Physical Fitness and Sports. Stock # 040-000-00371,
Superintendent of Documents, US Government Printing
Office, Washington, DC 20402; 60¢ea.* Includes chart
showing calories expended in various exercise activities.

An Introduction to Physical Fitness, The President's Council on
Fitness and Sports. DHEW Publication No. (OS) 79-50068,
Superintendent of Documents, US Government Printing
Office, Washington, DC 20402, $l.* Includes self-testing
activities, graded exercises and a jogging program.

Youth Physical Fitness, President's Council on Physical Fitness
and Sports. Stock # 040-000-00400-9 Superintendent of
Documents, US Government Printing Office, Washington,
DC 20402; $2.25 ea.* Suggestions for school programs.

The Fitness Challenge in the Later Years, The President's Council on Physical Fitness and Sports, Stock # 017-062-00009-3
Superintendent of Documents, US Government Printing
Office, Washington, DC 20402, 75¢ ea.* Exercises and
activities to combat problems of aging and to promote flexibility, balance and cardiovascular fitness.

Presidential Sports Award, President's Council on Physical
Fitness and Sports. Includes qualifying sports and standards, fitness logs to receive certificate and patch in
personally tested program. Information available from Presidential Sports Award, P. O. Box 5214, FDR Post Office,
NY,NY. 10022.

Food & Fitness, Blue Cross Association. Articles on all areas
of nutrition and physical fitness. Available from local Blue
Cross Association. Single copies free. Quantities. 25¢ each.*

Aqua Dynamics, President's Council on Physical Fitness and
Sports. Stock # 040-000-0036-6, Superintendent of Documents, US Government Printing Office, Washington, DC
20402.

Running "One Step at a Time", PCPFS. Stock # 017-001-00425.1, Superintendent of Documents, US Government Printing Office, Washington, DC 20402.

Walking. PCPFS, 400 6th Street, SW, Washington, DC 20201.

*Prices may vary

Films

The Athletic Institute. Produces and distributes more than 200 film and video presentations on fitness, sports, physical education, nutrition and health. Write 200 Castlewood Drive, North Palm Beach, Florida 33408 (305-842-3600) for free catalog.

The following three films are available on a 3-day rental basis for $12.50 from the National Audio Visual Center (NAC), General Services Administration, Washington, DC. 20409, Attention: Order Department. (301) 763-1891.

Alive and Feeling Great: (Order No. 008107). 13 minutes. The film shows Bonnie Prudden and Lenna M. Payton teaching 25 unrehearsed members of the Girls Club of America how to do basic body-building exercises that improve flexibility and muscle strength and prepare girls to enjoy sports of all kinds.

Aquadynamic Conditioning: (Order No. 007871). 19 minutes. Developed by C. Carson Conrad of the PCPFS, the film presents a series of vigorous water activities which can make a major contribution to flexibility, strength and circulatory endurance. The activities can be done in a small pool or in limited space in large institutional pools. Recommended for groups of all ages which have access to a pool. Produced by the National Varsity Club in cooperation with the PCPFS.

The Fun of Your Life: (Order No. 008277). 19 minutes. Charlton Heston narrates this film which deals with the importance of remaining physically active throughout life. Vignettes of various adult sports activities are shown. Presidential Sports Award Program is explained. Film recommended for all ages and groups. Developed by the PCPFS and the Montgomery Ward Company.

The following three films, produced by The Prudential Insurance

Company of America, are available on a free-loan basis from: Modern Talking Picture Service, Film Scheduling Center, 2323 New Hyde Park Road, New Hyde Park, NY 11040. (203) 277-4874.

Ahead of the Crows: 28 minutes. The film explores the motivation and goals of 10 outstanding athletes including Bob Griese, Stan Smith, Julius Erving, Bill Toomey and Kyle Rote, Jr. Recommended for all ages.

The Name of the Game is . . . Basketball: 28 minutes. The film features 11 great stars of the National Basketball Association who encourage physical fitness among young people. Appropriate for primary and secondary school boys and girls.

The Name of the Game is . . . Hockey: 28 minutes. The film features 15 National Hockey League stars and stresses the value of physical fitness. Appropriate for primary and secondary school boys and girls.

The following films are available on a free-loan basis from: The Travelers Film Library, c/o Modern Talking Picture Service, Inc., 2323 New Hyde Park Road, New Hyde Park, NY 11040. (203) 277-4874.

I Hope I Get a Purple Ribbon: 15 minutes. Stars Olympic medal winner Bill Koch and conveys the fun and excitement of participation in the Bill Koch Ski League, a Nordic ski program for children 13 years of age and under. Focuses on low-pressure competition and Bill Koch's beliefs about introducing young children to Nordic skiing. (PEPI Film).

The following four films are available from: Educational Media Services. Brigham Young University, Provo, UT 84602. (801) 374-1211, ext. 2713. Rental fees: $7 for one day, $1 each additional day in the following states: Arizona, Colorado, Idaho, Montana, Nevada, New Mexico, Utah, and Wyoming. In all other states: $14 for one day, $2 for each additional day. Films are also available for purchase by calling extension 4073.

Coronary Counter Attack: 21 minutes. The film demonstrates the risk involved in coronary artery diseases and measures to prevent these diseases. The need for exercise is explained and methods are suggested. Statistics by Dr. Kenneth Cooper are included. Appropriate for high school and adult audiences.

Run Dick, Run Jane: 20 minutes. The film shows how regular vigorous exercise can be insurance against heart disease.

Much of the subject matter is based on Dr. Kenneth Cooper's book, The New Aerobics. Presents exercises to prevent heart disease and become physically fit. Appropriate for intermediate grades through adults.

What Makes Millie Run: 15 minutes, produced by Brigham Young University in 1977. Millie Cooper's husband (Dr. Kenneth Cooper), who started the aerobics movement, encouraged her to jog. She is shown speaking to women's groups and describing her conversion to jogging. The film provides personal stories of women and families who have become more fit and gained feelings of satisfaction and well-being from aerobic exercising. Film encourages viewers to develop their own fitness program.

Bigger, Faster, Stronger: 25 minutes, produced by Brigham Young University in 1974. Power weightlifting is given a light-hearted treatment as its effects are demonstrated. Highlights extended capabilities it develops in practitioners. For competitive athletes of all ages and sexes.

The following three films are available on a 3-day rental basis for $18 for sale for $220 from: BFA Educational Media, 2211 Michigan Avenue, P.O. Box 1795, Santa Monica, CA 90406. (213) 829-2901.

Everyone's a Winner: Heart-Lung Endurance: 15 minutes. The film demonstrates the importance of heart-lung endurance and why these organs need exercise. Shows the best methods of keeping the heart and lungs in good shape: running and jogging. Suitable for elementary and junior high students.

Everyone's a Winner: Muscular Strength & Endurance: 16 minutes. The film describes a program for developing strength and endurance of the upper body, arms and abdominal muscles. Shows correct ways to exercise, including warm-ups. Suitable for elementary and junior high students.

Everyone's a Winner: A Program for Physical Fitness: 15½ minutes. The film shows why exercise helps for an active, interesting life. Describes a balanced program of exercise to meet the needs of active young people. Appropriate for elementary and junior high students.

The following film, sponsored by National Car Rental Systems,

Inc., the Minnesota Distance Running Association and Minneapolis Parks and Recreation Board in cooperation with the PCPFS, is available on a free-loan basis from: Modern Talking Picture Service, Film Scheduling Center, 2323 New Hyde Park Road, New Hyde Park, NY 11040. (516) 488-3810.

Run for Yourself: 26 minutes. Explains the personal drives that make three prominent physicians decide to run in a marathon. They not only explain their personal philosophies about running, but also go into the psychological, medical, practical, and historical aspect of the sport. In addition, you'll see action shots of the 547 runners who participated in the "City of Lakes Big Green Team Marathon."

Fitness Fever: 28 minutes. Features mass participation in diverse physical fitness activities sponsored by the Jacksonville, Florida recreation department, schools and other local agencies.

Take the Time: 18 minutes. Film features profiles of four working women, and how each has managed to fit a personal fitness program into their lives. It is a self-help motivational film that demonstrates to working women the importance of getting and staying in shape. Available from West Glen Films, 565 Fifth Avenue, New York, NY 10017 on a 30-day free loan basis or purchase. Appropriate for adult women.

AGENCIES FOR ASSISTANCE AND INFORMATION

Physical Fitness

American Alliance for Health, Physical
    Education, Recreation & Dance
    1900 Association Drive
    Reston, VA 22091
American College of Sports Medicine
    534 Clinical Drive
    Room 212
    Indianapolis, IN 46223
    (317) 264-3701
American Heart Association
    7320 Greenville Avenue
    Dallas, TX 75231
    (214) 630-7400

American Hospital Association
   Health Promotion Department
   840 N. Lake Shore Drive
   Chicago, IL 60611
   (312) 280-6000
American Medical Association
   Department of Health Education
   535 N. Dearborn Street
   Chicago, IL 60610
   (312) 751-6000
National Recreation & Park Association
   1601 North Kent Street
   Arlington, VA 22209
Blue Cross Association
   840 North Lake Shore Drive
   Chicago, IL 60611
President's Council on Physical Fitness
   and Sports
   400 Sixth Street, SW
   Suite 3030
   Washington, DC 20201
   (202) 755-7947

Running & Jogging Program

American Medical Jogger's Assn.
   P.O. Box 4704
   North Hollywood, CA 91670
   (213) 833-2265
National Jogging Association
   919 18th Street, NW—#820
   Washington, DC 20006
Road Runners Club of America
   2737 Devonshire Place, N.W.
   Washington, DC 20008

Walking & Hiking Program

American Volksport Association
   National Headquarters
   P.O. Box 107
   Fredericksburg, TX 78624
   (512) 997-7513

American Hiking Society
    323 Pennsylvania Avenue, S.E.
    Washington, DC
The Walking Association
    4113 Lee Highway
    Arlington, VA 22207

**Programs for Elderly
and Public Services Person**

National Association for Human
    Development
    1750 Pennsylvania Avenue, N.W.
    Washington, DC 20006
    (202) 833-2265
Administration on Aging
    Department of Health and Human Services
    330 Independence Avenue, S.W.
    Washington, DC 20201
Travelers Insurance Company
    One Tower Square
    Hartford, CT 06115

CHAPTER 4

INTRAMURAL
AND
EXTRAMURAL
SPORTS

The documented origin of intramural sports may be traced
back to the earliest form of physical education and athletic interest in the United States. Several sports were organized on
an intramural basis by colleges founded in the 19th century.
Not until 1913 did the first organized intramural sport program
with a faculty advisor begin, when the University of Michigan
and The Ohio State University, offered intramural competition
in various sports. Dr. Elmer Mitchell, the "Father of Intramurals," authored the first intramural textbook in 1925.

Historically, intramural sport has been a traditional term
for collegiate recreational sport. By 1975, the identification,

development and resulting popularity of informal sport programs, club sports, extramural sports and other programming
divisions required an expansion in terminology. Thus the um-
brella term "recreational sport," with intramural sport
representing just one of its programming divisions, surfaced.
The intramural principles and policies originally documented
by Dr. Mitchell are relatively unchanged. This new term
"recreational sport" is more representative of the diverse
recreational needs and interests of participants and relates
well to both theory and practice.

Another interpretation of intramural sport, outside of the
collegiate setting, occurred at the turn of the 20th century. A
variety of sport events were offered then by municipal and
community recreation departments, churches, elementary and
secondary schools, industries and private clubs. Although programs within these settings have not been traditionally termed
as "intramural sport" they meet the definition as presented.

The word "intramural" is a combination of the Latin words
"intra" meaning 'within' and "muralis" meaning 'wall'. When
used as an adjective in conjunction with the term sport, it
refers to those sport events that are planned and organized on
a recreational basis for members confined within the walls or
jurisdiction of a setting. Intramural sport represents structured
sport participation which requires design and external leadership for its provision. The term intramural sports may be used
in virtually any recreational sport setting. For example, a
sports program sponsored by a community parks and recreation department could be referred to as "intramural sports".
The same is true for such agencies as the Boys Clubs, Girls
Clubs, or YM/YWCA's which provide structured sport participation. Youth sport is more appropriately termed youth intramural sport.

Extramural sports are considered to be an extension or
outgrowth of the intramural sports program. Participants,
usually champions of organized intramural programs, compete
outside of the setting against champions from other institutions. Extramural events include sport days, play days or other
structured events that are conducted without a season-long
schedule, league competition or championship.

A high-quality intramural or extramural sport program encourages maximum participation in voluntary, satisfying, enjoyable and wholesome sport activities for all. Equal opportunities in sport should be available to all interested individuals regardless of age, sex, race, religion, creed, employment or economic status. The motto "Sport for Everyone" represents the philosophy of intramural and extramural sports. They provide a natural but yet wholesome outlet for satisfying the desire for competition and challenge.

Both intramural and extramural sport programs exist today because of popular demand. Simply stated, they endure because they are fun. The following sections of this chapter discuss general operational guidelines that ensure an effective sports program.

PROGRAM OF EVENTS

The development of a program of events is an important ingredient to the success of the intramural and extramural sports program. Although many activities are possible, the successful program reflects only those most suited to the majority of participants. It is more beneficial to offer a few well-selected and popular activities than a large number of poorly-administered ones. Quality of programming is far more important than the quantity or number of events offered. The following guidelines or principles may aid the development of program offerings:

1. *Needs, Interests, and Preferences of Participants.* The program content should be developed with participant input. When conducting surveys on interests, ask questions that determine what people do now, what they would like to see added or changed, what skill level they possess, and what activity they would actually participate in if it were offered.

   A good starting place in program development is a varied offering of basic events that are traditional in nature and have wide appeal based on programs offered by similar agencies elsewhere. The programmer may begin to modify the content as new input indicates.

2. *Balance of Offerings.* Individuals have different sport interests and skill levels. Consequently, the programmer should provide for individual differences by striving to offer a balance between: individual, dual, and team sports; non-traditional events, special events, and meets; indoor and outdoor sports; competitive and casual emphases; strenuous and less strenuous events; and the number of events offered during a season, session, or term.

3. *Flexibility.* Remain open-minded in selecting events to meet the needs and demands of the participants. What is appropriate one year changes the next. Factors affecting program selection include:

Age	Number of events
Sex	Time factors
Skill levels	Climate and season
Levels of competition	Budgetary limitations
Physical capacity	Area and facility availability
Safety	Equipment restraints
Number of participants	

Leadership and trained supervisory personnel

These factors may not apply to every sport setting. Institutions have unique restrictions or limitations. The effective programmer seeks to offer well-conducted events serving the majority of the clientele.

TYPES OF EVENTS

Events composing the sports program may be classified in various ways. Among them are:

1. *Individual sports*, such as swimming, golf, bowling and archery, allow the individual to participate alone.

2. *Dual sports*, such as table tennis, racquetball, badminton or handball require at least one opponent.

3. *Group sports*, such as relays, allow for various size groupings of individuals to participate.

4. *Team sports*, such as flag football, basketball or soccer require a specified number of players who play as a unit or organized team.

5. *Meets* are organized competition that include separate events and are usually completed within a specified period of time ranging from several hours to several days. Swimming, track and field, and wrestling are examples of a meet.

6. *Special events* consist of non-traditional events usually not practiced by the participant. Special events are excellent ways to promote positive public relations.

7. *Co-intramural sports*, applicable to many sport events, offer a balanced programming area that places emphasis on fun, team spirit and social interaction with members of both sexes.

Events may also be categorized according to actual types of games such as:

court games	gymnastics
net games	track and field events
lead-up games	outing events
floor games	water sports
field games	skill tests
combative sports	

UNITS OF PARTICIPATION

Units of participation are the select groupings which categorize participants for intramural or extramural play. These units are essential for a well-balanced program. Every effort should be made to develop reasonable and realistic units which will foster unit esprit de corps and enthusiasm, and maintain tradition in a wholesome competitive setting. Suggestions for units of participation in their respective programming settings are found in Figure 4-1.

SETTINGS AND UNITS OF PARTICIPATION

A. Church
Religious denomination
age groups

B. Community
residential zone
district
underprivileged
early bird
senior citizen
class A, B, C
church
business organization
sponsor
    YMCA/YWCA
    Hi-Y/TRI-H-Y
    GRA-Y
    Boys Club
    Scouts—Girl and Boy
special interest group
industrial
pony league
Babe Ruth league

C. Correctional
ward
cell
block
floor
wing
precinct

D. Education
**High School/
Elementary**
homeroom
class
grade
clubs
    Glee
    Honor
    Debating
    Drama
    Music

Science
physical education clas.
military
    'age
weight
height
alphabetical
bus route

College
living units
    dormitory
    floor
    quad
    hall
    graduate
    undergraduate

off-campus
community
faculty/staff
independents
geographic area
class groups
physical education class
college
department
academic session
    fall
    spring
    summer
    quarters
religious affiliation
military
    company
    battery
    squad
campus zones
home states
foreign students

E. Industry
plant
section
shift
division
union membership

F. Military
Air Force
    squadron
    group
    wing
    division
Army
    squad
    platoon
    company or squadron
    battalion
    regiments
    brigade
    division
    corps
Marine
    battalion
    squadron
    base
    regional
    All-marine
Navy
    division
    department
    element
    unit
    group
    force
    squadron
    fleet

G. Therapeutic
wheelchair
blind
mentally retarded

Figure 4-1. Units of participation.

Regardless of the setting, units of participation should be as equal as possible in size for a system to function effectively.

PROGRAM POLICIES AND REGULATIONS

The program policies and regulations of the intramural and extramural sport programs should be clearly stated and available to all participants *prior* to the start of the sport event. Some programmers have found it helpful to prepare these statements and make them available as a written handout in the form of "guides to participation." Whenever possible, the most pertinent information should be discussed with participants, perhaps at a participants or team captains meeting prior to the start of play. Examples of topical areas, comments and specific policies and regulations regarding each topic follow:

Eligibility

Eligibility rules for intramural and extramural sports need to be developed and enforced in order to assure fair competition and eliminate controversy. Theoretically, every member of an institution should have the right to participate in the program. Realistically, however, regulations must be established governing individual and organizational eligibility.

A. *Individual Eligibility.*
1. An individual is generally permitted to play for only one team per sport or contest. The team first represented should be the sole team for which a person may play for the remainder of the sport or contest.
2. Any player using an assumed name should be declared ineligible and the team for which they played under the assumed name should forfeit any contest in which the individual played.
3. Only individuals living, working, or attending a specified unit of participation would be allowed to play for that unit. Examples of this eligibility requirement are: employment for a particular company or industry; regular attendance at a specified church (unit of participation) or union membership.

B. *Skill Level Eligibility.*
   1. *Professional Eligibility.*
      a. Any person who has established oneself as a professional in any sport should be ineligible in that intramural sport or its related counterpart.
      b. Definition of a pro: A professional is any person recognized as such by the USLTA, PGA, NCAA, or a designated professional member of the NFL, CFL, NBA, major or minor league baseball, NASL or other professional or semi-professional organizations.
   2. *Intercollegiate Athletic Eligibility.*
      a. A person who has won a collegiate letter or award (i.e., trophy, plaque, jewelry, certificate, jacket) in a sport or its related sport should not be eligible to compete in that sport or its related counterpart for a period of three (3) calendar years after the awarding of the letter. Upon termination of the three (3) year grace period, only one (1) varsity letter winner is eligible to compete for a team in their sport or its related counterpart.
      b. A person who has received an athletic scholarship or is considered a member of an intercollegiate athletic team, but did not receive a collegiate letter or award as stated above in a sport or its related counterpart, should not be allowed to compete in that sport for a period of one (1) calendar year following such competition.
         1. A person is considered to be a member of collegiate team if they have practiced three (3) weeks prior to the first regularly scheduled athletic contest.
         2. Athletic coaches are considered members of their teams and are, therefore, restricted from participation.
         3. If an individual practices with a collegiate team for a period of one year and does not letter, but is subsequently dropped from the team the following year three (3) weeks prior to the first regularly scheduled athletic contest, he or she should be inelgible to compete

in that sport and in its related counterpart in the intramural sport program during that year.

3. *Club Sport Eligibility.*

Club sport members may participate in their specific or related sport. However, it is suggested that a limit of one (1) past or present member of a club sport be allowed to compete per team during an actual game in order to prevent domination by the club sport.

a. A club sport member is defined as any individual registered with a club (on the roster in the club sport office), or pays dues, or practices with the club within 3 weeks of the first game or match of the club season.

b. Upon termination of a one (1) year grace period, a past club member should return to a regular status for that specific or related sport.

4. *Related Sports.*

The following is a suggested list of sports and their related counterparts which refer to the above areas of professional, intercollegiate athletics, and club sport eligibility:

Professional, Athletic, Club Sport,
Related Intramural Sports

Badminton . . . . Badminton
Baseball . . . . Softball
Basketball . . . Basketball, Free Throw, Super Shoot,
One-On-One
Billiards . . . . Billiards
Bowling . . . . Bowling
Cross Country . . . . . . Cross Country, Track, Jogging
Diving . . . . Diving
Field Events . . . . Field Events
Football . . . . Flag Football, Touch Football
Frisbee . . . . Frisbee
Golf . . . . Golf, Miniature Golf
Handball . . . . Handball
Judo . . . . Judo
Racquetball . . . . Racquetball
Soccer . . . . Soccer
Softball . . . . Softball, Baseball

Swimming . . . . Swimming, Water Polo
Table Tennis . . . . Table Tennis
Track (Running Events) . . . . . . Track, Cross Country,
                                    Jogging
Volleyball . . . . Volleyball, Cageball
Water Polo . . . . Water Polo, Swimming
Weightlifting . . . . Weightlifting
Wrestling . . . . Wrestling

C. *Organizational Eligibility.*
   1. Individuals belonging to one or more organizations or units must declare membership with only one organization before the start of the event. Individuals who change organizations during the event should have the option of completing the specific schedule with their original team if they have participated in an event before moving.
   2. Participants for an organization must be listed on the official entry form or scoresheet kept in the sports office prior to participation.
   3. Only affiliated members are eligible to compete for an organization. Others may participate in an open division in the program.

Protests

Inevitably, there are going to be times when participants feel a mistake has been made by an official, someone has used an ineligible player, or some other situation (real or perceived) has occurred which seems unfair and prompts a verbal protest. In anticipation of protests, the sports programmer should have a predetermined procedure for receiving, documenting and reviewing them.

Accept protests, but do not encourage them whenever someone feels a wrong has been committed. Regardless of the ruling which results, the programmer has an opportunity to review the program and personnel objectively to reveal its strengths and improve upon its weaknessess. A protest process brings the programmer into direct contact with participants and provides an opportunity to establish better understanding and rapport with them.

1. Protests may be made once an ineligible player has participated or when improper interpretation or enforcement of the rules has occurred. Protests due to a judgement call of a sport official are usually not accepted. In some situations, protests arise from judgement calls as a way to take a break in the action and permit the participants to let off steam by writing out a grievance instead of directing emotion toward an offical. Although the programmer generally does not accept a protest on a judgement call, a review of the protest and discussion with participants may reveal a need to work more closely with official(s) on their mechanics or some other aspect of performance.

2. Any team or individual protesting the eligibility of an opposing player should provide evidence that the player is, in fact, ineligible. Such evidence may consist of:
   a. Written and signed testimony of a witness.
   b. Days, dates and times validating illegal participation.
   c. Pictures, rosters, etc., that depict ineligibility. Usually this evidence must be filed by a deadline designated by the sports staff.

3. If the protest does not involve eligibility, it should occur upon the field of play and be duly noted by the sport officials or supervisors on duty. The protesting team should make sure that the exact time of the contest, score and particulars of the play in question are noted by the officials and/or supervisors in charge before resuming play. (See Figure 4-2) If the protest is sustained, be it other than eligibility, it is suggested that the contest by replayed from the point of protest.

4. All protests should be verified in writing and submitted to the sports staff by 2:00 p.m. during round robin play, or by 9:00 a.m. during single elimination tournament play in team sports, and by 9:00 a.m. on the day following the protest in meets, dual and individual sports. No protest may be considered once filed after the time period has expired.

PROTEST FORM

SPORT: _____   Date: _____

● **TEAMS INVOLVED:**

Protesting Team A: _____   Team B: _____

Team Captain _____   Team Captain _____

Phone _____   Phone _____

Time Outs Remaining _____   Time Outs Remaining _____

Score _____   Score _____

● **DETAILS:**

Period: _____ (Volleyball)   Game: _____ (Softball)   Inning: _____

Time Remaining: _____

Team in Possession: _____ (Softball)   At Bat: _____

Explanation of Protest and What Occurred:

_____

_____

_____

_____

_____

How and Where Is Ball to be Put Into Play? _____

_____

Protesting Team Captain: _____
                                    Signature

● **OFFICIALS:**

Referee: _____ Phone: _____

Umpire: _____ Phone: _____

Officials' Comments: _____

_____

_____

Supervisor: _____ Phone: _____

Figure 4-2. Intramural sport protest form.

In many intramural and extramural programs, each protest must be accompanied by a specified "protest or sincerity fee." This fee is returned to the protesting team if the protest is sustained. Otherwise, it is retained by the department. Such a fee tends to discourage a large number of unwarranted protests.

Upon receipt of an initial written protest and documentation of evidence from the participant, the staff should further investigate the complaint. After reviewing all materials, an appropriate staff member should make a decision. Note: staff should always have the authority to investigate any alleged violation of any policy without the formal filing of a protest by a participant.

If an "invalid protest" ruling is made by the staff member, the participant should have the right to appeal the decision to an Appeals or Governing Board. This Board serves as a ruling body for all intramural or extramural sports programs. In making their final decisions, the Board should be governed by the same rules and regulations adopted by the program. To reach its decision, the Board may request the attendance at a meeting or hearing any staff, sport official, supervisor, witness or representative from the teams involved in the protest. All decisions rendered by this Board should be final and not subject to appeal. (See chapter on Program Control for further explanation of this system.)

Disciplinary Action

Persons who engage in sport participation may encounter disappointments or experience frustrations which bring them to a level of emotional agitation that they are unable to keep under control. Unless the programmer has an objective and consistent procedure for dealing with negative behavior and has the personnel capable of properly implementing this procedure, behavior problems will continue. Other participants may lose interest in the program, and the programmer may encounter problems securing officials. The effective control of negative behavior is a major factor in judging the success of a program in terms of enjoyment for participants and personnel.

1. In the event an individual or spectator acts in an unsportsmanlike manner during intramural or extramural competition, the game official has complete authority to take action, as deemed necessary, to keep control of the game. Depending on the severity of the incident, an official may take the following action according to his or her judgement: give a warning, eject from the game, eject from the area, or suspend the game.

2. All incidents should be reported to the intramural supervisor and documented for use by the staff in investigating the incident. Incidents which indicate unsportsmanlike conduct (examples: using an ineligible

player; theft of or damage to facilities or equipment; physical or verbal abuse toward officials, supervisors, players, or spectators) should be investigated by the staff. Question the individual(s) or team(s) involved and require a written statement of the incident on the day following the incident. Obtain detailed written statements from the officials and supervisors on duty, in addition to the Disciplinary Action Form. At the conclusion of the investigation, the staff may rule on the individual(s) and team(s) involved. Penalties could include: suspension from a game, games or season; temporary or permanent probation; and/or suspension from the sports program for a given time period. Only action relating to the intramural or extramural sport program is suggested. However, any incident judged to be of serious concern should be referred to the appropriate legal or law enforcement office.

Forfeits

Forfeits have a detrimental effect on the intramural and extramural sport programs and are a frustrating experience to those individuals or teams who were ready to play and no opponent appeared. In order to minimize forfeits the programmer should strive to schedule events at the most convenient times for participants, communicate schedules to participants well in advance, categorize participants by skill level or age, and utilize a system to remind participants of their scheduled event whenever possible.

1. All contests should be played on the scheduled date and hour. A team not ready to play within a specified period, usually *five minutes* after the scheduled time, is charged with a forfeit, subject to the discretion of officials, supervisor, or staff. Games lost by forfeit are not rescheduled for any reason.

2. If a team leaves before the forfeit is duly noted by an official or supervisor, then both teams should be charged with a forfeit.

3. The team that is present at a forfeit must have a full complement of players required for that sport or both teams are given a forfeit.

4. In the event one team is short the required number of players for that sport, the other team captain or manager should have the option to agree to play the game if provided for by the rules of that particular sport. It would then become a legal game and could not be protested on the grounds that an illegal team was fielded.

In the event both teams and the staff agree to play the game after the scheduled starting time has elapsed, no protest which is based on the starting time of the game is considered.

Disciplinary policies which may be taken in case of a forfeit include the following:

1. One forfeit results in the elimination of an individual or team from playoff competition in that sport.

2. Two forfeits results in the elimination of an individual or team from all further competition in that sport.

3. The individual or team may be assessed a forfeit fee.

4. A forfeit means reduction of a certain number of league or tournament points if a point system is in effect.

Regardless of forfeit procedures and policies adopted, communication plays a vital role. Both the forfeiting individual

---

Dear _Mr. Smith,_

According to our records, your _Flag Football_ team, _Smith's Team,_ has forfeited one of its regular season games. The rules governing intramural play state that any team forfeiting one game during regular season play will be disqualified from post-season play, and a team forfeiting two regular season games will lose all entry points and be dropped from further competition.

Forfeits are very disruptive to our program and a frustrating experience to those teams ready to play who receive the forfeit. Therefore, please make every effort to be ready to play the remaining games on your regular season schedule.

If you think your team will not be able to play your remaining games or if our records are in error, please contact us as soon as possible so that we may make the necessary arrangements.

Sincerely,

Figure 4-3. First forfeit letter.

or team and their opponents should be notified immediately via a personal phone call or written forfeit letter.

Dear _Mr. Smith,_

According to our records, your _Flag Football_ team, _Smith's Team,_ has forfeited two of its regular season games. The rules governing intramural play state that any team forfeiting two games during regular season play will lose all entry points and be dropped from further competition.

If our records are in error, please contact us as soon as possible so that we may make the necessary arrangements.

Sincerely,

Figure 4-4.   Second forfeit letter.

This personal approach might eliminate any future occurrences as well as indicate to the participants the concern of the staff in providing the best possible program for all.

Postponements and Rescheduling

All sport events should be played at the scheduled time unless major problems occur which affect the majority of participants. Inform teams to have an ample number of players on their roster since several of their members may not be available for a game because of conflicts with other activities.

1. If rescheduling is necessary, a scheduled contest should be postponed only with the consent of the opposing participant(s) and the staff.

2. A Rescheduling Request Form, providing all pertinent information, should be presented to the staff at least 24 hours prior to the originally scheduled contest so that all participants and game officials may be notified of the cancellation.

Postponements may occur because of poor playing conditions due to inclement weather. In this case, the intramural staff should notify all affected participants if possible. One method of notification gaining in popularity by both sport agencies and participants alike is the use of 24-hour recorded telephone messages. The obvious advantage to this system is that it affords up-to-date game schedules and postponement or rescheduling information _after_ regular office hours which is

when most intramural and extramural programs are conducted.

3. If a participant has not received postponement notification due to inclement weather prior to the scheduled
contest, it should be his or her responsibility to be present for the game or contact the sport office for a ruling.

4. Any games postponed by the staff should always be
rescheduled, not cancelled.

Medical Examinations

All participants should be urged to obtain a physical examination before participating in the intramural and extramural sport

---

RESCHEDULE REQUEST

Directions:

1. All games will be played at the schedule time unless *major* problems are present.
TEAMS SHOULD ANTICIPATE HAVING A PLAYER (OR PLAYERS) NOT AVAILABLE
FOR A GAME (OR GAMES) BECAUSE OF CONFLICTS WITH OTHER ACTIVITIES
AND HAVE AN AMPLE NUMBER OF PLAYERS ON THEIR TEAM ROSTER.

2. If rescheduling is necessary, a scheduled contest may be postponed only with the
consent of both teams' captains and the Intramural Staff.

3. This form must be completed and signed by both team captains and returned to
the Recreational Sports Office by 5:00 p.m. the day previous to the contest.

Team Initiating Request _____

Reason for Rescheduling _____

The team of _____ and _____
                  (Team Name)   (Team Name)

agree to reschedule their _____ game originally scheduled for _____,
                                (Sport)   (Day)

_____, at _____, on _____ to a time to be decided by the
   (Date)   (Time)   (Field/Court)

Intramural Sports Staff.

(Team)	(Team/Captain/Manager)	(Phone)

(Team)	(Team Captain/Manager)	(Phone)

FOR OFFICE USE ONLY

League # _____

The above game has been *rescheduled* to:

_____, _____ at _____ on _____
   (Day)   (Date)   (Time)   (Field/Court)

Figure 4-5. Reschedule request form.

program as a safeguard to their health. Since the majority of programs are voluntary in nature, participants are responsible for knowing their physiological limitations prior to the competition and are held accountable for their involvement in the program.

In situations where participants are considered minors, have the parents or guardian sign a statement indicating approval for their participation. If medical examinations are required prior to participation, the programmer may need a mechanism for keeping a copy of the exam on file or some other way to verify that the exam has been conducted.

DESIGNING TOURNAMENTS

There are several different types of designs that may be used in staging tournament competition. In order to determine the most appropriate type of tournament plan, many factors should be taken into consideration prior to implementation. These factors are:

1. *Objectives of the tournament.* Is it to:
    a. determine a winner quickly?
    b. provide for maximum participation?
    c. encourage social interaction?
    d. determine a true champion?
    e. emphasize the element of competition?
    f. motivate participants for a long period of time?
    g. increase skills in a particular sport?
    h. provide for equal number of matches per entry?
    i. rank all entries according to ability?

2. *Characteristics of the participants.*
    a. Age level—child, youth, adolescent, adult, or senior?
    b. Sex—Will the tournament be offered to men, women or co-intramural groups?
    c. Playing ability—Will the beginner, intermediate or advanced player be separated to ensure fair and even matches?
    d. Interest/desire—What is the participant interest level for the sport being offered?

e. Attention span—Is the attention span short (youth) or manageable (adult)?
f. Intensity of competition—Will tournaments be of a competitive or informal nature? Will contestant lose interest or a degree of sportsmanship if defeated and placed in a consolation bracket?

3. *Facility, equipment and personnel requirements.*
   a. policy for facility reservation
   b. number of available facilities
   c. availability of fields or courts
   d. condition of facility and all costs incurred in preparing the facility for participation
   e. accessibility to locker room facilities
   f. provisions for equipment rental and check-out procedures
   g. adequate number of sport officials and supervisors
   h. funding for personnel

4. *Time parameters.*
   a. length of time available to complete tournament
   b. specific dates, days and hours available
   c. provisions for inclement weather, rescheduled games and championship play-offs, if applicable

5. *Type of event.*
   a. individual sport
   b. dual sport
   c. group sport
   d. team sport
   e. meet
   f. special event
   g. co-intramural

6. *Other factors.*
   a. budget restrictions
   b. coaches' qualifications, if applicable
   c. administrative personnel requirements
   d. medical supervision
   e. publicity and promotion
   f. efficient maintenance staff
   g. program control
   h. governance procedures
   i. spectator (crowd) control

All tournaments have advantages and disadvantages, strong and weak points with one serving one objective well and another, others. The following discussion reviews various methods of designing tournaments, each with its own schematic, advantages, disadvantages, applicable formulas and an explanation of programmatic procedures.

I. ROUND ROBIN TOURNAMENT

Teams Entered	Rounds							Total Games Per Team
	1	2	3	4	5	6	7	
7	BYE - 7 1 - 6 2 - 5 3 - 4	BYE - 6 7 - 5 1 - 4 2 - 3	BYE - 5 6 - 4 7 - 3 1 - 2	BYE - 4 5 - 3 6 - 2 7 - 1	BYE - 3 4 - 2 5 - 1 6 - 7	BYE - 2 3 - 1 4 - 7 5 - 6	Bye - 1 2 - 7 3 - 6 4 - 5	6

Figure 4-6. Schematic: round robin tournament.

The round robin type of tournament provides for maximum participation since each entry plays against each other entry an equal number of times. The winner of the round robin tournament is usually determined on a won-loss percentage basis.

Advantages

1. Most popular type of tournament format.
2. Easily organized and administered.
3. Allows for complete pre-scheduling of entries into leagues.
4. Participants are informed in advance of opponents and game times.
5. Emphasis is on maximum participation for an extended period of time.
6. Each entry competes against each other on a scheduled basis, regardless of won-loss record.
7. A single round robin produces the true champion.
8. Entries may be ranked at the conclusion of the tournament.

9. Effective for outdoor sports programming when weather is a concern since postponed games may be replayed at a convenient date later in the tournament.
10. Easily understood by the participants.
11. It is not neccessary for rounds to be played in consecutive order, although it is preferred.
12. Participants get a chance to become better acquainted because of the extended season.

Disadvantages

1. Most time consuming of all tournaments.
2. Requires large amount of facility utilization.
3. Significant number of forfeits may occur toward last rounds when an entry realizes there is no chance of winning league championship.
4. Usually eight entries or fewer are most desirable. When used with a larger number, participant interest is hard to maintain.
5. If a large number of entries are divided into smaller leagues, several winners result with no true champion. An elimination tournament must be used to determine winner or have co-champions.
6. It is possible for a league to end in a tie which would require extra contests to decide a winner.
7. Does not provide "instant winner".

Formulas

With N = total number of entries, the following formulas may be used:

		Ex. If $N = 7$
A.) Number of games per league:	$\dfrac{N(N-1)}{2}$	$\dfrac{7(7-1)}{2} = \dfrac{42}{2} = 21$ games
B.) Number of games per entry:	$N - 1$	$7 - 1 = 6$ games
C.) Number of rounds:		
Even number of entries	$N - 1$	
Odd number of entries	N	$7 = 7$ rounds
D.) Number of games per round:		
Even number of entries	$\dfrac{N}{2}$	
Odd number of entires	$\dfrac{N-1}{2}$	$\dfrac{7-1}{2} = 3$ games/round

E.) Determining percentages:

$$\frac{\text{Games won}}{\text{Games played}} = .000 \qquad \frac{5}{6} = .833$$

NOTE: Ties should count as a half game won and a half game lost.

F.) Number of games behind:

$$\frac{(W_a - W_b) -)L_b - L_a)}{2}$$

W = Number of wins

L Number of losses

a = 1st place entry

b = Specific entry in question

Standings

	Won	Loss
Al	6	0
Jeff	4	2
Rob	2	4
Lee	0	6

Number of games Rob is behind?

$$\frac{(6 - 2) + (4 - 0)}{2} =$$

$$\frac{(4) + (4)}{2} = 4$$

Procedures

The first step in scheduling the round robin tournament is to develop a master tournament calendar which indicates playing dates, times and facilities that are available for the completion of the tournament. Special note should be taken to exclude days or hours in which no games may be played; i.e., religious holidays or conflicts.

Once a master tournament calendar has been prepared, pairings for the tournament are constructed by arranging all entries, either by name or assigned number, into two vertical columns. They should be listed consecutively down the first column and continue up the second. When an odd number of entries are scheduled, a "bye" should be placed in the fixed upper left position. This means that the entry scheduled against the bye is "standing by" and has no scheduled game in that particular round. For example:

7 - Entries		8 - Entries
Bye - 7		1 - 8
1 - 6	or	2 - 7
2 - 5		3 - 6
3 - 4		4 - 5

To obtain pairings for subsequent rounds, rotate the names or numbers COUNTERCLOCKWISE around the participant located in the upper left position of the column.

Round 1	Round 2	Round 3
Bye - 7	Bye - 6	Bye - 5
1 - 6	7 - 5	6 - 4
2 - 5	1 - 4	7 - 3
3 - 4	2 - 3	1 - 2

Another method of establishing rounds is the graph method as shown in Figure 4-7.

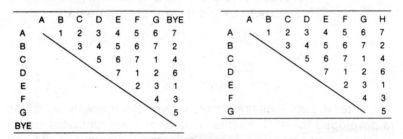

Figure 4-7. Graph method for round robin pairings.

The letters in Figure 4-7 represent entries while rounds are represented by numbers. The procedures for developing the graph are as follows:

Step 1. List the letters in alphabetical order both horizontally and vertically. For odd number of entries include the word "bye" at the end. Also, eliminate each entry's intersecting square.

Step 2. Begin with vertical column "B", on horizontal row A number across one less than the total number of entries including the bye. (numbers 1-7)

Step 3. Begin with vertical column "C", horizontal row "B" and start the vertical numbering with a number one higher (3) than the number immediately above it (2). Continue this process up to but *not* including the last vertical column.

Step 4. For the last vertical column, start with the number 2 and count down vertically by two until the highest round of the tournament is reached but not exceeded. For example:

If the number of rounds = 7
number 2 - 4 - 6
Stop at 6 because there is no eighth round. After
the last even number has been entered (6) start
with number 1 and count down by two.

Step 5. Matches in a round are determined by pairing intersecting entries who have the same number.
For example, Round 1 in a seven entry round robin
tournament would have these contests:

A   vs   B
D   vs   F
C   vs   G
E   vs   Bye

After the pairings are made, a round robin league schedule
is developed for each league. This form communicates to the
entries their appropriate game times and locations. At the end
of this chapter, appendices 4A, 4B, and 4C have examples of 4-7
entry round robin worksheets.

Record Keeping. A simple form used in notifying the participants of the progression of the tournament is shown in
Figure 4-8.

SPORT **_Softball_**   LEAGUE **_Church_**   DIVISION **_Men_**

Name of Team	All-Stars	Sluggers	Rejects	Batboys	Heroes
All-Stars					NOV 8 1-0 W [F]
Sluggers			NOV 1 12-2 W		
Rejects		NOV 1 2-12 L			
Batboys					
Heroes	NOV 8 0-1 L [F]				

Figure 4-8. League record-keeping chart.

All entries in the league should be listed at both the top and left side of the chart. At the conclusion of a contest, the date and score is recorded in the appropriate boxes. The chart is read horizontally with the score of the horizontal team recorded first. The examples would be read:

— All-Stars defeated Heroes by the score of 1-0 (forfeit) on November 8
— Rejects lost to Sluggers by the score of 2-12 on November 1

Note: Wins and losses should be written in different colors for sake of distinction.

Once all rounds have been completed, the league champion is determined. In the event two or more entries have an identical won-loss record at the completion of the tournament, several methods may be employed to determine the winner:

A. Play a single elimination playoff between the entries that tied.

B. The winner of the contest in which the tied entries played during league play is declared the tournament champion.

C. Allow tie to stand and award co-champions.

D. Utilize a point differential system in which each entry's total amount of points (runs, goals, etc.) allowed opponents is subtracted from the entry's total amount of points scored. The entry with the largest total is declared the champion.

ROUND ROBIN TOURNAMENT PROGRAMMING TIPS

1. The most desired number of entries per league ranges from four to eight. Remember, divide larger number of entries into several smaller leagues.

2. If several entries have similar playing time conflicts, group these entries together for easier scheduling.

3. Try to schedule each entry to play at least once a week.

4. Designate several open dates for rescheduling purposes.

5. Double check all work!

A variation to the traditional round robin tournament is the Lombard tournament. In this round robin format the entire tournament is completed in several hours. The entries play an abbreviated time frame which is a fraction of the regular game. For example, if the regulation time for volleyball was 40 minutes and eight teams entered, there would be eight 5-minute games. At the conclusion of 40 minutes, each entry's scores are recorded and the entry with the largest total is the winner. The Lombard tournament usually works best when the entries number 6 to 12 and there are 2 or 3 courts/fields being used at one time.

II. ELIMINATION TOURNAMENTS

II.A. SINGLE ELIMINATION

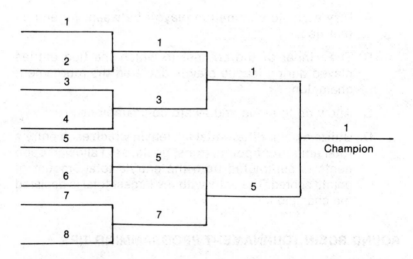

Figure 4-9. Schematic: single elimination tournament.

A single elimination tournament is a well-known and very simple tournament to design. All entries compete in the first round, but only the winners of each round compete in the subsequent rounds with the winner of the final contest becoming the champion. Often there is a drawing for position placements with the best entries being "seeded" to provide better competition as the tournament progresses towards the finals. Also, "byes" are awarded in the *first round* if the number of entries is not equal to a power of 2.

Advantages

1. Easily understood by the participants.

2. Simplest tournament to conduct.

3. Useful in determining a champion for preliminary tournaments such as a round robin.

4. Determines champion in the shortest amount of time in comparison to other tournaments.

5. May be conducted with limited facilities.

6. May accommodate a large number of entries.

7. Interesting for spectators.

8. Most appropriate format for a one-day event.

9. Economical to conduct.

Disadvantages

1. Minimum participation.

2. Maximum emphasis on winning.

3. Champion may not necessarily represent the best team or player. This also applies to the second place finisher since entries in the other half of the bracket may be better.

4. Does not allow for an "off-day."

5. Competition may become too intense due to the fact that the entry must win every contest or face elimination.

6. Outdoor sports programs, with their potential for weather related postponements, cause scheduling problems due to the sequential order that contests must be played.

7. Provides least amount of flexibility for the participant.

Formulas

With N = total number of entries, the following formulas may be used:

Ex. If N = 13

A.) Number of tournament games: N − 1   13 − 1 = 12 games

B.) Power of Two: Number of times 2 has to be multiplied to equal or exceed the number of entries.

$$2 \times 2 = 4 \text{ or } (2^2)$$
$$2 \times 2 \times 2 = 8 \text{ or } (2^3)$$
$$2 \times 2 \times 2 \times 2 = 16 \text{ or } (2^4)$$
$$2 \times 2 \times 2 \times 2 \times 2 = 32 \text{ or } (2^5)$$
$$2 \times 2 \times 2 \times 2 \times 2 \times 2 = 64 \text{ or } (2^6)$$

16

C.) Number of byes: (power of two) − N   16 − 13 = 3 byes

D.) Number of rounds: The power to which 2 must be raised. (2^4) or 4 rounds

E.) Number of 1st round games:

N − (next lower power of two)   13 − (8) = 5 games

or

$$\frac{N - Bye}{2} \qquad \frac{13 - (3)}{2} = \frac{10}{2} = 5 \text{ games}$$

The design of a single elimination tournament is totally dependent on the number of entries entered. Development of a tournament schedule or bracket arrangement cannot be completed until all possible entries have been accepted.

Procedures. The following is a guide to use in developing a single elimination draw:

1. Check and re-check to make certain that all names listed on the entry form are spelled correctly and are correct in regard to units of participation, divisions, and affiliation. *MISPLACING OR OVERLOOKING ENTRIES IS UNEXCUSABLE.*

2. Select the appropriate sized draw sheet. (4, 8, 16, 32, 64, etc.)

3. Determine the "seeds." The purpose of seeding is to separate the stronger entries so that they will not compete against each other until the later rounds by distributing strength throughout the draw. Although there is no requirement to have seedings, a seeded tournament assures a fairer tournament when the superior players meet in the final rounds. The general rule of

thumb for the number of seeds is no more than one seed for each four entries. The top seed, chosen according to ability, previous performance and ranking, should be placed in the top of the upper bracket with the second seed placed at the bottom of the lower bracket (see Figure 4-10).

To check the draw placement of seeds, the seeds at the extreme of each bracket should equal a consistent number when totalled. For example, in a 32 entry draw, seeds should be placed so that the eight quarters of the bracket equal 17 (1 + 16, 9 + 8, 5 + 12, 13 + 4, 3 + 14, 11 + 6, 7 + 10, 15 + 2).

An alternative method of placing seeds is to place the first seeded entry on the top line of the upper bracket and the second seed on the bottom line of the lower bracket, the third seed placed at the bottom of the upper bracket and the fourth seed at the top of the lower bracket and so on.

In utilizing this method, no attempt is made to equalize the upper or lower brackets. If the seeding procedures actually ranked entries according to ability, etc., it would be advantageous to require the first seed to play a weaker opponent, i.e., fourth seed instead of third seed.

4. Determine the number of byes. When the number of entries is not an exact power of two (2, 4, 8, 16, 32, 64, etc.) the first round should have "byes" so as to avoid having an uneven number of contestants remaining in the final rounds. *ALL BYES MUST BE PLAYED IN THE FIRST ROUND.* The number of byes should assure the number of contestants to be equal to a power of two (full brackets) in the second round.

5. Placing the byes. All byes should be distributed as evenly as possible between the upper and lower brackets. Seeded entries should be granted byes in order of their ranking. First seed receives first bye, second seed receives second bye, and so on. In other words, the placement of byes should complement the placement of seeded entries.

Figure 4-10. Seed placement for single elimination tournaments.

Figure 4-11. Alternative seed placement for single elimination tournament.

Ex: N = 11

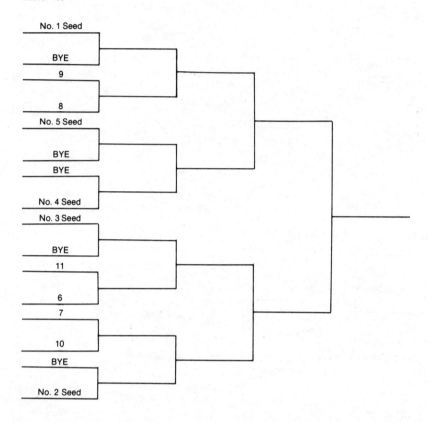

Figure 4-12. Bye placement for single elimination tournament.

6. **Number the games.** The numbering of games should progress by rounds in sequential order. If several bracket sheets are being used simultaneously, all games in the first round on each sheet should be numbered first before proceeding to the second round.

   Game numbers are usually placed where the winner's name will appear.

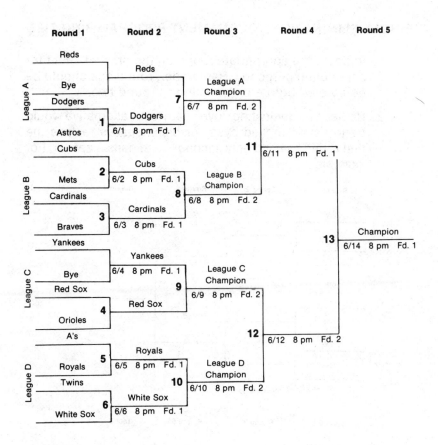

Figure 4-13. Sequential numbering of contests.

As indicated, the date, time and location of the game should also be listed on the bracket sheet. An alternative to placing the game informaton on the actual bracket sheet is to attach an additional sheet which only contains this type of information.

SINGLE ELIMINATION TOURNAMENT PROGRAMMING TIPS

1. Indicate the appropriate round on the bracket sheet for scheduling purposes. Remember, round one should be completed before progressing to round two.

2. Rather than indicating "bye" games an alternative would be to have "implied byes" or blank spaces replace the first round bye and only second round games appear. For example:

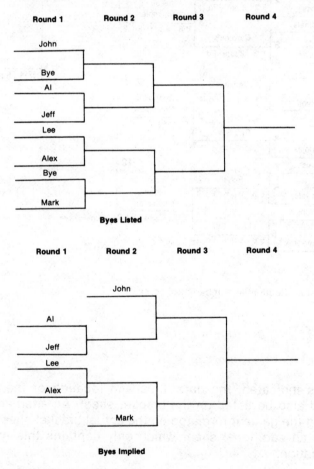

Figure 4-14.   Listing of byes.

3. The placement of byes starts at the extremes and moves toward the center.

4. When the number of entries is only a few over the number on a draw sheet, (power of 2), for example 17, it is less confusing to add one game to a 16 entry draw than it is to have a large number of byes listed on a 32-entry draw. To accomplish this, start at the center of the bracket and create two-line pairings until you have provided as many lines as there are entries.

5. Assignment of positions on the bracket sheet may be determined:

   a. at random
   b. on the basis of known ability (seeding)
   c. in the order the entries were received

II.B. DOUBLE ELIMINATION

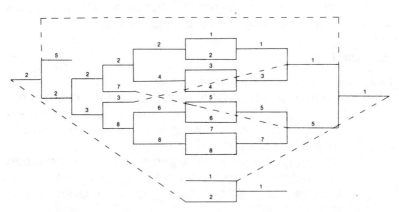

Figure 4-15.   Schematic: double elimination tournament.

The double elimination tournament, also known as the "two loss and out" tournament is an adaptation of the single elimination with consolation format; no contestant is eliminated until two losses occur. An entry which loses in the championship or winners bracket is scheduled to play other losers in a losers bracket or second elimination tournament.

Play continues until there is a winner of both the championship bracket and the losers bracket. These two winners are then matched to determine an overall winner. If the champion of the losers bracket defeats the champion of the winners bracket, an additional contest is required since both have one loss.

Advantages

1. One of the fairest types of tournaments since each entry must be defeated twice before being eliminated from the tournament.

2. Provides at least twice as much participation as the single elimination tournament.

3. Participant interest is maintained for a longer period of time than the single elimination or consolation tournament.

4. Affords entry who has had an "off day", been upset, or received a poor pairing a chance to win the losers bracket and play for the championship.

Disadvantages

In addition to those disadvantages associated with a single elimination tournament, double elimination tournaments are:
1. Complicated to show graphically since the losers rounds keep adding new contestants as they lose in the winners rounds.
2. Confusing to those participants that have a difficult time understanding the format of tournaments.
3. More time consuming than a single elimination tournament.

Formulas

With N = total number of entries, the following formulas may be used:

1. Number of games: Minimum = 2N − 2

Ex. N = 13
= 2(13) − 2
= 26 − 2
= 24 minimum games

Maximum $= 2N - 1$ | $= 2(13) - 1$
| $= 26 - 1$
| $= 25$ maximum games

Note: The maximum number of games occurs when the champion of the losers bracket defeats the champion of the winners bracket thus creating an extra game.

2. Number of rounds: Twice the power to which two must be raised to equal or exceed the number of entries plus an additional round if an extra contest is required. | $= 2(2^4)$
| $= 2(4)$
| $= 8$ rounds

In conducting a double elimination tournament, the basic procedures of a single elimination tournament generally apply to the winners bracket of the double elimination tournament. However, entries into the losers bracket are somewhat more involved. Byes must be arranged so that a second bye is not given to an entry that has already had a bye. Special attention should be given to "crossing" losers from the upper and bottom halves of the winners bracket. This prevents the pairing of entries who might have played each other in the winners bracket from playing each other a second time in the losers bracket until the latest possible opportunity. This "crossing" may be achieved by using either of the following two scheduling methods.

A.) *Back-to-Back*. As was seen in the previous schematic, the winners and the losers bracket are arranged side-by-side with the winners progressing to the right and the losers following the broken lines to the left. This assures that the earliest two previous opponents may meet would be late in the losers bracket.

B.) *Over-Under*. This method arranges the losers bracket under the winners bracket and eliminates the need for the often times confusing broken lines. An example of this bracket may be seen in Figure 4-16.

The method requires that each pairing of the winners bracket include the words "Loser to ____" followed by a letter of the alphabet. In the losers bracket, the line of the pairings are indicated by a consecutive listing of respective letters. This method is by far the simplest to read and understand by participants, spectators and tournament directors. However, regardless of the method chosen, the result of the brackets are the same.

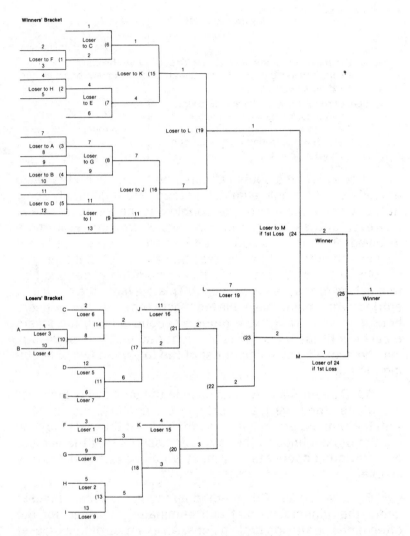

Figure 4-16. Double elimination *over-under* bracket.

DOUBLE ELIMINATION TOURNAMENT PROGRAMMING TIPS

1. After the first round in the losers brackets, each additional round in this bracket must have a number of contests which are equal to 2.

2. Contests should be numbered consecutively, as best as possible, depending upon the facility limitation and playing times.

3. List the times and playing locations and game numbers of each contest on the actual bracket. This lessens the possibility of a participant losing any additional sheets of information.

4. In numbering the contests, make sure an entry is never scheduled to play two contests in succession.

A variation to the double elimination format is the semi-double elimination tournament.

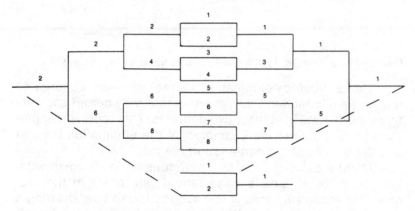

Figure 4-17. Schematic: semi-double elimination tournament.

This tournament is very similar to the double elimination in that all first round losers and those entries which were scheduled a first round bye, but lost in the second round, are placed in the losers bracket. However, from this point on in the tournament both the winners and the losers brackets continue on a straight single elimination basis with the winners of each bracket playing for the championship. In other words, each entry is guaranteed a minimum of two contests but not necessarily two losses.

II. C. CONSOLATION TOURNAMENT

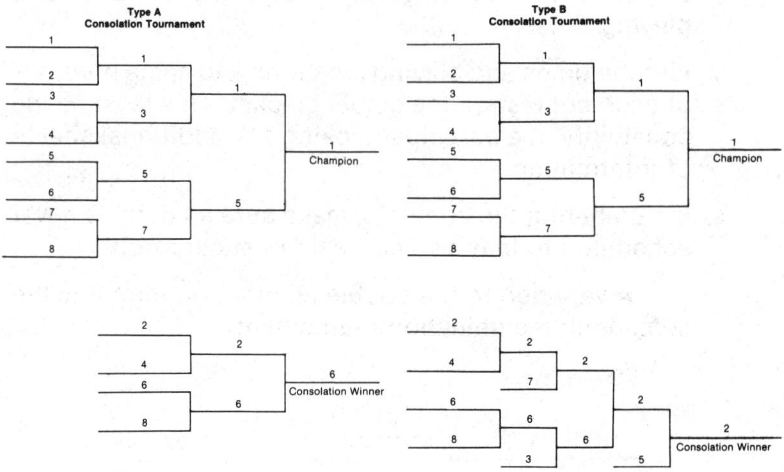

Figure 4-18. Schematic: Type A and Type B consolation tournaments.

These types of elimination tournaments are superior to the single elimination tournament in that they permit each entry to participate in at least two contests. This tournament produces two winners; the champion of the elimination bracket and the winner of the consolation bracket.

There are two general types of consolation tournaments. In Type A, or a "simple consolation", all losers in the first round (or those who lose in the second round after drawing a bye in the first) play another single elimination tournament. The winner of the second single elimination tournament is declared the consolation winner.

Type B consolation elimination tournaments or "second place consolation" provides an opportunity for any loser, regardless of the round in which the loss occurred, to win the consolation championship. This is similar to double elimination tournaments except that the winner of the consolation tournament is considered the third place finisher and does not play the winners bracket champion.

Advantages

1. Each entry is guaranteed at least two contests.

2. Additional participation is provided in comparison to straight single elimination.

Disadvantages

1. Interest is sometimes lost because there is no chance for winning the championship.

2. Forfeits are higher than in single elimination tournaments.

The basic rules which apply to the single elimination tournament are also applicable to a consolation tournament.

II. D. BAGNALL-WILD ELIMINATION TOURNAMENT

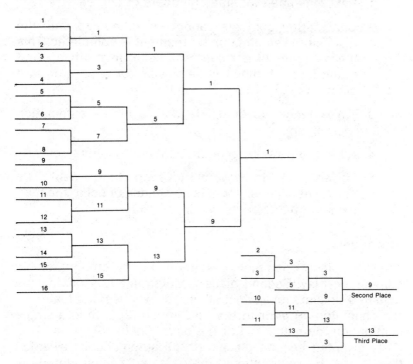

Figure 4-19.   Schematic: Bagnall-Wild elimination tournament.

The Bagnall-Wild tournament is an adaption of the single elimination tournament format. As well as determining a champion, this type of tournament design selects a true second and third place finisher. All entries who were defeated by the champion in the straight single elimination tournament compete against each other in mini-single elimination tournaments.

Advantages

1. Selects a true second and third place finisher.

2. Suitable for events such as wrestling meets where points are awarded to second and third place winners of each weight division or class.

Disadvantages

1. Recommended for small numbers of entries.

2. Consolation contests cannot be scheduled until the main single elimination tournament is completed. This means there is a significant delay in notifying first round losers if they will be playing for second or third place.

3. Takes longer to complete than a single elimination tournament.

4. All entries are not guaranteed more than one contest.

5. Forfeits, as in any consolation tournament, are prevalent because there is no chance of being the tournament champion once a loss occurs.

Procedures

The first place champion is determined by straight single elimination play. Second place is determined by pairing the defeated finalists (9) against all entries who were defeated by the champion (1) prior to the final round (2, 3, 5) in a single elimination tournament. If the defeated finalist (9) loses to (3), (3) is awarded second place with (9) automatically awarded third place. However, should the defeated finalist win, (9) is awarded second place and all entries defeated by (9) in the original single elimination tournament (10, 11, 13) compete in a third elimination tournament, the winner of which plays the defeated finalist from the second elimination tournament for overall third place.

BAGNALL-WILD TOURNAMENT PROGRAMMING TIPS

1. The playoffs for second and third place could begin before the final contest is even played. As soon as entries (1) and (9) are determined to be finalists, competition between the entries defeated by these two should begin. Thus, entries (2) and (3); and (10) and (11) should play contests. This will help reduce the wait for these entries.

II. E. MUELLER-ANDERSON PLAYBACK

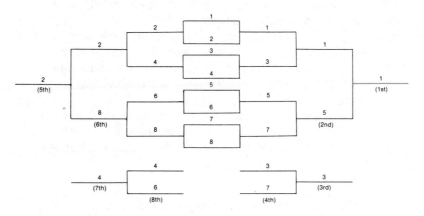

Figure 4-20. Schematic: Mueller-Anderson playback tournament.

This tournament is very similar to the single elimination-consolation format. However, instead of being eliminated after a first or second round loss, entries continue to play for an overall tournament ranking or position.

Advantages

1. Places rankings for all entries.

2. Each entry plays the same amount of games.

3. Emphasis on participation is maintained.

4. Provides for a more equitable distribution of points.

5. Forfeits are usually lower than in consolation tournaments because there is a motivation factor to finish the tournament with a highest ranking as possible.

Disadvantages

1. Requires more games than single elimination-consolation tournament even though the number of rounds may remain the same.

2. No established formulas for computation purposes.

CHALLENGE TOURNAMENTS

Challenge tournaments, or ongoing tournaments, place emphasis on participation rather than on winning. Contestants issue and accept challenge matches from each other with the ultimate goal of winning all challenges and advancing to the top of the tournament structure. However, all contestants continue to play regardless of the outcome of the challenge. This type of tournament is used primarily with individual and dual sports—but may be utilized in team sports as well. Challenge tournaments are often used by commercial recreational institutions and have proven to be an excellent tournament design for individuals with busy and fluctuating schedules.

Advantages

1. Easily organized and programmed.

2. Minimum of supervision.

3. Emphasizes maximum participation.

4. Winning is not a requirement for continued participation.

5. Does not eliminate any participant.

6. Encourages participants to choose opponents, and engage in social interaction.

7. Affords greater opportunity for social interaction.

8. Won-loss records need not be maintained.

9. Participants play at their convenience.

10. Useful for ranking participants.

11. Each contest is self-programmed.

12. No formal scheduling is required.

13. All ages and skill levels may be involved.

14. Participation is informal in nature.

15. Tournament may be terminated at any time by the programmer.

Disadvantages

1. Participants must contact each other to arrange date, time for match. Communication can become a problem.

2. Lack of challenges for some participants.

3. Suited for small number of entries.

4. Could appear complicated to participants.

5. Often need external awards or motivational incentives to continue interest and participation.

6. Limited amount of security pertaining to the operation of the actual challenge board.

Formulas

Formulas are not required for this tournament format.

Procedures

A challenge tournament begins by transferring from the entry form all names and telephone numbers to cards, circular discs, or other suitable material that permits removal into slots or being hung on hooks. Once this process is completed, there are several methods that can be used to position or rank the players on the tournament board. These methods involve:

1. The order participants entered or registered.

2. A random draw.

3. A ranking according to ability. (If this method is used, the top player is usually placed at the bottom of the tournament structure.)

4. Rankings derived from other tournaments.

Once placement is determined, the tournament is conducted by a series of challenges issued by the participants.

The main objective is to advance to the top of the structure and remain there. In general, movement to the top is gained by issuing a challenge to an individual on a higher level, defeating that individual and changing positions.

In conducting a challenge tournament, establish rules and regulations prior to the start of competition and inform the participants. Although these rules may vary according to the design of the tournament, the following are applicable:

1. Specific sport rules. Use sanctioned rules governing play with any local intramural modification.

2. Challenge Rules:

   a. Participants initiate their own challenges.
   b. All challenges must be accepted and played within or at an agreed upon time (usually 3–5 days.)
   c. A participant may challenge only those one level above

   or

   A participant may challenge those one or two levels above

   or

   A participant may challenge any one in the tournament (not recommended).

   or

   A participant must challenge someone at their own level and win before challenging a level above.
   d. If the challenger wins, the individuals exchange positions in the tournament. If the challenger is defeated, both individuals remain in their original position. However, the loser usually may not rechallenge the winner until a designated period of time passes, or until he or she has played at least one other match.
   e. It is the winner's responsibility to update the tournament board.
   f. Challenges may not be refused and should be met in the order that they were issued.
   g. If a challenge has been accepted and one of the contestants fails to appear, declare a forfeit and exchange positions.

3. Keep the position of each entry up-to-date so that challenges may be arranged at any time.

4. Add late entries to the lowest level.

5. Establish a minimum and maximum number of contests that may be played during any given period.

6. Announce a definite date for completing the tournament prior to the start of play in fairness to all participants.

7. The ranking of all players at the conclusion of the tournament determines the winner.

CHALLENGE TOURNAMENT PROGRAMMING VARIATIONS

Ladder Tournament. This is probably the most popular format of a challenge tournament.

LADDER TOURNAMENT

Al
Jeff
Rob
Lee
John
Jack
Don
Jim

Figure 4-21. Schematic: ladder tournament.

In the ladder tournament, the entries' names are listed on a horizontal rung and placed in a vertical column usually with the best player at the bottom. Similar to climbing a ladder, the rungs are used to advance players from one position to another in accordance to challenge procedures previously outlined.

The winner of the tournament is that individual at the top rung of the ladder when play is stopped.

If you receive a large number of entries, group the entries into several smaller tournaments that provide for both horizontal and vertical movement.

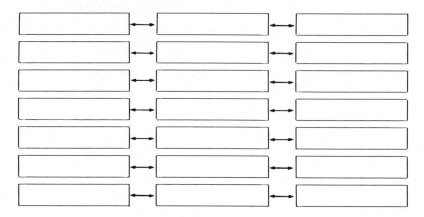

Figure 4-22. Multiple ladder tournament.

At the conclusion of the tournament, each ladder winner may participate in a playoff to determine the overall champion.

Pyramid Tournament. The pyramid design provides more participation and permits greater freedom to challenge than the ladder format.

PYRAMID TOURNAMENT

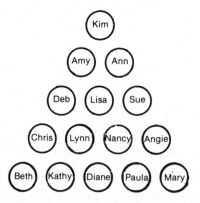

Figure 4-23. Schematic: pyramid tournament.

The names are arranged in rows, with one at the top, two in the second row, and so on with the number of rows depending on the number of entries. This type of design allows for an infinite number of entries by simply adding another base level to the pyramid. However, a realistic number should be determined based on the time available to complete the tournament and allowance for the base level entry the opportunity to reach the top.

King or Crown Tournament. As was the case in the ladder tournament, several smaller tournaments may be appropriate. This variation of the pyramid tournament is suitable when large numbers of entries are competing. Entries are grouped into three smaller pyramids at different levels. After an individual has reached the top of the lower units, he or she may challenge horizontally into a higher unit and then vertically again to advance to the crown or first position.

KING OR CROWN TOURNAMENT

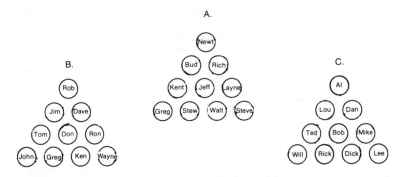

Figure 4-24. Schematic: king or crown tournament.

Funnel Tournament. The funnel tournament design is a combination of both the ladder and the pyramid tournaments. In the example, the top seven positions are played as a ladder tournament while the bottom positions follow the rules similar to that of a pyramid tournament. Additional entries are placed on the bottom row of the pyramid section. This tournament format provides for a large number of entries as well as a ranking of the top seven individuals.

FUNNEL TOURNAMENT

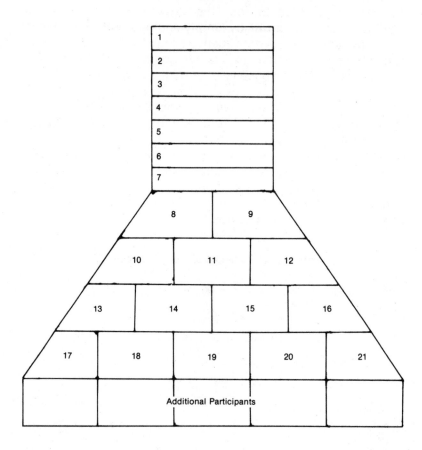

Figure 4-25. Schematic: funnel tournament.

Spider-Web Tournament. This hexagon form of tournament design affords greater opportunity for participation and involvement than traditional ladder or pyramid methods.

Although this format is conducted similarly to the pyramid tournament, its main disadvantage is that the number one or middle position is constantly being challenged by six players. To reduce this number of direct challengers to the middle position, challenges should be required to defeat an individual or individuals on their level before issuing a challenge.

SPIDER WEB TOURNAMENT

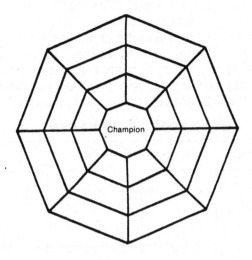

Figure 4-26.   Schematic: spider web tournament.

Round-the-Clock Tournament. This design is similar to a face of a clock. All entries are assigned an hour number represented on the clock.

ROUND-THE-CLOCK TOURNAMENT

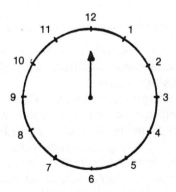

Figure 4-27.   Schematic: round-the-clock tournament.

The object of the tournament is for a player to advance completely around the clock, challenging no more than two players (hours) ahead, and be the first to return to their original starting position. Variations could require two or three revolutions of the clock face or in the case of excessive entries, several clocks with the winners of each "clock" playing in an elimination tournament to determine the champion.

Bump Board Tournament. Rather than participating against each other, the contestants in this tournament participate against existing records previously achieved in that specific sport which are posted on a result board.

BUMP BOARD TOURNAMENT

EVENT	RECORD	#1	#2
Free Throw Shooting	Al 177	Bill 125	Mike 119
Dribbles	Rob 26	Stu 24	Ron 21
3 Point Shot	Rich 48	Lee 41	Alex 40

Figure 4-28. Schematic: bump board tournament

The contestant who "breaks" one of the posted records is placed in that respective position with the others being "bumped" one position lower.

Progressive Bridge Tournament. This challenge tournament is a self-operating tournament which works exactly like bridge or other card sports. It is best suited for sports which have three or more playing facilities (courts, fields) located close together, i.e., tennis, badminton, or volleyball.

A number one or head court should be arbitrarily established prior to the start of participation with the contestants placed according to traditional challenge rule procedures for the first match. Following this initial match, the winner moves over one court towards the head court. The losers remain on the court that they lost except for the loser on the head court who moves all the way over to the last court to

PROGRESSIVE BRIDGE TOURNAMENT

Court 1   Court 2   Court 3   Court 4

(1)   3   5   (7)

2   (4)   (6)   8

*Circled letters indicate match winners, while arrows
show how participants exchange courts for next match.

Figure 4-29. Schematic: progressive bridge tournament.

begin the long battle again. It is best to time the matches so
that all players are ready to change at the same time. This type
of challenge tournament is very useful when supervision is to
be at a minimum and when motivation is needed to keep the
participant interest maintained.

Tombstone Tournament. The tombstone or "marker"
tournament involves a cumulative score or long-term goal that
is established prior to the start of the tournament for all contestants to strive to achieve. These goals may be listed in
terms of time, total points, and distance.

TOMBSTONE TOURNAMENT

	BASKETBALL FREE THROW									
	Day 1		Day 2		Day 3		Day 4		Day 5	
Entries	Daily Results	Accum Total	Daily Results	Accum Total	Daily Results	Accum Total	Daily Results	Accum Total	Daily Results	Accum Total
John	20/25	20	17/25	37	19/25	56	20/25	76	20/25	96
Sally	18/25	18	20/25	38	20/25	58	21/25	79	20/25	99
Mike	23/25	23	20/25	43	21/25	64	20/25	84	21/25	(105)
Sue	18/25	18	19/25	37	20/25	57	18/25	75	20/25	95

Figure 4-30. Schematic: tombstone tournament.

In the example of basketball free throw shooting, a goal of 100
successful free throws could be established with a limitation of

only 25 free throw attempts per day for five days. The first contestant to record 100 free throws (Mike) is declared the winner.

CHALLENGE TOURNAMENT PROGRAMMING TIPS

1. A challenge board may be constructed from wood, cardboard, peg board, or other similar sturdy material. Small nails or "eyehooks" can be arranged to suit the design of the tournament with wood tongue depressors (ladder) or circular price tags or discs (pyramid, crown) to record the participant's name and telephone number. Instead of using nails or eyehooks, 3″ × 5″ card holders may be used in which case the participants' name cards are inserted in the card holder and moved about as players change places in the tournament.

2. If several skill levels are evident, it is advisable to set up multiple challenge tournaments; one for beginners and others for more skilled players.

3. Awards may be given for: (a) top position; (b) player with the greatest number of recorded wins; or (c) the player who issued the largest number of challenges regardless of the outcome.

4. A message board, located adjacent to the challenge board, serves as an excellent communication device.

5. Placing entries on the challenge board in the order that they were received encourages players to register as quickly as possible.

MEETS

The intramural or extramural sports meet is organized competition in which individuals participate in separate events conducted in several sessions over a period of usually one to four days. A meet can take on such different characteristics as a highly sophisticated championship representing months of training for the finals, a season-long program, or an informal play day in which no special preparation is required and the contestants are there primarily for the sake of participation. Meets also lend themselves to a variety of sport settings, i.e., military, educational, and community, in which only minor modifications must be observed because of the setting.

There are basically two types of participation in a meet event: individual and team. A contestant who enters an event with no team affiliation solely represents himself or herself as an individual. In team participation, teams may be represented by an equal number of participants who win points for placing in specific events. The team accumulating the largest amount of points is the meet champion.

The following lists common meets which may be utilized in a recreational sport program:

Meets with several events:
Track and field
Swimming and diving
Wrestling
Gymnastic
Ice skating
Skiing
Play day
Martial arts

Meets with one event:
Cross country
Golf
Surfing

The design and nature of meets could result in undue fatigue and stress if a participant is expected to remain at the site for several hours prior to participating in an event. Consequently, the programmer must carefully schedule the meet events in order to avoid unnecessary delays, prolonged waiting periods, or back-to-back participations, each of which could pose a threat to safe, enjoyable participation.

Meet sport programming tends to be specialized to suit the particular interests, population and resources of the setting. We will discuss the major programming areas of concern common to all meets, accompanied by a more detailed application using a track and field meet as an example. In this way, the programmer may better sense the type of detail inherent within meet sport programming. This work is accomplished in a more concentrated time span than required for such other program designs as round-robin, ladder, or single elimination tournaments.

Concerns of Meet Organization

Prior to the actual organization of the meet, the programmer should "walk-through" mentally every facet of the meet event, from meet personnel to vehicular parking. This process is a valuable aid in programming and alleviates many potential problems. Once you have selected the type of meet, determine the program of events. Several factors which influence this selection are:

Age of the participants. For young children, events which are fun-oriented are more suitable than events which emphasize strength or endurance. Relays and unusual events utilizing game skills are very popular with the younger age group.

Physical capabilities of the participants. Events such as the discus, hammer throw or javelin throw would not be appropriate for a community meet because of the unique physical skills required.

Level of competition. A highly competitive meet with official sanction may require prior approval from an appropriate governing body.

Class groupings. If several groupings are used, care should be taken that each class competes at intervals so no participant is required to compete in consecutive events.

Time factors. Know the time required to complete each event by estimating the approximate number of entries. If these variables can be decided in advance, it is possible to determine both the total number and the order of events. Conduct as many events on a simultaneous basis as possible.

Facilities and equipment. Proper space and meet facilities suitable for the events on the program and adequate in size to accommodate the estimated number of participants are essential to a successful meet. All facilities should be carefully prepared for each event. For example, in a track and field meet, running lanes should be properly marked as well as the start and finish lines; the jumping and vaulting pits should be in good condition and the locations for the field events should be clearly designated and in proper condition prior to the meet competition.

Quality signs should indicate locations for various activities of the meet as well as stations for the participants and meet personnel. Provision for spectator and participant seating is especially important if a large crowd is anticipated. It is customary to distribute a map of the indoor or outdoor facility which indicates where participants are to report for registration, an outline of the course, (if applicable), spectator seating arrangements or other pertinent information (see Figure 4-31).

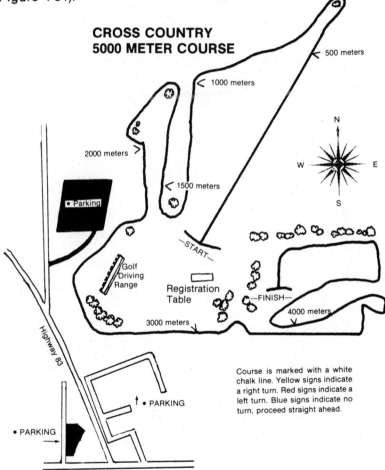

Figure 4-31. Cross country facility map.

TRACK AND FIELD

SPORT: Men's and Women's Track and Field

ENTRY DEADLINE: Thursday, March 4, 1984, 4:00 pm.

ENTRY FEE: $5.00 per team (See minimum numbers under eligibility)
$1.00 per individual

COMPETITION: Individuals are limited to 3 events, including the relays. Not more than 2 field events or 2 running events may be entered by an individual. No team may enter more than 2 individuals per event. An organization may only enter 1 team per relay.

ELIGIBILITY: To be eligible for team competition and points at the Divisional Level and/or the All-Meet Championship, a team must be comprised of the following:

Minimum number
A - 6 members
B - 6 members
C - 5 members
D - 6 members

MANDATORY MEETING: Intramural Sports Office, Room 119, 7:00 pm, Wednesday, March 10, 1984.

DATES & PLACES:
Tuesday, March 16, 1984, 7:00 pm
Divisional Track Preliminaries
Men's and Women's

Wednesday, March 17, 1984, 7:00 pm
Divisional Field Finals
Men's and Women's
**The one mile and two mile events will be run on this day.

Thursday, March 18, 1984, 7:00 pm
Finals - Track Events
Men's and Women's

FURTHER INFORMATION: 335-8359 or 335-2371

ENTRY FORM

☐ TEAM ENTRIES ONLY   ☐ INDIVIDUAL ENTRIES ONLY

Team _____   Individual _____

Manager _____   Address _____

Address _____   Phone Number _____

Phone Number _____

PROGRAM: **DIVISION:**
☐ MEN   ☐ A
☐ WOMEN   ☐ B
                                       ☐ C
                                       ☐ D

ELIGIBILITY STATEMENT

This certifies that I know and understand the Intramural Sport eligibility rules and have completely checked the eligibility of all participants listed on the reverse side. If there is any discrepancy, I will assume full responsibility. Failure to comply with these rules will result in disciplinary action as outlined in the Guides to Participation.

Individual/Manager Signature   Date

Figure 4-32. Track and Field entry form.

Conducting a meet. Once you have chosen the program of events and the specific location of the meet, distribute a meet entry form and a participant information announcement at least two or three weeks prior to the meet. The entry format should provide the following information:

Date and place of the meet
Entry fee
Eligibility restrictions
Required meeting dates and places for participants
Entry deadline
Brief rules governing the specific events
List of events
Roster of team members

The participant information sheet may cover such items as:

Participant entrance to the facility
Reporting time
Location of registration table
Location of locker rooms (if applicable)
Schedule and order of events
Brief explanation concerning the rules and regulations for each event
Method of scoring
Specific eligibility rules
Equipment policies
Parking information

After accepting entries, place individual names on a "heat result" form used during and after each event.

MEET SPORTS
OFFICIAL HEAT RESULT FORM

Event _____ Division _____ Heat _____

Lane	Place	Division Points	Final Points

Figure 4-33. Heat result form.

Meet personnel. The success of any meet depends upon the quality of the officials or meet personnel and their leadership ability. Each should be familiar with specific rules which govern their events as well as responsibilities necessary in performing specific functions and each must anticipate problems.

The number and type of officials or employees required depends upon the type of meet, the level of involvement and the events on the program. In general, the following personnel are needed to conduct a successful meet:

Meet committee. This committee's responsibility for supervising the meet includes:

1. Forming heats

2. Determining number of contestants

3. Deciding on the order of events

4. Ruling on appeals

5. Suspending meet because of weather, poor facility conditions, etc.

Meet coordinator. This individual closely monitors the organization and implementation of the meet and supervision of personnel. In the event there is no meet committee, the meet director usually assumes all administrative and organizational duties.

Meet personnel. There are a number of individuals who serve a variety of functions in a meet. These positions include:

Referee. In charge of activities during the meet and also responsible for assigning officials to specific duties and explaining their responsibilities.

Starter. Controls the start of each event.

Clerk of the course. Responsible for recording the name and/or number of each contestant and assigning them to proper heat and starting positions. The clerk is also responsible for giving instructions concerning specific rules for each event.

Other:
Clerical staff
Judges
Scorer

Announcer
Marshals
Timers
Inspectors
Press stewards/runners
Supervisors

Once meet personnel have been identified and properly instructed as to their specific responsibilities, the meet may be started. At a designated time prior to the start of the meet, all contestants in the first event must report to the clerk of the course. The clerk verifies each entry and informs them of the heat and lane assignments. At this time, an event card is completed for each participant.

EVENT CARD

Men _____   Women _____

Division: A B C D

Track Event: 60 yd. Hurdles 100 yd. Dash

Mile Run   440 yd. Dash   880 yd. Run   220 yd. Dash

800 yd. Relay   Mile Relay   2 Mile Relay

Name(s) _____

Name(s) _____

Team Name: _____

Timer #1 _____   Official Time _____

Timer #2 _____   Place _____

Heat _____ Lane _____   Race _____

Recorded By: _____

Figure 4-34. Meet event card.

While the first event is being conducted, the announcer informs contestants of the second event to receive their assignments so the event can follow immediately. Conducting a meet in this fashion reduces the amount of non-use time between events. Allow participants to warm-up prior to the start of their event in an area designated for that purpose. Assign appropriate personnel or attendants to set up and remove equipment such as hurdles, barriers, mats, standards or other equipment as soon as the use of the equipment is through. Make arrangements with the press steward or runner to record the results of each event promptly for the participant and the meet announcer.

Scoring. There are two basic types of scoring systems. The first type is "event scoring". Each event in the meet is assigned a scoring system to indicate the points awarded for overall placement. For example, for the long jump of a track and field meet, the scoring system may be based on the twelve best places within each division such as:

Place	1	2	3	4	5	6	7	8	9	10	11	12
Points	15	12	10	9	8	7	6	5	4	3	2	1

The second type of scoring is "divisional scoring" in which points are assigned for performance during preliminary and final events.

After the final event of the meet, the meet committee or meet coordinator should make sure that the following details have been attended to:

1. All scoresheets have been collected

2. Tabulations of results have been made official

3. Proper awards have been distributed

4. Press releases announcing winners and other items of interest have been prepared

5. All equipment and supplies have been collected and returned

6. Facility has been cleaned and equipment placed in original place

In conclusion, meet programs may encompass a wide variety of events according to the nature and age groupings of the participants. The possibilities for arranging and conducting a meet are limitless and depend primarily on the setting or environment. The sports programmer should ensure that every meet, regardless of its type, contributes to the enjoyment of the participants and spectators. Proper preliminary planning, competent meet personnel, suitable facility site and necessary equipment assures a successfully conducted meet.

EXTRAMURAL SPORT

Although extramural sports are very similar in nature to those of the intramural sports program regarding programming policies or procedures, the extramural program is separate and distinct in many ways. Extramural sport may be defined as an extension or outgrowth of the intramural sport program. Intramural champions or groups of outstanding players from various institutions compete against each other to determine an extramural champion. Participation in extramurals may be conducted either on an informal basis emphasizing fun and social interaction or a formal, highly organized basis which stresses winning and recognizes individual champions.

The extramural sport concept has tremendous potential in terms of providing visibility for the host institution and recognition for the participants. Traditionally, extramural sport programming has received minimal attention and emphasis within the total recreational sport operation. Major reasons are the amount of time, resources and planning required to host and accomodate others from outside the setting as well as the amount of resources required to send participants to extramural sport events. In essence, programmers tend to discourage extramural sport events when participation by the few, more highly skilled, is as or more expensive than events which provide opportunities for a majority of individuals with varying skill levels. Although this principle is a good guideline, the programmer should explore alternative sources of funding, perhaps through donations or commercial sponsorship, to provide for extramural sport. A quality extramural sport event may be a valuable mechanism for generating greater public awareness regarding recreational sport and may also serve to facilitate positive relations with other settings.

Scheduling

Schedule the extramural sport event as far in advance as possible to obtain housing accommodations suitable for the number of participants expected. When reviewing facility availability, make plans to schedule facility times prior to the tournament to allow for practice.

Investigate any conflicting events also scheduled in the proposed time period to prevent possible problems. Once preliminary approval of dates, times, and facility availability has been secured, begin developing entry forms and invitations to distribute one to two months in advance of the established date. Develop an effective publicity and promotion campaign to help secure participation as well as spectator interest in the event.

The host institution, with assistance from participating institutions, should be primarily responsible for coordinating all pertinent details of the extramural sport event. These would include:

a. specific events to be held
b. number of participants allowed per team
c. eligibility rules
d. modified rules of the sport, if applicable
e. type of participation
f. number of institutions invited
g. housing accommodations, transportation and hospitality
h. liability insurance
i. personnel requirements
j. finance and budgeting
k. equipment needs
l. registration procedure
m. recognition
n. promotion and publicity

Letters of invitation and entry forms. The invitations and entry forms should include all pertinent information. Since communication is usually handled by mail or by telephone, it is important that this literature be as complete as possible to eliminate breakdowns. The common items to include follow:

a. Type of event and specific activities to be conducted
b. Date, time, place and the duration of the event
c. Eligibility requirements
d. Expected entry fee and other costs
e. Approximate costs for housing accommodations including travel distance to the sport facility
f. Insurance coverage, if applicable
g. Travel information concerning planes, trains, buses and route directions for those driving
h. Facilities for both event and practice

i. Appropriate clothing or personal sport equipment and supplies needed for each event
j. Entry deadline date and the return address

In addition to an entry form, request the name and phone number for the agency's event coordinator, and a signed affidavit verifying participant eligibility.

Follow-up letter. After an agency accepts the invitation to attend the extramural event and forwards the completed entry form, send a follow-up letter. This correspondence provides more specific information and any new points of information such as:

a. Registration time and location
b. A tentative schedule of activities
c. Appropriate attire for social events
d. Parking arrangements and costs
e. Restaurant information including approximate prices
f. A city and facility map.

Finance. A finance committee should be organized to handle the business transactions involving the expenses and income of the event. Examples of the types of financial transactions requiring attention or provision follow:

Expenses	*Income*
Office supplies, mailing expenses	Entry fees - team or participants
Duplicating	Sponsors' contributions
Facility rental, if any	Donations
Equipment and supplies	Gate receipts
Maintenance	Business advertising in program
Personnel - Supervisors and officials	Concessions
Insurance	
Awards	
Publicity	
Hospitality functions including banquet	

Generally, participants attend an extramural event at their own expense rather than at the expense of the host agency, unless some financial support has been provided by a sponsor.

Officials. The number of officials will vary from sport to sport, but the customary number of game officials used for an intramural event should suffice. The host institution is generally responsible for securing all officials. However, it is not unusual for each institution to provide one or more qualified officials.

Facilities and equipment. Official regulation facilities should be available for the conduct of the event. Make special arrangements at the facility site for a registration table or tent, locker rooms, shower facilities, rest rooms, concession stand, lounge area for officials, and spectator seating.

Equipment, such as scorer's table, standards, timing devices, public address systems may be needed prior to the start of a specific event.

Rules and regulations. Whenever an extramural sport event is organized, make every effort to establish the rules and regulations early and communicate them to potential participants when entry forms and invitations go out.

When the event being offered is an outgrowth of intramural sport tournaments, pay special attention to rules and regulations to see if participating teams or individuals will be asked to learn any modifications. Unless differences are communicated well in advance, participants will not have adequate time to adapt to different rules and regulations. Such a situation places undue pressure on participants and officials, results in possible disciplinary problems, makes the whole tournament less than fair, and reflects negatively upon the host agency.

Travel and liability. If any form of funding for travel is being provided by a host agency or agency sending a representative to the event, the programmer should be fully aware of any liability factors associated with this assistance. For example, if participants have access to a vehicle through an agency, are precautions necessary to take regarding insurance, adult supervision, and counseling for proper use?

The host agency should also carefully review other potential liability concerns stemming from facility and equipment use and the handling and treatment of injuries.

Recognition. Design recognition efforts to highlight achievement rather than the cost of the award. Extramural awards can be similar to those distributed at an intramural event. Even though the focus of an extramural sport should be on participation and not on the award, the events lend themselves to designing a recognition ceremony at the completion of participation. This type of ceremony may be designed to recognize tournament finalists and also capitalize on the opportunity to recognize such other performances as good sportsmanship, the greatest number of participants representing an agency, most valuable players from each agency, an all-star team, etc. Finally, the ceremony can serve as a way to recognize persons responsible for organizng the event or for making some type of contribution to its provision.

Since extramural sports are an extension of the intramural sport program, the specifics on tournament scheduling, seeding, bye placement, officiating, and facilities supervision are the same as those employed in intramural sport programming.

MASTER TOURNAMENT CALENDAR

MONTH _____ *MAY* _____

SUNDAY	MONDAY	TUESDAY	WEDNESDAY	THURSDAY	FRIDAY	SATURDAY
1	2	3	4	5	6 NO GAMES	7 NO GAMES
8	9	10	11	12 Religious Holiday No Games 5:00-8:00 pm	13 NO GAMES	14 NO GAMES
15	16	17	18	19	20 NO GAMES	21 NO GAMES
22	23	24	25	26	27 NO GAMES	28 NO GAMES
29 Hold for Rescheduling	30 Hold for Rescheduling	31 No Games Team Captain's Meeting for Playoffs				

Figure 4-35. Master tournament calendar.

FACILITY SCHEDULE

Figure 4-36. Facility schedule.

INTRAMURAL AND EXTRAMURAL TOURNAMENT SCHEDULING

After selecting the appropriate tournament design, the programmer may proceed with the actual scheduling of the tournament. The first step in constructing the tournament schedule is to develop a master tournament calendar illustrating the time period in which the tournament will be conducted. After assigning days and dates, the programmer designates times that may not be played for various reasons, i.e., holidays, team captains' meetings, other sport conflicts. If specific dates are going to be assigned for practice times, include these too. Because postponements are inevitable, it is wise to allocate extra playing dates for rescheduling purposes as well as league tie-breakers and playoff schedules. Figure 4-35 is an example of a master tournament calendar.

After creating the tournament calendar, develop a facility schedule (Figure 4-36) indicating one week of playing times for each court or field. The example in Figure 4-36 indicates that there are 36 game openings per day or 144 game openings in one playing week of four days. In other words, 288 teams could participate in one game each during the first week of the tournament. Using this type of schedule helps the programmer determine the maximum number of entries that the tournament could accommodate.

Once entries have been received, sort them into appropriate units of participation. For example, an initial step is to place all men, women and co-intramural entries into separate groups. Then each of these groups may be further divided into smaller subunits such as advance, intermediate and novice classes. This process continues until all entries are separated into the smallest units possible with consideration being shown to place entries with special scheduling requests together as much as possible. Now that the entries have been sorted, it is possible to assign entries into leagues (round robin) or place them on elimination brackets.

The task of league assignment plays a major role in the success of a tournament. The programmer must have a thorough knowledge of the requirements of each sport event, the availability of facilities and to what degree is the interest level of the participants. If, for example, 28 teams signed up for a bowling tournament but only 5 team leagues were desired, how would the leagues be created? Would you structure:

$$\begin{array}{c} 5-5\text{ team leagues} \\ +1-3\text{ team league} \end{array} \text{ or } \begin{array}{c} 3-6\text{ team leagues} \\ +2-5\text{ team leagues} \end{array} \text{ or } \begin{array}{c} 4-5\text{ team leagues} \\ +2-4\text{ team leagues} \end{array}$$

The solution is based on the effectiveness of the programmer in recognizing such factors as: number of available facilities and their available operating hours, the maximum length of time required for each event, and the days in which participants have potential conflicts. Creative planning is a must in developing the league structure. Maintain equal playing opportunities for all entries, however.

After formulating the leagues, attach each league's entries to a scheduling worksheet. (see appendices 4A, 4B, 4C). On the cover of the worksheet, complete the league number, division, names of the entries and any special scheduling request. Once this task has been completed for all leagues and entries, construct a master schedule.

The process of scheduling each league's round robin contests is relatively simple if schedulers display care and accuracy. As one scheduler reads aloud the first league number and two corresponding team numbers, a recorder transcribes these figures on a master schedule while responding aloud the date, time and the proper field or court assignment for that contest. In the following example, at 5:00 p.m. on Court 5, team numbers 1 and 2 from League Number 1 will play. At 6:00 p.m. on Court 2, team number 3 and 4 from League Number 2 will play.

	CT 1	CT 2
5:00 p.m.	League 1 1 - 2	League 2 1 - 2
6:00 p.m.	League 1 3 - 4	League 2 3 - 4

Figure 4-37. Example of master tournament schedule.

This process continues until all entries and contests have been scheduled. Whenever possible, schedule all leagues on the same day and times throughout the tournament. Also, when scheduling several different units such as men's, women's and co-intramural, develop special codes for each or use different colors of pencil.

With the completion of the rough draft league schedules, check and double-check all work for accuracy. A single error in this step may cause mass confusion for the scheduler. Once organized, the schedules are typed (once again double-checked), duplicated and distributed to the participants.

An alternative to this process of tournament scheduling is instant scheduling. Instant scheduling is a method in which scheduling responsibilities are placed with the team captains or participants. After following a specified entry procedure, the participant schedules himself/herself into a league. League scheduling forms complete with playing days and specific game times are posted on a bulletin board usually outside of the sports office. Individuals merely look for openings in leagues where they can play. Once a suitable league is found, the individual writes in his/her or the team name and copies down the playing date, time and precise facility location. Thus, the individual has a copy of the league schedule.

Maas (1979) suggests several advantages and disadvantages of using instant scheduling. Advantages of this system include:

1. The brunt of responsibility in the scheduling process shifts from the intramural programmer to the team captain or participant.

2. Participants may select from a variety of available times. They can play and their schedule will be consistent from week to week for the entire season.

3. Selection of alternate playing times if the preferred time is not available is done by the participants.

4. The system encourages entries well before the final deadline.

5. Participants do not need to be contacted again until play-offs unless there is a schedule change.

6. Intramural programming time is reduced substantially and scheduling is finished on the deadline date except for late entries.

7. Schedules do not need to be typed and copied for the participants.

The disadvantages of instant scheduling include:

1. Need to predict the breakdown of leagues needed in each classification, or the need for flexibility to change league designations/classifications if an imbalance occurs.

2. Need for physical setting (hallway, large room, bulletin board space) to conduct the process with large numbers of people.

3. Initiation of this process may have problems until participants familiarize themselves with the procedure.

Instant scheduling provides a unique concept for the sports programmer in tournament scheduling. Although this method may not be applicable for all sport settings, it should be considered by the programmer as an optional choice.

PERSONNEL CONSIDERATIONS

Leadership, paid or volunteer, is the greatest single factor determining the success of a sports program. The term leadership may suggest a broad range of responsibilities within the realm of the sports program. Among them are found four distinct leadership levels; the functional level, the supervisory level, the administrative level and the executive or policy making level. Discussion in this chapter will focus primarily on the functional level of leadership: the employees and volunteers that deal with the participants on a face-to-face basis in an intramural or extramural event.

Leadership, by definition, implies that an individual has job duties and responsibilities that involve authority to influence participant's habits or attitudes. A person achieves this authority in two basic ways. First, the person it involves is placed in a leadership position and is given thorough training and knowledge about all details involved with the job. Second, the leader's ability to gain the respect, trust and admiration of the participant depends upon demonstrated competence on the job. Explain to your leaders that the authority of a position does not equal influence.

With these ideas in mind, we will focus on two of the most important leaders in the intramural or extramural sports program: sport officials and sport supervisors.

Officiating is one of the most difficult leadership positions in sports. Some consider it a thankless task while to others, it is a personal challenge that results in individual satisfaction knowing that one's presence was responsible for participants abiding by the rules of the sport.

A good official strives to extend his or her influence upon the participants without being noticed. To this extent, officiating is an art.

A good official should possess the following characteristics:

Quick reaction time. An official must make split-second decisions. The tempo of most games allows little time to make a decision.

Confidence. An official can portray confidence in such ways as speaking in a strong, firm voice, making positive motions in announcing decisions or blowing a sharp and loud whistle.

Emotional control. By using poise, calm and control, a good official will have a relaxing effect upon participants as well as spectators.

Consistency. One of the finest attributes of a good official, consistency assures that calls or decisions will be exactly the same regardless of participants or circumstances.

Integrity. An official should be honest at all times.

Knowledge of the rules. An official must understand the rules of the game, the mechanics of the job duties and the human relation aspects of officiating prior to refereeing sports at any level.

An official's checklist, developed by Richard Schafer (1977, p 20), illustrates several key points in officiating:

OFFICIAL'S CHECKLIST

1. BE COMPETITIVE—the players give maximum effort, so should you. Tell yourself, "I'm not going to let this game

get away with me. I am better than that." You are hired to make the calls that control the game—Make Them!

2. HAVE YOUR HEAD ON RIGHT—Don't think your striped shirt grants you immunity from having to take a little criticism. It's part of officiating. Plan on it. Successful officials know how much to take. Ask one when you get the chance.

3. DON'T BE A TOUGH GUY—If a coach is on your back but not enough to warrant a penalty, then stay away from him (or her). This is especially true during time-outs. Standing near an unhappy coach, just to "show him," will only lead to further tensions. Some officials develop irritating characteristics. Don't be one of them.

4. GET INTO THE FLOW OF THE GAME—Each game is different. Good officials can feel this difference. Concentrate on the reactions of the players. Take note if the tempo of the game changes. A ragged game calls for a different style of officiating from a smooth one.

5. DON'T BARK—If you don't like to be shouted at, don't shout at someone else. Be firm but with a normal relaxed voice. This technique will do wonders in helping you to reduce the pressure. Shouting indicates a loss of control—not only of one's self, but also of the game.

6. SHOW CONFIDENCE—Cockiness has absolutely no place in officiating. You want to exude confidence. Your presence should command respect from the participants. As in any walk of life, appearance, manner, and voice determine how you are accepted. Try to present the proper image.

7. FORGET THE FANS—As a group, fans usually exhibit three characteristics: ignorance of the rules, highly emotional partisanship and delight in antagonizing the officials. Accepting this fact will help you ignore the fans, unless they interrupt the game or stand in the way of you doing your job.

8. ANSWER REASONABLE QUESTIONS—Treat coaches and players in a courteous way. If they ask you a question reasonably, answer them in a polite way. If they get your

ear by saying, "Hey ref I want to ask you something," and then start telling you off, interrupt and remind them of the reason for the discussion. Be firm, but relaxed.

9. CHOOSE YOUR WORDS WISELY—Don't obviously threaten a coach or player. This will only put them on the defensive. More importantly, you will have placed yourself on the spot. If you feel a situation is serious enough to warrant a threat, then it is serious enought to penalize, without invoking a threat. Obviously some things you say will be a form of threat, but using the proper words can make it subtle.

10. STAY COOL—Your purpose is to establish a calm environment for the game. Nervous or edgy officials are easily spotted by fans, coaches and players alike. Avidly chewing gum, pacing around, or displaying a wide range of emotions prior to or during a game will serve to make you seem vulnerable to the pressure.

RECRUITMENT OF OFFICIALS

Recruiting competent sport officials may be a taxing, yet satisfying experience. Finding individuals for leadership positions first requires the agency to know the specific number of sport officials needed as well as a detailed job description explaining responsibilities and requirements of the position.

It is advisable to distribute and post position announcements or notices pertaining to the openings. Ads, such as those in Figure 4-38 placed in local newspapers, can attract new officials to the sports program.

Another good practice is to have an applicant complete an Official's Information Card (Figure 4-39) indicating sports desired, daily availability and the number of hours desired per week.

Such cards are an excellent way of providing a quick reference source once the season begins.

IN-SERVICE TRAINING

After recruitment, the applicants should attend an in-service training program designed to familiarize the new official with policies, procedures and rules relevant to their job description.

Figure 4-38.   Officials' advertisement.

Several meetings are suggested with the new official beginning with an initial orientation meeting. At this meeting, discuss the agency's goals, philosophy, benefits, on the job conduct, uniforms, safety, scheduling, and other general information pertaining to the job. This is also an ideal time for the employee to complete any necessary payroll or personnel forms.

A second meeting or "class session" is held to review rule interpretation, mechanics and positioning utilizing slides, films or other audio-visual aids. This meeting is vital to the success of the program since it assures that all officials are familiar with specific interpretations and are uniform or consistent in enforcement during actual game situations.

After a rule interpretation meeting, provide an on-the-field or court practical clinic in which the potential sport official officiates a practice game working on floor, hand, and verbal mechanics. The use of experienced or senior officials as instructors or evaluators is an excellent way of providing leader-

---

OFFICIAL'S INFORMATION CARD

Date _____

Name _____
　　　　　　Last　　　　　　　First　　　　　　Middle

Address _____

Phone _____ Registered Official ____ Yes ____ No

Sports Desired

MEN	WOMEN	CO-INTRAMURAL
___ Basketball	___ Basketball	___ Basketball
___ Flag Football	___ Cageball	___ Innertube
___ Soccer	___ Flag Football	___ Water Polo Softball
___ Softball	___ Kickball	___ Volleyball
___ Volleyball	___ Innertube	
___ Water Polo	___ Water Polo Softball	
	___ Volleyball	

Availability

MONDAY	TUESDAY	WEDNESDAY	THURSDAY	SUNDAY
___ 5-8 pm	___ 5-8 pm	___ 5-8 pm	___ 5-8 pm	___ 1-4 pm
___ 8-11 pm	___ 8-11 pm	___ 8-11 pm	___ 8-11 pm	___ 4-7 pm
___ Either	___ Either	___ Either	___ Either	___ 7-10 pm
				___ Any

Approximate hours per week desired: _____

Figure 4-39. Official's information card.

ship opportunities for these individuals as well as a means for strengthening the relationship and rapport between new and veteran officials.

Following these meetings, give all officials both written and practical knowledge tests developed either by the Intramural Staff or by a state or national officials' association. Require passing scores rated on proficiency and knowledge on both tests prior to scheduling, provide individual counseling for those scoring below the minimum.

After the tournament or season has begun, schedule periodic in-service sessions for the officials. The purpose of these sessions is to strengthen skills and to build upon what the official has learned through experience as well as to review persistent problems or errors in rule interpretation that might be occuring.

Whatever method is used, in-service training is a necessity to ensure a sound, quality officiating program. More and more agencies are deciding not to conduct these training sessions because of staff time and budget limitations. However, the dividends, reinforcement, morale and positive public relations obtained is far more valuable than the cost. When thought of as an investment, in-service training is a very worthwhile and recommended practice.

Scheduling. Methods of assigning officials vary among institutional settings. Several methods such as contract scheduling, weekly scheduling, etc., are discussed in detail and may be found in the Personnel chapter. However, whatever method is chosen, a carefully developed assignment plan is necessary.

Once this master schedule is completed, a daily list of scheduled officials (Figure 4-40) can be attached to the sport supervisor's clipboard indicating assigned courts and shifts at the facility site. The officials' names and hours worked from this form are later transferred to a master payroll form.

Sport Official Evaluation

Evaluating officials is a difficult task that occurs on a continuous basis throughout the season. Evaluations should be considered with a positive attitude to achieve maximum performance in job effectiveness. When the evaluation process is

VOLLEYBALL OFFICIALS

SCHEDULE 1983

Supervisor: _____   Day _____
Sport: _____   Date _____
Location: _____

	COURT 1	COURT 2	COURT 3	COURT 4
6:00 pm to 8:00 pm	REF. Smith In ___ Out ___ UMP. Jones In ___ Out ___	REF. Murphy In ___ Out ___ UMP. Long In ___ Out ___	REF. Hudson In ___ Out ___ UMP. Howell In ___ Out ___	REF. Flinn In ___ Out ___ UMP. Cline In ___ Out ___
	COURT 5	COURT 6	COURT 7	COURT 8
	REF. Burk In ___ Out ___ UMP. Roberts In ___ Out ___	REF. Johnson In ___ Out ___ UMP. Moore In ___ Out ___	REF. Frye In ___ Out ___ UMP. Evans In ___ Out ___	REF. Boyd In ___ Out ___ UMP. Baker In ___ Out ___

Figure 4-40. Daily official's schedule.

looked upon by the officials and administrators as an "aid" instead of a "threat" to employment, the overall quality of the program is enhanced. Presenting positive solutions and helpful suggestions rather than reprimand and criticism is important.

A popular method of evaluation used in intramural sports is a written evaluation form. There are probably as many official evaluation forms available as there are intramural departments. Figure 4-41 illustrates one example of an official's evaluation form.

BASKETBALL OFFICIALS' EVALUATION

DATE: _____

EVALUATOR: _____

CHECK APPROPRIATE RATING
7 = excellent   6 = very good   5 = good
4 = average   3 = fair   2 = poor   1 = bad

OFFICIALS' NAMES	SMITH	JONES	MILLER	JOHNSON
I. Attitude:				
enthusiasm	7 6 5 4 3 2 1	7 6 5 4 3 2 1	7 6 5 4 3 2 1	7 6 5 4 3 2 1
hustles	7 6 5 4 3 2 1	7 6 5 4 3 2 1	7 6 5 4 3 2 1	7 6 5 4 3 2 1
II. Rapport with Participants:				
courteous	7 6 5 4 3 2 1	7 6 5 4 3 2 1	7 6 5 4 3 2 1	7 6 5 4 3 2 1
takes criticism	7 6 5 4 3 2 1	7 6 5 4 3 2 1	7 6 5 4 3 2 1	7 6 5 4 3 2 1
self-control	7 6 5 4 3 2 1	7 6 5 4 3 2 1	7 6 5 4 3 2 1	7 6 5 4 3 2 1
III. Mechanics:				
position as LEAD OFFICIAL	7 6 5 4 3 2 1	7 6 5 4 3 2 1	7 6 5 4 3 2 1	7 6 5 4 3 2 1
position as TRAIL OFFICIAL	7 6 5 4 3 2 1	7 6 5 4 3 2 1	7 6 5 4 3 2 1	7 6 5 4 3 2 1
jump ball administration	7 6 5 4 3 2 1	7 6 5 4 3 2 1	7 6 5 4 3 2 1	7 6 5 4 3 2 1
free throw administration	7 6 5 4 3 2 1	7 6 5 4 3 2 1	7 6 5 4 3 2 1	7 6 5 4 3 2 1
throw-in administration	7 6 5 4 3 2 1	7 6 5 4 3 2 1	7 6 5 4 3 2 1	7 6 5 4 3 2 1
call and report fouls	7 6 5 4 3 2 1	7 6 5 4 3 2 1	7 6 5 4 3 2 1	7 6 5 4 3 2 1
switching at dead balls	7 6 5 4 3 2 1	7 6 5 4 3 2 1	7 6 5 4 3 2 1	7 6 5 4 3 2 1
use of signals	7 6 5 4 3 2 1	7 6 5 4 3 2 1	7 6 5 4 3 2 1	7 6 5 4 3 2 1
whistle	7 6 5 4 3 2 1	7 6 5 4 3 2 1	7 6 5 4 3 2 1	7 6 5 4 3 2 1
eye contact w/partner	7 6 5 4 3 2 1	7 6 5 4 3 2 1	7 6 5 4 3 2 1	7 6 5 4 3 2 1
IV. Consistency:				
calls both ways	7 6 5 4 3 2 1	7 6 5 4 3 2 1	7 6 5 4 3 2 1	7 6 5 4 3 2 1
no hesitation in calls	7 6 5 4 3 2 1	7 6 5 4 3 2 1	7 6 5 4 3 2 1	7 6 5 4 3 2 1
TOTAL				
V. Comments				

Figure 4-41. Officials' evaluation form.

Evaluations may be completed by fellow officials, sport supervisors, participants or teams. It is a good practice to employ quality, experienced officials as "daily evaluators" to provide another form of leadership opportunity. Whatever evaluation method is chosen, the official should have the opportunity for positive feedback and an opportunity to examine the report.

Officials' Club. The purpose of an officials' club is to advance, encourage and improve all phases of sports officiating, to develop further the ability of each of its members, and to promote a better working relationship among those persons interested in the area of sport officiating. Membership may be restricted to individuals who have successfully completed both written and verbal rule tests.

Club meetings may be devoted to informing officials of unusual rules and plays in an effort to prepare the officials for these circumstances. Other activities include social events with fellow club members, the conduct of clinics open to the general public and the assessment of fines or discipline upon officials for misconduct.

In conclusion, officials represent their employer *and* themselves. Make sure they are aware of this fact. Participants and spectators know who the officials are and observe them while they work and socialize. Officials should set an example for all to follow in the competitive atmosphere of organized sports.

SPORT SUPERVISORS

Although the characteristics necessary in becoming a competent sport official generally apply to a sport supervisor, several other qualifications are needed.

First, require all supervisors to obtain sports emergency training encompassing basic first aid skills. This training may be conducted by the Intramural Sport Office itself or by an appropriate health agency. First aid training allows the supervisor to provide immediate first aid care to an individual who has been injured or suddenly taken ill while participating in the sports program. It does not allow a supervisor to practice medicine, but it provides the knowledge and skills to handle life and death threatening situations. In addition to their sports emergency training, supervisors are responsible for accident reporting. A discussion on safety and accident reporting procedures may be found in the Safety in Sports chapter.

Along with proper safety training, a supervisor should have experience as a sport official. This allows the supervisor to provide advice pertaining to interpretations and protests, as well as to have a better appreciation of the difficulties in officiating. Since a sport supervisor is an extension of the office and the person in authority at the activity site, a thorough understanding of office policies, procedures and rules of the game is also essential. Supervisors must be alert and anticipate hazards that may be dangerous to the players, officials or spectators and eliminate them before play begins. More specific job responsibilities follow:

Pre-Game Responsibilities

Check to be certain all needed sports equipment and supplies are present and in good condition.

Determine if all sport officials are signed-in on the appropriate work-time form.

See that the games are started on time observing the forfeit time rule.

Verify the team's roster on the official scoresheet.

Game Responsibilities

The sport supervisor is the person responsible and in charge of all games and situations on the field or court.

The supervisor should be alert for disputes, protests or other problems and should prevent them before they occur. Circulating from field to field or court to court he or she may determine if all games are progressing properly. The supervisor should attach an extra sheet of game rules to a clipboard which he or she may refer to in case of a dispute.

Questions of eligibility are handled by a sport supervisor. If a participant is ineligible, the supervisor should insist that he or she not participate. Report any situation to the sports office.

In case of unfavorable weather conditions after the games have begun, play should not continue if it becomes too dangerous or hazardous. Supervisors must exhibit good judgement in these cases.

Supervisors are also responsible for improving the quality of officiating and working with the officials in developing proficiency whenever possible. In rating the officials, use an evaluation form accurately.

Supervisors should prevent the misuse of any sport facility. If participants are misusing a facility, the supervisor should inform them of the proper use of the facility. If they fail to comply with the supervisor's request, request law enforcement assistance.

If a protest occurs while the supervisor is on duty, complete the *Protest Form* upon the field of play and return to the sports office.

Post-Game Responsibilities

The supervisor is responsible in making sure each official signs the completed game scoresheet. If there are numerous games, the supervisor should circulate and collect scoresheets after *each* game is completed.

Report all cases of unsportsmanlike conduct by a team or individual to the proper authority. Submit a written report to the sports office to document such behavior.

Complete equipment sign-out forms at the time of equipment check-out and file them properly.

Supervisors should also complete a *Maintenance Repair Form* when reporting facilities in need of repair. Without the help of the supervisors in this area, maintenance problems will increase.

SUMMARY

The sports programmer at an operational level plays a significant role in the success of the intramural and extramural sports program. A sound philosophical foundation is a prerequisite for effective programming. The programmer should have the capabilities and knowledge in human relations, decision making, conflict resolution, specific rules and regulations, establishment and implementation of tournament scheduling procedures, and the many internal organizational policies and procedures involved in the program. Above all, the programmer must have a genuine interest in the field of recreational sports and specifically, intramural sports.

Each institutional setting has its unique programming approach. The material presented in this chapter should be considered general or basic programming tools aiding in programming efforts. It is up to the programmer to apply these principles to daily situations.

Intramural and extramural sports are an enjoyable and rewarding phase of recreational sports for the programmer and the participant. Both disciplines, with their diversity of sport events, offer a basis for wholesome competition and cooperation regardless of the skill and interest level of the participant.

PROGRAMMING TERMINOLOGY

With the tremendous diversity and involvement of sport, words often become confusing and acquire overlapping meanings for the programmer, but are relevant because of tradition and popularity of use. The following glossary presents terms with brief descriptions to assist in resolving this concern:

amateur—a participant in sport that does not receive the income, ranking, or status that results from professional sports.

bracket—a pair of parallel lines used in designing a tournament chart which designates opposing participants.

bye—a single position on an elimination bracket which indicates no opponent and results in an automatic advancement.

call—a verbal action demonstrating a decision made by a sport official.

captain—a designated member of the team who serves as spokesperson for that team during a sport activity.

challenge tournament—an on-going tournament in which participants issue challenges, usually with limitations, to other participants with the ultimate goal of reaching the highest level of the tournament design.

clerk—a sport official responsible for recording the names and identification number for each participant and assignment.

coach—a leader who is recognized for fulfilling various functions in individual or group management, covering such areas as instruction, training and strategy.

consolation tournament—a modification of a single elimination tournament in which losers in the first round, continue to participate for a consolation championship instead of being eliminated from the tournament.

contest—sport involvement and interaction where individuals or groups participate.

court or field—an area set aside for sport participation.

dead heat—when two or more sport participants finish at exactly the same time.

default—a loss resulting from sport participation due to participant inability to begin or continue because of injury, illness or unsportsmanlike conduct.

defeat—a loss resulting from sport participation.

disqualification—inability of a participant to continue involvement in sport because of a rule infraction or misconduct.

division—a major grouping or classification within a setting carrying a larger number of participants.

double elimination tournament—a modification of a consolation tournament in which no participant is eliminated until two losses have been registered.

doubles—a form of sport participation in which two participants compete as a team against two other participants.

draw—a process in which participants' names are drawn by a random procedure and are part of a tournament draw sheet.

draw sheet—an official chart listing tournament participants and their individual assignment on the first round with the remainder of the open tournament brackets following.

entry—a participant or team for a sport tournament.

event—a sport in which individuals or teams participate.

fees—
> entry—a required prepayment to a sport tournament.

> forfeit—a deposit held in escrow to be used as a fine for an individual or team who does not meet their responsibilities for sport participation.

> protest—a payment that accompanies a formal sports grievance to verify its sincerity.

field event—all events in a track and field meet that are not considered running events.

finals—concluding contests designed to determine the winner of a tournament or league.

flight—several small tournaments or round in which a group or participants are competing together.

forfeit—the loss of a sport event because of violation of the rules of the sport.

foul—an infraction of the rules and regulations of a sport.

handicap—point or points given to a participant in a sport event to equate ability in a unified fashion.

heat—one of a series of preliminaries of qualifying contests within a sport to reduce a large number of participants.

implied bye—an alternate method of indicating the placement of a bye in which a blank space is substituted for the bye's parallel bracket line.

lane—a designated stripe or alley which is perpendicular to the starting and finishing line of which participants must remain during the course of their event.

lap—one complete counter-clockwise circle of a track or designated area.

league—a group of participants composed of individuals or teams which participate against each other in a regular schedule. The team with the highest percentage of contest wins is the winner.

match play—sport involvement where participants compete against each other and compare respective skills.

match point—final scoring point.

medley—an event which carries a series of different sports skill within the same contest.

meet—structured sport participation that includes several different events in which individuals and/or teams participate simultaneously with each event contributing to the total score and an overall winner.

official—designated leader whose responsibilities are to enforce the rules and regulations of a sport.

open division—a tournament league section not restricted to any individual because of sport ability or eligibility limitations.

period—a time division for some sports.

player—an individual who participates in sport.

point—a unit of scoring.

postponement—a delay of participation in a sport event for acceptable reasons such as bad weather or facility repair.

preliminaries—a process that allows participation to occur before the regular competition begins.

professional—an individual who participates in a sport for financial gain in order to earn a living.

protest—a formal disagreement of a sport rule, regulation or interpretation between participants and an official generally voiced when the incident may affect the outcome of a sport event.

roster—an official list of team members.

round—a term used to indicate the tournament progress of an individual or team. Rounds in an elimination tournament include quarter finals: 8 teams or four contests remaining. Semi-finals: four teams or two contests remaining. Final: two teams or one contest remain to determine the champion.

scratch—a withdrawal of an official entry.

section—a sub-division that often demonstrates a difference in skill level and ability and provides special consideration for those circumstances.

seeding—a process of ranking participants according to their previous records or abilities in a sport.

semi-professional—an individual who is compensated for participation in sport, but may not take on the full dimensions of participating in a specific sport only to earn income.

singles—a form of participation in sport in which one participant plays directly against another.

sudden death—a period of extra play to decide a tie between individuals or teams.

team or individual—the smallest unit for tournament structure.

time trial—a process of clocking participants in order to determine their starting positions within an overall field.

tournament—a designed participation structure of cooperative and competitive play activity in the game form.

unsportsmanlike conduct—action not conducive or acceptable to the spirit of the game.

REFERENCES

Colgate, J.A. *Administration of Intramural and Recreational Activities: Everyone Can Participate.* New York: John Wiley and Sons, 1978.

Daughtrey, G. and Woods, J.B. *Physical Education and Intramural Programs: Organization and Administration,* 2nd edition Philadelphia: W.B. Saunders Co., 1976.

Gerou, N.E. *Complete Guide to Administering the Intramural Program.* West Nyack, N.Y.: Parker Publishing Co. Inc., 1976.

Hyatt, R.W. *Intramural Sports: Organization and Administration.* St. Louis: C.V. Mosby Co., 1977.

Kleindienst, V.K. and Weston, A. *The Recreational Sports Program: Schools . . . Colleges . . . Communities.* Englewood Cliffs, N.J.: Prentice-Hall, Inc., 1978.

Leavitt, N.M. and Price, H.D. *Intramural and Recreational Sports for High School and College,* 2nd edition New York: The Ronald Press Co., 1958.

Mass, G. *Instant Scheduling for Intramural Sports.* Paper presented at the Big Ten Recreational Sports Director's Conference, Chicago, December, 1979.

Means, L.E. *Intramurals: Their Organization and Administration,* 2nd edition Englewood Cliffs, N.J.: Prentice-Hall, Inc., 1973.

Mitchell, E.D. *Intramural Sports.* New York: A.S. Barnes and Co., 1939.

Mueller, P. and Resnik, J.W. *Intramural-Recreational Sports: Programming and Administration,* 5th edition New York: John Wiley and Sons, 1979.

Peterson, J.A. and Pre, L. (eds.) *Intramural Director's Handbook.* West Point, N.Y.: Leisure Press, 1977.

Rokosz, F. M. *Structured Intramurals.* Philadelphia: W.B. Saunders Co., 1975.

Shafer, R.C. "Thinking Right," *Referee,* Jan.-Feb., 1977.

APPENDIX 4A

Sport _____
League _____
Division _____

Team	Won	Lost
1. _____	_____	_____
2. _____	_____	_____
3. _____	_____	_____
4. _____	_____	_____

Team Team	Date	Time	Ct/Field
1 vs 4			
2 vs 3			
1 vs 3			
4 vs 2			
1 vs 2			
3 vs 4			

Appendix 4-A. Four entry round robin league worksheet.

Sport _____
League _____
Division _____

Team	Won	Lost
1. _____	_____	_____
2. _____	_____	_____
3. _____	_____	_____
4. _____	_____	_____
5. _____	_____	_____

Team Team	Date	Time	Ct/Field
1 vs 4			
2 vs 3			
5 vs 3			
1 vs 2			
4 vs 2			
5 vs 1			
3 vs 1			
4 vs 5			
2 vs 5			
3 vs 4			

Appendix 4-B. Five entry round robin league worksheet.

Sport _____
League _____
Division _____

Team	Won	Lost
1. _____		
2. _____		
3. _____		
4. _____		
5. _____		
6. _____		

Team vs Team	Date	Time	Ct/Field
1 vs 6			
2 vs 5			
3 vs 4			
1 vs 5			
6 vs 4			
2 vs 3			
1 vs 4			
5 vs 3			
6 vs 2			
1 vs 3			
4 vs 2			
5 vs 6			
1 vs 2			
3 vs 6			
4 vs 5			

Appendix 4-C. Six entry round robin league worksheet.

Sport _____
League _____
Division _____

Team	Won	Lost
1. _____	____	____
2. _____	____	____
3. _____	____	____
4. _____	____	____
5. _____	____	____
6. _____	____	____
7. _____	____	____

Team	Team	Date	Time	Ct/Field
1 vs 6				
2 vs 5				
3 vs 4				
7 vs 5				
1 vs 4				
2 vs 3				
6 vs 4				
7 vs 3				
1 vs 2				
5 vs 3				
6 vs 2				
7 vs 1				
4 vs 2				
5 vs 1				
6 vs 7				
3 vs 1				
4 vs 7				
5 vs 6				
2 vs 7				
3 vs 6				
4 vs 5				

Appendix 4-D. Seven entry round robin league worksheet.

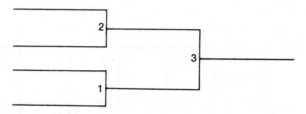

Appendix 4-E. Four entry single elimination bracket.

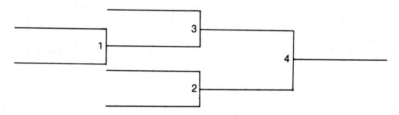

Appendix 4-F. Five entry single elimination bracket.

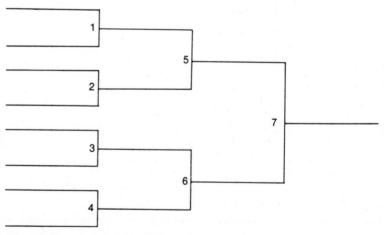

Appendix 4-G. Eight entry single elimination bracket.

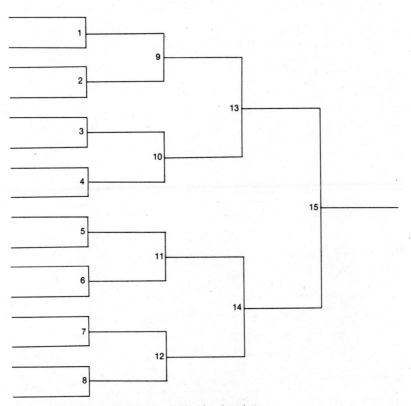

Appendix 4-H.   16 entry single elimination bracket.

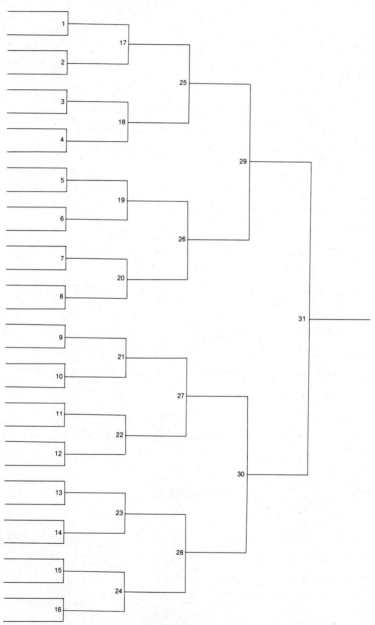

Appendix 4-I. 32 entry single elimination bracket.

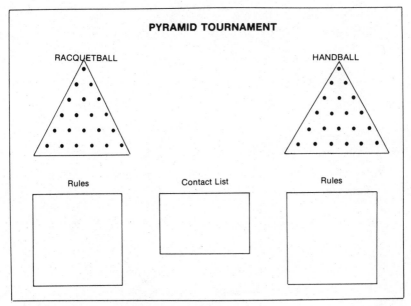

Sport: _____ Ending Date _____

LADDER

TOURNAMENT

Rules/Regulations

| JOHN |
| MARK |
| BILL |
| JACK |
| DAN |
| LEE |
| TOM |
| AL |

Contact List

Appendix 4-J.   Ladder tournament board.

PYRAMID TOURNAMENT

RACQUETBALL

HANDBALL

Rules   Contact List   Rules

Appendix 4-K.   Pyramid tournament board.

CHAPTER 5

CLUB SPORT

Club sport participation is a major program area within recreational sport. Club sport involves special interest groups that organize because of a common interest in a particular sport. Self-administration and self-regulation are characteristics common to all clubs, whether they revolve around bridge, chess, sailing, hot-air ballooning, track, rugby, or spelunking. Those who desire club sport membership seek regular participation under a more coherent design than informal, intramural or extramural programs offer.

Historically, club sport in America may be traced to the strong community club sport tradition that still exists in Europe. European clubs provide the main source of sport participation and instruction for all ages, interests and skill levels. Members customarily participate with or compete against those representing other communities. The clubs are self-governed by volunteer, elected, or paid personnel. Clubs obtain financial support through membership dues and utilize community facilities for practice and structured events.

Although Colonial America maintained a club sport format similar to the European system, club systems in the United States today vary depending on the setting in which they are found. Clubs in municipal settings are organized by age group. Clubs in a military setting parallel athletic sport in terms of sponsoring the most skilled participants to compete against those from other military bases. Clubs in a commercial setting may incorporate more than one sport. They are privately owned and operated on a profit basis through membership fees. Clubs within a correctional setting operate on one site with restricted or no opportunity for travel. Clubs in an educational setting are found at the collegiate level and at the high school level on a limited basis. Perhaps the biggest reason for the diversity in approach to club sports in America is that all sport programs were developed independently through educational or municipal settings. In Europe, all sport programs developed through the community-based clubs.

A club sport organization is typically formed when people within a setting organize themselves to share a common interest in a particular sport activity. All clubs desire an opportunity to operate independently, determining their own activities, leadership, and internal operating policies. Self-determination, unity and common interest are most appealing aspects of club sports for potential members. Such characteristics distinguish club sport from informal, intramural and extramural sport. Additional factors associated with club sport programs include: an ability to provide sport participation unavailable elsewhere, a better opportunity to engage in the sport of one's choice, service to special interest groups and extramural opportunities distinct from those offered in the intramural sport programs.

As club members pursue their sport interests, specific types of emphases emerge, including: tournament participation, socialization, instruction and skill development, or a combination of the three. Factors that influence the type of club that evolves include: traditions associated with the sport, interests and abilities of the membership, capabilities of selected leadership personnel, type and availability of facilities and equipment, mechanisms utilized for financial support and the proximity of opponents. The following descriptions of each major club type may help identify their characteristics:

ATHLETIC CLUB SPORT

Clubs that demonstrate an interest in scheduling and hosting tournaments, leagues or structured events operate similarly to athletic or professional sport teams. Club members tend to be goal-oriented and enjoy the rivalry and competition stemming from structured tournaments. Consequently, clubs hold regular practice sessions, often hire a coach, and maintain an organized schedule. Sometimes, clubs hold tryouts to select a traveling team or individual for the purpose of competing against others having a similar skill level. In some instances, club-sponsored teams or members participate in structured events through avenues such as the NCAA, NAIA, AAU, ACU-I and Olympics. In order to maintain a recreational sport philosophy, however, membership in this type of club should not be denied if the participant does not have the interest or ability to play at a high skill level.

The biggest difference between clubs which focus on tournaments and athletic sport is the degree of administrative support and complexity of the rules and regulations governing their operations. Clubs bear the bulk of the responsibility for generating and managing their finances, developing leadership, and determining guidelines and activities. If these functions were being performed for the club, it would more closely resemble an athletic sport system. In fact, where resources permit, many clubs take an athletic sport approach. In community youth support programs such as soccer, traveling teams are often selected, coached and financially supported to participate in scheduled tournaments. Similarly, commercial racquetball clubs may sponsor individual members to participate in tournaments on behalf of the club.

While enthusiasm and resolve for high skill-level performance should be encouraged, this may lead to participation by too few club members. Since involvement in scheduled activity requires a number of fund-raising mechanisms to handle the costs of entry fees, uniforms, equipment, travel and lodging, officials' and judges' fees and so on, each club member should be guaranteed an opportunity to choose how the resources of the club meet such expenses.

INSTRUCTIONAL CLUB SPORT

Another popular type of club concentrates on instruction, knowledge and skill development. While some form of teaching or information-sharing takes place among the membership in every club, learning here is not left to chance or dealt with in a haphazard way. Instructional clubs hire or recruit qualified personnel to structure lessons or clinics at practice sessions appropriate for the interests and abilities of their membership. Some clubs will often design testing situations and in-house tournaments so that the members may see what they have learned and where they need improvement. Other avenues for the display of newly-acquired or polished skills include demonstrations, clinics and extramural participation.

An instructional club may meet its financial needs through membership fees, lesson charges and fines. The biggest expenses arise from instructors' wages and equipment purchases. If a club is interested in supporting members or a team in tournaments or renting a facility, they may have to mount fund-raising efforts.

SOCIAL CLUB SPORT

In social club settings, participants seek membership in order to meet others who enjoy the same sport. The major interest shared by members is a specific sport, but participation becomes more a means for socializing than learning, skill development, fitness, or tournament play. Enjoyment arises more from rapport and comradery among members than from performance or an outcome of competition. The fun of participation may diminish if too much structure and competitive rivalry is present, although some clubs maintain regular intramural tournaments for their members as occasions to encourage social interaction. Other social club activities include sponsoring clinics, giving demonstrations, and traveling together to watch other demonstrations or tournaments. Members of socially-oriented clubs commonly provide their own equipment and support their activities through membership dues.

Some club sports may not fit completely into one of these categories. Most clubs choose to design activities for socializing, learning and tournament participation. The preceeding club types comprise a basic frame of reference for categorizing clubs and the diverse attitudes and modes of operation they represent.

GENERAL PROGRAM CONSIDERATIONS

In order for a club sport organization to remain in operation from year to year, it must maintain its resources. Changes in membership levels and interests, funding, facility availability, and leadership will influence its longevity. Consequently, an external support system may reinforce the club's internal leadership, helping provide continuity, organization, and programming assistance to clubs within a particular setting.

External administration for the club sport program should be centralized under one board, department, unit or agency. (Where applicable, the administration should occur where the other recreational sport programming areas are housed.) A central approach maintains continuity, standardizes operational procedures, establishes equitable access to resources, allows an assessment of needs and permits an evaluation of the total club program. Although external leadership support is not always vital to the continuation of a club sport, it may make valuable contributions to the stability and quality of club sport operations.

The degree to which external administration and program services exist depends on the philosophy of the institution, agency or board assuming administrative responsibility, as well as the potential of the setting for providing program resources. When these decisions regarding extent of support are determined at the higher administrative level, they are communicated to the club sport programming staff as policy or procedure. The club sport programming staff, and the administrator of the total recreational sport program, should seek an opportunity to influence these decisions.

While examining the type of program leadership and services to offer, consider possible legal restraints. At a minimum, a staff member should investigate the legal aspects of working with clubs within a particular setting, and serve as a resource person to solve problems for the club sport program. Examples of additional services that can be provided to clubs include partial or total support for: finances, instructional or coaching personnel, equipment, facilities, travel, office space, storage space, telephone access, clerical assistance and promotion-publicity.

Since the type and degree of program services provided to clubs varies, there are no established models dictating how club sports should be programmed. Two basic philosophical approaches to club programming exist: conservative, or formal; and liberal, or informal. The major principle of the conservative approach is that club members have little or no discretion in determining operational procedure. Characteristics of this approach include:

—Clubs receive financial support from the institution or agency having administrative responsibility.
—Club schedules and activities must receive administrative approval.
—Club travel must be approved, properly insured vehicles must be utilized for travel, and approved supervisors must accompany the club.
—Clubs must have an approved advisor or coach (may be a paid position).
—Clubs must maintain a formal document: for example, constitution or guidelines.
—Club members must have insurance coverage and a medical examination.
—Club financial transactions and purchases must be approved by a person within the administrative structure or a program staff person.
—Medical or athletic training supervision may be provided at club events.

Common characteristics of the liberal approach include:

—Club members control operations such as funding, travel, scheduling and purchasing.
—Clubs receive minimal or no external assistance in funding, equipment, facilities scheduling, office utilization, or medical supervision.
—Club members are responsible for their own insurance coverage and for knowing their own physiological limitations.

Institutions or agencies that provide partial or complete funding and adequate staff supervision usually select the conservative approach. The liberal approach is most frequently used when funding and staffing are limited or unavailable. The greater the financial dependence on an agency or institution, the greater the external leadership involvement in the club.

Quality club sport programs may flourish under either approach. The liberal approach relies heavily upon volunteer leadership, develops practices based upon the principle of voluntary assumption of risk, and is more limited in the extent and amount of program services that it can offer. When selecting a programming approach, make a firm decision to go in one direction or the other. Those who combine approaches may find themselves faced with legal liability because of indecisive or inconsistent administrative decision-making.

Organizational Structure

After considering the general program approach establish the specific organizational structures within which the various clubs will operate. These structures usually exist at two different levels—external and internal.

External Structure

Development of a sound external organizational structure involves documenting the policies of the setting that influence club operations, identifying the personnel considered responsible for supervising and coordinating the various club sports, and specifying the nature of services available to clubs. The latter function includes the procedures necessary to provide access to services.

Most club sport programs operating under a conservative, centralized system of administration have one supervisor who monitors and enforces operational policy, advises club leadership and employees, serves as a liaison between the club(s) and administrative personnel, shareholders or groups within the setting, supervises utilization of services provided within the clubs system, handles disciplinary problems, maintains proper reports and documentation for each club and the overall program, and works to meet the needs of the club(s). When the need exists, and resources permit, additional full or part time personnel may be involved on a paid or volunteer basis.

A number of club sport programs use a club sport council, federation or board to help shape and implement operational policy. Comprised of a representative from each club, the council and its executive officers may play an active role in policy development, club leadership and club governance (usually in conjunction with a liberal administrative approach.) Alternatively, the council may primarily function in an advisory or sounding board capacity for the programming personnel in charge of club sports (a conservative approach).

Regardless of the involvement of the council leadership and governance functions, the format allows for systematic input from each club. It keeps programming personnel appraised of club problems and needs, develops a sense of identity and unity, provides representative input for decision-making or operational procedures, facilitates the acceptance and adherence to policy and procedure and serves as a forum for problem-solving.

Internal Structure

Most clubs routinely identify or elect officers because they recognize the need for leadership. They know certain tasks must be accomplished in order for the club to function. Under a conservative approach to club sport programming, clubs are required to maintain elected officers. To an extent, the club sport staff dictates and supervises election procedures. This requirement reflects a desire to structure stability and establish an avenue or accountability to the club sport staff. The positions most likely to exist within a club, regardless of emphasis, include a president, vice-president, secretary, and treasurer. The general responsibilities of the officers include:

—convene regular club meeting for communication and business purposes
—be familiar with an approved code of parliamentary procedure
—monitor compliance with club operational policies
—maintain necessary records
—recruit new members
—initiate financial transactions
—prepare budget requests and annual reports where applicable
—serve as the liaison to the external administrative structure for the club sport program
—know agency or institution policies and procedures affecting clubs

—know legal parameters affecting club operations
—know safety precautions and accident reporting procedures

Specific duties for each club officer include:

President

—organize and conduct all club meetings
—appoint necessary chairpersons and committees
—serve as an ex-officio member of all committees
—coordinate and schedule all club activities
—supervise election procedures
—maintain contact with club officers and committee members
—call for oral and written reports as necessary
—represent the club to the agency or setting

Vice-President

—assume duties of the President in his or her absence
—oversee club equipment and purchase requests
—oversee all club committees
—assist President as required

Secretary

—notify members of meetings
—record minutes of all meetings
—handle all club correspondence
—maintain club membership roster
—maintain club records and files
—prepare club annual report for approval

Treasurer

—maintain accurate and up-to-date club financial records, salary schedules and payroll
—prepare purchase requests for approval
—collect membership dues
—prepare club budget request and annual financial report
—pay all club bills
—report club financial status to general membership upon request.

Other leadership positions that may be found in clubs include:

—a *club advisor,* serving as a resource person to approve club activities and to advise club members

—a *safety officer,* responsible for checking equipment and facilities for hazardous conditions and handling accident situations

—a *coach,* responsible for scheduling and coaching practice sessions and contests

—an *instructor,* responsible for designing structured learning experiences for club sport members

—a *publicity manager,* responsible for initiating and implementing all publicity for the club

Each club member should play a significant role in the success of the club. Without membership involvement, a club often grows stale, despite the enthusiasm of its officers. Each club member should help in the following ways:

—attend scheduled meetings and participate in decision-making

—help shape the club constitution and by-laws, membership requirements and dues

—select club officers and leadership personnel

—uphold club, agency, and institutional policies and procedures

Each club should develop written information on operations. This information aids continuity for a club when leadership and members change. It reflects the evolution of the club and the changes that occurred. A conservative program approach may require development of a constitution and by-laws. Once a document has been prepared, it is a common practice that it meet the scrutiny and approval of the club sport staff. In some instances, constitutions may need approval at an administrative level. Due to limited familiarity with the preparation of this type of document, a staff member may need to provide assistance. A format of a constitution and by-laws for a club sport follows:

CONSTITUTION

Preamble

States the purpose and aims of the group.

Article I—Name

States the name of the organization.

Article II—Membership

States the requirements and size limitations, if any.

Article III—Officers

Contains the list of officers and their terms of office in the group.

Article IV—Executive Committee

States the make-up of the executive committee (board or council), the method of their selection, and their term of office. Provision for vacancies of officers or other executive members may be included in a section under this article.

Article V—Meetings

States the regular meeting time and provisions for calling special meetings. If meetings cannot be held regularly, indicates authority to call meetings.

Article VI—Amendment

Requires previous notification, also a two-thirds or three-fourths affirmative vote of those present and voting, or of those present for its adoption.

Article VII—Ratification

May or may not be necessary. If more than a majority of those present is desired, a special article should so indicate.

By-Laws

The by-laws may involve the following:

1. Details on membership, such as rights, duties, resignation and expulsion procedures.
2. Provision for initiation fee, dues, and assessments; procedure for deliquencies.

3. Date and method of electing officers and duties of the officers.

4. Duties, authority and responsibilities of an executive committee.

5. Names of the standing committees and the method of choosing chairperson and committee members. Duties of each committee should also be stated.

6. Provision for use of accepted parliamentary manual, i.e., *Robert's Rules of Order, Revised.*

7. Number of members constituting a quorum.

8. Provision for honorary members or honorary officers.

9. Method to amend the by-laws. (Usually a majority vote.) For the sake of group stability, amending the constitution should not be a simple process, while amending the by-laws should be easier. The constitution should state the date of last revision. Insert after an amendment the date it was passed in parentheses.

For clubs that experience a turnover in personnel, change in focus, or expansion in programming, the constitution and by-laws should be reviewed annually to keep them current. Annual review keeps each club aware of its operating code.

Operational Guidelines

Guidelines provided by the board or agency should be as comprehensive as possible. They should not be so complex or strict that clubs are discouraged from organizing. Develop guidelines into a functional manual available to the officers of each club.

Since adherence to manual guidelines is important, review their content, highlighting the most important points, with the officers of each club. This task may be handled with each club individually or in a group. Either way, make personal contact with the officers and emphasize that guidelines exist to encourage the success of the club, not to obstruct enjoyment. Concepts necessary to develop successful club guidelines, consistent with a conservative program philosophy, follow. In this way, the reader can choose what is most applicable for his or her setting.

Procedure For Establishing a Club

Use a step-by-step approach for each prospective group seeking operation as a club. In settings where a legal bond exists between a club and sponsoring agency, require formal application prior to approval. Additional requirements may include:

1. Meeting with the club sport program staff to review requirements and guidelines for operation and application for acceptance. (See Figure 5-1)

2. Developing a club constitution and by-laws for approval.

3. Submitting an officers' list and membership roster. (See Figure 5-2, Figure 5-3)

4. Submitting a facility reservation request. (Sometimes unavailability of facility space prohibits a club from functioning.)

5. Obtaining a formal statement indicating approval or disapproval for club status. This step may also require the endorsement of an administrative unit within the setting or agency before final status can be determined. After reaching a decision to approve or disapprove the request, send a letter indicating the result to the club's leadership.

6. Meeting with the club sport program staff to review club status and discuss club responsibilities.

Once a club receives approval to function within the setting, it may encounter difficulties that jeopardize its ability to remain active. Consequently, operational guidelines should explain the conditions under which a club may be placed on an "inactive" list as well as how it may be re-activated. For example, there may be times when a club may not function due to disciplinary action. This situation may involve a specific penalty—a temporary loss of facility use, a fine, or a temporary hold on spending and club operations.

Other situations which may result in inactive status are loss of interest and inability to sustain operations. If this happens, plan to secure any left-over funds. In the event that the club remains inactive for an indefinite period of time, establish a date when the money is moved into a general fund for club sports programming. If the club is able to regenerate, the funds are customarily returned to the club for use by its membership.

Eligibility

The primary responsibility for determining membership and officer eligibility rests with the club. There may be situations where system wide eligibility statements are necessary in order to maintain the philosophy and purpose of the total club

---

CLUB SPORT STATUS APPLICATION

Date _____

Name of Club _____   Sport _____

I. **Status Desired:**

New Club _____   Approved _____

Maintain Status _____   Rejected _____

Reactivate _____   Date _____

II. **Purpose(s) of Club:**

_____

_____

_____

III. **Facility Request:**

Location 1st _____   2nd _____

Day(s)   1st _____   2nd _____

Time(s) 1st _____   2nd _____

_____

_____

_____

_____

IV. **Officer's List:** Name   Address   Phone

President _____   _____   _____

Vice-President _____ _____   _____

Secretary _____   _____   _____

Treasurer _____   _____   _____

_____   _____   _____

_____   _____   _____

_____   _____   _____

V. **Constitution and By-Laws:**

Approved _____   Date _____

Rejected _____   Date _____

Staff Signature _____

Figure 5-1. Club sport status application form.

sport program. Eligibility statements may prohibit membership by certain segments of a population or may specify the percentage of membership permissable by that segment. Examples of various settings that may warrant special eligibility statements are:

Military—off-base personnel, officers, non-commissioned officers, enlisted personnel, families.

Community—citizens of the community, age groups, skill levels.

CLUB SPORT OFFICERS' LIST

1. This information is to be completed by the club president and returned to the club sport office by the club's first meeting.

2. Any changes in officers, or addresses and phones must be recorded within one week of the change.

Club _____

Date Officers Elected _____

Date of Term Expiration _____

Date of Next Election _____

Officers	Name	Local Address	Phone
President			
Vice-President			
Secretary			
Treasurer			
Advisors			

Change of Officers

Date	Office	New Officer	Local Address	Phone

I acknowledge that all information is accurate and up-to-date.

_____
President's Signature

Figure 5-2. Club sport officers' list form.

College—non-university affiliates, faculty, staff, students, alumni.

Correctional—staff, visitors, inmates.

Another mandatory eligibility requirement might involve a medical exam and clearance prior to membership. All eligibility requirements should be available in writing to potential club members. The document must acknowledge a commitment to non-discriminatory membership practices regarding sex, race, religion and age.

CLUB SPORT MEMBERSHIP REPORT

1. This form must be completed, kept up-to-date, and on file in the club sport office by the first meeting of the club. Any additional members must be added before the next scheduled practice or meeting.

Club _____

	Name (Last/First)	S.S. Number	Address	Phone	Acknowledgement Form
1.					
2.					
3.					
4.					
5.					
6.					
7.					
8.					
9.					
10.					
11.					
12.					
13.					
14.					
15.					
16.					
17.					
18.					
19.					
20.					

Figure 5-3. Club sport membership report form.

Affiliation

Establish a standard procedure regarding club sport utilization of the agency's name to identify the club or associate the club with the particular setting. Make an investigation to determine at what point, if any, a legal responsibility exists, and to what extent it is dependent upon offical approval for the club(s) to exist, the formal sponsorship of the club(s), or merely the existence of the club(s) within the setting. This review should take into consideration activities within the home setting (community, campus, military base) as well as those activities engaged in outside of the setting.

If the club and the agency or institution do establish a legal tie, the clubs automatically become subject to the policies, rules and regulations governing the agency or institution. This situation means more control in managing a club program. On the other hand, the stipulations involved may hinder adherence. A large amount of stipulations may discourage clubs from organizing, so apply only those necessary to protect the safety and welfare of participants and eliminate legal problems for the agency or institution.

Meetings

Require monthly business meetings as a mechanism to facilitate communication within each club and keep club officers accountable to the membership. Maintain a copy of club minutes from each meeting as a good way to keep informed about each club. Good records on club functions help decision-making. (See Figure 5-4)

Safety

The safety and well-being of all club members has to be the primary concern of club officers and the club sport program staff or the program will cease to satisfy moral and legal requirements. Mechanisms used to ensure safety differ from program to program depending upon resources, legal requirements and the age groups involved. An examination of the following options may assist the practitioner in selecting those suitable for local conditions.

1. *Medical examinations.* Club sport programs utilizing the conservative approach require medical examina-

tions before participants are eligible to join a club team. The exam may be given by a local community doctor or by physicians employed by the agency. Time spans for up-dating exams vary from program to program.

Once the examination has been performed, a physician should note any limitations in participation on the participant's health record. In some club programs, members must carry a health clearance permit card to show officers prior to participation. Other programs require that this documentation be maintained with the program staff. If a program requires a medical exam, the staff is responsible for preventing participation without the proper clearance.

CLUB MEETING MINUTES

Club _____

Date _____ Location _____

Time Meeting Started _____ Time Meeting Adjourned _____

Number of Members Present _____ Number Absent _____

Report Submitted By _____ Office _____

Items Discussed:

A.

B.

C.

D.

Motions Made and Voted Upon:

A.

B.

Figure 5-4. Club meeting minutes form.

A more liberal approach to medical eligibility places the responsibility for determining health status and participation patterns with the participant. Since participation in club sport programs is voluntary, the individual is expected to understand the risks involved and participate within his or her physiological limitations. In this case, the program staff should inform all prospective members of the policy and record the policy in writing. Additionally, some programs require that participants sign a statement of acknowledgement regarding the policy. When a minor desires club membership, a parent or guardian must sign the form. The use of such a form does not release the staff or agency from liability for negligence.

2. Safety procedures. The best way to control accidents and hazardous conditions is by utilizing facilities and

---

CLUB SPORT MEMBERSHIP
ACKNOWLEDGEMENT OF PARTICIPATION STATEMENT
AND CONSENT FORM

I, _____ , as a current member of the _____ Club, a recognized organization and member of the Club Sport Council at _____ , affirm that I am aware of my physical condition, that I am voluntarily participating as a member of the aforementioned club, that I am aware that such participation may result in possible injury as a result of the nature of the sport, and that I am assuming any risk that may be involved in this sport.

I further acknowledge that I am aware of insurance policies that are available to me through private or institutional means, that I know and understand club and agency/institution policies and procedures, and that I will represent the club and agency/institution in such a manner that is expected. I have read and understand the above statements and will carry them out to my best abilities.

Signature _____ Date _____

Printed Name _____

Address _____

Birthdate _____ Phone _____

If club member is under 18 years old, then his/her parent or guardian must sign below.

Parent/Guardian Signature _____

Printed Name _____

Figure 5-5. Acknowledgement statement form.

equipment properly, providing adequate supervision and leadership, and by requiring proper conditioning. Each club program should develop an action plan for safety designed to prevent and manage problems effectively. The plan requires a regular inspection of facilities and equipment performed by the administrative staff, maintenance personnel, custodial staff, facility supervisor, or a club member designated as safety officer. Cost considerations and storage problems make it unlikely for many programs to provide and care for personal equipment. When club members provide personal equipment there is a greater possibility that they will use less protective and lower quality gear. An officer or appointed member should inspect equipment at each club function.

A staff member may organize and perform the inspection of facilities and equipment through the use of maintenance check lists. Club officers should understand the procedures for reporting problems and initiating requests for repair or replacement. In the event that a hazard remains, make a decision to cancel or postpone the club activity. This usually involves an on-site supervisor, or employee, a club officer, or a specially designated club safety officer. All personnel responsible for scrutinizing safety conditions should participate in a meeting or workshop as a way of training them to better assume their responsibilities.

A safe environment involves safe conduct. Developing safety awareness among club members may be difficult. Work through the officers of the club, or a club safety officer to develop an understanding of the attitudes and behaviors which may lead to accidents. The selection of proper officials and other event personnel who control unsafe conduct is important. Some programs will utilize the club person(s) responsible for inspecting facilities and equipment as the on-site supervisor trained to monitor the activity and handle unsafe conduct. More specific information on safety will be provided in a separate chapter.

Safety involves encouragement of continuous physical conditioning by club members. Few understand the role of conditioning in the reduction of injuries. Since club participation is voluntary, no sure way exists to know in advance whether a club member identifies with the values of conditioning or understands how to implement such a program. Therefore, the club sport staff may take some specific steps to familiarize clubs with the need for conditioning. Implement this idea in such ways as identifying medically-approved literature, announcing or offering presentations, lectures, clinics and workshops on fitness and related topics, designing basic conditioning programs specific to each club sport and informing clubs of fitness and conditioning opportunities provided through other approved sources. If the club staff chooses to sponsor or design conditioning programs, seek approval by qualified medical, exercise physiology, or sports medicine personnel.

Although we may reduce accidents and injuries, we cannot eliminate them. Each safety plan must specify a procedure for managing emergencies. Club officers should

---

CLUB SPORT SAFETY MEMBERS

Club _____

The following people have been designated as individuals responsible for safety of facilities and equipment. It is understood that at least one of these individuals must be present at all club functions.

Name	Phone
_____	_____
_____	_____
_____	_____
_____	_____
_____	_____
_____	_____
_____	_____
_____	_____
_____	_____

Submitted by:

_____
Signature

Office _____

Date _____

Figure 5-6.   Club sport designated safety members form.

understand that when they assume responsibility for handling accidents and injuries, they must know how to contact qualified help. They are also responsible for recording accident information for submission to the club sport staff.

The conservative approach requires that someone with First Aid and CPR training be in attendance at each club practice or event. This individual could be an athletic trainer, a physician, a facility supervisor or a club member. Regardless who assumes the responsibility, a designated person should review procedures to follow in handling the problem at the scene, securing additional help or transportation and documenting the incident on required forms. Written accident procedure should be available to avoid misinterpretation. Other liability safeguards include maintaining a record of each person's First Aid, CPR or W.S.I. certification, obtaining the signature of safety personnel on a statement showing they have agreed to perform the responsibilities of the position, and denying club access to facilities (when possible to do so) until emergency aid personnel have been identified.

CERTIFIED CLUB MEMBERS
IN EMERGENCY FIRST AID TREATMENT

Below are listed club members who have current certification in the indicated column. It is understood that at least one of these members will be present at all club functions. Copies of certification cards will be on file in the club sport office.

Name	CPR	First Aid	WSI	Other (Specify)
____	___	___	___	_____
____	___	___	___	_____
____	___	___	___	_____
____	___	___	___	_____
____	___	___	___	_____
____	___	___	___	_____
____	___	___	___	_____

Submitted by:

_____
Signature

Office _____

Date _____

Figure 5-7. Certified club members' form.

Facilities

Most recreation settings strain to meet the demand for access to facilities by clubs that lack their own resources. Facilities in most settings receive multiple use by many programs. For example, facilities may be shared by athletics and physical education at collegiate settings. Within a community setting, instruction programs, social programs, cultural programs and public school programs may share a single facility. Within the military setting, instruction programs and physical fitness and training programs use common space. Facilities within the correctional and industrial setting may house instructional programs, social programs, and cultural programs. The need to make maximum use of facilities has resulted in the use of standardized scheduling procedures. Information about facility reservations policy should include how, when and where to reserve the facility, the amount of user fees (if any), eligibility requirements, and rules governing proper use of the facilities.

Clubs should be aware of any scheduling policies which reflect priorities for facility utilization by all programs within the setting. Furthermore, a policy statement should establish a maximum amount of time a club may request for regular practices. This helps to distribute facility availability equitably and reduce any suspicion that preferential treatment exists. Factors to consider when developing this particular policy include: the number of club members, the type of facility and present demand for its use, the number of clubs seeking access to the facility, and the nature of the sport and the minimum amount of time needed to conduct a practice. Base adjustments in the amount of time allocated a club upon growth in membership or the availability of equipment.

When a club wants to conduct an event other than a regular practice, a separate facility reservation request is necessary. Establish a deadline for submitting any kind of reservation request—perhaps two weeks to one month in advance of the desired time. This allows the programmer an opportunity to coordinate maximum use of facilities and to avoid scheduling conflicts. It also provides an opportunity to counsel club officers on proper use of the facilities, responsibilities for supervision of the facility, and procedures for reporting accidents or maintenance problems. After the counseling session, a club officer may sign a statement accepting the conditions for facility use.

Once the club officers fully accept their role in protecting facilities, their membership may take pride in caring for the facility and contribute to anticipating and identifying maintenance problems.

EQUIPMENT

Club members either provide their own equipment, utilize what is available through the agency or institution, or purchase it through the club. Equipment-related areas of concern to program staff are purchasing, care and storage, and inventory and maintenance procedures. Equipment neglect results in waste, theft, loss, and other abuse.

Equipment purchased with club funds is considered as agency equipment reserved for club use. In this way, equipment is continually protected until it is no longer serviceable. Another safeguard that protects equipment and provides the best value for the money is channeling purchase requests through the staff for review and processing. This approach involves a staff decision regarding the appropriateness of the request. Whenever possible, identify three potential vendors to compare quality and cost. After selecting and ordering equipment, maintain a copy of the request to double check the order once it has arrived. Upon delivery have the equipment marked, coded, or engraved, inventoried and checked out to the club. This keeps staff current about club needs and equipment costs, provides an opportunity to develop positive business relationships with vendors and facilitates discussion regarding proper care and storage for equipment.

An up-to-date equipment inventory is a useful tool to foster accountability for the care and protection of equipment as well as to familiarize new officers or staff about club resources. The club should conduct an inventory once or twice a year. The validity of the inventory will be in question unless done in the presence of a staff person. An inventory documents the amount and types of equipment, purchase date and present condition. Such information is useful when considering additional purchase requests and evaluating merchandise quality.

Maximum use of equipment is furthered by proper care and storage. If the staff cannot handle this function, the responsibility rests with the club. The staff may retain some influence on proper equipment care by withholding funds, imposing fines, denying purchase requests or restricting facility use when a club demonstrates improper handling and protection of its equipment.

If the club needs equipment storage space, keep a record of its location and the person(s) responsible for its security. Obtain a signed statement from any individual accepting this responsibility. Finally, an equipment checkout system within the club itself may help reduce damage, theft or loss. This places financial responsibility on the user. A checkout system may be appropriate when equipment is used in different programs and is dispensed from a central location, or when the club issues equipment to its members for the year.

Although procedures regarding club equipment may be time-consuming, application of systems to protect and extend the lifespan of equipment is economically sound.

Insurance

Agencies often carry blanket insurance coverage for club sport participation, including those events conducted outside the particular setting. Other insurance practices include: requiring club members to have personal coverage, requiring each club to arrange for group coverage, or encouraging clubs and members to carry voluntary coverage. Once clubs or members are obliged to provide their own coverage, a system of verification is necessary. If clubs need not carry personal or group coverage, each member must sign a consent statement releasing the agency institution from responsibility for personal injury sustained while participating in a club function. When minors are involved, a parent or guardian must sign the statement. Such approaches place direct responsibility for obtaining health and accident coverage upon the individual.

Insurance should be taken seriously in the interest of proper coverage and protection from liability. Examine carefully present and possible alternatives to determine adequate and comprehensive coverage.

Travel

Clubs that receive funding from a board, agency, or institution have their travel interests and activities governed by specific policies addressing approval, funding or use of vehicles. The most common requirements utilized for club travel under a conservative approach include:

—an application for approval of travel
—a supervisor accompanying the club
—a roster of persons traveling on behalf of the club
—presence of personnel certified in First Aid and CPR
—use of vehicles carrying adequate liability insurance

Ideally, club transportation should involve commercially bonded vehicles or vehicles owned and insured by the agency. Clubs may use privately-owned vehicles. Some club programs permit use of money provided by the agency to cover funding for travel while others prohibit this practice due to liability concerns and the increased management load necessary to monitor club travel.

CLUB SPORT TRAVEL REQUEST

Date of Trip _____ Destination _____

Duration of Trip _____ Day _____ Overnight _____

Approximate Time Returning _____

Overnight Residence:

    Motel _____ Phone _____

    Hotel _____ Phone _____

    Campus/College _____ Phone _____

    Other _____ Phone _____

Drivers _____ _____

_____ _____

Owner(s) of Vehicle(s) _____ _____

_____

Vehicle(s) Registration _____ _____

_____

Company Insuring Vehicles _____

_____

Number of People Traveling _____ (Attach List of Names)

Purpose of Trip _____

_____

Emergency Numbers Where You Can Be Reached _____

Name _____ Date _____

Office _____

    Approve _____ Reject _____

Figure 5-8. Club sport travel request form.

Whenever possible, encourage clubs to limit travel to reasonably close geographic areas to reduce expenses and accident potential due to fatigue. Restrictions on distance and number of trips may limit access to vehicles owned by the agency. This stipulation typically occurs when the demand for travel exceeds the supply of vehicles, or the volume of requests hinders proper management.

SCHEDULES AND AGREEMENTS

Clubs organized to participate in leagues or tournaments seek and schedule regular opportunities for participation. Oppor-

---

REQUEST FOR MOTOR VEHICLES

Name of Organization _____ Account No. _____

Number of Vehicles Wanted _____ Types _____

Purpose of Trip _____

_____

_____

Destination _____

Equipment to be Carried _____

Date and Time Wanted _____

Date and Time to be Returned _____

Name of Driver _____

Driver's License No. and State of Issue _____

Address _____ Phone _____

Name of Driver _____

Driver's License No. and State of Issue _____

Address _____ Phone _____

Name of Driver _____

Driver's License No. and State of Issue _____

Address _____ Phone _____

List All Passengers _____

_____

_____

APPROVAL:

_____   _____
Director, Motor Vehicles   Club Sport Staff

_____   _____
Account Manager   Director, Recreational Sports

Complete in Quadruplicate.

Figure 5-9. Request for motor vehicle form.

tunities to schedule activity with other clubs or teams is influenced by facility availability, proximity, finances, skill level, conference regulations, and travel regulations. Scheduling input from program staff may occur when restrictions have to be imposed upon the number of home or away events. Restrictions may arise due to such limited resources as facility space and finances or an inability of clubs to manage their schedule. The staff may need to set an early timetable for finalizing scheduling plans for the current or upcoming year. The club and staff need time to prepare for events and utilize whatever means are available for promoting them. Often a club has such strong spectator appeal that a printed copy of its schedule is desirable.

When interested in a scheduling commitment for an event with other clubs, each participating club should sign a written agreement. The agreement specifies all of the conditions that each club is expected to fulfill and the particulars of the event such as purpose, day, date, time and location. A sample agreement is shown in Figure 5-10.

Before clubs choose to use written agreements, they should examine various aspects of legal liability. For example, under what conditions might the agency be responsible if a club does not fulfill its obligations? Under what conditions might the agency be held responsible for injuries that occur to representatives of visiting clubs? Must administrative or program staff people sign the contract or is a club officer sufficient?

In settings where the agency closely supervises all club activity, the agreements are designed and approved by the staff. Club officers may participate in a required review session with the program staff to ensure that the event has adequate planning and includes the appropriate safety precautions. Upon its conclusion, the club should submit an evaluation form describing the outcome of the event, identifying problems or accidents, making recommendations for improvements, and including a financial statement.

Another written agreement is utilized for securing qualified personnel to officiate or supervise the particular club event. The primary responsibility for obtaining personnel rests with the club. The program staff may make referrals or assume responsibility for this task. Any agreement should include the particulars about the event as well as the rate of pay and method of payment. An additional clause should indicate what

will happen should someone not fulfill specified obligations. A
sample agreement form is presented in Figure 5-11.

Morale is damaged when effort is put into hosting or
traveling to an event only to find that another club has not

CLUB SPORT CONTEST AGREEMENT

THIS AGREEMENT, made and entered into this _____ day of _____ 19 ____ ,
by and between the undersigned authorized representative of the _____
and the undersigned authorized representative of _____
stipulates:

FIRST: That the teams representing the above named organizations or
institutions agree to meet in _____ at:

_____ , _____
        Location of Contest   City and State

on _____ 19 ____ , at _____ o'clock ___ M., and at

_____ , _____
        Location of Contest   City and State

on _____ 19 ____ , at _____ o'clock ___ M.

SECOND: That the consideration binding the two teams to play the above
contest(s) shall be the appearance of each visiting team at the site of each home team
in the aforesaid contest; or, as indicated in paragraph NINTH, if applicable.

THIRD: That the contests shall be played under _____ rules.

FOURTH: That the Officials are to be mutually agreed upon.

FIFTH: That expenses of Officials are to be borne by the home team.

SIXTH: That the home management reserves the right to cancel the contest on
account of inclement weather or other unavoidable cause, two hours before the visiting
team leaves from its residence or the place of the previous game, notice of which time
had been given at least three days before.

SEVENTH: That in case a contest is canceled after the arrival of the visiting team
on account of inclement weather or other unavoidable cause, the home team shall pay
the visiting team _____ dollars.

EIGHTH: The day, time and location of any of the above contests shall not be
changed without the written consent of the authorized representative of the visiting team.

NINTH: _____

_____

_____

_____

IN WITNESS WHEREOF, we have affixed our signatures the day and year first above
written.

FOR: _____   FOR: _____

BY: _____   BY: _____
        Authorized Representative   Authorized Representative

Return one copy of completed contract to:

Figure 5-10. Club sport contest agreement form.

upheld its end of the arrangement. Written agreements may be helpful to formalize responsibilities and serve as a more binding commitment than a verbal agreement. There still is no guarantee that the event will happen as planned. Avoiding disappointment and problems which result from failure to

---

STATEMENT OF AGREEMENT FOR SPORT OFFICIAL

_____ of _____ Club
President

and _____ , hereby enter into the following assignment
Official

and terms for officiating:

   1. Said official agrees to be present and officiate _____ contest(s) of _____
sport

to be played at _____

on the dates listed during the year 19 _____ - 19 _____ .

Date	Day of Week	Time	Clubs Playing	Total Payment

   2. That in case of failure on the part of either one of the parties to fulfill the terms of this agreement, except by mutual consent, a forfeiture of twenty-five dollars ($25.00) shall be paid by the offending party to the other party within five days after the date set for each game in this statement. It is understood that there is a moral obligation to be considered in the making and breaking of agreements. Where obligations are not mutually adjusted, _____ reserves the right to review the facts and determine what these adjustments should be.

   3. This agreement is void if not returned on or before _____ .

FOR CLUB	FOR CONTEST OFFICIAL
Signature of President	Signature
Club	Address
Address	Social Security Number
Date	Date
Telephone	Telephone

Name/s of other official/s employed to work this contest (if available).

Figure 5-11. Club sport official agreement form.

meet obligations requires realistic planning and an ability to anticipate difficulties. No agreement is valid unless the club demonstrates an ability to fulfill its obligations and has an approved plan for meeting them.

Instruction and Coaching

Some degree of coaching and instruction occurs within any club context. When a club desires reliable, qualified and consistent leadership, they may appoint or hire an instructor or coach. Program staff may assist clubs in the selection process. Types of assistance may include: holding a discussion on selection and hiring, reviewing job descriptions, approving job descriptions, reviewing contracts, designing and approving contracts, handling or monitoring the payroll, approving use of club funds for employment of personnel, or serving as a resource for dealing with club personnel. When providing assistance, consider the following: maintaining a commitment to non-discriminatory employment practices, understanding whether the agency might be held liable for injuries sustained by club members performing activities designed by an approved or employed instructor or coach, and understanding what consequences exist if a written agreement is violated by any of the parties involved.

Regardless of the degree of staff involvement in approving or hiring personnel, the clubs should perform certain tasks, including developing appropriate job descriptions, receiving membership approval for use of funds, protecting funds allocated for employment purposes, using a reliable procedure for handling payroll, conducting an appropriate selection process and utilizing some form of documentation or agreement to specify the conditions of appointment or employment. Since most club members desire to learn more about their particular sport, or at least receive some leadership and direction while they participate, the selection and supervision of instructors or coaches is a most important process. Consequently, the program staff should be ready to assist clubs deal properly with personnel management.

Promotion and Publicity

When clubs fall under the supervision and jurisdiction of an agency, their public image reflects upon that of the agency.

Therefore, guidelines and stipulations for club public relations and publicity campaigns reflect a common desire for a positive image.

When the club bears full responsibility for the development and implementation of promotion and publicity, club sport staff should review ideas and rough draft material in advance to spot problems and assess the appropriateness of ideas. Require that plans and materials gain advance approval to allow time for revisions.

If the club sport program provides resources or personnel to assist in promotion, inform clubs on how to take advantage of opportunities and coordinate deadlines for approving and implementing requests. In order to organize requests and eliminate mistakes in information or design, the club should submit its requests in writing and then review them with the appropriate personnel. An advantage in managing club promotional efforts is the opportunity to directly influence the quality of the projects. A disadvantage occurs when promotional requests are submitted late or are unrealistic in terms of time, volume or cost.

Another aspect of promotion involves how materials are distributed or posted within the setting. Materials are often needlessly wasted, and the environment unnecessarily cluttered with notices hastily and unattractively posted resulting in negative image of the club, agency or institution.

Finance

A basic characteristic of club sport is financial self-support. Historically, clubs have sustained their own activities through dues, donations and fund-raising projects. Recently, clubs in some settings, particularly education, have received financial assistance from the agency within which they are administered. The amount of assistance provided to clubs depends on the budget and agency philosophy. Although such financial support may be useful, a greater dependence upon and accountability to the agency often results.

The process of identifying the financial needs of the club begins with a discussion about proposed activities. Strategies are established for securing the finances to cover club needs. Common sources include membership dues and fines, donations, fund-raising projects, and grants from an agency or institution. When seeking sources of income, the club may have to follow certain procedures to avoid violating laws or the regulations and policies of the setting. For example, clubs interested in soliciting donations through a street or a door-to-door canvass should check city or state codes to be sure the approach is legal. The primary functions of the club sport staff in the area of club funding are to identify acceptable funding approaches, inform club officers of policies and procedures governing fund-raising and establish a system to review and approve their ideas for securing income.

FUND-RAISING PROJECT APPLICATION

_____
                        Date Submitted

NOTE: Please complete in duplicate and return to the Club Sport Office. Depending upon the event additional information may be required.

Club _____

Project Chairperson _____

Local Address _____ Phone _____

Project Description _____

_____

Date(s) of Project _____ Location(s) _____

Time(s) _____ Income Source(s) _____

Total anticipated income from project $ _____

Expense Items _____

Total anticipated expenses from project $ _____

Total anticipated profit from project $ _____

Use of Proceeds _____

_____

Will the project be an annual event? _____

Does the organization have a local bank account?   Yes _____   No _____

The undersigned in connection with and as a part of the above application for a fund-raising project certifies that he or she is a club member and that the information listed is correct to the best of his or her knowledge and belief.

                        Signature _____

Comments _____

_____

Approved by _____

Date Approved _____

Figure 5-12.   Fund raising project application form.

FUND-RAISING PROJECT SUMMARY

To be submitted to the Club Sport Office within one week following the fund-raising project.

Project _____

Sponsored by _____

Date of project _____

Location(s) _____

Total income received $ _____

Expenses listed by major items:

_____

_____

_____

Total Expenses $ _____

Profit   _____

Use of proceeds _____

_____

Signature _____

Date _____

Figure 5-13. Fund raising project summary form.

A helpful tool for clubs to project expenditures and income is a budget proposal. A budget proposal requires careful planning and organization. It serves as a working blueprint for the club and a mechanism for holding officers accountable for financial transactions.

It is customary for the club officers, or a treasurer, to prepare a budget proposal for adoption by the membership. This proposal should include itemized expenditures and projected sources of income. The categories used to classify this information include the following:

Expenses:

1. Equipment—club equipment (not personally owned).

2. Supplies and expenses—telephone, stamps, paper, posters, trophies.

3. Hourly wages—payment for trainers, coaches, instructors, ticket takers.

4. Travel—gas, food, lodging.

CLUB BUDGET

ITEM	Actual Total 1982-83 cost/per x number Total	Projected Total 1983-84 cost/per x number Total
INCOME		
Allocated money		
Membership dues		
Donations		
Movie ticket sales		
Benefit game		
Total Income		
EXPENDITURES		
Hourly, Wage		
coach		
officials		
trainer		
Equipment		
balls		
sticks		
helmets		
knee pads		
nets		
Supplies and Expenses		
utilities		
facility rental		
stamps		
phone		
duplicating		
stationery		
trophies		
newspaper ads		
recognition banquet		
insurance		
laundry		
bank charges		
Travel		
gas		
food		
lodging		
bus. trip		
vehicle insurance		
Total Expenses		
Total Income		
-Total Expenses		
Balance		

Figure 5-14. Sample—club budget.

Income:

1. Membership dues.

2. Donations.

3. Fund-raising projects.

4. Grants.

We provide a sample budget in Figure 5-14 as a frame of reference. This particular format furnishes space to indicate the actual club expenses and income for the current year as a means of comparison with the budget proposal for the following year.

Before finalizing the budget proposal, the club should make sure it has identified reliable and acceptable sources of income and has made accurate estimates for projected expenditures. The club officers should be knowledgeable about policies regarding budget preparation, particularly if the club is eligible for grants from an agency or institution.

To date, recreational sports literature lacks a detailed explanation for setting up a grant allocation process. The rationale for club grants is based on a desire to support and perpetuate clubs as a vehicle for recreational sport participation. Financial support may provide a positive form of administrative control since clubs tend to abide with certain standards in order to maintain access to funding.

To assure that all clubs receive equitable treatment in the allocation of funds, uniform requirements regarding funding requests should be made available to all clubs. Additionally, the programmer should explain the criteria upon which allocation decisions are made to the clubs well in advance of the allocation process. Knowledge of the criteria aids in the preparation and organization of proposals and facilitates decision-making about the allocation request.

Allocations should be made by a committee of six to twelve objective people familiar with the club sport program yet not directly involved with any club seeking an allocation. The committee may be appointed by the club sport staff and approved by a Club Sport Council, or selected by a club council of representatives. The first option may be more desirable, since a professional staff member should not be biased in any way. The staff for club sport should not determine allocations.

This situation often invites conflict if a club is dissatisfied with its allocation. It is preferable for the staff to serve as a resource to help clubs prepare an appropriate budget and make a good presentation before the committee.

When seeking a grant, a club should prepare a budget. It is helpful to use a standard budget format and to respect the deadline for submitting budget proposals. The staff may hold a special meeting on budget preparation and make appointments to meet with clubs on an individual basis. Such preparation reduces the amount of time needed to make decisions and interpret budgets at the allocation committee meeting. Next, provide a way for members of the committee to review the proposals. Make copies of each budget for distribution to each member or establish a rotation system to review the originals. If committee members have questions about a club proposal or require further information, resolve these problems prior to the actual presentation. Hold a special training session for the committee members to resolve questions about the budgets and their duties. After the deadline for budget review has passed, schedule a time (date, time place) so that each club requesting funds may present a brief oral proposal (10–20 minutes) to the assembled committee and may respond to any questions. Prior to each presentation, a staff member or the Executive Officer of the Club Sport Council should indicate how well the club has met its responsibilities for the year. During the club's budget presentation, each committee member evaluates the club's justified needs in light of all criteria. The criteria utilized for determining a club's justifiable needs may be divided into: 1) the explanation and justification of budgets; 2) the nature of expenses; and 3) the performance of a club's duties to the agency, institution or Club Sport Council. Specific examples of the criteria follow, as if they were written for the club and allocation committee, to help clarify this aspect of the allocation process. Keep in mind that criteria are developed so that the process of budget preparation and review will be more objective and standardized.

Budget Preparation:

—Each club should include statements for the previous and current year, as well as a proposed budget for the coming year.

—Budgets should summarize club expenses vs. its revenues, indicating a balance. (Specify categories for expenses and revenue items at this point.)

—Estimate proposed needs as accurately as possible, based on a club's plans, justifiable expenses, and revenues. Do not underestimate or exaggerate requests.

Explanation and justification of budgets:

a. Hourly Wage
   —A club incurring expenses for instructors, coaches, officials, or trainers should give a detailed explanation (for example: rate, hours, days, number of people needed).

b. Equipment
   —Provide support only for equipment purchased for permanent club use and used only for club activities. This includes individual equipment (for example: uniforms) necessary for club activities that the individual member is not expected to provide.
   —Itemize and consider expenses in relation to the club's current equipment and its necessary maintenance or replacement.

c. Supplies and Expenses
   —A club incurring expenses for facility use should give a detailed breakdown (for example: rate, hours, days, utilities.)
   —Discourage the use of a miscellaneous category unless the club can provide an itemized breakdown.

d. Travel
   —Travel is defined as moving to a location outside the agency setting for the purpose of participation. A club should justify its travel, for instance, to obtain additional competition at its own level of ability or to further opportunities for training or instruction.
   —Clubs should attempt to combine matches in one geographical area to a single trip.
   —Give support only for the minimum number of players needed to participate. All expenses (food, gas, lodging) need explanation.

Performance of club duties:

The remaining examples provide a perspective of the allocation committee's considerations concerning factors less tangible than financial need. In general, such criteria reflect a club's dedication to its own stated goals, and those of the agency, institution or council. Since dedication and performance are difficult to define, the related examples of criteria receive broad treatment.

—No allocation will be made to any club which has not met its financial responsibilities (payment of dues and fines, if any).

—No allocation will be made to any club whose file is not complete. A complete file includes:

1) Constitution or operating guidelines.

2) Budget request and annual report.

3) General information sheet and membership roster.

4) List of officers.

5) Minutes from business meetings.

6) Consent forms.

7) Equipment inventory.

—The committee will consider whether a club has met such other responsibilities as attending meetings, keeping files up-to-date, and fulfilling obligations to committees. These constitute minimal standards required of all clubs, and failure to comply subjects them to a reduction of their allocation. The committee should note instances in which the club council, agency or institution may have established fines against a club's *current* allocation if responsibilities have not been met. Nevertheless, certain actions or gross neglect of responsibilities may also warrant decreasing allocations for the following year.

—Pay specific attention to a requirement that each club sponsor one special event per year. Failure to meet this requirement may reduce a club's allocation, while performance of this service beyond the required level may increase it.

A club's allocation often falls short of its needs. Encourage clubs to hold fund-raising activities since they will neither help nor hinder a club in terms of its allocation for a subsequent year. Some fund-raising activities may be regarded as an integral part of a club's purpose and function, and should be considered when making allocations. Accordingly, criteria governing fund-raising may be necessary. Several examples of statements used in the allocation process follow:

Fund-raising:

—A club should not include in their request fund-raising revenue or activities that are unrelated to the club's sport, or those activities that are not needed by the sports community (for instance, activities for which the club is not the only source.)

—A club should include fund-raising activities undertaken in the previous year or current year, and activities related to the club's sport and needed by the sports community (for example, a martial arts club serving as the only source for martial art uniform sales or the vollyball club serving as the only source of officials for the community intramural tournament).

In regard to the committee's evaluation of justified need, it should deduct a club's expected income via fund-raising from budgeted expenditures. However, the committee should not consider past fund-raising activities as a credit or deduction to the club's allocation.

Finally, criteria should indicate when a newly formed club is first eligible to request an allocation. One approach requires a club to be operational and "in good standing" for a year before seeking an allocation. In this way, the committee has a better opportunity to determine whether the club is well-organized, stable and responsible.

Once the committee makes a decision of justified need, it may determine each club's allocation through the following formula:

$$\text{Allocation to club A} = \frac{\text{Total allocated funds for } clubs}{\text{Total justified needs of all clubs}} \times \text{Justified need of club A}$$

Guidelines should explain how the club gains access to its allocated funds. The money may be provided as a direct payment to the club or retained in an account directly supervised by the club sport staff. A more conservative approach is usually selected when there are certain restrictions on how the money can be spent, when measures are needed to ensure that the money is being well spent, and when documentation of club financial transactions is necessary. When a club wants access to its money, it makes a written request to the club sport staff providing justification of need, potential vendors, and cost estimates. This information facilitates the decision-making process and saves time. The use of a request form assists in the bookkeeping and accounting process.

REQUEST FOR FUNDS
(Equipment, Hourly Wage, Others)

Club _____   Date of Request _____

Amount Requested _____   Date Needed _____

Funds Will Be Used For _____

_____

Justification Of Need _____

_____

Suggested Vendor(s)

1. _____
2. _____
3. _____

Specific Information (Size, quantity, color, etc.)

_____

_____

Projected Cost Per Item _____

_____

_____

Submitted By _____ , Treasurer

Amount Approved _____ Remaining Balance _____

Comments _____

_____

_____

Staff Signature _____ Date _____

Figure 5-15. Request for funds form.

Regardless of the mechanisms available to raise income, or the procedures required for fund-raising or making expenditures, the staff should make every attempt to eliminate opportunities for mishandling club funds. Such problems greatly damage the credibility of the club sport concept and often form the grounds for serious legal or disciplinary action.

Conduct and governance

Standards of conduct within the club sport program promote safety, social interaction, positive public relations and accountability. The type of expectations imposed upon clubs vary depending upon the program approach taken (conservative or liberal). It is unrealistic to assume that problems of conduct, alleged or proven, do not exist within club sport operations. Procedures must afford club members or the club as a whole a fair and objective review. Specific statements addressing behavior and duties expected of club members and officers should be part of each club's constitution. Penalties for violation of a code of conduct are often handled as an internal matter. When the actions of a club or some of the club members violate the policies, rules, or regulations of the agency, investigation and intervention may be warranted.

There are three reasons for delineation of club and staff responsibility for disciplinary action. First, a concept basic to club sport is self-governance. Staff intervention into club business weakens this principle and results in club dependency on the staff. Second, once the staff makes a ruling it should be a sanction affecting the club as a whole, not individual members. A club is expected to deal with internal problems and the staff will hold the club accountable for this responsibility. This requirement also places responsibility with the total membership for fulfilling club obligations. Finally, the staff should not manage internal club problems before the officers have had a chance to deal with them. Premature intervention hinders the ability of the staff to hear an appeal objectively.

Situations that may require disciplinary action, whether imposed by the club or staff, include:

1. Verbal or physical abuse by club members or club representatives.

2. Damage to equipment or facilities.

3. Mishandling of funds.

4. Violations of club, agency or institution policies, procedures, rules and regulations.

Disciplinary action requires a commitment to fair treatment, a predetermined set of guidelines and an informed club system which recognizes its responsibilities and the consequences of failing to meet them. There are a number of models to choose from when setting up disciplinary procedures. One such model involves an initial investigation and ruling by the staff, allowing an appeal to a hearing board comprised of a body of club sport representatives. This board or council comprises of five to ten people selected from a pool of club representatives trained to serve on an appeals committee. Suggested guidelines for implementing this model follow. They are an effort to demonstrate how such a process works. A more detailed discussion on governance appears in the material on Program Control.

Club Sport Disciplinary Guidelines

Grounds for Disciplinary Action: Complaints may be considered against a club for any action in violation of policies and regulations concerning club sports (whether committed by the club, club representatives, or individual members involved in a club function). Proven violations become grounds for penalties that may be assessed against the club. Once a complaint has been referred to the club sport staff for an investigation and ruling, the club should be notified of the complaint, preferably in writing.

Staff Investigation and Ruling: When a complaint is referred to the club sport staff, written statements should be obtained from the plaintiff, accused club, witnesses and any other appropriate parties. In addition, verbal conferences should be conducted with the plaintiff, accused club(s), witnesses, other appropriate parties, and the executive committee. Upon completion of an investigation, the Club Sport Staff should make a ruling based on the evidence uncovered during the investigation. Finally, the staff should notify the club of the ruling in writing.

Appeal Procedure: If the club wishes to appeal the staff decision it may do so through written notification either to the staff, or to the Club Sport Council President (where applicable). The case may then be referred to a Club Sport Hearing Board. This board consists of five to seven club representatives unrelated to any of the clubs involved. The Council President customarily appoints these representatives at the beginning of the year, one of whom acts as a secretary. Next, the Club Sport Staff or Council President, arranges a time and place for the hearing that is mutually convenient for all parties involved.

The Hearing: At least three (3) Board members, including the chairperson and secretary, should be present throughout the entire hearing, and only these members may vote after the Board's deliberation. The Hearing Board secretary should keep a record of the hearing, including a list of those present and the substance of all evidence and arguments. If possible, make a tape recording to avoid error. Suggested guidelines for the hearing follow:

a) The chairperson states the purpose of the hearing.
b) Opening statements proceed, first by a representative of the plaintiff, then by a representative of the accused club.
c) The respective parties may then present additional evidence of any sort, subject to questions by those present.
d) The parties may make final statements.
e) The Board may conclude with questions to any party.

Once the Hearing Board begins its deliberation in private, no record need be kept. Upon conclusion of the deliberation, the chairperson may entertain motions to increase or decrease penalties against the club, to sustain the Club Sport Staff's rulings, or to exonerate the club. The decision should have the support of at least three (3) of the members to lend legitimacy to the ruling. Within one (1) week of the hearing, the decision, together with a rationale, should be presented in writing to the Club Sport Staff, to be forwarded to the club. The club may obtain a transcript of the hearing record, bearing the cost of its provision.

Penalties: Penalties imposed on a club should have administrative approval. Examples of penalties include fines, temporary loss of funding or facility privileges, suspension from specified facilities, probation for a specified period under certain conditions, or recommendation for continued review.

Enforcement: A staff person commonly has responsibility for enforcing disciplinary rulings. In some instances, an administrator has the prerogative to overrule a decision, if it can be shown that due process was violated or significant new evidence has arisen that could alter the decision. A "veto" power is a positive tool because it may motivate the staff and hearing board to be more thorough and conscientious in their deliberations. If an administrator intervenes unnecessarily or frequently, the hearing board procedure becomes suspect.

These guidelines are models. When followed, they should result in a fair and appropriate decisions. Unless the staff is genuinely committed to due process, the best of models may be turned into a mockery of justice. Take disciplinary measures when necessary to improve the club system, not to demonstrate power and authority. If the clubs view the process as fair and just, they will participate in resolving problems in the same fashion.

Annual report

Each club ought to complete an annual report for historical reference and for planning its future goals and objectives. From an administrative perspective, annual reports may also serve to update staff about club activities, identify participation trends, specify problems faced by clubs and solicit ideas on improving services to clubs. An annual report form, developed for use by each club, assures that proper information is obtained. Establish deadlines for receiving the completed reports prior to election of officers and allocation funds. In this way, current officers are responsible for documenting the information that will assist new officers. Finally, an annual report provides additional insight into a club's performance when considering the criteria for allocating funds.

(See Annual Report forms in Appendix A of this section.)

Program assistance

The final subject covered in the club sport operational guidelines should explain the types of assistance each club may receive and how to use this support. Assistance may include partial or complete provision for mail, telephone, typing, storage, duplicating and office space services. These services not only contribute to the effectiveness and success of club operations, but also facilitate interaction and the development of rapport among staff and club members.

CONCLUSION

Club sport programming is a challenging, yet rewarding function. The challenges involve promoting diversity in sport interests and purposes, securing resources for funding, facilities and personnel and maintaining appropriate operational guidelines. It is gratifying when a quality club program results from the combined efforts of members, officers and staff. It is also rewarding to observe participants gain experience in decision-making, time management, leadership and social skills, finding satisfaction in their involvement.

Club sport in America will continue to be influenced by the state of the economy. In times of financial stress, clubs may experience cutbacks in activity. Sport programs that depend upon an agency for financial support and staff direction, such as intramural, extramural and athletic sports, may be sharply reduced or even terminated. It is possible that maintenance of club sport programs may require the pooling of resources from members and commercial or corporate sponsors.

Clearly, the recreational sport programmer is in a position to influence decisions regarding strategies for perpetuating the club sport concept. Although the challenges may be difficult, the programmer must recognize that clubs represent a distinctive avenue for sport participation, worthy of support.

REFERENCES-CLUB SPORTS

Hyatt, R. W. *Intramural Sports Organization and Administration*. St. Louis: C. V. Mosby Co., 1977.

Mueller, P. and Reznik, J. W. *Intramural-Recreational Sports: Programming and Administration*. New York: John Wiley and Sons, 1979.

Peterson, J. A. (ed.) *Intramural Administration Theory and Practice*. Englewood Cliffs, N.J.: Prentice Hall, Inc., 1976.

APPENDIX 5A

CLUB
SPORT
ANNUAL
REPORT

ANNUAL REPORT

Club _____

Club Officers	Fall	Spring	Fall (if elected)
President	_____	_____	_____
Vice-President	_____	_____	_____
Secretary	_____	_____	_____
Treasurer	_____	_____	_____
Advisor	_____	_____	_____
Coach	_____	_____	_____
Council Representative	_____	_____	_____
Instructor	_____	_____	_____

What is the total club membership? _____ Men _____ Women _____

How much is club dues per person? _____ year or semester?

What was this year's total budget? _____

What is next year's projected budget? _____

Are you seeking money from the council? _____ How much? _____

What facilities did the club use on a regular or part-time basis?

_____

When were practice times? _____

_____

When and where did the club meet other than for practice or games (i.e., business meeting).

_____

How many competitive events were held against other clubs? List matches and results (away and home competition).

_____   _____

_____   _____

Where did the club travel to? _____

_____

What was the average personal expenditure for each club member not paid by the club?

Travel _____

Equipment _____

Entry fees in meets _____

Appendix 5-A.   Annual report form.

Who can someone interested in joining the club contact? Name and number if possible.

_____

List any noteworthy accomplishments or awards received by the club.

_____

Write a paragraph explaining club activities. (200 words maximum.)

_____
_____
_____
_____
_____
_____
_____
_____
_____

Briefly summarize the club's activities this past year. Include club's short and long-range goals.

_____
_____
_____

Briefly state the club's goals and objectives for the coming year.

_____
_____
_____

List recommendations for improving club internal operations.

_____
_____
_____

List recommendations for improving assistance to the club by the club sport staff.

_____
_____
_____

Report submitted by _____

Position _____

Date _____

CHAPTER 6

PROGRAM PERSONNEL

The number of people involved in the provision of recreational services is staggering. Over five million full or part-time positions exist for recreational services, the manufacture, distribution, sales, and repair of recreational goods, and the construction of recreational facilities. While no data exists to describe the number of recreational sport programs requiring personnel supervision, Chubb and Chubb (1981, p. 637) state that physical activity programs, including recreational sport, are more numerous than any other recreation programs. This position is also supported by Tillman (1981, p. 85) who reports that "sport accounts for the largest number of participants, capturing from 60 percent to 75 percent of all active involvement."

As with other recreation program areas, those involved with the provision of recreational sport are not necessarily full-time professionals. Given the magnitude and diversity within recreational sport, most agencies rely heavily upon part-time employees and volunteers to assist in the delivery of programs. A tremendous need exists for procuring and training persons capable of providing supervision for:

1. Program divisions - informal sport, intramural sport, extramural sport, club sport

2. Skill levels - beginner, intermediate, advanced

3. Age groups - children, youth, adolescent, adult, senior

4. Sport formats - individual, dual, team, meet

5. Sport interests - aikido to white water canoeing

Consequently, skill in personnel management is essential because a recreational sport operation having an excellent array of programs and facilities but lacking quality personnel cannot be successful.

Program variety requires specialization of personnel. A total recreation program is often divided into social, cultural and sport areas of emphasis and personnel participate in the delivery of each recreational program. While similar in function, positions will vary from setting to setting and program to program depending upon the nature and size of the program as well as the number of facilities. In general, the larger the recreation program, the greater the number and specialization into administrative and program positions.

The preceding staffing principles apply to the specific program area of recreational sport. There is variance in the numbers, kinds, and types of responsibilities and in the systems used for classifying positions within a recreational sport program. Some programs choose to classify positions according to the size of the agency, while others classify positions by function or location.

The classificaton model that follows suggests a career ladder for advancement within recreational sport. Not all programs have each type of position, and some have significant overlap in roles: a single individual may serve such diverse functions as a coach, official, programmer and facility manager.

Our classification model is based upon a study by Young (1980) which identifies three levels of positions within a recreational sport staff. Job responsibilities within each classification are adapted from a listing by Kraus (1977, pp. 60, 61).

Auxiliary Staff—Personnel in this category may hold hourly wage, volunteer, or intern-trainee positions. They are directly involved in face-to-face relationships with participants either through the delivery of program activities or facilities.

Examples of auxiliary staff positions include officials, lifeguards, coaches, organization officers/managers, equipment attendants, ticket takers, desk attendants, intramural sport supervisors, club sport officers, informal sport supervisors, playground supervisors, and program aides. Intern-trainees, unlike hourly wage or volunteer personnel, serve the agency while participating in a learning situation or field work experience for academic credit as part of professional preparation for a career within recreational sport. Auxiliary staff positions may be seasonal, full-time, or part-time.

Level I: Program Staff—This is an entry-level position responsible for direct contact with participants and the delivery of services in the form of programs, facilities, or areas. Specific functions include organizing and directing a variety of indoor or outdoor sport activities; monitoring facility use and operations; handling equipment utilization, purchasing, and inventory; initiating publicity-promotion and effective public relations; providing participant/personnel recognition; monitoring operating budget; recruiting, hiring, training and scheduling support staff; monitoring adherence to agency/institution rules, policies, and procedures; implementing policies for safety, participant control, and governance; maintaining program-facility records and evaluations; and preparing statistical or analytical reports of operations. These specialized functions may provide full-time professional employment opportunities in larger operations.

Level II: Program-Administrative Staff—Personnel at this level direct administrative policies, guidelines, and resources and monitor programs, facilities and program staff. Functioning in a middle-management capacity, staff members may help plan policies and procedures; prepare budget proposals and annual reports; serve as an administrative assistant; monitor personnel practices; supervise program-facility expenditures and fee collections; participate in long-range planning; receive and review requests and reports from subordinates; coordinate the distribution of resources (facilities, personnel, equipment); serve as a liaison between the top administrator and subordinate employees; and participate in the provision of staff development programs. Positions of this nature are usually full-time professional staff positions.

Level III: Administrative Staff—the administrator is responsible for directing the operation of the recreational sport program and its resources. Customary functions include planning, approving, and supervising a diversified program of activities and services; developing personnel standards and procedures; supervising the total staff development program; directing or influencing the planning, acquisition, design, construction and maintenance of facilities; developing policies for utilization of resources; initiating planning, assessment, and evaluation studies; preparing, presenting, and monitoring annual budgets; maintaining positive relations; interpreting to the public the philosophy and specific programs of the agency; and maintaining complete and accurate records and reports of the total operation in terms of personnel, funding, facilities, and equipment. These responsibilities typically require a full-time employee in all settings and embody the only professional staff position in most small programs.

Another position classification suggested by Kraus (1977, p. 61) is logistical. While these positions are not traditional in the career hierarchy within recreational sport, they do provide administrative, managerial or operational assistance. Among positions in this category are: budget officer, personnel officer, public relations director, publicity-promotions specialist, clerk-typist, custodian, and switchboard operator.

Personnel Functions

Since the quality of personnel has a direct impact upon the quality of the program, the programmer must concentrate on ways to attract outstanding individuals and retain them through practices that facilitate their integration into the program, utilize their abilities, and support their development. We will discuss several functions the programmer may perform or oversee in the procurement, preparation and development of auxiliary staff personnel: job descriptions, recruitment, selection, placement, orientation, training, scheduling, and supervision.

Since volunteers constitute a considerable portion of the work force at the program operational level, we provide additional information to illustrate their role and several tips on how to work with them.

Job Descriptions. Personnel management begins with the development of clear, concise job descriptions which reflect the essential duties and responsibilities of each position, serve as a useful frame of reference during the personnel selection and training process, and help resolve differences of opinion regarding duties and responsibilities. The job description may be used as a yardstick to assist in gauging personnel performance. Examples for selected auxiliary staff positions, provided in Appendix 6A following this chapter, are intended to represent duties frequently required for key positions.

Recruitment. Recruitment is a process designed to maximize the chances for securing quality personnel. Based upon a clear understanding of current personnel strengths and weaknesses, expected turnover, position responsibilities, and requirements, recruitment involves the preparation of position announcements and advertisements. An effective job announcement provides essential information about the position that attracts appropriately qualified candidates and deters those whose interests and abilities do not mesh with the requirements. The following is typical of a format for a job announcement. (NRPA, 1978, p. 4).

IDENTIFICATION OF AGENCY:
(Mailing address) (telephone number)

CLASS OF POSITION TILE:
Should be descriptive of the job

SUMMARY:
General statement of major duties

SUPERVISOR:
To whom and for whom individual is responsible

EXAMPLES OF DUTIES AND RESPONSIBILITIES:
An indication of the important tasks within the position, yet broad enough to include anticipated supplemental assignments

QUALIFICATIONS:
Required knowledge, skills and abilities

SPECIAL REQUIREMENTS:
Technical or professional certification

EDUCATION AND EXPERIENCE:
Required education, training and experience

SALARY RANGE:

CLOSING DATE FOR RECEIPT OF APPLICATIONS:

CONTACT:
Full name, title, agency and address for submitting applications

In keeping with a commitment to affirmative action, each job announcement may include the following statement:

Equal Opportunity Employer. Employment will be based on merit as it relates to position requirements without regard to race, color, sex, religion, or national origin.

Personnel selection occurs through two major channels— internal and external. Individuals who are qualified for a position may already work in some internal capacity. Post job announcements where personnel within the agency may learn of opportunities in addition to making verbal announcements at meetings and inviting referrals. Consider the following recruitment methods through external channels:

1. Notices in such print media as newsletters, newspapers, and brochures.

2. Public service announcements on radio and television.

3. Mailings to employment agencies, placement centers, selected colleges and high schools, and colleagues in other recreational sport agencies.

4. Cooperative job referral with other surrounding recreational sport agencies.

To learn the qualifications of candidates, develop and use a job application form. When taking applications at the work site, use a form similar to the one in Figure 6-1.

After the deadline for applications, conduct a preliminary review to screen out unqualified applicants and group others by an estimate of potential.

After rating applicants on education, experience, and references, select a number for interviews. Check references after an interview to make comparisons between your assessment of the applicant and that of the reference(s).

Finally, rank the applicants. One way to accomplish this involves assigning a point value to each qualification being evaluated. The point total received by each applicant determines a placement among eligible candidates.

Personal interview. The personal interview is the critical factor in personnel review and selection. It affords both the interviewer and applicant an opportunity to determine compatability and potential for a successful working relationship. Use the interview wisely to discover as much as possible about the personality of applicants and the image he or she projects. A pre-determined outline of the interview session affords optimum use of your time.

Hold the interview in a relatively private, comfortable setting free from interruption. Put the applicant at ease by being attentive and congenial. Begin by having the candidate describe past experiences or comment on these aspects about the particular position that are most appealing. If a description on the application form is novel or interesting, discuss it to "break the ice." Balance direct questions with ones that are more open-ended. Use case studies to examine a candidate's knowledge or experience on a more in-depth basis. This technique encourages an unrehearsed response to a hypothetical situation.

Other items to explore during the interview include:

1. *Motivation for seeking the position.* Is it compatible with the needs of the agency?

RECREATIONAL SPORTS
PERSONNEL APPLICATION FORM

Last Name	First	Initial	Date	Year

Address	Phone

City	State	Zip Code

POSITION DESIRED

Place in rank order with 1 representing first preference.

_____ Coach   _____ Lifeguard   Other _____

_____ Instructor   _____ Official

_____ Labor crew   _____ Supervisor   Other _____

Place the proper number beside the sport that corresponds with your interest or ability to:

1 = Lead   4 = Officiate/Judge
2 = Instruct   5 = Supervise
3 = Coach

_____ Aerobic Dance   _____ Judo
_____ Archery   _____ Karate
_____ Badminton   _____ Lifesaving
_____ Baseball   _____ Racquetball
_____ Basketball   _____ Rifle
_____ Bowling   _____ Roller Skating
_____ Bridge   _____ Sailing
_____ Canoeing   _____ Scuba Diving
_____ Chess   _____ Skiing
_____ Diving   _____ Soccer
_____ Fencing   _____ Softball
_____ Fishing   _____ Swimming
_____ Football   _____ Table Tennis
_____ Golf   _____ Tennis
_____ Gymnastics   _____ Track
_____ Handball   _____ Volleyball
_____ Horseback Riding   _____ Water Polo
_____ Ice Hockey   _____ Water Skiing
_____ Ice Skating   _____ Weightlifting

EMPLOYMENT HISTORY

From	Employer and Location	Supervisor
To		

From	Employer and Location	Supervisor
To		

From	Employer and Location	Supervisor
To		

Figure 6-1. Personnel application form.

RELATED EXPERIENCE OR CERTIFICATION

PERSONAL REFERENCES

( )

Name   Address   Phone

( )

Name   Address   Phone

RECREATIONAL SPORT BACKGROUND

List special interests, hobbies, sport activities, etc.

SCHEDULE OF AVAILABILITY

	Monday	Tuesday	Wednesday	Thursday	Friday	Saturday	Sunday
Morning							
Afternoon							
Evening							

Comments

Signature _____ Date Available _____

2. *Position job description.* Does the candidate have a grasp of requirements? Does the person seem enthusiastic to join the agency given the job requirements, job and conditions?

3. *Education, preparation, experience, or background.* Does the candidate have the necessary credentials? What type or extent of orientation and in-service training may be required? What contributions can be made to the position or agency?

4. *Expectations of the immediate supervisor or the job.* Are they realistic? Will the candidate require close supervision or extensive consultation? How might the person respond to constructive criticism?

5. *Interest in the position.* How long does the candidate envision staying? Does the individual desire upward mobility? How many hours per week is he or she willing to work? When is it possible to begin?

6. *Interpersonal relations skills.* Will the candidate relate well to others? How will others perceive him or her? Does the candidate possess acceptable communications and listening skills? Can the person handle interpersonal relations problems appropriately?

7. *Public relations image.* Is the candidate neat and well-groomed? Does he or she show an interest in serving others or being served?

Questions which may not be used in employment inquiries, application forms, and interviews, unless their use is *job related* and non-discriminatory in effect include:

1. Race
2. National Origin
3. Religion
4. Education
5. Arrest and Conviction Records
6. Credit Rating
7. Sex, Marital and Family Status
8. Physical Requirements
9. Experience Requirements
10. Age

11. Relatives
12. Appearance (photo)

Advice regarding civil rights, discriminatory practices and equal opportunity employment guidelines is available from personnel managers, municipal officers and lawyers.

Use the interview to sell the program and review expectations of personnel. Take written notes throughout to facilitate complete and accurate recall, especially during a series of interviews.

Testing. When considering candidates who must lead an activity or perform specific skills as an exercise leader, official, or lifeguard, try-outs or other testing procedures often supplement the interview. The results provide a better indication of the skills, knowledge and leadership ability necessary than does the interview alone. Such tests take place before qualified judges who rate each individual on a standardized form (See Figure 6-2).

Reference check. An excellent resource for candidate assessment is a reference. Reference checks may save time in such aspects of personnel management as orientation, in-service training and consultation.

References supplied by the applicant tend to accentuate the positive. When speaking with a recommendation source, emphasize the importance of knowing as much about a candidate as possible in order to assure compatibility. If a reference relates a significant concern, check it out with a different one before reaching a conclusion. Reference checks made by phone reveal more than written ones because the phone provides an opportunity to discern tone, inflection, and sense of conviction. In addition, you may control the content of the discussion.

Personnel selection. A comparison of qualifications leads to a decision on selection. If it is difficult to choose between two or more applicants, conduct additional interviews. When it is not possible to find a position for an extremely qualified applicant, refer him or her to a colleague at another agency. Placing persons in positions for which they may be considered "over-qualified" may result in discontent later.

At some point during the interview, inform each applicant of the decision date for selection. If time or circumstances make it difficult or awkward to inform unsuccessful candidates,

AEROBIC RHYTHM LEADER TRY-OUT

Date _____

Individual's Name _____

Judge's Name (optional) _____

Please rank-order your answers on a scale of 0 to 10 with 10 being excellent and 0 being very poor. Use area next to question to provide any comments you feel are necessary. (Please be as specific as possible.)

	Rank	Comments
A. **General**		
1. Good role-model		
2. Poise, self-assurance		
3. Strong leadership characteristics		
4. Pleasant personality		
5. Motivating; encouraging		
B. **Exercise Selection**		
1. Variety; non-repetitious		
2. Safe/beneficial exercises		
3. Proper form and technique of movement		
4. Original or unique exercises		
5. Equal number of exercises on each side of body		
C. **Music Selection**		
1. Variety of music selections		
2. Motivating; fun		
3. Compatible with exercises done		
4. Smooth music transition between songs		
D. **Routines**		
1. Easy to follow		
2. Catchy routines; fun		
3. Original or creative movements		
4. Smooth transition between moves		
E. **Voice Quality/Presentation**		
1. Projects clearly		
2. Pleasant voice		
3. Explains movements clearly		
F. **Rhythm**		
1. Stays with beat of music		
2. Moves well; smoothly		
3. Apparent knowledge of music and/or dance		
4. Easy to follow and copy movements		

TOTAL _____

AVERAGE _____

Figure 6-2. Standardized judge's form for aerobic dance leader try-out.

post a list of the successful ones expressing appreciation for the interest shown in the program. Retain all applications for future reference. When an unexpected vacancy occurs, an on-call file may be useful.

Probation. Probation allows the programmer and the new employee or volunteer time to evaluate each other for suitability. The probationary period may vary from six weeks to six months.

Orientation. Adequate preparation of personnel greatly increases the likelihood for quality job performance and job satisfaction. The specific order of presentation, number of sessions, and the type of orientation (individual or group) is at the programmer's discretion. The following topics are appropriate for personnel orientation after providing routine information about payroll, withholding tax procedures and time sheets:

1. Introduction of each person participating in the orientation session.

2. Overview of the agency.

3. Flow chart of line and staff responsibilities.

4. Orientation to the setting and nature of the participants.

5. Introduction to co-workers or others with whom the position affords frequent contact.

6. Review of a personnel manual containing agency policies and procedures affecting personnel, position, job description, and sample forms commonly used.

7. Tour of the facilities or area in which the individual will work.

8. Question-answer period.

A checklist is a practical way to keep track of what needs to be discussed with probationary personnel (figure 6-3 is an example of such a checklist).

If a large number of people need accommodation for orientation and coordination of schedules to conduct a group session is impossible, videotape portions of the orientation for small group or individual review. Maintain an opportunity for a staff-directed question and answer period.

ORIENTATION CHECKLIST

Name _____   Position _____

INTRODUCTIONS

DATE ___
- Immediate Supervisor
- Fellow Workers

PAYROLL

DATE ___
- Pay Rate
- Pay Periods
- Pay Check
- Tax Forms
- Time Sheets

POSITION INFORMATION

DATE ___
- Job Description
- Job Expectations and Standards
- Agency Policies and Procedures
- Securing Supplies and Equipment
- Uniform-Special Attire
- Certification(s) Obtained

WORK SCHEDULE

DATE ___
- Schedule of Availability
- Minimum-Maximum Hours
- Overtime
- Breaks
- Substitutions
- Meals

BENEFITS

DATE ___
- Discounts
- Holidays
- Sick Leave
- Insurance
- Time Off

MISCELLANEOUS

DATE ___
- Appearance-Image
- Parking
- Lockers
- Meetings

Figure 6-3. Personnel orientation checklist form.

Training. This personnel practice covers in-service training for new and senior personnel and may involve some of the following aspects:

Apprenticeship—Schedule the new employee or volunteer to work with an experienced person before going it alone. Place the newcomer with the best role model available.

Clinics—Clinics enhance learning through observation and participation. Use them to illustrate such tasks as officiating techniques and mechanics, equipment use, lifeguard rescue skills and maintenance.

Meetings—Use personnel meetings, scheduled on a regular basis (weekly, monthly) to disseminate information, review concerns, and obtain feedback. Do not schedule them out of habit. Special meetings may focus on a particular job description responsibility.

Workshops—Workshops afford an opportunity to treat topics of concern in more depth, and are expecially useful in encouraging personnel involvement. They may focus on job preparation, assertiveness training, conflict resolution, communication and listening skills, problem-solving, racism and community relations.

Retreats—Retreats provide a series of workshops held in succession over a number of days in a non-work related setting. Usually reserved for personnel holding key positions of responsibility and more complex jobs, retreats are a beneficial way to build esprit de corps and improve job performance.

Individual Sessions—Personnel should receive regular observation and feedback sessions to reinforce strengths and eliminate weaknesses. Encourage them to reflect upon the program and their own needs.

Short Courses—Short courses focus on a skill or topic over an extended period of time. Attendance may be voluntary or mandatory, depending upon importance to job performance. Topics include first aid, sport skill instruction, alcoholism and drug abuse, sexism and racism, spectatorship, personnel and the police, conflict resolution, and accident and injury prevention.

Inservice training programs help eliminate future problems when their content relates to the knowledge and skills needed on the job. They also contribute to confidence and stimulate interest in the job.

Although some differences exist among positions, there are principle duties common to all positions (accident reporting, maintenance and repair, discipline, complaints and suggestions, special or unusual situations and lost and found).

When conducting a training session to prepare personnel to adequately handle these duties, emphasize the importance of consistency in performance.

1. Accidents—Establish a specific procedure for handling and documenting accidents. In some instances supervision within the recreational sport environment is general instead of direct. General supervision indicates that personnel cover multiple facility areas or functions, while direct supervision means that personnel oversee a specific function or facility. For example, an informal sport employee may be responsible for overseeing a large facility, a number of activities, and many participants. Consequently, place alert personnel in accessible and visible locations and instruct participants how to locate appropriate personnel in the event of an accident.

   All personnel should receive special training on the procedures for recording and forwarding accident reports to an immediate supervisor. When a serious accident involves ambulance or emergency first aid treatment, both a detailed written statement and a follow-up report are required. Accident records are essential due to the incidence of law suits, insurance claims and inquiries into safety and accident prevention measures.

   The accident report form provides blanks for the name, address, phone number of the injured party, parent's name, address, phone for minors, insurance company, social security number, day, date, time and place, location of the injury, explanation of how injury occurred, recommendations for prevention, immediate action taken and by whom, mode of transportation for delivery to hospital or physician, name, address and phone number of witness(es), and name, address, title, and phone number of person submitting the report.

2. Maintenance and Repair—While recreation budgets include funds for facility maintenance and repair, they rarely meet the need. Regardless, all personnel should participate in regular facility and equipment inspection for the purpose of identifying maintenance needs and facilitating repair work. Develop standardized forms

that note the date, time, location, problem, possible cause, recommended action, and person submitting the report.

Familiarize personnel to whom the forms should be sent and the need for follow-up. They should use a filing system to keep track of all requests for maintenance and repair. A workload file containing copies of submitted forms helps because:

a. the original could get lost.
b. participants and personnel sense that something tangible is being done to correct problems.
c. the file serves as a record of steps taken to correct a safety hazard.
d. a special request for priority consideration may be made if delays jeopardize safety or morale.
e. the completed tasks reveal a dollar value useful during budgeting.

In addition to a routine procedure for handling minor problems, personnel need training to handle such emergency situations as power blackouts, flooding, tornado, chemical leakage, fire and major property damage.

They need to know how to respond to equipment or facility emergencies that result in safety hazards, whom they should contact for assistance or notification, what the emergency phone numbers are and how to evacuate an area if necessary. They should also be prepared to stay at the scene to maintain control until more qualified assistance arrives. This may include locking access doors, roping off hazard areas, posting warning signs, making public address announcements and appointing on-site supervisory personnel.

3. Discipline—Reporting of discipline problems must be prompt and thorough. Appropriate action requires documentation of the date, time, and location of incident, person(s) on duty and home phone number, person(s) involved in incident and phone number, a description of the incident, signatures, and witnesses.

Encourage personnel to interview as many witnesses as possible to obtain a perspective of the incident. Record all information as soon as possible to avoid the problems of memory lapses and inaccurate recall. Discipline situations most often encountered in the recreational sports environment include verbal and physical abuse toward personnel and participants and misuse or vandalism of facilities. Obtaining information for the report from the accused person(s) may be difficult to achieve. Minimize disciplinary problems by adopting the following strategies:

a. Train personnel to closely monitor activity and facility use and to keep a high profile.
b. Teach them to anticipate and recognize problems as they develop and then take appropriate preventative measures.
c. Train them to utilize effective assertiveness and conflict-resolution skills.
d. Establish parameters which assist personnel in knowing when to request law enforcement assistance.
e. Encourage them to obtain testimony from witnesses.
f. Punish employees who do not handle problems correctly or who avoid dealing with problems. Policy enforcement is a vital tool in minimizing repeat occurrences.

Regard discipline reports as confidential material. Upon review, retain these forms for use as case studies to train employees to establish precedents, to monitor potential repeat offenders and to provide evidence in the event of disciplinary action or legal suits.

4. Complaints or Suggestions—Personnel occasionally develop blind spots and do not report certain situations unless required to do so. One effective way to encourage thoroughness is by soliciting complaints and suggestions. They identify new ideas, involve participants in decisions, monitor personnel performance and inform staff about unexpected problems. Publicize your

---

COMPLAINT AND SUGGESTION

Date _____   Time _____

Concerning: Informal Sports _____   Intramural Sports _____
        Club Sports _____   Facilities _____

General complaint: _____
_____
_____
_____
_____
_____

Specific details or examples: _____
_____
_____
_____
_____
_____

Suggestion regarding what should be done: _____
_____
_____
_____
_____

If you desire to be contacted concerning your complaint, please complete this section.
Name _____
Address _____
Telephone # _____

Thank you for your time and interest in our program.

Figure 6-4. Complaint and suggestion form.

responses in a highly visible location within the facility, in a newsletter or newspaper column.

5. Special or Unusual Situations—Use a special reporting format to note situations that are not covered by existing policy or procedure, that are unexpected or that require priority attention. Examples of occurrences that could be reported under this category are listed in Figure 6-5.

 Any standard form for reporting special or unusual situations should include space for date, time, facility, program, person(s) involved and phone number(s), person

REPORTABLE OFFENSES AND INCIDENTS

Offense Against Public Order
Riots
Demonstrations
Drunkenness
Disturbing the Peace
Juvenile Drinking

Criminal—Persons
Assault
Child Abuse
Civil Rights
Extortion
Forgery
Murder
Manslaughter
Homicide
Impersonation
Kidnapping
Narcotic and Drug Violations
Perjury, False Swearing and False
   Official Statement
Robbery
Suicide
Traffic Fatality
Traffic Violations
Carrying a Concealed Weapon
Communicating a Threat
Miscellaneous Offenses in this
   Category, e.g., Malfeasance,
   Misfeasance
Accidental Death
Abandoned Property

Criminal—Sex Offenses
Child Molestation
Indecent Acts
Unlawful Possession, Selling, or
   Exhibiting of Pornography
Rape
Exhibitionism
Obscene Communication

Criminal—Property
Arson
Burglary
Unlawful Forced Entry (automobile, etc.)
Wrongful Appropriation of Private
   Property
Wrongful Disposition of Private
   Property
Wrongful Destruction
Sabotage
Attempted Sabotage

Criminal—Fraud
Bribery
Conflict of Interest
Accept Gratuities

Reservoir Violations
Fish and Game Violations
Fire Arms
Fire Violations
Trespass
Encroachment

Figure 6-5. Examples of reportable offenses and incidents in recreational sports.

submitting report, explanation of circumstance, action taken, and action recommended.

6. Lost and Found. Programmers should anticipate receiving many inquiries regarding lost and found items. While participants welcome a system for storing these items, this service is not necessarily a simple or secure one. Develop policy and procedures that consider:

   a. the location for the lost and found

SPECIAL OR UNUSUAL SITUATION REPORT

Date _____   Time _____

Concerning: Informal Sports _____ Intramural Sports _____
                       Club Sports _____ Facilities _____

Persons involved:

    NAME   ADDRESS   PHONE #

1. _____
2. _____
3. _____
4. _____
5. _____

Explanation of circumstances: _____
_____
_____
_____
_____

Immediate action taken: _____
_____
_____
_____
_____

Suggestions or comments: _____
_____
_____
_____

Reported by: _____ Phone: _____

Figure 6-6. Special or unusual situation report form.

      b. how and where items will be secured and stored
      c. the proof required for claiming an article
      d. the length of time articles may be kept (is there a legal requirement?)
      e. the disposition of unclaimed articles
      f. prevention of tampering with or use of articles
      g. education to help avoid loss

    Personnel need training to oversee a lost and found system. The report form used to log in a lost or found article should include a place for date, time, location where article was found, descriptions of article(s), signature of employee or volunteer receiving article, and signature, address and phone of person claiming article. Report all claims of theft to assist in improving security measures.

Scheduling. There are two basic approaches to personnel scheduling: short-term or long-term. Variables affecting scheduling decisions include nature of the position, number of personnel for the position, strengths or specializations required of personnel, availability of personnel, and number of personnel needed to cover a responsibility. Generally, once job conditions and personnel qualifications and availability are fairly consistent, consider the long-term, or "contract" method of scheduling. This system establishes work schedules for a specified time span (month, quarter, semester, 6 weeks, 8 weeks).

Personnel may work certain days, certain shifts, certain facilities, certain positions, or any combination thereof. Some personnel prefer a schedule involving the same slot week-by-week because it allows them to arrange other activities around their employment or volunteer service. For the programmer, consistency reduces confusion and leads to increased productivity on the part of personnel who work the same shift. As these individuals become familiar with situations and participants, they can provide reliable observations regarding their experiences and observations. However, anticipate the problems of complacency and boredom by providing personnel with needed changes of pace.

The actual scheduling of personnel may be achieved in two ways. Either the programmer collects schedules of availability from each eligible person and does the scheduling, or the volunteers or employees sign up individually for the days and shifts they prefer working. The latter approach is recommended when the requirements of the job can be handled adequately by all personnel.

Upon completion of the schedule, draw up an agreement, retain one copy and give another to the employee or volunteer.

Limiting the number of hours each person may take prevents the few from taking all the hours. Another way to provide incentive and structure is to permit personnel with the

**RECREATIONAL SPORTS
LOST AND FOUND LOG**

Date Received	Time Received	Item (Be Specific)	Supervisor's Name Receiving Item	Date Returned	Supervisor's Name Returning Item	Person Claiming Item and Phone Number

Figure 6-7.   Lost and found log form.

PERSONNEL AVAILABILITY WORKSHEET

MONTH _____   YEAR _____

SUNDAY	MONDAY	TUESDAY	WEDNESDAY	THURSDAY	FRIDAY	SATURDAY
E M L	E or L	E or L	E or L	E or L	E or L	E M L
E M L	E or L	E or L	E or L	E or L	E or L	E M L
E M L	E or L	E or L	E or L	E or L	E or L	E M L
E M L	E or L	E or L	E or L	E or L	E or L	E M L
E M L	E or L	E or L	E or L	E or L	E or L	E M L

E = Early Shift
M = Middle Shift
L = Late Shift

Figure 6-8. Personnel availability worksheet to be submitted prior to each scheduling session.

greatest seniority the first opportunity to select preferred slots. Such an approach has a better chance for success when

INTRAMURAL SPORTS SUPERVISOR CONTRACT

The Division of Recreational Sports and *Beth Coleman*, a Sport Supervisor employed by the Division of Recreational Sports, hereby enter into the following agreement. The said supervisor agrees to be present and supervise the following *Flag Football* games listed below to be played on the agreed to dates and times during the said activity season.

	DATES	TIMES
1.	September 14	5:00- 8:00
2.	September 15	8:00-11:00
3.	September 21	8:00-11:00
4.	September 22	5:00- 8:00
5.	September 23	5:00- 8:00
6.	September 28	5:00- 8:00
7.	September 29	8:00-11:00
8.	October 1	5:00- 8:00
9.	October 4	8:00-11:00
10.		

It is agreed that the Division of Recreational Sports will pay the Activity Supervisor so mentioned for fulfilling his or her obligations in supervising the games listed above.

Signed this _5th_ day of _September,_ 19_83_.

X _____
      Supervisor

X _____
      Coordinator of Supervisors

Figure 6-9. Supervisors contract scheduling form.

each person maintains a favorable performance record. An example of a seniority system contract is shown in Figure 6-10

Contract scheduling is unrealistic for use when positions require specialization. If a particular program or function involves a large work force or varying levels of proficiency, such as intramural basketball tournament officiating, the flexibility afforded by a short-term scheduling procedure is needed. Programmers who schedule personnel on a short-term basis often specify a deadline for the submission of information on availability. After this point, a number of scheduling options are possible:

SENIORITY CONTRACT SCHEDULING

DISTRIBUTION OF SENIORITY POINTS

1.) 7 points—each season worked as a supervisor.
2.) 4 points—each season worked as an intramural sport official, (NOTE: in order to be credited with seniority points, officating duties must have been assumed prior to becoming a supervisor or have taken place during a season in which you were officiating only and had no supervisor duties.)

3.) Grade on supervisor's exam:

       7 points = score of 97 - 100
       6 points = score of 94 - 96
       5 points = score of 91 - 93
       4 points = score of 88 - 90
       3 points = score of 85 - 87
       2 points = score of 82 - 84
       1 point = score of 79 - 81

4.) Evaluation points—

    Eight performance factors will be rated in the following way:

       Outstanding .... 4 points
       Above Standard .... 3 points
       Standard .... 2 points
       Below Standard .... 1 point
       Unsatisfactory .... 0 points

    (to be used only during tournament contracting and will not be carried over to future seasons.)

FAILURE TO ATTEND ASSIGNED WORKDATE

First Offense .... Verbal Reprimand
Second Offense .... Written Reprimand and/or Termination*
Third Offense .... Termination
*depends on each individual circumstance

SCHEDULING

    In case of a **tie** in the overall points at any level, the numbers 0-9 will be assigned to those individuals for use in the following randomly selected draw for seniority, and order of priority in the scheduling process for their level. For example, the employee assigned #1 would go first, then #9, etc.

WEEK 1	WEEK 2	WEEK 3	WEEK 4	WEEK 5	WEEK 6
1	5	0	3	2	4
9	2	1	4	9	6
0	8	4	7	1	3
7	6	6	1	3	8
3	9	8	9	5	2
8	3	5	2	4	9
6	1	7	5	8	0
5	4	2	0	6	7
2	0	3	6	7	1
4	7	9	8	0	5

Figure 6-10. Seniority contract scheduling form.

1. Programmers may prepare schedules on an individual notice slip (Figure 6-11) and issue them on a certain date. They handle and confirm adjustments in scheduling on an individual basis with staff.

   Comments: This method may be most effective when the need exists for close quality control, the personnel are few in number, or personnel availability is very sporadic and diverse. Since handled individually by a staff member, this task may require a great deal of time and effort. If schedules need to be mailed or use special forms, the process is more expensive.

PERSONNEL SCHEDULE

Name _____ Phone _____

Job	Location	Day(s)	Times	Approved

I hereby accept or reject the hours given me as noted above.

_____
(Signature)

Figure 6-11. Personnel scheduling form.

2. Programmers may prepare schedules in advance and post them at a regular time (Figure 6-12). If individuals can work as scheduled, they circle their name, or put an "x" on their name. The staff person has the option of rescheduling the vacancies, leaving them open for personnel to sign up on their own, or both. While this method still requires initial staff work, it permits an opportunity to work additional hours. The staff reschedules any unfilled slots.

3. On a specific day, programmers post a schedule showing only the slots to be filled (no names). Personnel

BASKETBALL OFFICIALS WORK SCHEDULE

DAY: _____ DATE: _____

COURT	1	2	3	4	5
TIME 5:00 TO 8:00	Nigh Circle	Dusing Erdman	Butler Sparks	Schutz Esckilsen	Piercefield Clensy

ROVERS: B. McMinn

TIME 8:00 TO 11:00	Ellard Leubert	Napoli Hank	McManus Damer	Ravensburg King	Peterbaugh Phillips

ROVERS: R. Hailey

*Schedules will be posted every Wednesday by 12:00 noon for the following work week (Sunday through Thursday). You must circle your name by 12:00 noon Friday.

Figure 6-12. Example of a work scheduling form.

sign up for work, restricting themselves to a limited number of hours to allow everyone an equal opportunity. After another specified time, vacancies may be claimed by any qualified worker. After completing a personal schedule, an individual files a confirmation card with the staff and retains a copy for reference (Figure 6-13).

Comments: The staff member may schedule those individuals who cannot come in for a legitimate reason or those who are needed to fill a particular slot. Since personnel schedule their own hours, they can work around commitments. This method may leave staff short-handed. Specifying a minimum number of hours worked per scheduling period helps avoid this problem.

Among several other scheduling techniques meriting attention is the use of a substitute roster. Invariably, situations arise when personnel are unable to fulfill their assignments. If other regular workers are not available, call in a substitute worker. When holidays or special events drain off personnel, scale down programming, use supplemental, part-time help or

MONTH _____ YEAR _____

TIMES	MONDAY	TUESDAY	WEDNESDAY	THURSDAY	FRIDAY	TIMES	SATURDAY	SUNDAY
7 - 8:30	22	23	24	25	26	10-12:30	27	28
11:30- 1:30						12:30-3		
6-9						3-5:30		
9-11						5:30-8		
7 - 8:30	1	2	3	4	5	10-12:30	6	7
11:30- 1:30						12:30-3		
6-9						3-5:30		
9-11						5:30-8		

Figure 6-13. Alternative work scheduling form.

reschedule regulars to perform different functions. Finally, in the case of last minute shortages, maintain a list of those available on an "on-call" basis.

Supervision. Historically, the supervisory role involved making observations and formulating strategies to see that work was accomplished and that workers did not loaf on the job. Recent studies in the behavioral sciences indicate the need to modify or replace this orientation with a view of the personnel supervisor as a facilitator of competent performance, rapport, and personnel growth.

A staff supervisor is responsible for helping subordinate personnel improve their work, while adhering to agency objectives. The role of the supervisor who mediates between the staff who administer the agency and the auxiliary staff who implement its functions at the program or operational level is primary to our discussion.

Personnel supervision is a multifaceted function which includes the following types of responsibilities:

Guidance. Orientation and in-service training efforts cannot fully prepare personnel for handling every circumstance, nor do they guarantee that the knowledge or skills taught will be understood, properly applied, or consistently performed.

One way of determining whether personnel need assistance is to make performance observations. A common technique is the unannounced observation. It should be a way to monitor operational needs and concerns rather than a strategy for catching personnel doing something wrong. If you notice a problem with personnel performance during an unannounced observation, address it later or handle it discretely, so the individual is not embarassed in front of co-workers or participants.

Another technique of personnel observation is the expected or routinely-scheduled check. Use this procedure to witness a situation, to answer first-hand an employee or volunteer request for assistance, to help solidify relationships with personnel, or to complete a structured evaluation process. In rejecting the "snoopervisor" concept, this method enables personnel to view a supervisor as a resource.

In order for personnel to accept guidance and assistance, a supervisor must project competence and legitimacy as a role model. Supervisors need a knowledge of all the duties and responsibilities of the positions under their supervision, an ability to anticipate problems for which a worker may be unaware and a capacity to help devise a plan of action for use in resolving problems. Furthermore, a supervisor should be careful to distinguish between domination, guidance, and avoidance. If the supervisor demands control and usurps personnel duties and responsibilities, morale drops, creativity declines, and learning suffers. Such domination also implies lack of confidence, disinterest in personnel growth, and a "know-it-all" attitude. On the other extreme, neglect of the responsibility to provide needed guidance to personnel implies a lack of confidence or knowledge, inaccessibility, or disinterest on the part of the supervisor which has a negative impact upon morale and performance. Effective guidance requires an ability to anticipate, analyze, explain, consult, and offer solutions while cultivating these same qualities in personnel.

Development. Provide opportunities for personnel to learn, develop, upgrade, and refine various skills and receive evaluation on performance. Since we have already reviewed some of the methods commonly used for these purposes under the training section, we will make just one additional suggestion. The opinion of your personnel is a valid resource in determining the appropriateness of the content and approach selected for training, review and evaluation sessions. Combining personnel and supervisor perspectives should result in a more relevant program, one which everyone can support.

Communication. Two-way communication must exist between a supervisor and his or her subordinates. The success and quality of supervision suffers when one party functions with partial information. A supervisor's success in maintaining morale, sustaining quality performance, and contributing to the development of personnel depends heavily upon the reciprocity of the communication process in effect.

The following suggestions describe ways to improve communication. (adapted from Dooher and Marquis, found in Kraus, 1975, pp 323, 324)

1. Have a purpose for the communication and select an avenue for it that will convey the desired message effectively and efficiently. For example, if you want to

change someone's attitude, do you send a memo, talk over the phone, or meet on a face-to-face basis?

2. Consider whether or not your thoughts are well-organized, clear, and concise before communicating. Understand your audience. By placing yourself in another's position, you will increase the likelihood that your message will be received and understood.

3. Whenever possible, determine whether the communication was received as you intended. The sender does not always select the proper words or style that conveys the message and the person receiving the message may not always interpret it accurately.

4. Be a good listener. Concentrate on what others are saying and seek to understand not only the message but the motivations underlying it. Demonstrate a genuine interest in the ideas, opinions and concerns of others.

5. Be mindful of situations where it is appropriate to obtain additional information before taking action.

6. Recognize the fact that body language and tone of voice affect the communication process.

7. Consider environmental factors that affect communication. Is the setting too hot, too cold, too noisy, or distracting in any other way?

8. Consider psychological factors that affect communication. Does the individual act preoccupied, does emotional stress exist between the supervisor and subordinate, is there adequate time for the communication, does the person feel threatened?

9. Develop lines of communication that are as direct as possible to reduce the chances of message distortion.

10. Inform subordinates of your interest in their input and the available channels of communication.

11. Envision communication as an important avenue for building and maintaining positive interpersonal relations.

12. Provide an effective mechanism for airing complaints.

13. Communicate by action. Support your words with consistent behavior.

Personnel relations. There are two aspects of relations referred to in this discussion: relations between supervisor and subordinates, and relations among co-workers. The primary responsibility for maintaining positive relations in both instances rests with the personnel supervisor.

The major factors contributing to success in the relationship between supervisors and subordinates include a clear understanding of the expectations and objectives of each party and a genuine concern by the supervisor for the needs and interests of subordinate personnel. As a supervisor, seek to integrate your expectations and objectives with those of your subordinates and involve them in decisions and the setting of goals. Justify all policies and procedures that personnel must observe. Build good working relationships by:

—developing an incentive system which reinforces and recognizes quality performances.

—furnishing challenges which stretch personnel beyond their usual capabilities.

—establishing good working conditions in terms of salary, scheduling and pleasant work surroundings.

—keeping subordinates informed about new information or changes in procedure that effect their duties and responsibilities.

—supporting actions of subordinates whenever possible to do so.

—being consistent, fair, and objective with all personnel and show no favoritism or preferential treatment.

Logical outcomes of these strategies are an increased commitment to the job and greater satisfaction.

High morale, quality performance and progressive supervisor-subordinate relations do not develop instantly. They result as personnel and supervisor undergo experiences with one another that demonstrate commitment and competence.

Despite efforts to the contrary, problems develop ranging from a petty policy infringement to an overt violation or behavior which has a disruptive effect upon other personnel. In such situations, disciplinary measures are appropriate. Inaction perpetuates negative behavior, demoralizes personnel, jeopardizes rapport and damages the supervisor's credibility. Equally damaging is a disciplinary measure that is inappropriate, biased, or retaliatory. More detailed references to disciplinary action and procedures are made in the Program Control chapter.

Measures taken to facilitate positive interpersonal relations among auxiliary staff depend upon the degree of interdependence that exists. When personnel function as a unit and need to cooperate in order to accomplish their duties and responsibilities, strategies, such as the following, enhance esprit de corps:

1. Plan occasional functions outside the job environment such as a party, picnic, movie, or a sport activity.

2. Make careful placement decisions. Knowing as much as possible about each employee or volunteer will help you put them in positions commensurate with their abilities and compatible with their personalities.

3. Provide inservice training on human relations and teamwork. Help personnel assess themselves and others realistically.

4. Anticipate problems. Stay in-tune with personnel concerns. Make regular observations and interact frequently with subordinates on a one-to-one basis. Explore their attitudes.

5. Resolve problems. Encourage personnel to work out their differences, providing direction as needed. Serve as an arbitrator if it helps resolve the problem. Be prepared to reassign, or relieve personnel when conflict persists.

Volunteerism. We mentioned earlier that volunteers provide a considerable portion of the work force within public and private recreational sport programs. Historically, volunteer leadership has provided a major role in the organized recreation movement and it will continue to do so for years to come. Volunteerism is important because:

1. Volunteers may supplement or complement professional staff in maintaining or expanding services under

difficult economic conditions and providing skills or knowledge not possessed by professional full-time staff.

2. Volunteers, motivated by a genuine desire to serve, furnish fresh perspective, enthusiasm and sense of dedication that often stimulates others and generates participant interest.

3. Volunteers may assume the necessary routine tasks enabling full-time staff to focus on other important duties and act as liaisons between staff and various interest groups.

Volunteers hold a wide variety of positions and responsibilities. Their roles are grouped into the following three classifications:

1. Logistical services—Volunteers who meet the basic operational needs associated with the program, such as transportation, clerical, secretarial, maintenance, publicity, promotion, and financial functions.

2. Program delivery—Volunteers who help provide programs. In many instances, volunteers serve as the primary staff responsible for leadership, activities, personnel supervision, or facility management. In others, they assist staff on a supplemental, short-term basis. Examples of program delivery roles include sport officials, club officers, sport instructors, community center coordinators, program supervisors, special event assistants, tournament coordinators, and contest judges. Volunteers in this group correspond to auxiliary staff and program staff levels.

3. Administrative-advisory—Volunteers who are involved in the direct administration of recreational sport programs or who assist with decison-making in an advisory capacity. Members of a Board of Directors, committee appointees, technical or legal consultants, governing board members, and advisory council members are examples of such roles. Volunteers in this group correspond to program-administrative staff and administrative staff levels.

Although it is difficult to standardize the positions and responsibilities for volunteers holding logistical services or program delivery roles, it is possible to describe volunteer roles in the adminstrative-advisory classification in such a way as to be relevant to a variety of settings. Volunteers involved in an administrative capacity work on boards or councils with, or in place of, professional staff to determine policies and oversee program operations. Such adminstrative involvement is found in the Board of Directors structure at the Y.M.C.A. and Boys' Club; the Employee Recreation Association in the industrial setting; the Parks and Recreation Board (Commission) in the municipal setting and the Executive Board in the commercial club setting.

Volunteer leadership also exists at the program operational level through committees, councils, or boards responsible for hearing appeals concerning protests or disciplinary action. We treat this important role in more detail in the chapter on Program Control.

Volunteers who fill advisory roles exist on an individual or group basis. Individuals who possess special skills or knowledge often volunteer their expertise as consultants. Examples include an accountant who helps set up the bookkeeping process, the newspaper advertiser who helps create a publicity campaign, the lawyer who advises on legal liability, the space utilization expert who reorganizes an office, or the architect who helps plan a new sports facility.

Volunteers who staff advisory councils, boards, or committees do not have final authority or responsibility for policy or administration. They do provide such important functions as:

—conducting studies which help advance programs, facilities and services
—serving as a liaison between staff and participants or staff and employees
—making recommendations regarding policy and procedure
—serving as a sounding board to influence decisions.

Advisory groups are usually composed of representatives from all interested areas of a program and may be elected by participants, appointed by staff or appointed by special interest groups as their representatives.

The titles council, board, federation, or committee are interchangeable descriptions of advisory groups. Such groups may utilize standing or ad hoc committees to delve more fully into specific topics or responsibilities on behalf of the whole group. Some of the topics considered by sub-committees include funding, promotion, facilities, governance, membership, constitution and by-laws. In the examples of advisory groups that follow, we discuss each briefly, since a programmer will likely work with one or more advisory groups.

Recreational Sport Council or Association. Members of this group may be representative of each program area (club, intramural, informal), participant group (employee, management, students, faculty, staff, township, squadron), personnel function (supervisor, official, lifeguard, unit manager, program assistant, instructor), or a combination thereof. It may recommend policy, evaluate programs, facilities, and services and serve as the representative voice for a particular constituency. Often used as a sounding board, the council solicits feedback from its constituency on proposals and priority needs. Although primarily advisory in nature, it often wields tremendous influence upon administration policy, particularly in the area of finances and facilities. Persons who serve in this group usually have the most experience and involvement within the recreational sport program. Figure 6-14 traces the function of this group through an organizational flow chart.

Informal Sport Council. Members of this council may represent different participant groups, facilities, activity interests, or a combination thereof. Functions performed by this group may include: policy and procedure recommendations; review of participant/employee complaints, appeals for facility services or utilization; liaison between participants and staff; evaluation of facilities and operation; and identification of priorities regarding facility needs.

Intramural Sport Council. Commonly composed of representatives from various units of participation, intramural sport supervisors and officials, the council serves as an important link between staff and participants. The council endeavors to provide staff with feedback and evaluations concerning programs, facilities, and personnel. They may make recommendations for changes in specific sports and the over-all intramural sport programming area.

RECREATIONAL SPORTS ASSOCIATION

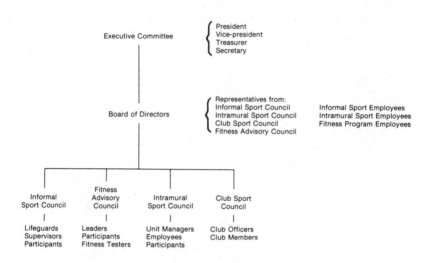

Figure 6-14. Recreational sports organizational flow chart.

Club Sport Council. This council includes representatives from each club falling under the jurisdiction of the staff, or agency. These individuals meet to make recommendations on policy and procedure while representing the various interests of member clubs. A Council Executive Committee often will appoint sub-committees to study and propose recommendations to staff on ways to improve club funding, facilities, or other support services.

Working with volunteers in an advisory capacity requires time and adequate preparation. By providing avenues of involvement to express and direct their interest for program improvements, the programmer includes the volunteer as a valuable resource who shoulders some of the responsibility of sport management. When those affected by decisions participate in making them, the end results are easier to accept.

Group Organization. The degree to which rapport and high productivity may be attained within a group depends largely upon the personalities, attributes, and skills of professional staff volunteers. While in-service training may improve group dynamics, select volunteers who already possess such important qualities as:

1. A sincere interest in and commitment to the importance and value of the program(s).

2. A willingness and ability to give time and effort.

3. An ability to work well with others.

4. Sound judgment, an ability to speak out on issues after careful analysis, and a desire to offer solutions to problems.

5. A commitment to representing the opinions of one's constituency—not personal opinion.

Whenever possible, the programmer should see that boards, councils, and committees are as broadly representative of the population specific to its function as possible, whether it be from an age, gender, occupational, educational, social, economic or racial standpoint. Consider the length of terms of office so that you can plan to secure capable replacements. Generally, the more complex the responsibility, the longer the term must be due to the time it takes for the person to gain expertise. Stagger or overlap terms in the interest of maintaining continuity and operating ability.

Orientation, Training, and Evaluation. Unfortunately, once volunteers are selected, their preparation and evaluation as a group is too often neglected. In view of the significant responsibilities and contributions volunteers represent, the programmer should devise a training and evaluation program for them.

A helpful tool for orientation and training is a manual that includes a statement of purpose, an organizational flowchart, the history of the group and program, constitution and by-laws or operational guidelines, executive officer job descriptions, program policies and procedures, agency policies, and a directory of staff and group member names, positions, and phone numbers. Organize special sessions to review this material. Discuss each volunteer's role, anticipated responsibilities, and potential priority projects.

Volunteers who hold positions of responsibility for logistical services or program delivery also require some degree of on-going supervisory attention in terms of guidance, development, communication and interpersonal relations. Supervisory responsibility often rests with a professional staff member who, by nature of the position, provides an element of continuity from year-to-year.

Special Considerations. The motivation for volunteering one's time and services arises from many reasons—a desire for practical experience, personal recognition, prestige, job recommendations, academic credit and other psychological or social needs. Since the volunteer does not depend upon the position for income, problems may result.

1. When a volunteer refuses to identify with the priorities or philosophy of the setting, performs in an unreliable fashion, or lacks the abilities to handle an assignment, corrective or disciplinary measures may have little impact since he or she is not a regular employee.

2. A volunteer worker may perform tasks in a highly acceptable manner, act as an excellent role model, and accept additional responsibilities only to feel resentment when an employee does not measure up to the same standard.

3. Personal priorities may interfere with commitment to volunteer duties.

4. Unruly volunteers can be difficult to control or remove.

5. Volunteer leaders may try to usurp the authority of a professional staff member working in the same project or program.

Volunteers do have many positive attributes and contributions to offer, and the programmer must learn how to tap them in order to make maximum use of their potential. The following suggestions may help establish a mutually beneficial relationship (adopted from Kraus, 1975). In addition to these guidelines, refer to the section on personnel practices for more detailed information.

1. Since volunteers do not always seek out opportunities for service, the programmer may need to develop an outreach program for recruitment. During this process, the programmer should consider these motivational factors: a feeling that the job is an important one, a sense of relating to and participating in the setting, an agreement with the basic objectives of the agency, a feeling that the job will contribute to self development and career ambitions, the need for approval and recog-

nition and the desire to make a contribution to society or satisfy the needs of others. Factors that deter volunteers include timidity, shyness, lack of confidence, a fear of taking risks, a reluctance to associate with certain types of participants, a fear of not being needed, doubt concerning qualification, laziness and fear of boredom.

2. Review a volunteer's background and qualifications carefully to make the wisest possible decision about selection and placement. During a personal interview, explore the individual's motivations and evaluate his or her personality. In addition, give the potential volunteer adequate insight into agency and job expectations.

3. Upon selection and placement, involve a volunteer in the same training process recommended for employees in terms of introductions to colleagues, tour of the agency or site of work, review of precise responsibilities, review of other regulations or legal limitations to the work of the volunteer (safety, first aid, discipline), and review of participant population with whom he or she will come in contact.

4. Afford volunteers inservice training opportunities to strengthen their skills and help them further identify with their role and relationship to the agency or institution.

5. Provide volunteer workers the same supervision from professional staff as given other employees. However, observe their performance in an atmosphere of support and genuine appreciation for their contributions; not in a casual, off-hand or harsh manner. Sound comunication and proper supervisory assistance helps motivate quality job performance.

6. A key factor in positive volunteer-agency relationships is the provision of recognition and reward for volunteer contributions. Some derive satisfaction from doing a good job, and others appreciate concrete expressions of appreciation. Recognition may take a number of forms, including: an agency uniform or other type of apparel, reduced rates for food services or facility use,

newspaper or newsletter recognition of work, letters of commendation or recommendations for other positions, praise and encouragement before peers or at staff meetings, increased responsibilities or change of title, awards of pins, certificates, or placques of appreciation and a reception or other special event to acknowledge volunteer contributions.

Personnel Policies. Personnel policies are statements which govern on-the-job performance. They may specify expectations, accepted ways of carrying out duties and responsibilities, information regarding compensation and benefits, rules of conduct, disciplinary action and grievance procedures, evaluation duties and other topics specific to the particular program and setting. While the programmer at the operational level usually does not establish these policies, he or she interprets and enforces them. All personnel policies and procedures should be published in an administrative manual. Figure 6-15 lists the possible categories and topics included in such a manual.

CONCLUSION

The programmer working with personnel at the operational level may need to invest considerable time for the training and supervision of those who serve the agency on a part-time basis or for a short duration. Decisions or recommendations regarding the selection, placement, training, scheduling, supervision, evaluation, and recognition of personnel require careful thought and preparation in order to contribute to quality performance, positive morale, and a reduction in personnel turnover. Unless the programmer continually recognizes, and demonstrates through action, that the jobs performed at the operational level are important and meaningful to the total recreational sport program, both paid and volunteer personnel may lose their motivation and view their work as demeaning and unpleasant.

Programmers need to understand personnel management and the impact that their decisions or actions have upon subordinates. Effective implementation of personnel practices assures the overall quality of a recreational sport program.

PERSONNEL MANUAL

TABLE OF CONTENTS

Figure 6-15. Sample table of contents indicating suggested topics for a recreational sports personnel manual.

REFERENCES

Chubb, M. and Chubb, H.R. *One Third of Our Time? An Intro-duction To Recreation Behavior and Resources.* New York: John Wiley & Sons, Inc., 1981.

Kraus, R. G. *Recreation Today: Programming and Leadership,* 2nd edition. Santa Monica, California: Goodyear Publishing Company, Inc., 1977

Kraus, R. G. and Bates, J. *Recreation Leadership and Super-vision: Guidelines for Professional Development.* Philadelphia: W. B. Saunders Company, 1975.

National Recreation and Park Association. *National Personnel Guidelines for Park, Recreation and Leisure Service Posi-tions.* Arlington, Virginia: N.R.P.A., 1978.

Tillman, A. *The Program Book for Recreation Professionals.* Palo Alto, California: National Press Books, 1973.

Young, L. J. *A Competency Analysis of Recreational Sports Personnel in Selected Institutional Settings.* Unpublished doctor's thesis, Bloomington: Indiana University, October, 1980.

AUXILIARY STAFF JOB DESCRIPTIONS

TITLE: Aerobic Dance Leader

REPORTS TO:

SUMMARY: Serve as a facilitator, continually emphasizing that participants exercise within their own personal limits.

Duties and Responsibilities:

1. Serve as a leader of exercise and dance routines in a gymnasium (or similar) environment. It is the leader's primary responsibility to ensure that the environment is safe for par-

ticipants at all times during the program. Any concerns should be directed immediately to the Recreational Sports Staff.

2. Have a complete and thorough understanding of all policies and procedures concerning the Aerobic Dance program. Such policies and procedures are covered in the training sessions offered prior to employment.

3. Attend each designated weekly practice session. Each leader is to be attired in clothing appropriate for exercise, as the practice sessions are designed so that the leader can learn new routines. It is the responsibility of each leader to have a complete understanding of each routine learned, *prior* to leaving the meeting.

4. Develop exercise and dance routines which follow a format provided by the program coordinator. Each routine developed should be designed in the best interest of the participant; it may become necessary for the coordinator to adjust routines used in the program.

5. Be prepared for each session. This includes being properly attired (leotards, tights and gym shoes), being thoroughly prepared to lead each routine, having cassette recorder, stop watch and music tapes on hand, and having the participants' Weekly Record Sheets available before the session begins.

6. Arrive at the designated facility at least five (5) minutes before the session is scheduled to begin. This is important in order to handle participant questions or concerns, and to provide each participant with their Weekly Record Sheet.

7. Maintain current certification in Cardio-Pulmonary Resuscitation. Follow stated policy for handling and reporting accidents.

8. Secure the facility and equipment before leaving or wait to be relieved from your position by an incoming employee.

TITLE: Fitness Tester

REPORTS TO:

SUMMARY: Perform fitness assessments for the Fitness Program and serve as a Fitness public relations person at special events.

Duties and Responsibilities:

1. Attend all training sessions and meetings as designated for fitness testers. Employment shall be delayed until sufficient training for fitness assessments has been completed.

2. Provide physical fitness assessments to individuals and refer individuals to the proper normative charts for each assessment.

   The fitness tester's position is not designed to provide participants with a subjective evaluation of their fitness level and/or any form of exercise prescription. The fitness assessments shall serve as normative tests by which the individual may judge their own current level of physical fitness based upon medically accepted norms provided by the program.

3. Assist the Fitness Testing Supervisor in setting up and taking down equipment used for fitness assessments. Employees should plan to arrive and leave the area approximately fifteen minutes earlier and later than the time block scheduled for actual testing.

4. Perform only fitness assessments that have been specified and that the individual has been trained to perform. If a situation should arise in which there are an insufficient number of testers available, the Fitness Testing Supervisor must assume responsibility for performing the assessment or for contacting additional trained employees to assist.

5. Serve as a volunteer fitness tester at special events such as the S.O.S. All Nighter, Health Fair, Fitness Awareness Week and other similar events.

6. Maintain an up-to-date summary of all fitness programs offered. This is imperative since the position requires answering individual's questions concerning other fitness programs.

TITLE: Exercise Leader—Senior Position

REPORTS TO:

SUMMARY: Fitness Coordinator with the implementation of the Aerobic Dance program, and serve as liaison between the Coordinator and all Aerobic Dance leaders.

Duties and Responsibilities:

1. Assist with the screening and auditioning of applicants for Exercise Leader position.

2. Assist in the design and implementation of outlines concerning the weekly routines used in the program.

3. Oversee each weekly practice session; handle all concerns related to routine development, music selection, and other program concerns.

4. Assume responsibility for maintaining weekly payroll for each of the leaders.

5. Attend each leader's session on a pre-determined rotation basis to observe and evaluate the performance of the leaders.

6. Distribute, explain, and collect the program evaluation forms given to all participants at the completion of each program.

7. Serve as a liaison for the organization, implementation and evaluation of all exercise demonstrations performed within the setting.

8. Maintain documentation of all tasks undertaken and submit a complete written summary and list of recommendations at the end of each program.

9. Attend a weekly meeting with the immediate supervisor to discuss all concerns and needs of the program; highlight employee evaluations.

TITLE: Weightroom Supervisor

REPORTS TO:

SUMMARY: Supervise proper use of the weightroom during informal sport hours.

Duties and Responsibilities:

1. Report to work 5 minutes prior to the start of the shift.

2. Check to see that the facility is properly organized and equipment in its appropriate place.

3. Check for safety hazards and correct problems. Close the facility if the conditions warrant.

4. Curtail improper use of equipment; correct improper or unsafe techniques but absolutely refrain from prescribing work out or conditioning programs.

5. Enforce courtesy policies governing wearing shirts or draping towels over benches while in use; and the policy requiring the use of a "spotter" for lifts/presses.

6. Organize participants to assist in placing weights in their proper location at the completion of a shift.

7. Closely monitor equipment use to prevent thefts or damage. Conduct an inventory at the completion of the shift.

8. Initiate proper emergency first aid when necessary. Follow stated policy for handling and reporting accidents. Follow up with a written report on serious injuries.

9. Complete maintenance repair forms as necessary.

10. Strive to maintain positive public relations. Provide participants with complaint-suggestion forms; refer to the appropriate staff when necessary.

11. Secure the facility when working the final shift or wait to be properly relieved from your position.

TITLE: Lifeguard

REPORTS TO:

SUMMARY: Monitor the safety and participation of swimmers during informal sport pool hours.

Duties and Responsibilities:

1. Maintain participant safety through preventive lifeguarding. Check the area for safety hazards and try to eliminate them. Close the facility if a hazardous condition warrants.

2. Utilize appropriate rescue techniques and follow-up procedures. Provide emergency first aid when necessary. Call for ambulance assistance as warranted.

3. Report any accidents or disciplinary problems on the appropriate forms. Curtail misuse of the facility.

4. Strictly enforce pool policies, regulations, laws and ordinances governing the conduct of persons using the facility.

5. Position yourself at the assigned locations at the pool for maximum visibility.

6. Maintain a neat, clean area. Assist in the proper maintenance and sanitary operation of the facility.

7. Complete maintenance repair forms as needed.

8. Strive to maintain positive public relations. Provide participants with complaint-suggestion forms, or refer to staff.

9. Do not leave your post until properly relieved, or secure the facility if yours is the last shift.

10. Keep W.S.I., C.P.R. and First Aid certifications current.

TITLE: Internship, Informal Sports

REPORTS TO:

SUMMARY: The staff assistant will work with the Assistant Director in the planning, organizing, conduct, and evaluation of the Informal Sports program.

Duties and Responsibilities:

1. Assist with the scheduling of informal sports employees.

2. Maintain bi-monthly payroll for informal sports employees, and submit to program-administrative staff for approval.

3. Maintain daily, weekly and monthly procedural/programming forms.

4. Observe and report on informal sport employee performance.

5. Maintain accurate statistical analysis of program participation.

6. Assist in the recruitment and training of employees; attend regular employee meetings.

7. Assist in the operation of the I.D./Fee Collection Process.

8. Submit revisions for the Informal Sports Employee Policy Manual.

9. Assist with the Informal Sports Advisory Council.

10. Maintain and organize the Complaints and Suggestions forms, and provide an answering service.

11. Assist in the collection of information for budget preparation, the annual report, and other documents as required.

12. Assist in other projects within Informal Sports as requested by the Program Administrative Staff.

13. Maintain daily office hours.

TITLE: Intramural Sport Manager (volunteer position)

REPORTS TO:

SUMMARY: Communicate the general philosophy and content within the Recreational Sport Program to the residents within your participation unit; facilitate participation in the intramural sports program.

Duties and Responsibilities:

1. Maintain a personal approach in encouraging and organizing participation in recreational sport from your area.

2. Implement activity interest survey for your unit.

3. Be familiar with intramural entry procedures and fee system.

4. Submit all intramural entry forms from their area to the Recreational Sports Office prior to the deadline.

5. Inform intramural team captains of their responsibilities and assist them in their role as a leader.

6. Serve as a consultant in regard to intramural eligibility, policies, and procedures in the Intramural Sports Program.

7. Monitor the recognition and/or point systems for their unit.

8. Coordinate and supervise assistants.

9. Attend meetings as established by the Intramural Sports Staff.

10. See that promotion/publicity materials get posted and/or communicated to residents within your area.

11. Assist with program evaluation and feedback.

12. Assist with special projects/committees relevant to Recreational Sports Programs within the unit.

13. Encourage high standards of sportsmanship for your unit.

14. Visit the Recreational Sports Office regularly.

TITLE: Intramural Sport Official

REPORTS TO:

SUMMARY: Utilize appropriate mechanics for officiating and enforce the sport rules and regulations in effect for the particular sport.

Duties and Responsibilities:

1. Report to work ten minutes prior to the start of the scheduled contest. Check in with the sport supervisor and obtain necessary equipment and supplies.

2. Locate the team captains and have them complete the roster on the score sheet. Locate scorekeepers.

3. Double check the condition of the facility for hazards. Report problems or maintenance concerns to the on-duty sport supervisor.

4. Issue equipment to team captains if needed. Conduct the pre-game meeting to handle introductions and highlight important rules, regulations, or modifications.

5. Anticipate problems and seek to prevent or minimize them through quality officiating.

6. Attempt to resolve disputes if possible. Receive any requests for protest and report to sport supervisor for documentation. Continue the game as soon as possible. Submit written report.

7. Report any misuse of the facility or discipline problems from participants or spectators to the sport supervisor. Submit a detailed written report on serious situations.

8. Send for the sport supervisor in the event of an accident. Remain with the injured party until relieved. Follow-up with a written report for serious accidents.

9. Check with the sport supervisor for reassignment in the event of a forfeit, or a personnel shortage at the beginning of a new shift.

10. Maintain a neat, clean environment.

11. Strive to maintain positive public relations.

12. Return equipment, supplies and completed score sheets to the activity supervisor at the completion of your shift. Sign-out.

TITLE: Intramural Sport Supervisor

REPORTS TO:

SUMMARY: Supervise the participants, spectators and employees during assigned intramural sport events; curtail any misuse of the area; remain alert for safety hazards and try to eliminate.

Duties and Responsibilities:

1. Arrive thirty minutes prior to the scheduled start of games.

2. Check the facilities and equipment for safety hazards. Postpone games if the problem can not be eliminated or unfavorable weather conditions prevail.

3. Issue necessary equipment to sport officials, monitor its use, and secure it at the completion of the shift.

4. Coordinate the sign-in for sport officials, and the re-assignment of personnel from games not being played.

5. Collect score cards after each game.

6. Follow employee procedures for handling and reporting accidents and injuries. Complete the accident report form. Call for ambulance assistance as needed. Follow up with written report for serious injuries.

7. Be alert for disputes, protests, and other problems. Try to curtail or prevent them from occurring. Document problems on the appropriate forms as required for handling protests or potential disciplinary action situations. Contact the police for assistance as the last measure.

8. Complete the officials performance rating sheet for employees under your supervision.

9. Complete maintenance repair forms as needed.

10. Maintain a clean, neat area.

11. Strive to maintain positive public relations. Provide participants or spectactors with complaint-suggestion forms, or refer to appropriate staff.

12. Contact your immediate supervisor in the event of an unusual circumstance requiring prompt resolution.

TITLE: Club Sport President

REPORTS TO:

SUMMARY: Organize, delegate, initiate, or conduct actions in the interest of serving the club membership and maintaining quality club operations.

Duties and Responsibilities:

1. Conduct all club meetings following accepted code of parliamentary procedure.

2. Appoint necessary committees and chairpersons as provided within the club operational guidelines.

3. Coordinate and schedule all club activities.

4. Maintain regular contact with club officers and committee members; request oral and written reports as necessary.

5. Organize and supervise the election procedure.

6. Review, seek adoption, and present the club annual report and budget request as required.

7. Monitor compliance with agency or club policies, rules, regulations, and ordinances.

8. Arrange for and monitor use of facilities, equipment, and supplies.

9. Arrange for and monitor a safety and accident prevention program. Follow approved first aid or accident reporting procedures as required.

10. Serve as the representative of the club to the agency or setting.

TITLE: Recreational Sport Instructor

REPORTS TO:

SUMMARY: Plan, organize, and conduct instruction of a specific sport activity at a single facility or variety of facilities and localities.

Duties and Responsibilities:

1. Prepare and propose content and session outlines for review by program-administrative staff.

2. Arrange for and monitor use of facilities, equipment, and supplies.

3. Initiate and assist with the preparation of promotional materials and hand-outs.

4. Train and supervise auxiliary staff in the conduct of the sessions.

5. Maintain discipline and safety; follow appropriate first aid measures as required.

6. Prepare, administer, and interpret evaluation instruments of participant learning and skills development.

7. Check for and report any maintenance-repair needs on the appropriate form.

8. Maintain appropriate records, inventories, reports, and information as required.

9. Prepare and submit budget proposals, evaluations and recommendations, and other reports as required.

CHAPTER 7

PROGRAM CONTROL

Program control involves identifying and managing negative factors that exist within recreational sport while promoting desired patterns of behavior on the part of participants, spectators, and program personnel. Negative or stressful situations in sport range in degree of severity and intensity. Situations producing a negative impact over a period of time include: unauthorized use of limited access facilities, inconsistent adherence to a club constitution, forfeits in structured tournament play and unrealistic expectations of officials. Negative situations within sport requiring prompt, decisive action include vandalism, verbal or physical abuse, insubordination or incompetence by personnel, and violation of established policy or procedure.

When faced with a stressful situation, the programmer may be tempted to avoid the responsibility for resolving the problem. Avoidance only perpetuates and compounds a conflict when the programmer is capable of handling it. Although conflict resolution is often unpleasant, it is a necessary programming function. Time commited to analyzing problems and becoming familiar with the methods and techniques used to establish or restore control helps the programmer maintain a positive sport environment for participants, spectators, and program personnel. Without control, a potential exists for disorder, personal injury, conflict and destruction of property.

There are two factors affecting program control within the recreational sport environment: one relates to self-control or self-discipline, while the second pertains to external control techniques. Our main focus centers upon external control: the roles, responsibilities and sphere of influence of program personnel within sport. While self-control is a matter of individual responsibility, the programmer should consider factors which affect individual behavior as the basis for selecting external control methods and techniques. For example, individuals or groups engaging in sport events often meet frustration—a state of mind associated with disappointment in the pursuit of goals. Participants unable to control frustration or alleviate stress may exhibit such behavior as violence, apathy, withdrawal, hostility or aggression.

For many years, sport psychologists have contended that abnormal aggressive behavior stems from deep psychological problems. The competitive nature of sports may also account for some deviant behavior. As Leonard (1973, pp. 45–46) suggests, competition is similiar to salad dressing in that ". . . it adds zest to the game and to life itself. But when the seasoning is mistaken for the substance, only sickness can follow."

The sport programmer has a responsibility to analyze probable causes for negative behavior. Avoid assuming behavior problems always result from lack of self-control or such personal factors as inadequate ability, unrealistic expectations, or different standards of behavior. Misconduct may result from such external factors as rules, regulations, opponents and program personnel, conduct, classification systems, or governance procedures. When trouble develops, use the situation to evaluate program design and delivery. Perhaps a rule is unfair, a sport offical is biased, a classification system is inequitable. Be creative in your efforts to minimize, alleviate, and control negative behavior.

PRACTICES FOR GOOD PROGRAM CONTROL

Program control begins with a basic understanding of human behavior and the establishment of standards and expectations. Some differences of opinion exist regarding acceptable or unacceptable behavior, but the programmer who exhibits a professional, conscientious approach will be able to identify and establish suitable standards. Among the aspects of desirable behavior are:

Respect for self
Respect for others
Respect for position
Respect for property
Respect for rules and regulations
Respect for law and order

Publishing a list of expectations for conduct is not sufficient to cultivate adherence. Desirable behavior within the recreational sport environment is attainable if specific objectives and strategies are established. We suggest several guidelines using the aforementioned categories.

RESPECT FOR SELF

Research suggests that the ability to demonstrate respect for others is derived from respect for self. Since there is a positive correlation between positive feelings about one's body and self-respect, programs that seek improvement in posture and fitness are useful. When participants have opportunities to experience competence by mastering skills, they may develop greater self-esteem. Helping individuals develop a positive self-image provides a good foundation for program control.

RESPECT FOR OTHERS

Thoughtfulness, courtesy, and consideration are attributes associated with respect for others. Care for others and sensitivity to their needs is a quality that should be encouraged by any sports program. The courteous behavior or "etiquette", associated with tennis or golf is indicative of an attitude applicable to other sport and life situations.

Sport participation has negative social consequences when participants dwell upon the differences and peculiarities of others. Accentuate the positive by emphasizing the similarities between people. Demonstrate an ability to accept the different interests and sport skill levels of others.

RESPECT FOR POSITION

Positions of responsibility including official, supervisor, officer, programmer, or volunteer should command respect. When an individual in one of these roles fails to live up to expectations of participants, respect for the position diminishes.

Sport programmers hold a position of authority and need the respect of participants and fellow staff members in order to bring about control within the program. Abuse of authority jeopardizes the respect for the total operation. It is unprofessional and unacceptable when someone in authority extends special favors to friends or relatives.

RESPECT FOR PROPERTY

Respect for public or private property is characteristic of good program control. Such an attitude discourages theft and vandalism by emphasizing consideration for what others own. Disrespect for sport facilities, equipment and supplies leads to increased repair and replacement costs and infringes on the right of others to use the resources.

Conservation is relevant to this discussion. How often do volunteers or employees waste or misuse resources? How often have softball field lights been turned on when there is insufficient interest to warrant their use? After using lights, do people forget and leave them on all night? Is equipment consistently lost or misplaced because of a poor check-out system or poor equipment inventory management?

RESPECT FOR RULES AND REGULATIONS

The most significant aspect of control in sports programming, respect for rules and regulations, recognizes the necessity for specific criteria that govern the conduct of individuals, teams, and groups in sport. No sport may be played and enjoyed without this structure. The more conscientiously participants observe the rules, the easier it is for them to focus on participation. Imagine what a basketball contest would be like without violations and fouls! The first action a group takes when participating in informal basketball is to establish such ground rules as the calling of fouls, the number of baskets needed to win and the handling of jumpballs.

For most participants, specific rules and regulations governing behavior and conduct are usually unnecessary. However, some individuals like to challenge the system and ignore or deliberately break the rules for their own personal gain.

Appropriate rules and regulations guarantee and protect the rights and welfare of all. Participants need to understand that they do not have the privilege of picking the rules they choose to follow. While they have a right to propose changes when rules and regulations seem unjustified or inappropriate, they should respect and follow them until they are changed by an objective process of review and revision.

RESPECT FOR LAW AND ORDER

Law and order involves a judicial system that represents one of the oldest techniques of program control. Such deviant behavior as assaulting an official or player, stealing or selling drugs is illegal and unacceptable in a sport program. Participants and personnel should know the procedures and possible penalties involved when a violation of the law occurs. Prompt, decisive and appropriate action on the part of program personnel conveys a clear message: disrespect for law and order will not be tolerated.

Respect, consideration and responsible behavior within a sport environment requires cultivation. Reinforce volunteers, employees, participants, and spectators as they practice socially acceptable behavior. Principles which illustrate desirable behavior include:

—considering the rights of others

—contemplating the consequences of an action before committing it

—being truthful and dependable

—being fair and just, moral and ethical
—avoiding objectional dress, speech and gestures

PRACTICES FOR CONTROL

Standards of behavior serve as one measure contributing to control within sport. The following categories describe other practices which have demonstrated effectiveness in establishing program control.

Personnel. A professional image among personnel in terms of dress and manner is essential. Participants have little respect for the sloppily-dressed or rude staff member. The success of any individual often depends on good personal habits: dress, grooming and manners.

All sports personnel should understand thoroughly the need for and purpose of program policies, rules and procedures. If they cannot explain them to participants or serve as proper role models, compliance suffers.

Policy, Rules and Regulations. Delete irrelevant rules from operational guidelines. Obsolete rules hamper the creation of a positive attitude among participants. Enforce the relevant policies, rules and regulations with consistency. Erratic enforcement results in program control problems. Participants should have the opportunity to take part in policy formulation and review based on their degree of maturity and responsibility.

Governance. All disciplinary action should be fair, consistent and understanding. When considering the punishment to impose after a rule violation, the level of maturity of the individual involved is more important than the age. Penalties too lax for an adult or too stringent for a child may perpetuate problems. Precedents furnish perspective in determining the severity of a penalty. As you consider what penalty to impose, prepare to justify and defend your decision. Always provide an opportunity for appeal.

Programming. Provide opportunities for participation regardless of specific sport interest or skill level. Structure programs without bias or preferential treatment and involve participants and program personnel in the decision-making and evaluation process affecting program development or modification.

Develop leadership characteristics on the part of staff that facilitate participant willingness to adhere and conform to behavioral expectations. Among the desired characteristics are: a professional image, a genuine interest in the participants and program, competence and knowledge regarding program responsibilities, and an ability to create a challenging, interesting and enjoyable sports program.

In addition to the preceding general principles governing conduct, the following checklist is useful in describing recommended practices for dealing with problem conduct situations.

CHECKLIST FOR PROBLEM SITUATIONS

1. *PUBLICIZE RULES FOR CONDUCT EARLY.* By listing, describing or explaining *firm* behavioral expectations in advance, through team captains' meetings, organizational meetings and manuals, the participants and program personnel are fully aware of what is expected of them and the consequences of any infraction.

2. *USE SUSPENSION AS A LAST RESORT.* Think twice before ejecting a participant from the sport event or terminating program personnel from the program. Do so only after exhausting every available alternative. Once a participant, employee or volunteer is suspended or ejected from the program, he or she is usually lost forever.

3. *DON'T OVERREACT.* Making every incident a crisis only lessens the respect for the programmer and creates more problems. Be careful that less significant incidents do not "snowball".

4. *DISCUSS MISBEHAVIOR, NOT THE INDIVIDUAL.* The personality of the employee, volunteer, or participant should not be the issue in a disciplinary case. Disapprove of the misbehavior and not the person. Never label an individual as an "instigator" or "trouble-maker" without giving him or her a chance to prove otherwise.

5. *PRAISE PUBLICLY, REPRIMAND PRIVATELY.* Humiliating an individual in front of his or her peers is a poor method of handling discipline. If a reprimand is necessary, always respect the participant's feelings and avoid using ridicule or sarcastic comments.

6. *BE FIRM, FAIR AND FRIENDLY.* Treat offenders as you would like to be treated. If you approach all situations in a positive, business-like manner, half the battle is already won. A poised demeanor is effective in problem situations, and a pleasant attitude is appreciated by others.

7. *ANTICIPATE PROBLEMS.* By staying one step ahead of a situation, many potential problems can be avoided. Mentally "walk through" responsibilities and try to anticipate the unexpected.

8. *DON'T PRETEND TO KNOW IT ALL.* The programmer will gain more respect by saying "I don't know, let me look it up" than by pretending to be a walking encyclopedia. Participants realize that no one is capable of knowing all sport rules, regulations and policies, so don't try to bluff your way through.

COMMUNICATION

The programmer should utilize every available avenue for conveying expectations for desirable behavior and the possible consequences of noncompliance. When communicating standards, avoid an extreme emphasis on consequences, otherwise, participants may lose interest in participation.

Communication about program control may take the form of verbal presentations to participants, spectators, and personnel through meetings, clinics or workshops, and the form of printed-presentations using pamphlets, brochures, handbooks and manuals. A handbook or manual is an excellent way to promote program control. Written material often contains a code of conduct or description of acceptable behavior. Content describes acceptable and unacceptable behavior and the consequences of violations. With the written material, there is less chance for misinterpretation. Mass distribution of manuals and handbooks is more effective way to reach people than informal verbal presentations.

Developing a handbook. The preparation of a handbook may involve different emphases, writing style, and size. Some handbooks address a general population; others, a specific target group. An intramural sport program may publish a unit managers' resource handbook, a club sport program may create an officers' manual and constitution and an informal sport program may utilize a manual to communicate guidelines for participation. Among the topics most often covered in a handbook format are the following:

—Facility descriptions and hours of operation.
—Sport program calendar of events.
—Rules and regulations regarding eligibility requirements, protests, forfeits, and postponements.
—Policies and procedures relevant to fees and charges, locker rooms, equipment, facility utilization, accidents and lost and found.

Participants need information describing specific rules regulating conduct, describing unacceptable behavior and the penalties that result from infractions. An example of a description that might appear in an intramural handbook follows:

"In the event an individual(s), and/or spectator(s) conducts himself/herself in an unsportsmanlike manner during sport competition, the official(s) on the game has complete authority in taking action, as deemed necessary, in order to keep the sport in control. Depending on the severity of the incident, the sport official may take the following action: give warnings, eject from the game, eject from the area, and/or suspend the game. Incidents of unsportsmanlike conduct (examples: using an ineligible player(s), theft of or damage to facilities or equipment; physical and/or verbal abuse toward officials(s), supervisor(s), player(s), or spectator(s)) will be investigated. The individual(s) and/or team(s) involved will be questioned and required to submit a written statement of the incident. Written statements from the officials and supervisors on duty will also be obtained. At the conclusion of the investigation, the staff will rule on the individual(s) and/or team(s) involved. Penalties include: suspension from a game, games or season; temporary or permanent probation; and/or suspension for a given time period."

A handbook should specify the procedural steps followed by the agency in the event of a disciplinary action (participants' rights, grievance procedures, the appeal process).

A careful handbook design and distribution increases its effectiveness as a communication tool. Key concepts of handbook design include simplicity, attractiveness, clarity, conciseness and relevance. A requirement that all personnel and participants sign a statement acknowledging they have read and understand the contents of a handbook furthers familiarity with the essential information.

After an initial distribution, retain extra copies of each handbook or manual for newcomers, for periodic redistribution at key locations, and for visible recreational sports office reference.

DISCIPLINARY ACTION AND PROGRAM CONTROL

Little recreational sport literature exists about a system for handling disciplinary situations. While programmers understand that discipline problems exist and that corrective action is often necessary, some lack confidence in coping with them. Consequently, we will now consider the foundations of a disciplinary action process, and examine an example of implementation.

Due Process in Sports. Due process is fundamental to American constitutional law. It is a concept that safeguards equality, fair treatment and rights for all. Although most people are quick to assume they know their rights, few can define them.

Most individual rights derive from the original ten amendments of the Constitution, known as the Bill of Rights, and extend through subsequent amendments. The Fifth Amendment guarantees that "no person shall be . . . deprived of life, liberty or property, without due process of law." The Fourteenth Amendment extends the Fifth Amendment protection to state government and reads ". . . nor shall any State deprive any person of life, liberty, or property, without due process of law."

Due process is delineated into two categories: substantive and procedural. Substantive due process involves program control, which includes the publication of rules and regulations, the specificity of regulations and the authority of agency personnel to deal with disciplinary cases.

Procedural due process pertains to the right to a trial by one's peers. The following decribes aspects of procedural due process applicable for sport participants, spectators, employees, and volunteers:

1. Provide ample opportunity for all to know the standards and regulations they must follow.

2. Once there is evidence of a violation, furnish a complete description of the charges.

3. Allow time for the accused to prepare a defense.

4. Establish an appropriate hearing opportunity to consider arguments for and against the accused.

5. Make a fair and impartial decision, and put it in writing. (Adapted from Forsythe, 1977 p. 354)

In addition to these procedures, include the right to obtain a list of witnesses and copies of their statements prior to a hearing, the right to counsel at the hearing, the right to hear all witnesses, the right to present a case, the right to remain silent, the right to appeal, (Alexander and Solomon, 1972), and the right to inspect in advance any written reports on the charges as well as the right to cross-examine all witnesses (Van Alstyne, 1970).

Although due process standards and theories have greater relevance to judicial settings, they apply to the non-legal sport environment. When a recreational sports disciplinary action system is based upon a commitment to fair treatment, it parallels that of the judicial system, even though a programmer lacks the legal expertise.

Greenleaf (1978, p. 34) suggests that professionals involved in discipline may assist "in developing an understanding of authority and in developing personal values and attitudes". Consequently, the agency should establish and maintain sound due process procedures.

THE DISCIPLINARY ACTION PROCESS

The following is an example of a process for handling situations which may merit disciplinary action. We first present an outline of steps involved in a disciplinary action, and then provide more detail about each step. Any approach to disciplinary action entails:

—Identifying and reporting the problem
—Investigating the cause
—Deciding appropriate action
—Providing an opportunity for appeal
—Maintaining documentation

Identifying the disciplinary situation or complaint. The first step in the discipline process begins with the source of a complaint. You cannot assume all complaints have equal validity, since they often arise out of personal dislikes or bias. Begin your review with an open mind. The assumption of innocence applies to the sport setting.

Once a situation warranting disciplinary action has occurred, verify the incident and obtain a detailed account of the alleged violation. Verification provides the foundation for subsequent investigation. Document all details on a Complaint Form or Disciplinary Action Form.

Investigating the Cause. For any investigation, collect and consider basic background information. If the accused is an employee, check into the length of employment, past performance ratings, similar complaints, previous personnel evaluations, and comments from peers. If the accused is a participant, information regarding previous involvement in the program, reports from other institutional settings, or past disciplinary records may provide insight. In any case, we cannot overemphasize this principle: *TO* THE INVESTIGATOR MAY FLOW MUCH INFORMATION; *FROM* THE INVESTIGATOR FLOWS A FEW CAREFULLY-SELECTED STATEMENTS.

If a situation involves an alleged violation of policy, rule or regulation, determine whether or not the violation was intentional and the extent to which external factors contributed to the problem. Was the rule or policy specified in writing to the individual prior to the act? Did the individual violate a written or verbal rule? For example, it is not fair to penalize an individual for smoking in a non-smoking section of the building when no sign is posted.

Enforce consistent policies and rules. Imposing a rule one day and ignoring it the next lessens its credibility and the disciplinary action that results. If the justification for a policy or

DISCIPLINARY ACTION FORM

Date _____ Time of Incident _____
Location of Incident _____
Type of Sport/Program _____

Witnesses: (1) _____   Phone _____
               (2) _____   Phone _____
               (3) _____   Phone _____

Personnel   (1) _____   Phone _____
on Duty: (2) _____   Phone _____

Persons Involved in the Incident:
   NAME   ADDRESS   PHONE NO.
(1) _____
(2) _____
(3) _____
(4) _____

Describe the Incident in as Much Detail as Possible
WITNESS #1:

                                 Signature _____

WITNESS #2:

                                 Signature _____

WITNESS #3:

                                 Signature _____

PROGRAM PERSONNEL #1:

                                 Signature _____

PROGRAM PERSONNEL #2:

                                 Signature _____

Additional Comments from Program Personnel:

Figure 7-1. Disciplinary action form.

rule is based solely on the fact that it is "office policy", its effectiveness suffers when the participant thinks it unreasonable or unwarranted.

Any investigation involves interviewing persons familiar with the situation. Prior to interviewing the accused, a sensitive investigator determines what occurred by pursuing all accounts of an incident from participants, witnessses and program personnel and records their statements for reference.

The first contact with the accused is an opportunity to review the case and to uncover discrepancies. This interview routinely involves informing an individual(s) of the complaint concerning his or her alleged behavior, and specifying his or her rights of due process. Most people cooperate when they are confident that due process is being followed.

Although the majority of disciplinary situations may be settled during an initial interview, the accused should have every opportunity to explain his or her side of the story. If confusion or uncertainty exists after the initial meeting, conduct subsequent interviews to clarify specifics.

Making the decision. After completing all interviews, formulate an initial decision regarding the complaint. Before going public with a decision, evaluate your process of investigation: have all the facts been gathered? Are there concrete answers to such questions as: what happened, who was involved, why, when and where did it happen, and who was in error? Prepare to substantiate the fairness of the investigation: have all persons, interests and points of view been fairly represented? Have personal feelings, likes, dislikes, or biases influenced the decision?

Assuming the investigation indicates a need for disciplinary action, assess the severity of the situation prior to specifying a penalty. The penalty should match the violation. Some violations may warrant harsh punishment. An incident involving an assault on a staff member is far more serious than a forfeit of a scheduled contest. Punitive options progress from less serious to serious; probation through suspension to expulsion. Variations in severity may exist within each type of penalty: probation does not prohibit the individual from continued involvement as an employee, volunteer or participant, but indicates an incident is a matter of formal record, warning that future problems may lead to more severe disciplinary action.

Suspension entails a temporary loss of privileges, benefits, or affiliation with the program. Examples of variations in this category include: suspension from participation in a single intramural sport or all sports offered during a specified time span; temporary loss of facility utilization or financial support for a club sport; and reassignment from employment as a central facility manager to a gymnasium supervisor.

Expulsion or termination is reserved for situations in which the severity of the incident requires total separation from the program. These involve violations of law, policy, rule or regulation that jeopardize safety or security: the use of alcohol or illegal drugs, assault and battery, unauthorized, unexcused absence from a supervisory assignment, theft, vandalism or falsification of payroll.

Prior to selection of a penalty, consider the concept of precedents. Review similar situations that have occurred in the past and impose a similar judgement. If precedents for a ruling do not exist with your particular program, contact other agencies for perspective. Regardless of the penalty, justify it to the individual to promote understanding for the basis of your action. Summarize the investigation and resulting disciplinary action in writing, forwarding a copy to the individual involved, and maintain another as a matter of record.

The appeal process. If an individual is dissatisfied with the decision or believes he or she received unfair treatment, provide an opportunity to appeal the decision to a peer group governing board or to an administrative staff member. A last recourse, the appeal process is valuable in the event of error, bias, or skepticism regarding the initial decision. One is more inclined to accept the decision of one's peers than that of the staff. However, the appeal process can fail if those involved are not committed to a fair, objective review.

Preparation. Provide a summary of the case and all pertinent reports and statements for each member of the appeals board. Plan to have separate presentations by the staff person involved with the case and the appellant.

Before the board begins questioning, inform the appellant of the procedure that will be followed. The appellant should sign a statement indicating an understanding of the procedure and the rights guaranteed by the appeals process.

The Hearing. The appellant presents an account of the incident, followed by questioning by the board. A hearing conducted in a formal, yet unaccusative manner demonstrates a commitment by the board to complete examination of the facts in the case and fair treatment. A board hearing is not a trial.

Deliberation. Once the interviews are complete, the board deliberates the case in private. Once a decision is reached, the board informs the appellant and the staff. Further appeal from this point on must be based on a violation of due process.

Maintaining documentation. Throughout each phase of the disciplinary action process, systematic collection of information is essential. The programmer needs to maintain thorough minutes of cases brought to appeals. Documentation facilitates the collection of information for historical reference, and the provision of case studies for the training of new appeals groups.

Establishing a governing or appeals board

Care in the selection and training of members is essential for effective board operations. When reviewing prospective applicants, identify those who have related experience and knowledge regarding program operations. Design selection to guarantee representation for those who are affected by board decisions. Provide training to familiarize new members with purpose, standards, duties, and operating procedures. More specific guidelines for implementing a governing or appeals board follow.

Purpose. The purpose of a governing board is to assure fair treatment and promote delivery of recreational sport programs to all those served by a setting. This responsibility includes adjudicating appeals and evaluating proposed program, policy or rule changes.

Ethical standards. In order to preserve the professionalism and objectivity of the board, members must observe certain ethical standards. Violation of these standards may constitute just cause for removal from the board. It is the responsibility of each board member to observe the following principles:

1. Information regarding a case is confidential.

2. The record of any participant may not be discussed or disclosed outside the hearing.

3. Members should never make accusations or statements unsupported by the facts.

4. In all cases, the vote of each board member is confidential. The vote of the entire board, including majority and dissenting opinions, is relayed to the appellant and recorded in the minutes of the hearing.

5. Members of the board must uphold the regulations and policies of the recreational sport program.

6. Members of the board who have a conflict of interest in a case must abstain from participating as a voting member of the board on that case. They may attend the hearing as an observer.

If a member of the board is found to be responsible for a violation of any policies or regulations, the board may discuss the incident with the member in a closed session to determine if the violation affects the credibility of the board. By a majority vote of the board and its chairperson, the following may result:

1. The board may issue the member a warning to indicate that any future violations of policies and regulations may result in removal from the board.

2. The board may remove any member. Members so removed will be ineligible for service on any board for a specified period.

3. The board may decide that the matter does not warrant further consideration and take no action against the member in question.

Duties and Responsibilities. Members should have a clear understanding of the duties and responsibilities of each board position.

Board Advisor (Member of the area program staff)

—Coordinates the selection and training of members.
—Coordinates the storage and filing of all documentation.
—Informs the appealing party of hearing procedures.

—Informs members about all meetings.
—Investigates or monitors recommendations.

Board Member

—Arrives on time for all scheduled meetings.
—Anticipates absences and informs advisor ahead of time.
—Assists with projects and committees.
—Comes prepared for all meetings.
—Participates in decision-making.

Board Secretary

—Maintains minutes.
—Records motions and the name of the member presenting or seconding a motion.
—Submits minutes to the board advisor.
—Prepares written statements of board rulings for program staff and the chairperson.

Chairperson

—Has command of Robert's Rules of Parliamentary Procedure.
—Handles opening comments and introductions.
—Facilitates discussion and maintains order.
—Reminds members of operating procedure.
—Helps the advisor organize agenda and material.
—Announces results of deliberations to the parties involved.
—Appoints an acting secretary when necessary.
—Assists with an evaluation of the board's performance.

Operating Procedures. The board chairperson ensures the efficient operation of the board. Prior to the start of a hearing, the chairperson reviews reports with other members to delete irrelevant material and identify areas of questioning. When the board is ready, the chairperson introduces the appellant to the board and outlines the procedures for the hearing. Once the board begins its questioning, the chairperson is responsible for maintaining its professionalism and objectivity.

The chairperson must also discourage emotional banter and outbursts among board members and witnesses. When board members are adequately trained, the task is not a difficult one. A seating arrangement which places the appellant in full view before board members and locates witnesses away from the board helps maintain order. This ensures that responses to questions are addressed to the board and not to spectators. Outbursts by spectators cannot be tolerated. Remove persons from the room who do not comply with protocol.

Normally, the chair does not participate in debate when serving as a meeting facilitator. In the case the chair wishes to join into a debate, a temporary chair should preside until the particular discussion or debate is completed.

During deliberations, the chairperson has a responsibility to see that each member of the board reaches an independent decision. The chairperson may not vote unless there is a tie in voting or the board decides to vote by secret ballot, and the chair informs the board of an intent to vote. The chair may also elect not to vote on a tie, thereby causing a motion to fail. The advantage of a multiple member board is the value of differing perspectives. Board members should voice dissenting opinions and ask for explanations when they disagree with other members. Both the majority and dissenting opinions on an issue require documentation for future reference.

The following outline of the process involved in a board hearing is offered as a review:

PRE-HEARING

A. Participant making appeal

    1. Participant given copies of:
        a. appeal statement (Figure 7-2)
        b. copy of the Recreational Sport Staff decision

    2. Participant given Statement of Rights and asked to acknowledge its receipt. (Figure 7-3)

    3. Participant informed of due process procedure.

    4. Participant shown roster of board members.
        a. Individual may disqualify a member from voting if so desired.
        b. Roster must be set 24 hours in advance.
        c. A quorum must be present to vote.

GOVERNING BOARD APPEAL FORM

CASE NUMBER _____

DATE _____

SPORT _____

NAME: _____

ORGANIZATION: _____

STAFF DECISION BEING APPEALED: _____

_____

_____

SUMMARY OF REASON FOR APPEAL (Be specific, include names, dates, locations and other pertinent facts; use additional paper if necessary):

_____   _____
Signature   Phone

_____   _____
Date   Mailing Address

Figure 7-2. Governing board appeal form.

B. Board Members (no participants or staff present)

1. Chairperson reviews philosophy of recreational sport.

2. Chairperson reviews principles of due process and parliamentary procedure.

3. Chairperson reviews questions requiring answers.

4. Appeal forms and all other written information are presented to board members for review.

5. Chairperson requests copies of the operating handbook or specific sport regulations for clarification of rules.

6. Chairperson leads discussion to clarify facts or situations, and identify questions.

GOVERNING BOARD: STATEMENT OF RIGHTS

CASE NUMBER _____

DATE _____

SPORT _____

1. Right to read the written decision of the Recreational Sports Staff regarding the case.

2. Right to give your reaction to this statement and to offer any additional information during the hearing.

3. Right to remain silent and this will not be used against you.

4. Right to hear all testimony regarding the case.

5. Right to present witnesses on your behalf.

6. Right to be accompanied by an advisor of your choice.

7. Right to object to the participation of any member of the board. (Must be in writing 24 hours in advance of hearing).

8. Right to a closed hearing (no observers).

9. Will receive written notification within 10 class days of the results of this hearing.

10. I understand that if I speak out of turn, or when I am not asked, that I may be removed from the hearing, and the decision may be made without any further input from me.

I have read and understand this statement of rights:

_____

Signature

_____

Address

_____

Phone

Figure 7-3. Participant statement of rights form.

7. Chairperson contacts staff representative and appellant and escorts them to the designated meeting room.

HEARING

A. The Chairperson introduces members and advisors.

B. The Chairperson explains the due process procedure and reviews appellant rights.

C. The Chairperson asks staff to present its decision. The staff may present supporting witnesses at this time.

D. During the staff presentation, questions and rebuttal are not allowed. Upon completion, the board questions the staff member, establishing the following:

1. Timing of incident

2. Facts of case

3. Sources of problem

4. Specific policies or rules involved, and record of enforcement

5. Precedents

E. The chairperson now allows the appellant to state his or her case. After any supporting witnesses have testified, the Board may pursue further questions.

F. Board may recall the staff member, the appellant and witnesses for further questioning. Do not allow further presentations, questions, or rebuttal.

G. The chairperson asks the appellant and staff member to present one-minute summary statements. Barring further questioning, excuse both parties from the room.

POST HEARING DISCUSSION (Board only)

A. The chairperson opens the floor for discussion.

B. The chairperson reviews the case.

C. The board determines if more testimony is necessary. The chairperson may recall any witness.

D. The chairperson encourages each board member to comment.

E. The chairperson refers to previous decisions that may apply as a precedent. It is the staff's responsibility to furnish the chair with this information.

F. A board member makes a motion to:
1. Uphold the staff decision
2. Overturn the staff decision

G. The chairperson solicits a second.

H. A vote is taken. The board determines whether it is a secret or open ballot.

I. A simple majority rules. The secretary records the specific vote count and notes any majority and dissenting opinions.

J. The board documents all accompanying recommendations.

PRESENTATION OF DECISION

A. The chairperson leaves meeting room and escorts both parties into a private office.

B. The chairperson presents decision and rationale to both parties.

C. The chairperson and secretary sign minutes of hearing. (Refer to the examples of minutes in Figure 7-4.)

D. The chairperson writes up the final decision of the board, complete with rationale, and submits it for final typing.

E. The chairperson and advisor forward a copy of the decision to all concerned parties within 7 to 10 days.

In some cases, the board is asked to evaluate a proposal to change an existing rule or program offering. To proceed with a case of this nature, consider the following:

1. The participant or interest group should present a written proposal for the rule or program change.

2. The staff member responsible for the area affected by the rule or program change reviews the proposal and determines whether the rule change is a major or minor departure from established policy.

3. If the staff member rules that the proposed rule or program change is minor, the participant or interest group may take their case directly to the board.

4. If the staff member rules that the proposed rule or program change is major, the participant or interest group appears before a *Program Change Committee* within a designated time period.

5. The Program Change Committee should consist of the following members:

362 RECREATIONAL SPORT PROGRAMMING

a. Specified members of a regular board.
b. Specified members of the full-time staff of the agency. One of these representatives should serve as committee chairperson.

MINUTES OF GOVERNING BOARD HEARING

CASE NUMBER _____
DATE _____
SPORT _____

Nature of Hearing: **Location of Hearing:** _____
_____ Appeal of staff decision
_____ Program change
_____ Rule change   **Time of Hearing:** _____

Staff Decision Being Appealed:

Governing Board Chair:

Governing Board Secretary:

Governing Board Advisor:

Members Present:

Staff Member Presenting:

Appealing Party(s) (names and organizations):

Hearing Minutes (Summary):

Proposed Motion (Give names of proposer and the second):

Rationale and Recommendations:

Vote on Decision: _____ For _____ Against _____ Abstained

Figure 7-4. Example of governing board hearing minutes.

CONCLUSION

Program control is essential in operating a successful sport program regardless of size, location or environment. Effective program control begins with personnel at the operational level.

Confidence, courtesy, knowledge and assertiveness are essential when program personnel communicate with participants. Other practices that foster a better relationship between participants, spectators, and personnel involve improvements in program design and delivery and effective governance. When we promote constructive behavior, control undesirable conduct, and apply appropriate disciplinary measures, we create an attractive work and play environment.

REFERENCES

Alexander, K. and Solomon, E.S. *College and University Law.* Charlottesville, Virginia: The Michie Company, 1972.

Appenzeller, H. *Athletics and the Law.* Charlottesville, Virginia: The Michie Company, 1975.

Brady, T.A. and Snoxell, L.F. *Student Discipline in Higher Education.* Washington, D.C.: The American Personnel and Guidance Association, 1965.

Forsythe, Charles A. and Keller, Irvin A. *Administration of High School Athletics.* 6th Edition, Englewood Cliffs, New Jersey: Prentice-Hall, Inc. 1977.

Greenleaf, E.A. "The Relationship of Legal Issues and Procedures to Student Development" in *The Legal Foundations of Student Personnel Service in Higher Education* edited by Edward Hammond and Robert Shaffer, Washington, D.C., The American College Personnel Association, 1978.

Hyatt, R.W. *Intramural Sports: Organization and Administration.* St. Louis: The C.V. Mosby Company, 1977.

LaPoint, J.D. *Organization and Management of Sport.* Dubuque, Iowa: Kendall/Hunt Publishing Company, 1980.

Leonard, G.B. Winning Isn't Everything, Its Nothing. *Intellectual Digest* 4 (2) 45–46, 1973.

Paratore, Jean. "Controlling Unsportsmanlike Conduct in Intramural Sports," *Journal of Health, Physical Education and Recreation.* January, 1979, p. 46.

Pennock, J.R. and Chapman, J.W. *Due Process.* New York: New York University Press, 1977.

Van Alstyne, W.W. "Student Activism, The Law, and The Courts," in *Protest! Student Activism in America,* edited by Julian Foster and Durwood Long, New York: William Morrow and Company, Inc., 1970: pp. 531–553

CHAPTER 8

FINANCE

Recreational sport programs and facilities depend upon timely acquisition and intelligent use of funds. Financial support does not guarantee quality—it merely determines the extent of programming, personnel and facilities that can be provided. Since a resourceful staff can stretch available funds to gain maximum return, a programmer needs a familiarity with revenue sources, expense categories, budgeting and control measures.

SOURCES OF REVENUE

Recreational sport program revenue sources vary according to political priorities, participant needs and interests, and staff philosophy. Recent changes in the economy have stimulated discovery of non-traditional revenue sources to maintain and expand current levels of programming.

For the purpose of our discussion, revenue represents income either produced or acquired by the agency. Among the various revenue sources for recreational sport are:

Taxes. Recreational sport programs sponsored by government, as in municipal, collegiate or military settings, receive tax monies. The taxes that generate the most funds are property, income, sales, and special assessments or mandatory fees earmarked specifically for sport.

Grants. The Federal government and many state governments provide grant-in-aid programs to municipalities, often requiring local matching funds. Private foundations furnish another source for grants. Since most grants have a time limit, once a program or facility loses its funding the agency may have to assume the financial responsibility to continue their operation.

Gifts and Donations. Gifts may include land, a building, or cash to support or sponsor a particular project or program. Occasionally, a trust fund provides an income to the agency. As with gifts, donations are sporadic and may involve so many restrictions that they are impractical.

Leases. A new source of revenue is the leasing of public land or facilities to private individuals or agencies to operate. In many of these arrangements the public agency receives a rental to offset their debt charges on the capital required to develop the operation plus an agreed portion of any profits.

Concessions. A traditional source of revenue is the sale of goods and services. Common forms of concessions include vending machines, pro shops, restaurants and equipment rentals. The practice of distributing profits through contractual agreements with private concessionaires is extensive although some programs prefer operating their own concessions.

Bonds. Bonds comprise a primary source of financial support in a municipal setting for such major capital development projects as land acquisition and sport facility construction. They are a form of deferred payment that spreads the cost of a government enterprise over a period of years rather than allocating it to a single year's budget. Bond approval is difficult to secure. Even the most well-organized campaign often fails to gain support from the general public or legislative body.

Fund Raising. An agency may raise money through special events or fund drives. Some settings maintain strict policies and procedures which govern fund raising. Since it requires considerable investment of agency time and effort with little guarantee of success, few rely upon fund raising as a primary source of revenue.

Commercial Sponsorship. Under this arrangement, a commercial establishment offers to underwrite the cost of personnel, equipment, facilities or programs. A commercial sponsor may package a program (such as a tournament or superstar competition) that can be implemented by the agency with little investment other than personnel. Sponsors often consider providing support as a marketing or public relations function. It is rare to find one, however, who does not expect some visibility, recognition, or return on the investment.

Fees and Charges. Revenue from fees and charges constitutes a large portion of income for municipal and non-profit agencies, colleges and universities, while providing the primary source of income for commercial agencies. A description of the common categories of revenue from fees and charges follows: (Hines, 1968)

Entrance Fees—Charges to enter parks, zoos and other developed recreational areas (fairgrounds, game preserves, and historical sites).

Admission Fees—Charges to enter a building or structure (concert hall, arena and grandstand) to observe specific exhibits or performances.

Rental Fees—Payments made for the privilege of exclusive access to equipment or property for a set period of time (canoes, bicycles, lockers, golf carts, skis, horses, boats, club rooms, tennis racquets, gymnasiums, swimming pools).

User Fees—Annual, daily or other prorated charges made for non-exclusive use of facilities and participation in sport. Examples of settings imposing user fees includes a swimming pool, lake, toboggan slide, roller rink, golf course, archery range, boat launch, skeet range, weight training facility or a skateboard area.

Special Program Fees—Charges in connection with certain kinds of programs or conveniences such as tournament entry fees, instructional classes, lighting, supplies or court reservations.

License Fees—Payment for official acknowledgment of permission to engage in a lawful sport. A license permits such activities as model plane flying, hunting, fishing and camping.

Sales Charges—Revenue obtained through the operation

of concessions: restaurants, sporting goods and equipment stores or other types of retail operations.

TYPES OF EXPENDITURES

An agency may categorize its expenditures in two ways: capital and current (operating).

Capital expenditures (or capital improvement and development) are outlays for projects of a nonrecurring nature having a life expectancy of at least ten years. Items in this category might include a major renovation of tennis court surfaces, the construction of a new sports complex, the acquisition of land for fitness trails, the refurbishing of a senior citizen center and the addition of racquetball courts to an existing structure. Projects of this scope are commonly financed through taxes, special assessments, and bond issues.

Operating expenditures represent the recurring costs for provision of sport programs and facilities. Examples of expense categories include personnel, contractual services, supplies, materials, utilities, repairs, properties, and insurance.

BUDGET

A financial plan is known as a budget. The recreational sport administrator is often called upon to prepare two budgets— one for capital outlay and the other for the annual operations. An operational budget provides an administrator with an allocation policy that accomplishes stated goals and objectives for the delivery of programs, facilities, and services. It is a tool for planning, implementation and control, reflecting a choice among priorities and a forecast of the cost of personnel and other resources needs. Regarding implementation, a budget organizes resources, standardizes operations and provides a frame of reference for clarifying or supporting decisions. As a control mechanism, the budget serves as an aid in determining the level of effectiveness and efficiency for a given area of the total program. Expenditures are evaluated by comparing results with stated objectives. Finally, the budget serves as a guideline for making adjustments due to emergencies or new priorities.

Budget preparation and management requires careful thought and detailed planning. Although the responsibility for developing, requesting and managing the budget remains an administrative function, the programmer is involved in the following ways. First, he or she complies with financial accountability by following budget control measures and preventing unnecessary expenditures or losses during daily operations. Second, the programmer provides feedback to administrative staff regarding operational concerns, recommendations and financial priorities.

Financial Accountability. The programmer often manages funds involving fees and charges, hourly wage payroll, equipment, supplies, and facility maintenance. He or she monitors expenditures for each of these categories to control waste or abuse. Specific recommendations for financial accountability within each category follow:

Fees and Charges. Responsibility for fee collection involves such tasks as:

1. Training and supervising collection personnel.

2. Requesting supplies and monitoring inventory.

3. Conducting financial transactions with participants and forming necessary cash register functions: sales, rentals, charges, voids, refunds.

4. Interpreting and enforcing policies including fee scheduling, waivers, refunds, service charges, eligibility and methods of payment.

5. Securing collected funds, making safety deposits, preparing end-of-shift report, reconciling differences.

6. Issuing tickets, permits, identification cards, hand stamps, badges and receipts.

7. Checking the eligibility of users.

8. Performing basic bookkeeping that records, posts, and files daily income receipts.

9. Providing feedback and receiving and channeling comments regarding fees and charge policies, supplies and procedures.

Since these tasks involve direct handling of money, the programmer should adhere to strict fee collection procedures, supervising personnel and supplies closely and double checking calculations and records for accuracy. Conscientious and careful performance helps reduce theft, minimizes waste of supplies and avoids costly losses in terms of time and money.

Hourly Wage. The programmer hires and assigns full-time or part-time employees to manage sport activities and programs, and to operate facilities. By careful monitoring of the rate of pay, number of personnel needed and the projected number of work hours, the programmer can stay within the allocation, or alert management of anticipated hourly wage expense overruns in sufficient time to explore alternatives.

A helpful aid for monitoring hourly wage needs is the use of an hourly wage worksheet. Formats used for informal sport and intramural sport programs are presented in Figures 8-1 and 8-2.

The programmer may have an additional responsibility for maintaining and submitting an hourly wage payroll for each employee, or for informing employees of the procedure used

INFORMAL SPORT
HOURLY WAGE WORKSHEET

Position ______________________

Pay Period ______________________

CURRENT Pay Rate: ________ | **PROJECTED** Pay Rate: ________

Days	Shift	Number of Employees	Number of Hours/Shift	Number of Days/Shift	Number of Hours/Mo.	TOTAL	Shift	Number of Employees	Number of Hours/Shift	Number of Days/Shift	Number of Hours/Mo.	TOTAL

	Total By Day		Total By Day
Monday-Thursday	________	Monday-Thursday	________
Friday	________	Friday	________
Saturday-Sunday	________	Saturday-Sunday	________
Grand Total	________	Grand Total	________

Figure 8-1. Informal sport hourly wage worksheet.

**INTRAMURAL SPORT
HOURLY WAGE WORKSHEET**

SPORT: _____   DIVISION: Competitive ___ Casual ___

PROGRAMMING AREA: JOB TITLE:

___ Men's Intramurals   ___ Official
___ Women's Intramurals   ___ Supervisor
___ Co-Intramurals   ___ Laborer
___ Other _____   ___ Other _____

Clinic	# projected employees _____ # hrs/employee x _____ = Total # clinic hours needed _____ Ave pay rate per hr x _____ = Total #Asst. Instructors _____ # hrs/employee x _____ = Total # clinic hrs needed _____ Ave pay rate/hr x _____ = Total + _____ Clinic total (A) _____	
Regular Season Format	# games/league _____ # leagues x _____ = # league games _____ # employees/game or hr x _____ = Total employees/game or hr _____ Ave pay rate per game or hr x _____ = Total (B) _____	
Play-Off Format	# of Teams _____ # of Games _____ # employees/game or hr x _____ = Total # employees/game or hr _____ Ave pay rate/game or hr x _____ = Total (C) _____	
	GRAND TOTAL (A + B + C) _____	

SUMMARY			
19 ___ - 19 ___ Allocation	19 ___ - 19 ___ Expenditure	Surplus/Deficit of Allocation	19 ___ - 19 ___ Request

Figure 8-2. Intramural sport hourly wage worksheet.

RECREATIONAL SPORT
HOURLY WAGE PAYROLL

EMPLOYEE'S NAME: _____   PAY RATE: _____

EMPLOYEE'S SS #: _____   SPORT CODE: _____

TITLE CODE: _____   FACILITY CODE (Informal Only): _____

PAY PERIOD	Sun	Mon	Tue	Wed	Thu	Fri	Sat	Total 1 Wk	Sun	Mon	Tue	Wed	Thu	Fri	Sat	Total Hr/Pay
6/6-6/19																
6/20-7/3																
7/4-7/17																
7/18-7/31																
8/1-8/14																
8/15-8/28																

GENERAL INSTRUCTIONS: Please complete all information. Be sure to indicate the ACTIVITY CODE as well as the TITLE CODE.

SPORT CODE:
FF Flag Football
VB Volleyball
BB Basketball
WP Water Polo
SE Special Event
      (indicate event)
SB Softball
SO Soccer
XC Cross Country
WR Wrestling
SW Swimming
J Jogging
AD Aerobic Dance
SC Scuba
IS Ice Skating
IH Ice Hockey
B Boating
SA Sailing
C Canoeing
SK Skiing

TITLE CODE:
O Official
S Supervisor
L Labor
SA Staff Assistant
LG Lifeguard

FACILITY CODE:
W Weightroom
FH Fieldhouse
TC Tennis Courts
OF Outdoor Fields
P Pool
IR Ice Rink
OP Outdoor Pool
L Lake
FT Fitness Trail
SS Ski Slope

Figure 8-3.   Hourly wage payroll form.

for recording and submitting their own hours. Accuracy in payroll matters is a necessity.

The programmer may record employees' hours in a number of ways, the most common being a time clock card, an individual employee time sheet, a signed scorecard or a sign-in sheet. Each method requires careful transfer of hours onto a payroll sheet, followed by accurate monitoring. A typical payroll sheet is reproduced in Figure 8-3. It is customary to retain original copies of time and payroll sheets in case there ever is a need to verify hours of work performed or to investigate discrepancies.

Equipment. The programmer distributes equipment through loan, rental or sales to individuals. He or she has the responsibility for the condition, security and return of equipment used in a program. Those who issue or sell equipment should keep daily records of use, sales, or rentals, assist with equipment storage and repair, handle financial transactions and reports for rentals or sales, maintain inventory, and submit purchase recommendations for additional or replacement items. Proper care and handling of equipment can result in significant financial savings.

Supplies. Regardless of the specific responsibility, any programming position involves the use of supplies; i.e., items that are consumed or worn out in a reasonably short period of time. Stationery, clipboards, pencils, fuel, food, clothing, rubber bands, staples, chemicals, ice, first aid supplies, cleaning supplies, tape, blotters and rulers all belong in this category. Supplies are often taken for granted through such wasteful activities as retyping materials requiring minimal correction, duplicating an excess number of copies and using paper and pens for personal business. Impress upon subordinate personnel the need for prudent and economical use of supplies.

Maintenance. While working in a facility, the programmer should develop a capability for spotting maintenance and repair needs. Reports forwarded to the appropriate staff prompt the necessary corrective action. In many instances, a regular facility maintenance-repair checklist is useful for this purpose. As participant behavior may result in damages to the facility or area, on-site supervision is a preventative measure.

BUDGET PREPARATION

It is customary for the programmer to receive instruction regarding how to identify, specify and justify budget requests. Make every effort to identify realistic needs regardless of previous allocations, and rank them by priority in anticipation of budget limitations. Whenever possible, relieve financial pressures through more efficient use of existing resources.

Rather than waiting until the start of the budget process before formulating recommendations, the programmer should contribute to an idea file throughout the year. This technique reduces the chance of forgetting a useful idea and helps develop perspective on the relationship between a function and its budget implications. Include budget modifications or recommendations with each evaluation statement written at the completion of a program.

CONCLUSION

The programmer should always cultivate sound fiscal practices and maintain a professional attitude toward participation in the fiscal process. As programs struggle to remain in operation during difficult economic periods, procurement of new revenue sources, fiscal accountability, and cost efficiency become important goals. Proper performance by the programmer will help avoid crisis management situations stemming from fiscal deficiencies and unexpected problems.

REFERENCES

Hines, T. I. *Budgeting for Public Parks and Recreation*. Washington, D.C.: National Recreation and Parks Association, 1968, No. 46, p. 23.

Johnson, N. S. The Budget. In S. G. Lutzin and E. H. Storey (Eds.) *Managing Municipal Services*. Washington, D.C.: The International City Management Association, 1973.

Kraus, R. G. and Curtis, J. E. *Creative Management in Recreation and Parks*, 3rd edition. St. Louis: The C. V. Mosbey Company, 1982.

Rodney, L. S. and Toalson, R. F. *Administration of Recreation and Leisure Services*, 2nd edition. New York: John Wiley & Sons, 1981.

CHAPTER 9

FACILITIES

Any space used to hold recreational sport participants or spectators is a recreational sport facility regardless of whether it is large or small, singular or multi-purpose, natural or man-made, indoors or out-of-doors.

Factors which influence the types of facilities available within a setting include geographical area, terrain, climate, ecology and finances.

A less obvious factor which significantly affects facility development and availability is politics. Many special interest groups sponsor programs which require access to facilities. Given the diversity of need, the expense of facilities and space limitations, it is often difficult to satisfy everyone. Maximizing the use of facilities while satisfying diverse interest groups often is complicated. Attempts to respond to political realities accounts in part for the great variety in the types, appearance and array of facility operations.

The goal of facility development and management is to provide facilities in sufficient quantity, diversity and quality to

INDOOR RECREATIONAL SPORTS
FACILITIES OR AREAS

Single Function	Specialized or Multi-purpose Function	
+Archery range	Country Club	Gymnasium
Badminton court	golf	gymnastics
*Basketball court	swimming	combatives
Billiards room	table sports	basketball
Bowling alley	weightlifting	volleyball
Combatives room	tennis	badminton
*Curling rink		table tennis
*Diving pool	Fieldhouse	
Electronic games arcade	basketball	Racquetball Club
Fencing salle	track	weightlifting
Gymnastics room	soccer	jogging
*Handball court	lacrosse	
+*Ice rink	jogging	Recreation Center
Racquetball court	archery	billiards
*Rifle-pistol range		table sports
*Roller skating rink	Fitness Center	table tennis
*Shuffleboard course	swimming	swimming
Squash court	weightlifting	gymnasium
*Swimming pool	jogging	
Table sport room	combatives	
Table tennis room		
*Tennis court	Key	
Weightlifting room	*Found outdoors	
Wrestling room	+Found in natural environment	
*Volleyball court		

Figure 9-1. Partial listing of indoor recreational sports facilities and areas.

fulfill the basic purpose of the recreational sport agency. Sound facility operation allows participant use in a way that fosters favorable attitudes toward the agency and toward sports themselves. Since the programmer is involved with daily facility operations, our topics cover safety, facility personnel, scheduling, use counseling, supervision, maintenance and repair routines.

Safety

A concern for safety and accident prevention influences decisions and actions executed in facility operations. Safety considerations determine the number of supervisory personnel needed, the type and frequency of equipment and facility inspections, the funding provided for maintenance and repairs, the extent of counseling for proper use, the mechanisms

OUTDOOR RECREATIONAL SPORTS
FACILITIES OR AREAS

Man-made environment

Airfield
Baseball field
*Basketball court
+Beach
Bicycle path
Boat launching ramp
+Bocce ball course
Bowling green
+Cross country course
*Curling rink
Deck tennis
*Diving pool
Field hockey field
+Fishing pond/lake
Fitness trail
Football field
Frisbee golf course
Go-cart track
Golf course
Golf driving range
*Handball court
Horseshoe pit

Hydro-slide
+*Ice rink
Lacrosse field
Marina
Miniature golf course
+Motocross course
*Riding paddock
+Riding trail
+Rifle/pistol range
*Roller skating rink
*Shuffleboard course
Skateboard ramp
Skeet & trap range
+Skiing course
Soccer field
Softball field
Speedball field
*Swimming pool
Team handball field
*Tennis court
Toboggan slope

Natural Environment

Air
Beach
Field
Jungle
Lake
Mountains

Ocean
Plains
Pond
River
Stream
Trees

Key
*Found indoors
+Found in natural environment

Figure 9-2. Partial listing of outdoor recreational sports facilities or areas.

developed for handling accidents and emergency situations, and the manner sport programs are scheduled into facilities.

More thorough coverage of safety within facility operations will be covered in Chapter 11.

Facility Personnel

The number of personnel and the functions they provide are influenced by the number and types of facilities, the magnitude of participation, and the diversity of programs seeking access to the facilities.

In smaller programs with limited facilities, the program staff, part-time employees and volunteers handle scheduling, supervision, and simple maintenance and repair jobs. More complex maintenance or repair work receive service through centralized physical plant personnel or private contractors. Larger programs with a greater number and diversity of facilities may require the attention of a full-time facility manager, a large maintenance staff and a substantial number of on-site supervisors.

Facility scheduling

Scheduling is a process for achieving maximum use of facilities within the resource and staff capabilities of the agency. A quality scheduling process is similar to solving a mystery or piecing together parts of a puzzle. All involve gathering the required pieces of information and finding the sequence and combinations that work.

Scheduling may accomplish shared use of facilities among different programs and agencies, provide different types of participation in the same sport, or furnish opportunities for participation in a variety of activities. The scheduling policy developed to handle the specific needs of the setting reflects the philosophy of the setting, the interests of participants, the availability of facilities and the capability of the staff and resources to handle facility operations efficiently and safely. Once priorities for facility use and eligibility statements are set, facility reservation requests may be processed. A mechanism for identifying the type and extent of requests for facility use is the written reservation form shown in Figure 9-3.

This form should specify how soon and where a request should be submitted. Advance notice of facility need gives the programmer adequate time to organize and schedule requests, eliminate conflicts, chart use levels, control use levels, and review the appropriateness of the design for the activity. It also

---

**RECREATIONAL SPORT
FACILITY RESERVATION REQUEST**

Date _____

To: Coordinator of facilities

From: Name _____   Phone _____

Organization _____

Address _____

The above organization would like to reserve the following:

1.) FACILITY: _____

2.) ACTIVITY: _____

3.) DATES: _____

4.) TIMES: _____

5.) NUMBER IN GROUP: _____

6.) RESPONSIBLE PERSON: _____

Signed _____

NOTE: Requests must be submitted in writing at least *two weeks* in advance of times
and dates requested.

Figure 9-3. Facility reservation request form.

allows those responsible time to make modifications or reject
a request (where applicable), and counsel the participants
regarding proper use.

All scheduling practices are ways to utilize time. Scheduling practices that accommodate various sports, programs and
user groups are commonly based on three time units:
seasonal, monthly, and daily.

Seasonal scheduling

The time of year and climate often influence facility scheduling. Seasonal scheduling most often corresponds to Fall,
Winter, Summer and Spring, or simply, Winter and Summer.
Consequently, it does not apply to parts of the country where
there is little variation in climate. In some geographical areas,
winter requires a move indoors for some sports signaling peak

use of indoor facilities for volleyball, basketball, roller skating, swimming and jogging. Winter also means peak facility use for such sports as sledding, skiing, tobogganing, ice skating and ice hockey. The return of warm weather causes a switch outdoors to enjoy such sports as softball, golf, hang-gliding, moto-cross, rugby, surfing, drag racing and scuba diving.

Seasonal scheduling helps coordinate availability of

KAP
Community Center Schedule

FALL SESSION I: September 13–October 31
   Registration: August 16

FALL SESSION II: November 1–December 19
   Registration: October 4

KAP COMMUNITY CENTER	123 Intramural Drive		333-3333	
SPORT	**DAY**	**TIME**	**FEE**	**WEEKS**
Aquatics				
Age 3-5	Mon/Wed	3:45-4:15 pm	Free	4
	Tues/Thurs	5:30-6:00 pm	Free	4
	Saturday	9:00-9:30 am	Free	4
Age 6 and over	Tues/Thurs	6:00-6:30 pm	$2.00	4
(Basic)	Saturday	4:00-4:30 pm	$2.00	4
Family Swim	Fri/Sat	7:30-9:30 pm	Free	6
	Sunday	1:30-3:30 pm	Free	6
Scuba	Tuesday	8:00-10:00 pm	$10.00	6
Tennis				
Beginning	Mon/Wed	7:00-8:30 pm	$4.00	6
Intermediate	Tues/Thurs	7:00-8:30 pm	$6.00	6
Volleyball				
"A" League	Friday	8:00-10:00 pm	$6.00	6
(2nd Session only)				
"B" League	Sunday	8:00-10:00 pm	$4.00	4
2nd Session only				
Karate	Mon/Wed	7:00-9:00 pm	$6.00	6

Figure 9-4. Seasonal program schedule.

facilities with sport seasons like football, soccer, wrestling, basketball and tennis. The scheduling of facilities according to calendar or sport season makes it easier to manage programs designed to meet on a regular basis over an extended period of time (8, 10, 12 weeks) for class, tournaments, or club participation. When a schedule covers a long time span, consider the effect of holidays upon plans. Figure 9-4 illustrates a seasonal scheduling pattern.

According to traditional scheduling practice, most major maintenance and repair tasks occur before or after a season. Functions involving emergency or preventative maintenance occur as required.

Monthly and weekly scheduling

Shorter duration scheduling accommodates a great variety of interests. Instead of a fixed schedule operating on a daily or weekly basis, the programmer may allow greater flexibility to meet user demands, although this practice may frustrate those accustomed to routine. In addition, fluctuating weekly schedules may be inappropriate for some sport activities and programs like skill development and structured tournaments that require continual participation. In these instances, consistent scheduling is preferable.

A monthly or weekly scheduling pattern is especially appropriate for such facility-centered programs as ski areas, pools, and golf courses where patron use is constant and regular. Since this pattern involves a shorter time period, reserve time for maintenance and repair, particularly for facilities in yearly operation. Figure 9-5 illustrates a typical monthly schedule for a swimming pool.

Daily scheduling

Daily scheduling practices divide the day into general time periods: morning, afternoon, and evening; or morning, early afternoon, late afternoon, early evening and late evening. This structure requires an understanding of participant lifestyles so that scheduling of facilities may be tailored for a sport activity, program, or age group. Figure 9-6 provides an example of a daily schedule.

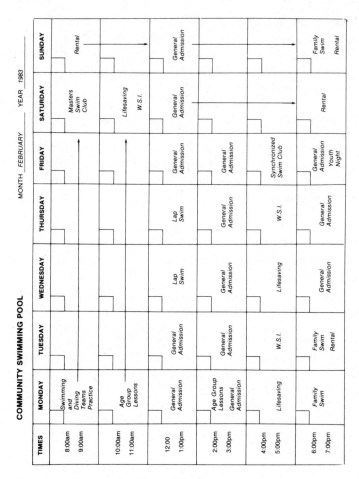

Figure 9-5. Monthly facility schedule.

In addition to these general time units for facility scheduling, specialized scheduling techniques exist that are useful within each time unit. The most common of these techniques are block and simultaneous use scheduling.

Block Scheduling

This scheduling technique recognizes different groups, programs or sports having priority for facility use within specific blocks of time during the day. In an educational setting, for example, training and instructional programs may have priority from 8:30 am through 11:30 am and 1:30 through 3:30 pm Mon-

MARCH 10, 1983

Time/Facility	Freeweight Room 092	Universal Gym Room 092A	Gym 095
7:00 AM	Informal Sport	Athletic Sport	Instructional Sport
7:30 AM	Informal Sport	Athletic Sport	Instructional Sport
8:00 AM	Informal Sport	Athletic Sport	Instructional Sport
8:30 AM	Informal Sport	Athletic Sport	Instructional Sport
9:00 AM	Closed	Closed	Closed
9:30 AM	Closed	Closed	Closed
10:00 AM	Closed	Informal Sport	Informal Sport
10:30 AM	Closed	Informal Sport	Informal Sport
11:00 AM	Informal Sport	Informal Sport	Informal Sport
11:30 AM	Informal Sport	Informal Sport	Informal Sport
12:00 Noon	Informal Sport	Informal Sport	Informal Sport
12:30 PM	Informal Sport	Informal Sport	Aerobic Rhythm
1:00 PM	Informal Sport	Informal Sport	Aerobic Rhythm
1:30 PM	Informal Sport	Intramural Sport	Aerobic Rhythm
2:00 PM	Informal Sport	Intramural Sport	Stretch Fit
2:30 PM	Informal Sport	Intramural Sport	Stretch Fit
3:00 PM	Informal Sport	Informal Sport	Closed
3:30 PM	Informal Sport	Informal Sport	Judo Club
4:00 PM	Informal Sport	Informal Sport	Judo Club
4:30 PM	Informal Sport	Informal Sport	Judo Club
5:00 PM	Informal Sport	Informal Sport	Judo Club
5:30 PM	Informal Sport	Informal Sport	Judo Club
6:00 PM	Weight Club	Informal Sport	Hapkido Club
6:30 PM	Weight Club	Informal Sport	Hapkido Club
7:00 PM	Weight Club	Informal Sport	Hapkido Club
7:30 PM	Weight Club	Informal Sport	Hapkido Club
8:00 PM	Weight Club	Informal Sport	Aikido Club
8:30 PM	Weight Club	Informal Sport	Aikido Club
9:00 PM	Informal Sport	Informal Sport	Wrestling Club
9:30 PM	Informal Sport	Informal Sport	Wrestling Club
10:00 PM	Informal Sport	Informal Sport	Wrestling Club
10:30 PM	Informal Sport	Informal Sport	Wrestling Club
11:00 PM	Closed	Closed	Closed
11:30 PM	Closed	Closed	Closed

Figure 9-6. Daily facility schedule.

day through Friday. Intramural and club sports take precedence from 3:30 to 6:00 pm, athletic sports from 6:00 through 8:30 pm, and informal sport from 11:30 am through 1:30 pm and

8:30 pm until closing. Similarly, a single facility may use block scheduling to accommodate a number of program formats with the same activity. For example, club sport swimming may be scheduled for early morning, instructional swimming for late morning, informal sport swimming during the early afternoon, structured meets for late afternoon, and informal sport swimming for the evening. Scheduling may designate age group access to the pool: pre-school children in the morning, youth teams in the afternoon, and adults in the evening.

Block scheduling may occur on a weekly, monthly, seasonal or annual basis. Since block scheduling identifies regular consecutive time spans of facility use for an activity, program or group, it establishes order and permits staff and participants the opportunity to set a routine. However, this procedure deters individuals whose timetables conflict with these schedules.

Simultaneous scheduling

This refers to scheduling of more than one group, sport or program in the same facility or area at the same time. This method applies when multiple units of the same type of facility exist (basketball courts, bowling alleys, racquetball courts or riding paddocks); where a multi-purpose facility handles simultaneous use (gymnasium, natatorium, fieldhouse, or stadium); and where a singular facility is of sufficient size or accoustical design so that multiple users do not distract or interfere with one another (golf course, ski slope, lake, mountain, or outdoor sport field). Although simultaneous scheduling accommodates a variety of sports and a potentially large number of users, the sports activities must be compatible. Pairing a martial arts class with an aerobic dance group in the same gymnasium is not wise.

Regardless of the method in use, the programmer needs accurate information regarding scheduling in order to submit and implement reservation requests, to monitor and supervise scheduled sport activities or programs, and to communicate general information to participants and personnel regarding reservations or availability. Since the programmer works closely with participants, he or she has ample opportunity to consider their opinions and attitudes concerning aspects of

EVANS FIELDHOUSE

	Monday	Tuesday	Wednesday	Thursday	Friday	Saturday
8:00 am			Physical Education			
9:30 am						
11:00 am			Recreational Sports		Recreational	
12:30 pm						
2:00 pm			Athletics		Sports	
3:30 pm			Physical Education			
5:00 pm						
6:30 pm			Recreational Sports			
8:00 pm						

Figure 9-7. Block scheduling.

facility scheduling and forward these sentiments to appropriate administrative staff. Sensitivity to feedback is essential for accurate asessment of interests and evaluation of services.

Reservation requests for facility use

When individuals or groups apart from the recreational sport staff design events and submit facility requests, establish a procedure for considering the request and for counseling in proper facility use. The responsibility for conducting the review and counseling process rests with a facility coordinator or a recreational sport program staff member.

In settings where a variety of interest groups share facilities, the recreational sport staff may not have complete responsibility for facility management and scheduling. Programmers work instead through a facility coordinator to review those requests that occur during established recreational sport hours or requests that require programming expertise to determine their suitability. Whatever the circumstance, provide for a formal review, decision and counseling process in the interest of safety and quality control.

When reviewing a request, the programmer should determine the suitability of the event or program in terms of organization, personnel, safety and format. In some settings, the programmer serves as a resource person aiding in the organization and implementation of an event or program. In other settings, the programmer simply states the conditions that must be met in order for the request to be granted. Upon completion, the review process may reveal that the time or facility requested is not available and alternatives are needed.

When reviewing requests for facility access during recreational sport hours, programmers need an objective way to consider how to fulfill the request without infringing upon agency-sponsored programs and special events. The following comments offer suggestions on how to make objective decisions in a simple manner.

Use levels. A record of daily participant facility use taken at 30 minute, 45 minute, or 60 minute intervals reveals use patterns that may allow transfer of time to other programs. When participation levels are consistently high, the request is usually denied. Low use levels permit flexibility regarding requests. Often a decision is influenced by the nature of the request. If it is a short-term event, or of benefit and interest to a large number of people, a request may be approved despite moderate to high use levels.

Facility alternatives. After consideration of participant and program use levels, the programmer may suggest a change in the time span requested in the facility reservation request. There are instances when an individual or group can use non-prime times or less convenient facility locations.

Nature of the request. On occasion, a reservation request for a structured event does not meet acceptable standards to warrant facility space, regardless of availability. For this reason, it is wise to prepare basic criteria to evaluate facility requests. Require individuals or groups to submit preliminary plans and information regarding intended use of the facility along with the reservation request. A sample of a format used to obtain preliminary plans is presented in Figure 9-8.

When the responsible party does not provide for proper safety, leadership and programming support, consider denying the request.

Once a decision on a request is reached, communicate it to the prospective user or to the facility coordinator. (See Figure 9-9).

Upon request approval, conduct a session with the responsible party to review final plans, expectations and responsibilities. Have a procedure ready to handle potential

**SPECIAL EVENT
FACILITY RESERVATION REQUEST**
Preliminary Information

Name _____Phone _____

Address _____

Additional Contact Person:

Name _____Phone _____

Address _____

Organization _____Date _____

1. Summarize previous facility reservations by your organization.
   (Include date, facility, time, event) _____
   _____
   _____
   _____
   _____

2. What kind of special event is to be conducted? (Tournament, clinic, etc.)
   Please explain _____
   _____

3. How many individuals or teams are expected to participate? _____

4. Will there be an entry fee? _____Spectator admission fees? _____
   If yes, how much? _____If yes, how much? _____

5. What facilities are being requested? (Please list) _____
   _____

6. When is the event to take place?   1st Choice _____
                                            2nd choice _____

7. What special equipment or facility preparation might be needed:
   (Please list) _____
   _____
   _____
   _____

8. How many people will be assisting in the operations of the event?
   _____

9. Does anyone in the group have first aid or CPR certification? _____
   If yes, please indicate name and phone number.
   _____

10. Are there plans to have any type of concessions at the event?
    If yes, please explain. _____

11. Is there a need to have assistance by personnel from Recreational Sports?
    If so, how many, what functions, and how do you plan to pay them?
    (If necessary) _____
    _____

12. Additional Comments: _____
    _____
    _____
    _____

Figure 9-8. Preliminary plans and information form.

RECREATIONAL SPORT FACILITY REQUEST REVIEW

A. General Information

Date Submitted to Facility Coordinator _____

Date Received by Recreational Sports _____

Name _____ Address _____

Organization _____

Facility _____ Phone _____

Dates _____ Times _____

B. Use Analysis

Previous use summary _____

_____

Recreational Sports use _____

_____

C. Programming Review

Meeting date _____Outline required _____ Approval _____

Groupleader _____

Equipment needs _____

_____

D. Final Status

Request approved _____ Denied _____

Reason(s) for denial _____

_____

Date returned to Facility Coordinator _____

Staff Signature _____

Figure 9-9. Facility request review form.

problems, accidents and emergencies. To confirm acceptance of the conditions for use, require the user(s) to sign an acknowledgement of responsibility form, such as the one shown in Figure 9-10.

At the conclusion of the counseling process, provide the user with a written confirmation of the reservation and a copy of responsibilities for facility use. The following summary itemizes all considerations for facility reservation requests by outside groups:

I. Planning
   a. Kind of event
   b. Dates and times
   c. Facilities needed
   d. Rental fees, damage charges

STATEMENT OF RESPONSIBILITY FOR FACILITY USE

The user, or his/her sponsor if one is deemed necessary, shall be responsible for cleanup, damage, injuries, supervision and any liability incurred during the use of facilities requested in the application received by this office. The specific responsibilities are listed below:

A. **Supervision:** The user agrees to supervise the use of the facility to ensure that there is no abuse to it nor any violation of the laws of the State or the rules and regulations of the agency. Assistance may be sought through the facility supervisors. Verification of reservation will be required (bring confirmation slip).

B. **Injury:** Any personal injury requiring immediate medical attention must be reported to facility supervisor, or the ambulance service. A written report describing the circumstances must be completed and returned to this office or facility supervisor. Accident report forms are available from the facility supervisor or from this office.

C. **Cleanup and Damage:** The facility will be inspected by a facility supervisor or this office both before and after use. If cleanup is necessary it will be done by:

    1) The user assuming the actual physical action of the cleanup. This will again be subject to inspection.

    2) Placing a work order for its cleanup. The user will accept financial obligations for this action.

Any damage to the facility, its furnishings, or equipment must be reported in writing to this office. The user will be responsible for the cost of repair or replacement.

I, _____ , acting as the responsible individual for
_____ have read the above statement and will ensure that these
      organization
stipulations are followed.

                            Date _____

                            Signed _____

Note: This statement must be returned by _____ .

Figure 9-10. Acknowledgement of responsibility form.

    e. Event rules and regulations
    f. Volunteer or paid assistance needs
        1. officials
        2. supervisors
        3. medical
        4. set up and take down
    g. Entry fees
        1. participants
        2. spectators

      h. Other expenditures
         1. publicity and promotions
         2. equipment
         3. supplies
         4. recognition
         5. facility preparation
         6. utilities
      i. Equipment and supply needs
         1. tables, chairs, bleachers
         2. equipment
         3. supplies
      j. Identification of responsible persons
      k. Concessions
         1. sanitation
         2. serving permit
         3. access to utilities
II. Organizing
      a. Development of rules, forms, publicity
      b. Food services approval
      c. Securing needed personnel
      d. Recreational sport staff approval
      e. Advising on facility utilization
         1. policies
         2. supervision
         3. safety, accidents, emergencies
         4. maintenance
      f. Signing statement of responsibility
      g. Payment of rental fee
      h. Transmission of approval to facility coordinator
III. Conducting the event
      a. Set-up
      b. Equipment pick-up
      c. Supervision and crowd control
      d. Clean-up
IV. Evaluation
      a. Follow-up and post-event inspection by staff
      b. Return of equipment
      c. Damage charges
      d. Recommendation for future use

    The programmer should monitor participant adherence to conditions of use, either through firsthand observation or supervision by subordinate personnel. Some settings require verbal or written follow-up reports, especially in the event of disorderly conduct, accidents, emergencies or facility misuse.

Supervision of Facilities

Theoretically, anyone present at a facility site may provide supervision, although such a tenuous arrangement is not always appropriate. In practice, the nature of the sport or program, age level or participants, group size and concern for safety determine the appropriate type of supervision. Common functions performed by on-site supervisory personnel include:

—preventing or controlling hazards

—reporting and managing accidents

—curtailing disruptive conduct

—communicating and enforcing policies and procedures

—organizing activity

—curtailing facility and equipment misuse

—providing equipment

—reporting suggestions, problems, maintenance needs and emergencies

—checking eligibility of users

—handling facility security

—enhancing public relations

Hourly wage employees, club sport officers, and volunteer workers who handle such on-site responsibilities as safety and conflict resolution require specialized training. Clearly, on-site supervisors are in direct contact with participants and serve as vital communication, safety and public relations links. Encourage them to obtain participant feedback regarding ideas, concerns and problems and channel comments to staff through such aids as suggestion and complaint forms.

In many settings the programmer has an assignment in on-site supervision as well as a responsibility for training, monitoring and evaluating other supervisors.

Maintenance

Natural deterioration requires attention to keep facilities, areas and equipment in good order for safe use. A total maintenance effort covers two broad areas: operations and repairs.

Operations refers to scheduled routines such as sweeping floors, dragging infields, picking up trash and debris, mowing grass, cleaning rest areas and replacing light bulbs. Other maintenance tasks are preventative in nature and involve regular inspections of facilities, areas and equipment to avoid costly or time-consuming repairs. Preventative maintenance involves tuning engines, painting, preserving adequate ground cover, applying protective floor surfacing, pruning dead tree limbs, replacing worn mechanical parts and cleaning filtration systems.

The second category of maintenance involves repair work that requires more specialized labor. Such repair work as replacing roofing, fencing or floor surfaces and seeding fields are anticipated and scheduled functions, while others such as those needed when vandalism, neglect, accidents and weather damage occur, are unpredictable. Many repairs are relatively simple and inexpensive to handle: clogged drains, broken windows, torn nets or broken bleachers. Other repairs may be expensive and require extensive work due to damage caused by such events as a tornado, fire, auto accident, roof leak, disrupted utility service or equipment breakdown.

The maintenance role of a programmer depends on the nature of the job and training, the type of facility, area, or equipment, the maintenance need and the maintenance staff available within the setting. It is not unusual for a programmer to perform or oversee simple custodial or housekeeping chores. Figure 9-11 indicates examples of routine tasks monitored by a programmer at a multi-purpose indoor facility.

The programmer plays a prominent role in preventative maintenance through activity supervision and facility inspection. Curtailing the costly problem of vandalism is a significant contribution to the maintenance effort. A supervisor should maintain a high profile. Both participants and spectators must understand that acts of vandalism lead to criminal or civil prosecution.

Preventative maintenance is furthered by regular inspections of facilities and equipment. In most instances, inspections

DAILY MAINTENANCE CHECKLIST

A.M.	Noon	P.M.	Maintenance
			RESTOCK BATHROOM
			Locker rooms (refill sauna pail)
			Main level
			Sub basement
			ALL SPORTS CENTER & ACTIVITY CENTER COURTS
			Sweep with dust mop
			Straighten out ping pong tables
			Pick up trash
			TRACK
			Sweep with vacuum
			Pick up trash
			POOLS
			Doors locked when pools are closed
			Supervise guards
			LOST & FOUND
			Deposit all lost articles at front desk until end of day
			Deposit all valuables to main desk
			Deposit all articles to lost & found at end of day
			FIRST-AID SUPPLIES
			(Use checklist—deposit list at Main Desk) Back door
			Front door
			RECEPTIONIST DESK
			Pick up trash
			Check supplies
			RACQUETBALL, HANDBALL AND SQUASH COURTS
			Turn off lights in all courts not in use
			MEN'S & WOMEN'S WEIGHT ROOMS
			Clean all vinyl parts
			Check equipment
			TV & MEZZANINE LOUNGE
			Straighten furniture
			Pick up trash
			TRANSIENT LOCKER ROOM
			Pick up trash
			Check bulletin boards
			Check lockers at closing that are missing keys. (Empty them out using master key.)
			BOXING ROOM
			Sweep floors
			Check equipment
			COMBATIVES/DANCE ROOM
			Sweep floors
			Inspect mats (mop when needed)
			ARCHERY/GOLF ROOM
			Straighten nets
			Put rooms in order

Figure 9-11. Daily maintenance checklist form.

require general knowledge and simple observation to detect situations needing attention. During these regular inspections, use a checklist like the sample in Figure 9-12.

Most repair tasks performed by the programmer and subordinate staff involve minor preventative maintenance rather than actual repairs. For example, the programmer may

---

**OUTDOOR FACILITY/AREA
MAINTENANCE REPORT FORM**

Location _____ Date _____

Checklist		Comments
Backstop		
Bleachers		
Fields		
Courts—Basketball		
Courts—Tennis		
Horseshoe Pit		
Nets		
Lights		
Fence		
Pavement		
Water Fountains		
Stairs		
Bike Path		
Signs		
Standards		
Driveways		
Other		
Other		
Other		

This report is to be filled out each morning by the first shift supervisor.

G - Good Condition
F - Fair Condition
N - Needs Attention

Submitted By: _____

Figure 9-12. Maintenance report form—outdoor.

be called upon to perform or supervise the manicuring and lining of outdoor sport fields, the back-washing of pool filtration systems, the lubricating or tightening of equipment parts, the

---

VANDALISM REPORT

Facility _____ Date of Occurrence _____

Specific Location _____

Detailed Damage Description _____

_____

_____

MAINTENANCE CREW—COST RECORD OF REPAIRS

Labor (List total hours of each different employee classification worked)

_____

Material _____

_____

Equipment (List total hours of each different type of equipment used)

_____

_____

VANDALISM PREVENTION

Do you think that this act of vandalism could have been prevented? _____

How? _____

_____

_____
                Supervisor

_____
        Recreational Sport Staff or
          Facility Coordinator

_____
        Maintenance Division

_____ DO NOT FILL IN BELOW THIS LINE _____

Labor _____   _____

Material _____   _____

Equipment _____   _____

  Maintenance Crew Totals (from above)   ====================

        Total Cost of Repairs   _____

Figure 9-13. Vandalism report form.

painting or staining of small structures or signs, the watering of outdoor fields, or the operating of ice resurfacing equipment.

When extensive repair work is required, the programmer specifies needed repairs on standard reporting forms. These forms, designed for general or specific use, ensure the collection of appropriate information. Figures 9-12 and 9-13 demonstrate the difference between these approaches.

Whenever a hazard exists at the site of repair work, the programmer should secure the area, remove the hazard, notify the proper authorities and initiate evacuation when necessary. When repair work requires closing a facility or area the programmer and subordinate staff should communicate this information through signs at the facility site, press releases and individual contact with users by mail or phone. Keep on-site subordinate staff informed of maintenance-repair timetables so that they may accurately respond to participant inquiries. Advanced notice of facility unavailability minimizes user disappointment.

Conclusions

Although the programmer may be removed from the planning, design, funding and construction responsibilities associated with facilities, he or she is concerned with essential daily operational tasks. The supervisory, maintenance and repair tasks associated with facility operations are often routine, yet necessary conditions for the availability, attractiveness and preservation of facilities as well as essential requirements for the safety and welfare of the participants. Care and protection of facilities combined with appropriate use policies and procedures result in favorable participant impressions and productive use of resources.

BIBLIOGRAPHY

Departments of the Army, Navy and Air Force. *Planning and Design of Outdoor Sports Facilities.* Washington, D.C.: U.S. Government Printing Office, 1975.

Murray, J. J. *Facility Maintenance Systems.* New York: Girl Scouts of the USA, 1980.

The Athletic Institute and the American Association for Health,

Physical Education, and Recreation. *Planning Areas and Facilities for Health, Physical Education, and Recreation.* Washington, D.C., 1966.

Sternloff, R. and Warren, R. *Park and Recreation Maintenance Management.* Boston: Holbrook Press, Inc., 1977.

CHAPTER 10

EQUIPMENT
AND
SUPPLIES

Sport programs require the availability of equipment and supplies that are safe for use and sufficient to meet participant demand. The large financial investment in facilities requires the
availability of equipment and supplies necessary for their maximum productivity. Even when facilities are inadequate, it is
still possible to provide quality recreational sport programs
through the use of appropriate equipment and supplies. Consequently, a programmer should concentrate on obtaining all
the materials necessary for the conduct of a quality program.

To better understand this area of management, we have
divided the physical resources of a sport environment into
three classifications for review: facilities, equipment and supplies.

Facilities. Facilities are areas or structures that accommodate a sport event. These are the media of sport participation: arenas, stadiums, rivers, coliseums, swimming pools,
ballfields, tennis courts, fields, golf courses and mountains.

Equipment. Equipment refers to permanent or expendable items required for the conduct of sport. Examples of permanent equipment are: lawnmowers, basketball backboards, softball backstops, volleyball standards, weightlifting weights, and tennis posts. Expendable items that require periodic replacement include: softballs, bats, table tennis balls, nets, roller skates, and hockey sticks.

Supplies. Supplies are supplemental and expendable items required for the orderly operation of a sports program. Items range from scoresheets, clipboards, towels, pencils and field marking chalk to mops, cleaning liquids and soap for the shower room. Water, gasoline, sand, gravel, grass seed, and fertilizer come under this definition when an agency is involved with maintenance of outdoor facilities.

Since equipment and supplies comprise a significant proportion of an operational budget, the programmer should apply sound management principles when selecting, buying, storing, distributing, and caring for them.

TYPES

When assessing equipment and supply needs, a programmer may divide equipment and supplies into three categories: sport program, area and office.

Sport Program

Equipment and supplies in this category are those items necessary for the conduct of a sport or required by the rules. In flag football, for example, this includes flags, belts, footballs, end zone and ball markers.

Area

This category includes permanent facilities and equipment that make an area a singular unit. In flag football, the area involves the field, goal posts, bleachers, and light poles.

Office

An office cannot function without adequate equipment and supplies. Bookcases, calculators, copying machines, desks, filing cabinets, cash registers, paper, pencils and pens, stationery, telephones, and typewriters are basic needs.

CRITERIA FOR PURCHASE

When identifying and recommending any item for purchase, consider the following:

—Is the item a necessity or a luxury?
—Will the item contribute to the quality, efficiency, and effectiveness of operations?
—Is the item of quality material and workmanship?
—Will the item pose any safety hazard?
—Is the item durable?
—Can the item be used for multiple purposes?
—Is the item economical?

Selection

The individual responsible for the selection of equipment and supplies may be a specially-trained purchasing agent or a sports programmer if the latter has the qualifications, time, and interest to do the job.

The purchasing agent has the responsibility to procure a requested item at an appropriate time at the best price consistent with desired quality. Current knowledge of design changes, new processes and products is important in the selection process. Examine new equipment catalogs as soon as they are received from the manufacturers. Have equipment dealers or representatives demonstrate samples of new items.

Each of the following influences purchasing decisions:

1. Specific program events. The nature of programs and specific events offered affects selection of equipment and supplies. What is appropriate for an outdoor program may not be suitable for an indoor one.

2. Available space and facilities. The extent of facilities, either indoor or outdoor, determines the type of items needed for an event. When a softball facility has a small field area, use a flight-restricted ball.

3. Age. Equipment and supplies should suit the needs of the age group using them.

4. Sex. Often the suitability of materials used in sports events varies with the sex of the participants. Volleyball standards, as an example, adjust to different net heights for men and women.

5. Skill. The skill level of participants may influence the selection of equipment and supplies. Trick skis, considered standard equipment for a professional water skier, are inappropriate for a beginner.

6. Leadership. The quality of supervision available to monitor equipment and supplies at an event affects what items to select. You cannot buy trampolines unless you can provide the proper supervision, security, and storage.

7. Cost. Budget limitations determine price ranges. Establish spending guidelines to avoid wasteful purchasing practices. Realistic budgeting aids in the long-range planning of equipment purchases.

8. Quality of material. Cost is not a fool-proof indicator of quality. Look for quality in terms of performance, craftsmanship, appearance and service warranties. The purchase of more expensive quality equipment and supplies often results in savings in the long run.

9. Reputable dealer. Select items from an established dealer recognized for reliable and efficient service. Manufacturers who market national brands of equipment and supplies usually guarantee their products. When selecting vendors, check the availability of merchandise. Consider dealer policy concerning quick delivery, service, exchange and adjustments.

10. Standardization of equipment. Selecting items of similar craftsmanship, style or color may mean considerable savings over time. Standardization makes items easier to replace and repair. Special order equipment and supplies result in higher cost; delay shipment and repair.

11. Timing. Order all equipment and supplies well in advance of need to allow for inspection, evaluation, possible replacement and inventory control.

12. Dealers. The main objective in selection is the purchase of quality merchandise at a competitive price. If a reputable local dealer offers a quality product or service competitive with the price of an out-of-town company, use the local dealer. Good will and quick delivery are important considerations here.

Additional considerations to pursue during selection follow:

1. Persuade your dealer to stock an item with distinctive nontraditional colors: the use of a yellow football, a blue water polo ball, or a white basketball deters theft.

2. Ask the dealer if the manufacturer can engrave your agency's identification marks or logo upon your items at the factory.

3. Purchase standard pieces of equipment and supplies in bulk and save money.

4. Take advantage of close-outs or sales on stock items. If you do not require equipment of exceptional quality, buy slightly blemished goods at considerable savings.

5. Take time when selecting equipment and supplies and consider all relevant information before placing an order.

6. When buying clothes, don't take a participant's word for a correct size. Always measure for yourself.

PURCHASE PROCEDURES

An efficient agency explains its specific purchasing system to appropriate personnel. In larger organizations, a staff member serves as a liason between the organization's purchasing agent and each department. In smaller organizations, one person acts as a part-time purchasing agent in addition to a full-time programming job. Any organization buying quantities of equipment or supplies can benefit from a purchasing policy manual providing explanations, purchasing policies, procedures, and examples of forms and records used in processing.

The following are general steps in the purchasing process.

1. Preliminary request. It is important that an administrator—such as a director or associate director— is aware of any purchasing requests before they are forwarded to the purchasing agent. A preliminary request form indicates the staff member initiating the request, the program charged, the date the equipment or supply is needed, the suggested vendor, the method of payment and the quantity, description and cost estimate of desired item. (see Figure 10-1).

PRELIMINARY EQUIPMENT REQUEST FORM

Requested By: _____   Approved By: _____

Date: _____   Date: _____

Date Needed: _____   Vendor Suggested: _____

Budget Charged: _____   Address: _____

_____

(Check one:) Purchase Requisition ____   Printing Plant _____

   Bookstore _____   Physical Plant Job Request _____

   Petty Cash _____   Central Stores _____

   Other _____ Specify: _____

Quantity	Brief Description of Item, Book Title, Work to be Performed, Etc. (catalog #, name of salesperson, etc., requested)	Estimate Cost

Figure 10-1. Preliminary equipment request form.

2. Justification. The programmer should be ready to provide administrative staff with a written or verbal justification for each purchase request. A justification answers the following questions:

— Why are the items needed?

— How will they improve operations?

— What are the advantages and disadvantages of the product?

— Can they be maintained and stored easily?

— Is there a need for special care or handling?

— Is the product a current or new (recommended) item?

3. Specifications. Upon approval of the preliminary request, include specification or bid sheets with a purchase requisition form to provide the necessary details for the purchasing agent.

   Specifications are needed to assure that the items *wanted* are the items *received.* When preparing item specs, provide as much information as possible about the product. Complicated specifications may discourage bidders. Strict ones may block the purchase of suitable items because they do not meet precise requirements.

4. Bids. After writing equipment or supply specifications, send them to the purchasing agent for competitive bidding. A bid system exists to eliminate favoritism and stimulate competition to reduce prices.

   Most state and federal organizations have an established policy, dictated by law, concerning purchases made with tax money. If the purchase item exceeds a certain amount, ranging from $100 to $1000, an intent to purchase must be advertised publicly to invite competitive bids. Other guidelines specify procedures governing formal and informal bids. When this process is geared towards the lowest bidder, an inferior or low grade quality of merchandise may result. By issuing invitations well in advance, responsible firms have sufficient time to prepare competitive bids.

   A competitive bid system results in competition from reliable vendors within a close price range. It is important to consider all vendors and to treat them fairly.

   "Once you've sent out signals you're only going to buy from one vendor, you can kiss competitive bidding goodbye... Decide your awards on logic and stick to it. (We) defend the awards, not the vendors or the users. Low bid is the most powerful argument, providing the bidder has met (our) qualifications. On any bids, if you do not take the low bid, be sure you list the reasons why you are not accepting the low bid. Always be prepared to

Indiana University Treas. Form 13 B-45—		PURCHASE REQUISITION			32 REQ. NO.

ACCOUNT TITLE AND NUMBER

Recreational Sports
12-345-6789

EXPENSE CLASS
5000

DATE REQUIRED
10-24

STATE COMPLETE DELIVERY ADDRESS (BOTH BUILDING AND ROOM NUMBER)

REQUESTED BY   DATE

VENDOR SUGGESTED:

I CERTIFY THAT FUNDS ARE AVAILABLE WITHIN THE ACCOUNT CHARGED.   DATE

Acme Whistles

VENDOR:

HEAD OF DEPARTMENT

OTHER APPROVAL   DATE

Smith's Whistles
0000 Avon
Anywhere, U.S.A.

SHIP VIA.   F.O.B.   TERMS:

QUANTITY	ITEMS (GIVE COMPLETE SPECIFICATIONS)	ESTIMATED TOTAL		ACTUAL TOTAL
5 Doz.	M-2 Plastic Whistles @ 65¢	39	00	
	Order phoned in on 10-24. Whistles were to be put in the mail on same date. Quoted 65¢ unit price on 10-24. Vendor's phone number is: 995-0799.			

ORDER NO.   APPROVED--TREASURER   ACCT. DEPT.

REQUISITIONS FOR EQUIPMENT MUST BE ACCOMPANIED BY SUPPORTING STATEMENT

Figure 10-2. Purchase requisition form. Source: Indiana University Purchasing Department (form).

explain your actions." (Athletic Purchasing and Facilities, 1981, p. 14).

5. Purchase orders. Upon acceptance of a bid, prepare a purchase order for the specific items. Standard business forms, containing from one to five duplicate copies, include name, address, and telephone number of the recommended vendor, the name, address, and

---

THIS PAGE FOR USE ONLY BY PURCHASING DEPARTMENT

REASON FOR CHOICE OF VENDOR:

☐ LOWEST PRICE   ☐ EARLY DELIVERY   ☐ BETTER QUALITY

☐ FIXED PRICE   ☐ FRANCHISE ITEM   ☐ REQUIRED DESIGN

☐ CURRENT OR COMPETITIVE PRICE   ☐ INSUFFICIENT TIME TO SECURE QUOTATIONS   ☐ REPLACEMENT PART FROM MANUFACTURER

☐ SMALL ORDER   ☐ ONLY AVAILABLE SOURCE   ☐ PROFESSIONAL SERVICES

☐_____   QUOTATION TAKEN BY PHONE_____

telephone number of the agency initiating the request, billing instructions, delivery instructions, the purchase order and requisition number, date of the order, the quantity, description, unit cost and total cost of the items requested and an approval signature from the purchasing agent.

INVENTORY

Once equipment and supplies arrive, check the accompanying merchandise packing list and count all cartons and items received. Open the cartons, inspect for damage and verify that the items coincide with the original purchase order. Report defects, damage, or shortages to the vendor immediately. If items are in order and acceptable, inventory them.

A good inventory system, indicating what is needed for bidding and purchasing, provides an efficient way to control the amount and condition of stock on hand. Before adopting any inventory system and its record-keeping requirements, consider future need for equipment.

Inventory records describe the condition, location and quantity of items on hand, the cost of each item, and the amount of stock to maintain at any one time. Keep a record of items that have been transferred, lost, discarded, destroyed, or repaired since the previous reporting period.

Mark all sports equipment and supplies for identification purposes before entering them in the inventory and allowing their use. Use permanent ink, waterproof paints, engravings or other durable marking methods. Identify the organization, unit number, date of purchase, serial number and size, when necessary.

With proper control, inventory systems are valuable sources for the preparation of financial reports and future budget requests. They can indicate the popularity of certain programs within a recreational sport operation.

STORAGE

After equipment and supplies have been inventoried and marked for identification, they must be properly stored. Use racks, bins, lockers and other structures to protect the items and to maximize the use of space. Regulate the temperature, moisture, humidity, and ventilation of the storage area for the protection of all equipment and supplies. Storage should be convenient to the sports facility or playing area where the items are used.

In a large facility, the storage area is usually a multipurpose room designed to warehouse, distribute, repair, and

RECREATIONAL SPORTS
INVENTORY OF EQUIPMENT AND SUPPLIES

EQUIPMENT INVENTORY	ITEM		PROGRAM				
	MODEL #		AREA				
SUPPLIER:			PHONE NUMBER:				
ADDRESS:			CONTACT:				

CATALOGUE PAGE		UNIT COST		MINIMUM ORDER		MINIMUM INVENTORY	
DATE OF TRANS-ACTION	RECEIVED		DISBURSED		BALANCE		
						DEFICIT	
	P.O. #	AMT.	AMT.	WHO	AMT.	C	D	L	S

DEFICIT:
  C = CONSUMED
  D = DISCARDED/BROKEN
  L = LOST
  S = STOLEN

Figure 10-3. Equipment and supplies inventory form.

launder equipment and supplies. For convenience, this room is typically located next to the locker and shower facilities.

DISTRIBUTION

Establish definite policies and procedures for issuing items and maintain check-out forms providing for their return.

There are several acceptable procedures for distributing equipment and supplies. Items needed for an intramural sport may be issed to a programmer having the responsibility for their distribution at the playing site. Figure 10-4 represents a model equipment check-out form suitable for an intramural event.

With a club sport, equipment and supplies may be issued to the club president or other representative for the season. Individual clubs maintain their own inventory since they are responsible for all items used in their program.

Informal sport activities and instructional sport sessions may use an equipment room for issuing equipment and supplies. In this case, participants need to present identification and complete an equipment check-out slip, providing their name, address, telephone number, social security number and locker number. Information on the form should indicate the quantity and name of the item, identification code, and date of distribution and return.

A check-out slip should contain an acceptance statement that indicates personal responsibility for the items and agreement to purchase or repair the items if they are lost or damaged. Some organizations require a security deposit while equipment is on loan.

Participants appreciate access to a variety of sports equipment and supplies on a check-out basis. Those who normally do not participate for lack of equipment now have what they need.

MAINTENANCE AND CARE

Proper handling, maintenance, and care extend the useful life of equipment and supplies. Constantly inspect equipment and supplies for faulty or broken parts and classify them according to condition. At the first sign of deterioration or damage, remove an item from use until it can be repaired. Simple repairs may be done by the equipment staff, while major ones should be handled through an authorized dealer. Dispose discarded equipment where it cannot be found and used again.

At frequent intervals, inspect used equipment to determine what can be kept and what has to be thrown away. Items in storage require periodic cleaning to improve their appearance and to maintain their usefulness. If additional equipment or supplies are needed, purchase them immediately. The end of a sports season is often a good time to take advantage of sales, discounts or close-outs of many seasonal sports equipment and supplies.

EQUIPMENT CHECK-OUT FORM

Date: _____   Phone: _____

Name: _____   SS #: _____ - _____ - _____

Address: _____   Activity: _____

Locker Number: _____

EQUIPMENT REQUESTED:

QUANTITY	**DESCRIPTION OF ITEM**

Office Use Only

Out | In

Staff Initial: _____|_____   Actual Return: _____

Date Equipment Needed: _____   Condition: _____

Initial/Date Return: _____

I hereby agree to pay for any equipment damaged or not returned. Failure to do so will result in legal action.

_____
Signature

Figure 10-4. Equipment check-out form.

CONCLUSION

Due to the variety of items, number of users, maintenance requirements and expense, a programmer must employ proper management techniques in the procurement, use and care of equipment and supplies. Such practices contribute to safe, efficient and economical use of resources necessary for quality program delivery. Constant advancements in technology will require the programmer to keep in tune with those changes that may alter current management practices.

BIBLIOGRAPHY

Bucher, C. A. *Administration of Physical Education and Athletic Programs.* St. Louis: The C. V. Mosby Co., 1979.

Daughtrey, G. *Physical Education and Intramural Programs: Organization and Administration.* Philadelphia: W. B. Saunders, 1976.

Kleindienst, V. and Weston, A. *The Recreational Sports Program: Schools . . . Colleges . . . Community.* Englewood Cliffs, New Jersey: Prentice-Hall, Inc. 1978.

McCurrach, D. "Don't Get Burned by Low Bids." *The American School Board Journal.* January, 1981, pp. 38–39.

Penman, K. A. "Where Do You Store Your Sports Equipment?" *Athletic Purchasing and Equipment.* January, 1979, pp. 38–41.

"Putting Inventory to Work for You," *Athletic Purchasing and Equipment.* January, 1982, pp. 10–14.

"Quick! Tell Me How to Buy Athletic and Playground Equipment," *The American School Board Journal.* February, 1977, p. 11.

Resick, M. C., Serdel, B. L. and Maron, J. G., *Modern Administrative Practices in Physical Education and Athletics.* Reading, Massachusetts: Addison-Wesley Publishing Co., 1979.

Schneider, E. "How to Cut Your Equipment Purchasing Costs," *Athletic Purchasing and Facilities.* October, 1978, pp. 58–60.

"Specifications: Important in Getting What You Want." *Athletic Purchasing and Facilities.* August, 1981, pp. 10–16.

"The Changing Face of Equipment Vendors," *Athletic Purchasing and Facilities.* October, 1981, pp. 24–26.

The Rawlings Sporting Goods Co., *Athletic Equipment Digest,* 4th edition. St. Louis: Rawlings Sporting Goods Co., 1966.

"Using Competitive Bidding to Your Advantage," *Athletic Purchasing and Facilities.* September, 1981, pp.10–14.

Chapter 11

SAFETY IN SPORT

One of the requirements of recreational sport programming is a safe, injury-free environment for participants, spectators and personnel. It is critical that a sound philosophy and knowledge of sport safety be implemented into all phases of program operations.

The amount of time spent participating in various recreational sport activities on a daily basis is overwhelming. Since most sport activity occurs with little supervision, it is nearly impossible to calculate the total extent of participation or the number of accidents and related injuries that occur as a consequence. Recreational sport activities are, by their very nature, potentially hazardous. An element of risk often makes sport activity more enjoyable, challenging and appealing to participants, many of whom consider the possibility of injury an acceptable risk of sport. Lloyd, Deaver and Eastwood, (1936, p. 174) explain the hazardous nature of sport:

Practically all activities involve hazards, athletics particularly so, since they are situations largely organized around the emotional tendencies of attack and retreat. Also, since athletics involve play with the emotional patterns characterized as fear and rivalry, cooperation and individual aggrandizement, defeat and success, it follows that much is at stake and risks will be incurred to achieve success. Some of the hazards found in athletics then will be due to the nature of the game; to remove these would be to dehydrate the activities until they become unrecognizable and uninteresting.

The same hazards found in athletics exist in a recreational sport environment. A sports safety program cannot eliminate hazards or risks, but may control activities so that accidents and unnecessary risks are minimized. The programmer has a responsibility to take every precaution possible to guard against potential hazards and reduce the risk factor, while preserving the value and popularity of the sport.

Sport safety requires an understanding of the term "risk" and the types of risk-takers. Fox (1961, pg. 50) explains:

Most people tend to use the term *risk* with two meanings. First, they mean the inherent danger in a situation. Usually the situation or action is called risky, implying in a mixed way both that there is danger and that the actor (participant) is behaving with likelihood of accident or injury as a result of this behavior. But if no one is actually misbehaving, people talk about the absolute risk of a situation. Secondly, people talk about a person's taking risk, implying that he has deliberately entered a dangerous situation. There is little implication here that the "risk" is attributable to the situation—more to the person's [behavior] in this dangerous [manner] situation.

[I] propose that we use two words here which will separate these meanings more clearly. They are "hazard" and "risk". "Hazard" will be objective danger or likelihood of failure, and "risk" will be subjective estimate of hazard. The usage proposed—that is, hazard = danger, and risk = estimated hazard—can become formalized easily.

A risk to one person may be a common occurrence to another. Such sport events as mountain climbing, sky diving and auto racing attract those who enjoy the risk and adventure associated with them.

In discussing risk-takers, Fox (1961 pp. 52–53) indicates three common types:

1. Those who are perfectly aware of the hazards;

2. Those who are only partially aware of the hazards;

3. Those who are ignorant of the hazards, assuming complete safety.

While all three types are of concern to the recreational sport programmer, the latter two are involved in the majority of sports accidents. When the programmer has an opportunity to recognize and educate these individuals regarding potential hazards, he or she may promote a significant decrease in the number of accidents.

"Of all the principles related to accident prevention, 'risk recognition' is probably the most significant. One must possess a clear understanding of the hazards and the potential dangers of the activity before one can establish control. It should not be presupposed that participants are aware of the inherent dangers of certain activities. It has been established without question that effective leadership reduces accidents." (Gabrielsen, 1978, p. 38)

The programmer must stress to all participants, especially among younger children for whom the dangers are usually higher, all of the risks involved. Furthermore, participants must understand that when they choose to participate, they undertake a normal assumption of risk, and cannot hold others responsible for the consequences. However, the programmer can minimize the amount of their risk by taking precautions and enforcing accident prevention policies.

Definitions

"Accident" and injury" are terms common to sport participation. The National Safety Council (Worick, 1975, p. 12) defines an accident as "that occurence in a sequence of events which usually produces unintended injury, death or property damage". Injury often results from an accident and is "a damage or hurt done or suffered—a detriment to or violation of person, character, feelings, rights, property, interest, or value of a thing. . . in the near future it seems likely that sport injuries will be more accurately defined as to the quantitative and qualitative limits of damage to person and/or property." (Elkow, 1967, p. 5)

The vast majority of sport accidents reported today are attributed to human behavior, often caused by carelessness. Consequently, we should not accept accidents as an inevitable part of sport. It is imperative for the programmer to know the primary causes of accidents in recreational sports and how to implement strategies for their prevention.

CAUSES OF ACCIDENTS

Safety experts agree that most accidents originate from two prime causes: unsafe behavior (the human factor) and unsafe environment. Of the two, unsafe behavior is considered by many persons to be a significant contributing factor in about 85% of all accidents (Strasser, 1973, p. 25). Anticipating and controlling unsafe behavior then, is essential in accident prevention. In order to design effective prevention measures the programmer needs to recognize the vital role individual differences in physical skills, emotions, knowledge and safety habits play in susceptibility to accidents or injuries.

Physical Skills

Sports require a degree of coordination, agility, balance, reaction time, speed, power and judgment. Individuals who possess more of these qualities tend to be less susceptible to accidents and injuries. When sport enthusiasts overestimate their abilities and physical skills, many accidents occur.

Emotions

Individuals who possess poor emotional control are more prone to accidents and injuries. Physical fatigue and such psychological factors as tension, worry, fear, anxiety, anger and nervousness may set the stage for an accident or injury. Watch for these symptoms and intervene when necessary by assessing penalties or even excluding troubled participants from further participation.

Knowledge

Sport participants who are unaware of potential hazards or specific rules, regulations, equipment, skills and strategies involved in an activity are also prone to accidents and injuries. Ryan (1975, pg. 6) contends:

> The individual engaged in a recreational sport, generally speaking, has no administrator, coach, trainer, or physician to guide him. He must take the responsibility for determining whether he is physically fit to participate, whether and to what extent he needs to condition himself, what learning of sport skills is required, what equipment he needs and what its quality should be, what facilities are safe for his use and under what conditions, and how he will prepare himself to deal with the emergency of an injury. The problems posed for the individual participating in an unsupervised sport are enormous.

Communicate information to participants to give them an understanding of the sport, necessary skills, and the required conditioning.

Safety Habits

Carelessness that becomes habit-forming results in repeated accidents. Participants need instruction in safe practices from the beginning to help them form positive safety habits. It is much easier to develop good habits than it is to break bad ones.

Unsafe Behavior

Specific conditions causing accidents and injuries which are attributed to the human factor follow (adapted from Gabrielsen, 1978, pg. 48).

Leadership

1. Forcing participants to do things that they are incapable of doing because of low skill level.

2. Adapting equipment to a use for which it was not intended.

3. Leaving an activity unsupervised.

4. Inadequate supervision of activities which are inherently hazardous.

5. Mismatching participants of different ages or skill ability.

6. Inadequate preparation for introduction of a new activity.

7. Lack of professional qualification for teaching or coaching the activity.

8. Allowing rough play.

Participants

1. Overweight.

2. Overly aggressive.

3. Awkward or poorly coordinated.

4. Overcrowding of equipment or apparatus.

5. Children in unsupervised situations.

6. Fatigue caused by too much activity or illness.

7. Horseplay.

8. Consumption of drugs or alcohol prior to participation in activity.

9. Overestimation of one's ability.

10. Pressure from peer group to try something beyond one's capability.

11. Failure to follow instructions or rules.

12. Failure to wear proper equipment.

13. Failure to intervene when a hazard cannot be removed immediately.

Unsafe Environment

Other major causes of accidents and injuries in recreational sport relate to unsafe environmental factors, and involve indoor and outdoor sport facilities and such natural forces as lightning, sun, heat, extreme temperatures and humidity. Although accidents resulting from an unsafe environment are fewer than those caused by unsafe behavior, they require strategies for prevention. The recreational sport programmer has no excuse for accidents that result from faulty equipment or poor maintenance. An adapted list from Gabrielsen reveals the most common causes of accidents involving equipment and facilities:

Equipment

1. Failure to inspect and evaluate the condition of equipment before use.

2. The improper placement of equipment.

3. Poor quality of equipment.

4. Improper use of equipment.

5. Modification of equipment by users or instructors.

6. Equipment defect.

Facilities

1. Poor condition of facilities: holes in the ground, gravel on hard surfaces, and debris on playing fields resulting from inadequate maintenance.

2. Overloading bleachers.

3. Insufficient buffer zone between field activities, and between indoor playing areas and walls.

4. Placement of rigid equipment too close to playing areas.

5. Soap on shower room floors.

6. Wet floors with painted surfaces in locker rooms.

7. Fences around tennis courts too close to side and end lines.

8. Improper surface on playing courts and fields.

9. Bicycles on playground where young children play.

10. Concrete curbing placed too close to play apparatus.

11. Side and/or end lines of football, soccer, lacrosse, and field hockey playing fields located too close to solid walls or concrete curbings.

12. Improper placement of light poles around tennis courts, football fields and baseball diamonds.

ACCIDENT PREVENTION

Once the programmer accepts the theory that accidents have causes and understands and recognizes their contributing factors, he or she makes accident prevention an integral part of a total recreational sport program. An effective accident prevention program involves proper planning and competent leadership.

Planning involves the proper layout of sports and playing areas, the selection of good equipment, the correct installation of equipment, and a proper maintenance program. A flow pattern of users as it relates to the placement of equipment is an essential ingredient in good planning. Effective leadership implies a knowledge of safety rules, the proper conduct of activities and the ability to control hazards and risks. (Gabrielsen, 1978, p. 34)

Hazard control, a major thrust of accident prevention, involves incorporating the following principles into sport programming. First, identify all potential hazards or risks involved in the recreational sport prior to program start. Eliminate or reduce these hazards if at all possible. Develop control methods or alternatives that will compensate for those hazards that cannot be eliminated. Finally, prevent any additional or unnecessary hazards in subsequent sport offerings.

Specific policy and procedural guidelines to help eliminate hazards and prevent accidents include:

Medical Examination

Recommend a thorough medical examination for those who wish to participate in strenuous recreational sports. Point out that involvement in these sports require appropriate skills, stamina and endurance.

Training and Conditioning

Encourage and provide proper training and conditioning for participants. Few understand the importance that fitness plays in safe, enjoyable participation.

Equity

Provide equitable participation according to similar age, weight and skill levels. A significant increase in injuries occurs when individuals of widely different backgrounds are grouped together, especially in contact sport programs.

Scheduling

Develop reasonable limitations on the number of games or matches scheduled for a team or individual during a structured tournament or season. Contests scheduled too close together increase the chance of fatigue-related injuries.

Sport Modifications

Modifying sport rules and regulations to suit the characteristics of the participants is the greatest single tool for reducing accidents in structured recreational sport programs. Modifications may involve the adjustment of rules, playing periods or playing areas. For example, "screen blocking" (similar to that of setting a "screen" in basketball) has resulted in significant decreases in accidents in flag football. This removes practically all physical contact at the line of scrimmage.

Quality Personnel

Provide quality personnel. Modifications to sport rules and regulations are futile unless competent sport officials or supervisors enforce them. The programmer should make every effort to furnish trained personnel for all sports. Stress that the safety of the players depends upon how well personnel interpret the rules and control the environment. Since the safety of the participant is their highest priority, empower officials to suspend play if necessary. Hold supervisors accountable for accidents that occur during their scheduled assignment.

Spectator Safety

Initiate safety regulations for spectators. Safe bleacher construction, restraining lines, effective crowd control procedures, and vehicular traffic regulations are only a few precautions that require consideration for spectator safety.

Environmental Safety

Maintain the environment to insure safe playing conditions. A programmer, sport supervisor or sport official should complete daily inspections of the sport facilities at the site. Close a facility if a hazard cannot be controlled or eliminated.

Typical considerations for facility or area inspection include:

—location of hazardous, sharp or protruding objects
—condition of the playing surface
—extreme environmental conditions
—ventilation and air circulation
—visibility and lighting conditions
—pedestrian or vehicular traffic patterns
—spectator seating and boundaries
—protective facility coverings and pads
—designated entrance and exit points to facilities or areas

Equipment Safety

Concern with the safety of equipment begins with selection and purchase. Carefully consider the durability, quality of workmanship, quality of materials, and suitability of equipment. Note that stationary equipment requires proper installation by trained maintenance personnel after purchase.

A regular schedule of inspection is essential to detect equipment hazards. Provide a safety maintenance checklist to assist their identification. Once faulty equipment is discovered, qualified personnel should perform proper repairs. Replace equipment requiring constant repair work. Attention to these details helps reduce the occurrence of injuries and increases the longevity of equipment.

Acknowledgement Forms

Use participant acknowledgment of responsibility forms, particularly if a sport involves young children or high risk. Although these forms do not guarantee legal protection, they point out risks and responsibilities associated with participation. They also illustrate that participants know the dangers and accept responsibility for risk prior to participation. These forms discourage the filing of law suits against the programmer and agency.

Participant Safety

Insist that each participant regard safety as a personal responsibility. The recreational sports agency plays a significant role in accident prevention through rules, regulations, policies and safety awareness efforts, but individual application of these principles, in conjunction with safety attitude and behavior, minimizes accidents and injuries. Several guidelines that participants should know to develop safety awareness in sports follow (adapted from Stack and Elkow, 1966, pp. 91–93):

1. Study the sport and the hazards it poses as you advance in skills and participation.

2. Determine your physical and emotional fitness to meet the demands of an activity.

3. Learn what the limitations are of the equipment and facilities.

4. Use equipment, facilities, and supplies for the intended purpose.

5. Refuse to participate in a hazardous activity unless protective equipment is properly provided and fitted.

6. Secure instruction from qualified personnel.

7. Keep others informed of where, and when you plan to go before entering an area known to be hazardous.

8. Act your age.

9. Use progressive skill development. Become proficient in simple skills before moving on to more advanced ones.

10. Be ready to send for assistance if it is needed.

11. Provide prompt and effective medical treatment of injuries and insist upon adequate follow-up treatment to facilitate a quick return to participation.

12. Accept responsibility for your fellow man. Assist others to achieve safety in hazardous situations.

Among such populations as pre-school, middle childhood, late childhood, or handicapped groups, participants may not be capable of assuming partial or full responsibility for their own safety, or the safety of others. The recreational sport programmer should take specialized safety precautions and supervision measures for these groups.

Guidelines for Handling Accidents

Since all programmers, supervisors, officials, coordinators, volunteers, and other leadership personnel are in a position to curtail accidents, they represent the single most important factor in safety and hazard control. When accidents do occur in the sport environment, they require adequate instruction to fulfill their responsibilities for swift and sure accident management.

Train personnel

Because of a need for on-site leadership, the selection and training of responsible persons in recreational sport safety is a high priority. Select mature, responsible workers with an ability to make quick and sound judgments. Require personnel to hold certification or provide for basic emergency training. At a minimum, employees should demonstrate proficiency in cardio-pulmonary resuscitation (CPR) and other techniques designed to sustain life until certified medical personnel arrive.

Content areas recommended for inclusion within a sports emergency training program include;

—accident prevention
—safety measures
—procedures at the accident scene
—accident reporting
—control of bleeding
—skeletal injuries
—CPR
—Mouth-to-mouth resuscitation
—Heat related illnesses
—Shock
—Hyperventilation
—Insulin shock
—Epilepsy

The knowledge and skills gained through proper training may mean the difference between life or death, temporary or permanent disability, rapid recovery or extensive rehabilitation. Sport emergency training prepares the leader to protect a participant from further injury, maintain or restore life, provide comfort and reassurance, and plan for transportation to a medical facility. Additional training in first aid is available at an authorized health agency. The extent of expertise and certification required by an agency for its program personnel often depends upon the immediate availability of qualified medical personnel.

Assess the Situation

First aid procedure at the scene of an accident or injury begins with an assessment by the leader. This in itself will help both the leader and the victim to remain calm. If the victim is conscious, determine what happened and the location of any pain. In the case of an unconscious victim find and question eyewitnesses. If there has been no fall or other trauma which makes you suspect a neck injury, check for respiration. If the

victim is not breathing, open the airway. (Procedures available from the American Red Cross or American Heart Association)
Examine victim for such obvious signs of injury as:

—bleeding
—deformity of limbs or body parts
—level of consciousness
—color of skin
—pupil size
—swelling
—burns
—medical alert tag

DO NOT probe for injuries or test for broken limbs. Determine the need for emergency assistance. In the case of minor injuries, assist the victim by rendering appropriate care at the scene.

Take appropriate action

The leader should summon an ambulance immediately if any of the following conditions exist:

—interruption of breathing or pulse

—unconsciousness, dizziness, loss of memory, stupor or loss of coordination

—suspected fractures other than fingers and toes

—severe bleeding

—heart attack—chest pains radiating down the arm, sweating, anxiousness, shortness of breath, or stroke—loss of function on one side of the body, loss of speech, one side of face droops.

—severe allergic reaction

If an ambulance is needed, notify the appropriate authorities. Many sports departments first contact a law enforcement office who relays the call. Explain the nature of the emergency, specific location, number of persons involved and your telephone number in case the ambulance service needs further directions. In most instances, a sport supervisor, sport official or competent adult may summon an ambulance while the program leader remains at the scene to care for the victim. When this is not possible, write down the necessary information and hand it to a volunteer assistant. Refrain from using a personal vehicle to transport an injured person to a medical facility. If the victim is unconscious, check for an emergency medical identification bracelet, necklace, medallion or card. This may help determine the nature of the emergency and such knowledge may help save a life.

In case of serious injury or sudden illness, program personnel should be prepared to provide immediate attention while help is being summoned.

1. Perform a prompt rescue when necessary. Transport the victim away from a hazardous location.

2. Ensure that the victim has an open airway and administer artificial respiration or CPR as needed.

3. Control severe bleeding.

4. Treat for shock.

5. Reassure the victim that medical assistance has been summoned and should be arriving soon. Do not discuss agency insurance coverage or liability. Report accident details only to authorized personnel.

6. Keep bystanders and other participants away from the victim(s).

7. Record all observable symptoms so that the ambulance attendants may report them to the doctor.

Whatever the circumstance, program personnel should have a reason to justify their every action. Above all, they should recognize the limits of their abilities and responsibilities. Finally, when a participant sustains an injury, programmers should follow-up with a telephone call or visit to demonstrate personal and agency concern.

Accident Records and Reporting

Sports safety requires an effective accident recording and reporting system. The National Safety Council (1966, p. iii) notes that a major purpose of accident reporting is to "reduce the number of accidents and injuries through effective and realistic planning and through effective and realistic improvements in the environment." The documentation of injury-producing accidents is essential in determining what activities, facilities, rules, and regulations contribute to unsafe conditions. Accurate reporting is also critical in situations where legal action results from accidents.

What accidents to report and record

In our opinion, report and document *ALL* accidents regardless of the severity of the injury. What may appear to be a minor or incidental injury might develop into a more serious one.

A consensus in current literature makes a distinction between 'reportable' and 'recordable' accidents. Reportable accidents are those which result in an injury to a participant, regardless of severity. Recordable accidents are those which result in injuries severe enough to disable an individual and interrupt sport participation for an indefinite period of time.

Whatever reporting or recording system you adopt, keep it simple. Staff should have a clear understanding of the policy so that reporting is uniform throughout the agency. Inconsistent reporting results in misleading statistical data.

When an accident or injury is not observed by those affiliated with the recreational sport program, participants need to report them. Unless they understand appropriate procedure, it is not possible to provide immediate care for the injured or have a comprehensive reporting and recording system.

Accident reporting forms

Once an accident occurs, complete an accident report form, documenting the pertinent facts of the incident, as soon as possible. This helps avoid inaccurate or conflicting descriptions of the accident.

The form should be a working document that is possible to complete in a minimum amount of time, containing all necessary information. The format depends on the information desired, the individual completing the form, and data processing requirements. If several copies of each accident report are required, color coding or carbon-backed forms are practical and time-saving. (See Figure 11-1 for an example.)

RECREATIONAL SPORT ACCIDENT REPORT FORM

Day _____ Month _____ Year _____ Su-M-T-W-Th-F-S
(circle day of week)

Name of Injured _____ Male ____ Female ____ Age ____

Soc. Sec. No. _____ - _____ - _____ Local Address _____

Phone _____

Time accident occurred: _____
A.M. _____ P.M. _____

Time accident reported: _____
A.M. _____ P.M. _____

Personnel Present: Yes ___ No ___
Instructor ___ Supervisor ___ Official ___
Professional Staff ___ Other _____

Part of Body Injured: Place √ in applicable line

___ Abdomen	___ Face	___ Leg
___ Ankle	___ Finger	___ Mouth
___ Arm	___ Foot	___ Nose
___ Back	___ Forearm	___ Rib(s)
___ Chest	___ Hand	___ Scalp
___ Ear	___ Head	___ Shoulder
___ Elbow	___ Hip	___ Tooth
___ Eye	___ Knee	___ Thigh
Other: Specify _____		___ Wrist

Nature of Possible or Suspected Injury:

Key word: _____

(sprain, fracture, bruise, etc.)
Brief description: _____
_____
_____
_____
_____

Specific Location:

___ Golf course	___ Outdoor pool
___ Gym no. ___	___ Indoor pool
___ Handball/	___ Stairs or inclines
squash courts	___ Tennis courts
___ Field A	___ Weight room
___ Locker room	___ Fieldhouse
___ Club field	
___ Intramural field	

Other: Specify _____

Brief Description of Accident and
Disposition: _____
_____
_____
_____

Probable Cause of Accident:

___ Caught in, on, between
___ Fall—same level
___ Fall—different level
___ Rubbing
___ Striking against
___ Struck by
Specify other _____

Activity: Check applicable line

Recreational sports
___ Intramural
___ Extramural
___ Club
___ Informal
Specify activity: _____

Immediate Action Taken: (Name & Title)

___ First Aid _____
___ Sent to Physician's Office _____
___ Sent to Hospital _____
___ Refused Attention _____
___ Other: Specify _____

Method of Transportation:

	Time: Reported	Time: Arrived
___ Ambulance	_____	_____
___ Private Vehicle	_____	_____
___ Law Enforcement Vehicle	_____	_____
___ Fire Department Rescue Squad	_____	_____
___ Other: Specify _____	_____	_____

Witness(es) Available: Yes ___ No ___

Name _____ Address _____ Phone _____
Name _____ Address _____ Phone _____

Report filed by: _____ Date _____

Approved by: _____ Date _____
(Department or Division Head)

Follow Up: Recommended: Yes ___ No ___
Completed by: _____ Date _____
(Name & Title)

Figure 11-1. Accident report form.

Regardless of the format, a recreational sport accident form answers essential questions covering the who, what, where, when, why and how of the accident. The information typically requested in an accident form includes:

1. Name of victim

2. Address

3. Telephone number

4. Social security number

5. Age

6. Sex

7. Date and day of accident

8. Time accident occurred

9. Time accident was reported

10. Nature of injury

11. Probable cause of injury

12. Brief description of accident

13. Part of body injured

14. Sport activity involved

15. Specific location of accident

16. First aid treatment, if any

17. Method of transportation to a medical facility, if required

18. Person completing report

19. Name, address and telephone number of witness(es) to the accident

20. Follow-up investigation

21. Agency signature

Provide instructions for accurate completion of the form. These instructions may be attached to the form, printed at the top or omitted in deference to in-service training.

"If your ideal, efficient and well-printed form is to be worth anything for accident prevention purposes, the persons completing and reviewing the report must know *why* they are to report accidents, *how* to fill out the forms, and *what* the items mean. Simple, clear and meaningful instructions must be given to all concerned." (National Safety Council, 1966, p. 12)

Evaluating accident report information

After completing each accident report, send copies to those appropriate individuals or offices who will USE the data. Accident reports are of little value if they are filed without further action. One of the most efficient and effective ways of eliminating safety hazards in your sport program is through careful analysis of these reports to identify causal factors. An accident report summary, for example, might indicate that equipment repair or replacement, modifications of playing rules, or improved supervision are needed. Accurate reports are essential in resolving a legal action. They provide the necessary background facts upon which to refute or support a claim of negligence on the part of the agency or programmer. The absence of a reporting process may demonstrate negligence in itself.

The recreational sport programmer at the operational level should promote a concern for safety among professional staff, leaders, volunteers, and participants. It is a credit to the safety-minded leader wheh the number of participants enjoying recreational sports increases year by year while the number of accidents and injuries in sport decreases. Safety is not an end in itself but a means to maximize enjoyment in sports activities.

REFERENCES

Effron, D. M. *Cardiopulmonary Resuscitation-CPR*. Tulsa, Oklahoma: CPR Publishers, Inc., 1978.

Elkow, J. D. The Injury Problem in Sports. In C. P. Yost (ed.), *Sports Safety: Accident Prevention and Injury Control in Physical Education, Athletics and Recreation*. Washington, D.C.: AAHPER, 1967.

Fox, B. H. *Behavioral Approaches to Accident Research.* New York: Association for the Aid of Crippled Children, 1961.

Frankel, L. S. Recreation and Park Program Safety. *Urban Data Service Reports,* April, 1980.

Gabrielsen, M. A. (ed.). *Blueprint for Safety In Sports and Recreation.* Waterford, Connecticut: The Knoll Press, 1978.

Haering, F. C. Recreation and Park Program Safety. *Urban Data Service Reports,* March, 1980.

Hyatt, R. W. *Intramural Sports: Organization and Administration,* St. Louis: The C. V. Mosby Co., 1977.

Kraus, R. G. & Bates, B. J. *Recreation Leadership and Supervision: Guidelines for Professional Development.* Philadelphia: W. B. Saunders Co., 1975.

Lloyd, F. S., Deaver, G. G., and Eastwood, F. R. *Safety in Athletics* Philadelphia: W. B. Saunders Co., 1936.

National Safety Council. *Student Accident Reporting Guidebook.* Chicago: National Safety Council, 1966.

Ryan, A. J. Prevention of Sports Injuries: A Problem Solving Approach. In *Selected Problems in Sports Safety.* Washington, D.C.: AAHPER, 1975.

Stack, H. J. and Elkow, J. D. *Education for Safe Living. Englewood Cliffs: Prentice-Hall, Inc., 1966.

Strasser, M. K., Aaron, J. E., Bohn, R. C., and Eales, J. R. *Fundamentals of Safety Education,* 2nd edition. New York: MacMillan Publishing Co., Inc., 1973.

Thygerson, A. L. *Safety: Principle, Instruction and Readings.* Englewood Cliffs: Prentice-Hall, Inc., 1972.

Worick, W. W. *Safety Education: Man, His Machines, and His Environment.* Englewood Cliffs: Prentice-Hall, Inc., 1975.

Yost, C. P. (ed.). *Sports Safety: Accident Prevention and Injury Control in Physical Education, Athletics and Recreation.* Washington, D.C.: AAHPER, 1967.

CHAPTER 12

PLANNING
AND
EVALUATION

Planning and evaluation, although separate in function, are interrelated in a cyclical way—planning leads to evaluation, evaluation leads to planning. While planning is a predetermined system for action, evaluation is the process used to determine effectiveness in achieving stated goals. Consequently, both functions are essential for providing programs which meet participant needs and interests.

Although we have already focused on how to organize and conduct specific programs, planning and evaluation are the two functions in programming that provide the concrete direction for decisions regarding program design and delivery. During our discussion of these topics, we include evaluation as a component within the planning process, then cover it in more detail as a separate category.

PLANNING

Planning is a lifelong process that involves such activities as organizing one's wardrobe, schooling, finances, shopping list and menu, marriage, vocation, family, vacation, and retirement. Planning may be subjective or objective, formal or informal, simple or complex in design, comprehensive or narrow in scope, effective or ineffective in outcome, and efficient or inefficient in operation. It involves envisioning a goal, identifying the steps and actions necessary to attain it, and making provisions for alternatives. Planning also entails organizing resources, taking action, and evaluating the effort.

Why plan? Planning for recreational sport improves the probability that the end product of our actions will serve participant needs and interests, solve problems, and utilize time and resources wisely. The programmer should consider planning not only as a process used to meet needs but also as a learning experience through which he or she can exercise and refine analytical, decision-making and organizational skills.

A PLANNING PROCESS

In general, administrative and middle-management level staff use planning and decision-making to control comprehensive program development and operation. This involves:

—specifying the participants to be served
—identifying participant needs and interests
—determining overall program philosophy, goals and objectives
—translating goals and objectives into a program design
—establishing the resources through which the program becomes operational.

A programmer should follow all of these planning steps within his or her own area of responsibility. For instance, although a decision to provide a basketball tournament, open an ice skating rink, sponsor a Hapkido club, or teach contract bridge is made at the administrative level, the programmer concerned with implementation continues planning to assure that each activity is provided in a way consistent with the overall program philosophy, each is appropriate for the intended participants, the particular activity has specific goals to meet participant needs, and evaluation takes place to determine the effectiveness of the activity to offer recommendations for improvement. There are a number of ways to approach planning. We suggest a process that has universal application to any task within program development or program operations.

A planning blueprint. We have prepared a blueprint for action to suggest planning steps to use when considering the various tasks associated with program operation. These steps indicate a general direction so that each programmer has flexibility to respond to conditions and resources within the particular agency and setting. The general principles of our planning blueprint include:

1. Understanding the circumstances surrounding the task.

2. Conducting an assessment.

3. Developing objectives and strategies.

4. Organizing a plan of action and timetable.

5. Implementing the plan of action.

6. Evaluating the plan and outcomes.

Although these steps are presented in a sequential order, they are interdependent. Since it is not impossible to control all variables that influence planning, new information and circumstances often necessitate a reassessment, modifying the original intention.

Step 1: Understanding the circumstances. When tackling a responsibility, whether it is solving a problem or fulfilling a need, gather as much information about the nature of the task as possible. Without a clear definition, you may waste a considerable amount of time, energy and other resources, and fail to realize desired outcome. The frustration caused by inadequate fact-finding is spoofed in Figure 12-1.

Fact-finding should begin with a clear understanding of the overriding philosophy, goals, and objectives of the agency. The numerous public, private, and commercial agencies involved in the delivery of recreational sport programs have differences in these areas. Ultimately, agency philosophy influences all staff decisions and actions.

In trying to grasp the evolution of a particular philosophy,

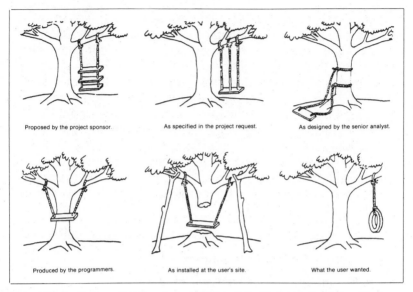

Proposed by the project sponsor.

As specified in the project request.

As designed by the senior analyst.

Produced by the programmers.

As installed at the user's site.

What the user wanted.

Figure 12-1. Source: Dundes, A. and Pagter, C.R. *Work Hard and You Shall Be Rewarded.* Bloomington: Indiana University Press, 1978, p. 168.

goal or objective, make specific inquiries: What is the history of this problem, need, group activity or program? Why are things the way they are? What is the intent or purpose of this activity, program, group or service? What are the expectations of me? Will anyone else be involved in the planning process and if so, who? After gaining a clear understanding of the framework for a given responsibility, the programmer can proceed to the next step.

Step 2: Conducting an assessment. When planning a program, specific activity, facility, or group function assessment of constituency needs, interests or problems is a logical prerequisite.

Through assessment, the programmer identifies interests, opinions, attitudes, habits or knowledge concerning the recreational sport program for which he or she bears responsibility. An assessment of current conditions and future needs serves as a status report on the efforts to date and a springboard for future action. Specifically, an assessment uses the following types of background information:

1. Demographic characteristics. Composition of the constituency: age, sex, income, education, occupation, and family size.

2. Resource availability. Resources needed to meet the needs of the constituency: personnel, facilities, equipment, and funds.

3. Time use. Insight into how individuals use their time: availability, preference, frequency and duration.

4. Attitudes and opinions. What people think about different aspects of the recreational sport program and operational issues—current or future.

5. Expressed needs and interests. What an individual would actually like to do or see take place.

Familiarity with the instruments and methods used in assessment is necessary to obtain the kind of information that is appropriate and pertinent to decision-making. This includes knowledge concerning their design and construction. Although you need not possess extensive research skills, you should know how to select methods or instruments that will yield accurate, dependable results. There are many instruments and methods currently available to help conduct an assessment.

The inventory. The inventory identifies existing resources and programs. By listing current funding, supplies, equipment, facilities, personnel expertise and program format, the programmer has a grasp of the resources and needs from which the conditions for planning are established.

Questionnaire. A questionnaire is a flexible tool for gathering information on one or more topics at a time. It may assess activity interests, participation rates, attitudes and opinions about existing or proposed services, procedures and priorities, participation patterns, and reasons for nonparticipation. While questionnaires are relatively easy to develop and distribute (mail, personal interview, or hand delivery), they have limitations. Responses only reflect the questions asked. What people say and what they really feel may differ. Respondents may not understand a question. Consider potential limitations in the design and construction of questionnaries. Keep your questions appropriate, understandable, relevant, and concise.

Meetings and hearings. Information is readily available when interest groups or individuals gather to discuss a particular topic. Give your target group sufficient notice and information about the location, time and purpose of the meeting or hearing. Anticipate the opinions of an assertive, vocal minority. Encourage discussion or input from different perspectives.

Advisory groups. Advisory groups act as sounding boards to help determine need. They provide input and feedback useful during assessment, implementation and evaluation. When soliciting information from advisory groups, see that responses are representative of constituencies and do not merely reflect personal opinions.

Referendum. A referendum seeks a consensus of all concerned parties on a given topic, proposal or issue. The result directs what action the programmer takes. Effective use of a referendum assumes that all who vote have a clear understanding of the topic because the process leaves little room for exploring alternatives. Consequently, the referendum is most valuable when persons primarily affected by the outcome vote.

Written evaluations. Written evaluations and recommendations from previous programming efforts provide useful historical perspective and direction for current planning efforts. Even though strategies used on past occasions may have yielded positive results, replication does not guarantee success unless the conditions which shaped the processes are similar.

All of these assessment methods are useful to the extent that the programmer knows how to design and administer them properly, interpret the results objectively and accurately, and make the proper conclusions. Unfortunately, assessment is often under-utilized due to the time, expense, or knowledge necessary for its conduct, or the desire to avoid arousing expectations.

Step 3: Identifying objectives and strategies. After defining the need, problem, or task to tackle, the programmer develops specific objectives and strategies. Objectives are the desired outcomes to be observed, measured, and attained, while strategies are the specific ways the programmer plans to achieve these outcomes.

The programmer needs to formulate two types of objectives: program objectives and performance objectives (Russell, 1980, pp. 112–119). Program objectives, also called operating, process, or production objectives, refer to the means used for accomplishing a responsibility and might focus upon materials, personnel, organizational methods and techniques, equipment, facilities and problem-solving strategies. They should be as precise and comprehensive as possible in terms of expectations and the minimum level of accomplishment. Examples of program objectives include:

Personnel

—Secure, prior to the start of practice, a first degree black belt as the instructor for the Judo club.
—Maintain a lifeguard-swimmer ratio of 1:25 during the indoor informal sport swim hours.

Facilities

—Achieve a 75% court reservation occupancy level during weekday evening hours.
—Expand informal sport time in the weightroom by two hours.

Organization

—Realize a 5% increase in participation by adult women in the aerobic dance class during the second eight week session.
—Achieve 80% attendance at monthly meetings by representatives of the advisory council.
—Reduce the number of forfeits within the spring intramural sport squash tournament by 15%.

Performance objectives, also known as behavioral or instructional objectives concern outcomes demonstrated by an individual in a sport activity, program, or function. They describe some skill, knowledge, or attitude that the individual should demonstrate at the conclusion of his or her involvement.

Performance objectives correspond to one of three specific domains: psychomotor, cognitive, or affective. The psychomotor domain involves physical skills and capabilities; the cognitive domain involves thought processes and knowledge; and the affective domain involves individual attitudes, feelings, and values.

Performance objectives need expression in precise terms, giving special attention to measuring the specific behavior, the conditions under which the behavior occurs, and the minimum level of performance. Examples of performance objectives include:

Skill (Psychomotor Domain)

—After receiving the ball from a teammate, the participant will be able to set the ball over a 12-foot net and have it land in a target 3 out of 4 times.

—At the completion of a six week instructional program, the participant will be able to correctly demonstrate a tennis serve by placing 8 out of 10 attempts in the proper service court, without any rule violations judged by the instructor.

Knowledge (Cognitive Domain)

—Upon completion of an officials' training program, the official will be able to sufficiently recall water polo rules and regulations by correctly answering 80% of the questions on a written test.

—At the end of an eight week program, beginners will be able to select the golf club appropriate for use in a given situation in the opinion of the instructor.

Attitude (Affective Domain)

—During a club sport ice hockey season, there will be a reduction in aggressive behavior as evidenced by a decrease in the number of altercations which take place between the players.

—The children within the neighborhood playground will demonstrate a sensitivity to the needs of others by voluntarily choosing to involve newcomers in playground baseball games.

A traditional programming orientation emphasizes the technical and procedural knowledge required for program design and delivery with little regard for its impact upon participants. By implementing sound objectives, the programmer may integrate procedural expertise with knowledge about participant behavior essential for contributing to participant development.

The creation of program and performance objectives need not be a complex or elaborate process. Put objectives and strategies in writing to permit evaluation of results. When identifying strategies, specify tasks that should lead to achievement of stated objectives. If the objective is to increase participation by adult women in the aerobic dance session by 5%, list the possible ways to meet this goal. Rank your ideas of feasibility and probability for success. A plan might appear as follows:

(Objective)

To realize a 5% increase in participation by adult women in the aerobic dance session during the second eight week session.

(Strategies)

1. Locate a suitable facility at a neighborhood site to promote accessibility.

2. Sponsor demonstrations at local civic and social functions.

3. Place public service announcements on radio and TV.

4. Offer discount rates on an introductory basis.

Concerning strategy development, we recommend that as many options and alternative plans be considered as possible, and that priorities be established within the list. Specificity in planning provides a clearer, more comprehensive frame of reference and direction for action, but maintain flexibility. Make the necessary adjustments to attain desired outcomes.

Step 4: Preparing a plan of action. An action plan entails specifying objectives and organizing the resources necessary for acting on them. When preparing the plan, identify what needs to be accomplished—how, when, by whom, where, and to what extent?

A comprehensive plan of action organizes tasks to attain stated objectives. We offer the following examples of possible tasks which might constitute plan preparation in a variety of situations with regard to: content, time factors, setting, equipment/supplies, cost, personnel, and publicity/promotion.

Format and Content:

—What is the best way to present a sport activity or topic—an elimination tournament, a challenge board, through brainstorming or small group discussion?
—What information should be developed for the participant—an orientation sheet, rules and regulations, entry forms, application form, articles of the association?
—What information should be obtained from and considered about the participant—age, sex, skill level, qualifications, certifications?
—How are participants to be grouped?
—How will problems be handled?

Time Factors:

—What should the duration be—one hour, two hours, three hours a day?
—How frequently should it be—daily, weekly, monthly, once a week, twice a week, once a month?
—When are individuals available—morning, afternoon, evenings, weekdays, weekends, winter, summer?

Setting:

—What type of facilities and areas exist?
—What does it take to reserve a facility or area?
—What facility, environment, or area is most desirable?
—Will the setting need to be prepared in advance?
—Can the setting handle multiple or simultaneous use?
—How many different facilities and areas are there?
—How many facilities and areas of similar type are there?
—How many people can be accommodated at one site?
—What kind and extent of supervision is needed?
—Is weather or climate a factor?

Equipment and Supplies:

—What is needed?
—What is available?
—Where are items located?
—How can items be obtained?

—What needs to be ordered or repaired?
—Are existing items adequate?
—Is there a sufficient quantity?
—Are special skills required for operating equipment?
—Who will supervise the items?
—Who will distribute and collect the items?

Cost:

—What costs will be incurred?
—How will costs be recorded and processed?
—What bookkeeping or accounting methods are required?
—Have funds been allocated for a specific purpose?
—Can fees and charges be assessed?
—Can revenue be collected—how—where—when—under what conditions—how is it to be secured?

Personnel:

—What functions need to be performed?
—How many people are needed per function?
—What skill level or qualifications are needed?
—How will duties and responsibilities be assigned?
—How will personnel be recruited, selected, trained, scheduled, supervised, and disciplined?
—What human resources are available?
—Will personnel be employees or volunteers?
—Will special testing be required?
—What type of incentives or recognition will be offered?
—What specific expectations will be established for personnel?
—What communication network is needed?

Publicity/Promotion:

—What constituency needs to be reached?
—How can a constituency be reached?
—What methods or media are available?
—What materials need to be prepared?
—What resources are available?
—Who will be responsible for preparing materials or information?

—How long will it take to prepare materials?
—What distribution process will be used?
—Where can materials be displayed?
—What is the best way to present the activity, program, facility, or function?

The preceding examples merely indicate the details involved in formulating a plan of action. Implementation requires that the programmer visualize responsibilities from start to finish in the most systematic and thorough way possible, seeking to identify every detail of each task to be performed, while anticipating problems that may develop. The final list should represent the programmer's best effort at specifying those tasks necessary for the attainment of objectives.

Step 5: Implementing the plan. Implementation translates the thought process into action. Even though the tasks are specified and detailed, it requires time, effort, and organizational ability to coordinate a plan efficiently. Implementation involves sound organizational and time management principles. Kraus and Bates, (1975, pp. 330, 331), adapting material published by the Boys' Club of America, make the following recommendations:

TWENTY WAYS TO GET THINGS DONE

1. Make a list of things to do, and cross off each item as you do it. Crossing off an item when you complete it shows that progress has been made, and also calls attention to tasks still to be done.

2. Keep the work you have to do right in front of you. This helps to eliminate competing distractions. Instead of having four projects on your desk at once, clear away everything except the one task that should be done first.

3. Break tasks down into segments. If a task is particularly long or laborious, break it down into segments and tackle them one at a time; that way, it can be handled by stages, and will not appear to be too overwhelming.

4. Have an effective reminder system. Develop a self-reminder system of events, deadlines, tasks to be accomplished, etc., and keep these notes in a place where they can be regularly checked.

5. Be decisive. Once you have all the facts on a given matter, take action on it. Don't bother to worry about whether or not your decision was the best possible one; move on to other tasks.

6. Don't exaggerate a job's difficulties in advance. Avoid building up all the problems in a given assignment beforehand, and you will find it easier to get at it, and to carry it out successfully.

7. Don't overplan. While it is necessary to plan carefully for each new project or task, excessive planning may be an excuse for not taking action. It is like the writer who keeps doing research, and avoids getting down to writing.

8. Set specific time limits for tasks. Be definite, rather than vague, about when projects should be undertaken and completed. If there are several activities to be done, put them in a time sequence based on their order of priority, their possible deadlines, and the degree and kinds of work it will take to carry them out.

9. Don't be a perfectionist. If you expect yourself to do everything perfectly, you may avoid new challenges for fear of failing. While your standards should be high, they should also be realistic, and should recognize that you, like others, have the right to make mistakes.

10. Strengthen your weak points. Recognize your areas of weakness, or performance skills in which you lack confidence. Concentrate on improving your skills in these areas.

11. Know when you work best. Many people function differently at different times of the day. Analyze your own energy, alertness and "ups and downs" throughout the day, and plan your most demanding

tasks for the times when you will be able to meet them.

12. Learn to say "No." When you are able to make a choice, avoid taking on commitments that you would rather not have, or are not essential.

13. Listen attentively. Avoid errors, backtracking and repetition by getting pertinent information right the first time.

14. Do it now. Many people put off getting started by such devices as sharpening pencils, day-dreaming, or window gazing. Avoid procrastination—use your working time to the fullest.

15. Seek short-cuts. This does not mean to "skimp" on doing a job right, but rather looking for the most effective and efficient way to carry out an assignment, no matter how it was done in the past.

16. Anticipate. Look forward to the next day and make sure that all necessary arrangements have been made. Keep extra change, keys, eyeglasses and stamps in your office, and in other ways eliminate minor frustrations that waste time and energy.

17. Make fullest use of time. Use travel time and similar periods to think out problems, read reports, make plans or jot down ideas for future implementation.

18. Vary your activities on the job. Many jobs become tedious because of repetition. It is best to alternate tasks in order to fight off fatigue and keep mentally alert. Most supervisors do not have to worry about this; their jobs are seldom boring.

19. Get an early start. Many supervisors find that they can get a great deal of paper work and planning out of the way by starting early in the day, before distractions and other job demands begin.

20. Gain a healthy respect for your own time. Recognize that your time is an immensely valuable asset; use it as fruitfully as possible.

In addition to these recommendations, the programmer may benefit from the use of a planning checklist form such as the one in Figure 12-2. By ranking tasks, the programmer can more systematically attend to each item.

THINGS TO DO TODAY !	Date: _____

Urgent
√

Done
√

☐ 1. _____ ☐
☐ 2. _____ ☐
☐ 3. _____ ☐
☐ 4. _____ ☐
☐ 5. _____ ☐
☐ 6. _____ ☐
☐ 7. _____ ☐
☐ 8. _____ ☐
☐ 9. _____ ☐
☐ 10. _____ ☐
☐ 11. _____ ☐
☐ 12. _____ ☐
☐ 13. _____ ☐
☐ 14. _____ ☐
☐ 15. _____ ☐
☐ 16. _____ ☐
☐ 17. _____ ☐
☐ 18. _____ ☐
☐ 19. _____ ☐
☐ 20. _____ ☐

NOTES

Figure 12-2. Planning checklist form.

Planning for maximum and optimal use of time is important. Stephanie Winston (Russell, 1982, pg. 240) recommends these eight timesavers:

1. Barter: Trade or exchange distasteful jobs with others.

2. Make use of services: Rely on professionals as much as you can afford.

3. Double up on time: Do several small tasks at the same time (for example, sign letters while on telephone hold).

4. Make use of bits of time: Plan small projects during waiting periods or while riding the bus.

5. Plan ahead: Make sure everything is at hand before starting a project.

6. Pool resources: Experiment with cooperative arrangements.

7. Consolidate: Combine errands, telephone return calls, and as much movement as possible.

8. Labor-saving devices: Use modern technology as much as possible.

Implementation strategies. In recognition of the potential number, variety, and complexity of details and tasks associated with plan implementation, we urge the programmer to adopt an implementation strategy. Three strategies taken from the fields of business and management apply to planning within the field of recreation: the Program Evaluation and Review Technique (PERT), the Critical Path Method (CPM) and the Flow Chart Method (FCM). The PERT was developed jointly by the U.S. Navy, Lockheed Aircraft Corporation, and a private management consulting firm for weaponry development (cited in Russell, 1982, p. 241). The primary element of PERT appropriate for use as an implementation strategy is a flow chart that illustrates the steps to achieving a finished product. In the PERT chart, all the tasks involved with the activity, program, or function are listed. The time estimated to complete each task is indicated between tasks. The estimate of time is expressed in the following manner (cited in Edginton, Compton, and Hanson, 1980, p. 360).

1. Optimistic Time (OT)—the length of time required without complications or unforeseen difficulties arising in the activity.

2. Most Likely Time (MLT)—the length of time in which the task is most likely to be completed.

3. Pessimistic Time (PT)—the length of time required if unusual complications or unforeseen difficulties occur.

If these three estimates are taken into consideration, then a realistic time (rt) may be calculated and included in the PERT chart between activities, using the following formula (cited in Farrell and Lundegren, 1978, p. 104):

$$\frac{PT \; + \; 4\,(MLT) \; + \; OT}{6} \; = \; RT$$

The next step is to plot the information using the Critical Path Method or Flow Chart Method. These techniques provide a systematic way of separating a responsibility into segments which consider what is to be done, when it is to be done, who is to do it, and how long it will take (Russell, 1982, p. 241). For example, Figure 12-3 presents the components of a sample bridge class as a checklist. Placement of the checklist on a timeline for the Flow Chart Method is presented in Figure 12-4 while the same checklist is applied to the Critical Path Method in Figure 12-5. The placement of tasks onto a timeline or time path in sequence gives the programmer a view of the progression for their implementation. Persons who lack an interest in a graphic ordering of tasks for implementation stop once the tasks are assigned a priority and timetable for completion.

Although the Critical Path and Flow Chart methods require time to develop, they facilitate the delegation of responsibility once tasks are determined, and serve as a frame of reference for recurring responsibilities. The major difference between the two methods is that the Critical Path Method illustrates tasks which are implemented simultaneously.

These organizational aids, combined with experience in time management, enables the programmer to approach implementation with greater effectiveness. However, the relative

CHECKLIST FOR IMPLEMENTATION
Eight Week Bridge Class

COMPONENT	TASK	TIME REQUIRED TO COMPLETE (WEEKS)	DEADLINE
Personnel	Determine leadership needs	2	1/19
	Advertise	2	2/4
	Interview	1	2/12
	Test	1	2/14
	Selection	1	2/16
	Complete Forms	1	3/29
Materials	Arrange for storage	1	2/11
	Order equipment	1	2/19
	Deliver equipment to the site	1	4/2
Facilities	Determine needs	2	1/21
	Explore sites	2	2/6
	Reserve times	1	2/13
Program	Set times and dates	1	2/22
	Accept registration		3/9
	Registration completed	2	3/26
	Prepare and deliver class list	2	4/5
	Evaluation	1	5/28
Publicity	Design plans	2	2/17
	Distribute publicity	1	3/4
	Alert media	1	3/7

Figure 12-3. Implementation checklist.

success of program operations remains dependent upon the appropriateness of decisions made prior to implementation and the effect of decisions and actions which occur during implementation.

The fact that all the details and tasks for implementation have been specified and prioritized still does not guarantee success. For example, proper planning and organization may lead to the selection of qualified personnel, but training and placement does not automatically guarantee success in terms of their productivity, morale, and job satisfaction.

Step 6: Evaluating the plan and outcomes. Even though a great deal of thought, time, and effort is put into the planning and implementation of sport activities, programs, and other

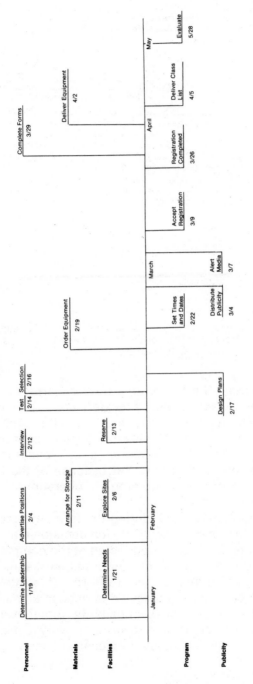

Figure 12-4. Flow chart method schematic.

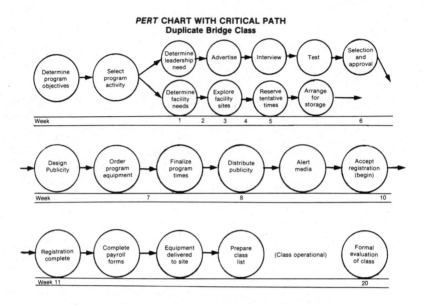

PERT CHART WITH CRITICAL PATH
Duplicate Bridge Class

Figure 12-5. Critical Path Method schematic. Source: Farrell, P. and Lunde-gren, H.M. *The Process of Recreation Programming Theory and Practice.* New York: John Wiley and Sons, 1978, p. 302.

responsibilities, the same does not hold true for evaluation. Perhaps the reason relates to anxiety about possible results, confusion about how to design evaluation instruments, frustration in identifying what to measure, lack of confidence in the accuracy of evaluation, inexperience in evaluation, or lack of money to support the effort. Yet because of the time, effort, cost, and resources put into program operations, it is illogical not to judge the results.

Evaluation may occur during the formative steps of planning providing useful feedback for decision-making or plan modifications. Evaluation conducted at the completion of program operations yields useful information leading to recommendations for future planning efforts. This interdependent relationship between planning and evaluation stimulates quality throughout each area of responsibility. Since evaluation is a process that can be applied to virtually every aspect of recreational sport, we will discuss it extensively here.

EVALUATION

Evaluation implies making a judgment or appraisal of worth. In terms of relevance to the programmer, evaluation concerns an assessment of program operations in terms of their efficiency and their effect upon participants and personnel compared to stated objectives. Unless clearly and appropriately stated objectives have been identified, the usefulness, accuracy, and credibility of evaluation efforts are questionable.

The focus, then, of evaluation is to determine how efficient and effective our program efforts are in terms of the process (means) used and the outcomes (ends) obtained.

The process. Process encompasses those factors used in and required for program delivery. The major areas to evaluate within process include personnel, program content, and physical resources. More specific examples of items for evaluation include the following:

1. Personnel—qualifications, performance, in-service training, scheduling, public relations.

2. Program—appropriateness, sufficiency, acceptance, scheduling, safety, promotion-publicity, rules/regulations, policies, recognition, governance.

3. Physical Resources—availability, adequacy, accessibility, appropriateness, safety, attractiveness, maintenance, policies/procedures.

Approaches used in analyzing process include evaluation by attainment of program objectives, evaluation by standards, and evaluation by cost-benefit analysis. Program objectives, discussed in step three of the planning process, are expectations regarding the conduct and content of program operations and the minimum level of accomplishment. Standards express criteria which represent a desired practice or level of performance. For example, standards may specify a certain number of courts per person, sit-ups per minute and lifeguard ratio to swimmers. Evaluation by cost-to-benefit ratio quantifies the benefits (objectives) of a program, in economic terms so that a ratio can be established between it and the fixed costs associated with providing the program.

The outcome. Evaluation within recreational sport tends to focus more upon process than upon outcome. This is because process objectives are more precise and quantitative, while outcome objectives tend to be qualitative. Nonetheless, evaluation of outcomes is extremely important in terms of accountability and effectiveness as it focuses on the impact involvement has on individuals (leaders or participants). Examples of parameters involved in evaluating the effect of participation include the following:

1. Physical—skill, strength, endurance, stress, injury.

2. Emotional—attitudes, opinions, behavior, stability.

3. Social—affiliation, friendliness, cooperation.

4. Mental—knowledge, application, synthesis.

Evaluation of outcomes centers on the degree to which performance objectives are met. Performance objectives specify the desired skill, knowledge, or attitude the individual should be able to demonstrate at the conclusion of involvement. Evaluating how effectively performance objectives are met is easier for the physical or mental, than for the social or emotional.

Data Collection in Evaluation

Evaluating effectiveness of process or outcomes requires expertise in selecting appropriate instruments for measuring a specific quality, trait or action. Although the programmer is not usually expected to fulfill this responsibility, he or she is frequently involved in the collection of data and interpretation of results. Typical data collection techniques used in evaluation follow. References containing details regarding their development, meaning, and interpretation are contained in the bibliography of this section.

Questionnaire. A common method to collect data, a questionnaire solicits responses from individuals to a written or oral series of questions. It may obtain demographic information about a sample population, assess opinions or attitudes, or provide information about participant behavior. Questionnaires appear in a fixed alternative (yes/no, multiple choice, etc.) or open-ended format. While the first alternative is easy to administer, it restricts responses to specific questions that may be superficial. The second alternative provides more in-depth questioning and better reflects true opinion. Since it requires greater verbal and written skills, it may evoke responses too broad or complex to interpret and discourage a respondent from taking the time to answer questions.

COUNTY YOUTH RECREATIONAL NEEDS
SPORT QUESTIONNAIRE

Recreational sport opportunities are advantageous for our youth. This is your opportunity to make suggestions and to have a responsibility in developing a sound recreational sport program.

This could be the beginning of an orderly, long-range development plan to improve the recreational sport opportunities for our young people. THEREFORE, WE INVITE YOU TO SPEAK OUT ON YOUR OPINIONS OF RECREATIONAL SPORT NEEDS. YOU NEED NOT SIGN THIS SURVEY.

1. Are you familiar with present sport facilities?   Yes _____ No _____

2. Are you familiar with the recreational sport program?   Yes _____ No _____

3. Are your recreational sport interests
   indoor _____
   outdoor _____
   equal _____

4. What type of sport supervision and sport instruction do you feel is best? _____
   a. adult
   b. committee of youth and adult
   c. youth _____
   d. other _____

5. Do you feel youth has a responsibility for the conduct, clean-up and prevention of vandalism for your recreational sport facilities and opportunities?
   Yes _____ No _____

6. Would you be interested in participating in a special activity or event?
   Yes _____ No _____
   If *yes* list in order your preference?
   _____ a. 4th of July   _____ d. All Nighter
   _____ b. Youth Fair   _____ e. Christmas
   _____ c. Halloween   _____ f. Other _____

7. Do you feel transportation is a problem for youth in attending activities?
   Yes _____ No _____

8. In your opinion, do you feel that parents, *in general*, are interested in the youth of the county?   Yes _____ No _____ Don't Know _____

9. If you feel there is room for improvement in parental interest, what are the ways you feel it can be improved?
   _____
   _____

10. Do you feel our schools are interested in the youth of this county?

Yes _____ No _____ No Opinion _____

11. Do you feel the schools should make their facilities available for recreational and educational activities under responsible adult supervision?

Yes _____ No _____ No Opinion _____

12. Do you feel there are enough recreational sport activities available for young people in this county? Yes _____ No _____ No Opinion _____

13. Of the following, which recreational sport activities would you participate in if given the opportunity?

_____ Croquet	_____ Roller Skating
_____ Volleyball	_____ Bowling
_____ Badminton	_____ Chess
_____ Basketball	_____ Water Safety
_____ Ping Pong	_____ Gymnastics
_____ Tether Ball	_____ Judo
_____ Shuffle Board	_____ Karate
_____ Movable Back Stop	_____ Checkers
_____ Baseball	_____ Canoeing
_____ Horseshoes	_____ Others _____
_____ Tennis	_____ _____
_____ Fly & Bait Casting	_____ _____
_____ Swimming	_____ _____
_____ Archery	_____ _____
_____ Target Shooting	_____ _____
_____ Gun Safety	_____ _____

14. As of this date do you plan on living in this county after high school graduation?

Yes _____ No _____ Undecided _____

15. If *no*, would you share your reasons with this committee?

_____

_____

_____

_____

_____

_____

Figure 12-6. Recreational sports questionnaire.

Rating scale. The rating scale asks the individual to assign a value to a statement on a continuum. The values have numbers assigned to them to permit results to be quantified. Words commonly used to categorize values are:

a. Strongly agree, agree, neutral, disagree, strongly disagree
b. Excellent, good, fair, poor, very poor
c. Always, sometimes, never

Rating scales are used to collect data on program content and operations, physical resources, personnel, and policies.

While they are easy to develop and administer, they contain bias. For example, the rating of one factor may influence the rating given to succeeding ones so that the majority of responses fall on one side of the continuum. In addition, one person's interpretation of excellent, may differ from another person's.

EMPLOYEE PERFORMANCE RATING

Name _____ Position _____

Date _____ Evaluator _____

Date of Last Evaluation _____

Evaluation Factors		Rating				
		1	2	3	4	5
A. Personal						
1. Ability to work without supervision		—	—	—	—	—
2. Ability to work with others		—	—	—	—	—
3. Dependability		—	—	—	—	—
4. Ability to constructively influence others		—	—	—	—	—
5. Diplomacy and tact		—	—	—	—	—
B. Task-related						
1. Ability to organize tasks		—	—	—	—	—
2. Quality of written reports		—	—	—	—	—
3. Knowledge of program skills		—	—	—	—	—
4. Planning ability		—	—	—	—	—
5. Initiative		—	—	—	—	—
6. Relations with participants		—	—	—	—	—
7. Willingness to try innovative approaches		—	—	—	—	—
C. Effectiveness						
1. Effectiveness compared to others in a similar capacity		—	—	—	—	—
2. Effectiveness compared to previous performance		—	—	—	—	—
3. Potential and advancement		—	—	—	—	—
4. Overall effectiveness		—	—	—	—	—
Totals		—	—	—	—	—

A = _____   5 = Excellent

B = _____   4 = Good

C = _____   3 = Fair

Total _____   2 = Poor

   1 = Very Poor

_____   _____   _____
Evaluator's Signature   Personnel's Signature   Date

Figure 12-7. Employee performance rating form. Source: Adapted from Graham, P.J. and Klar, L.R., Jr. *Planning and Delivering Leisure Services.* Dubuque, IA: William C. Brown Company Publishers, 1979, p. 140.

RECREATION INTEREST CHECKLIST

Date completed _____

Name _____ Date of birth _____ Sex (M) ____ (F) ____

Address _____ Phone: Home _____ Business _____

Sunday School Department _____

To assist our Recreation Staff in planning a program of recreation that will best fill the needs of our church family, we ask that you complete this survey as promptly and as completely as possible. Please indicate your interest and participation in each of not more than 5 activities. Use the number 1 for the activity which interests you most, placing this number in the column which corresponds to your experience and ability. Use the number 2 for your second interest, etc.

If you check the column some experience (SE), please, if you feel that you are qualified, also check the column for could provide leadership (L).

Use the blank spaces for any activity in which you are interested, and which is not listed.

TEAM SPORTS		(SE)	(L)	ARTS-CRAFTS		(SE)	(L)
Baseball	☐	☐	☐	Ceramics	☐	☐	☐
Basketball	☐	☐	☐	Painting	☐	☐	☐
Volleyball	☐	☐	☐	Leathercraft	☐	☐	☐
_____	☐	☐	☐	Woodwork	☐	☐	☐
_____	☐	☐	☐	Candlecraft	☐	☐	☐
				Decoupage	☐	☐	☐
GYM ACTIVITIES				Poster Making	☐	☐	☐
Tumbling	☐	☐	☐	Home Decorating	☐	☐	☐
Weight Lifting	☐	☐	☐	_____	☐	☐	☐
Karate	☐	☐	☐	_____	☐	☐	☐
Boxing	☐	☐	☐	_____	☐	☐	☐
Wrestling	☐	☐	☐	_____	☐	☐	☐
Slimnastics	☐	☐	☐	_____	☐	☐	☐
_____	☐	☐	☐	_____	☐	☐	☐
_____	☐	☐	☐	_____	☐	☐	☐
DRAMA				OUTDOOR ACTIVITIES			
Skits & Stunts	☐	☐	☐	Family Camping	☐	☐	☐
Major Production	☐	☐	☐	Water Skiing	☐	☐	☐
Lighting	☐	☐	☐	Fishing	☐	☐	☐
Sets	☐	☐	☐	Nature Study	☐	☐	☐
Puppetry	☐	☐	☐	Swimming	☐	☐	☐
_____	☐	☐	☐	Bicycling	☐	☐	☐
_____	☐	☐	☐	_____	☐	☐	☐
_____	☐	☐	☐	_____	☐	☐	☐
INDIVIDUAL SPORTS				HOBBIES			
Racquetball	☐	☐	☐	Photography	☐	☐	☐
Handball	☐	☐	☐	Ham Radio	☐	☐	☐
Tennis	☐	☐	☐	Quilting	☐	☐	☐
Golf	☐	☐	☐	Flower Arranging	☐	☐	☐
Bowling	☐	☐	☐	Stamp Collecting	☐	☐	☐
Badminton	☐	☐	☐	Coin Collecting	☐	☐	☐
Badminton	☐	☐	☐	_____	☐	☐	☐
Skating	☐	☐	☐	_____	☐	☐	☐
Ping Pong	☐	☐	☐	MISCELLANEOUS			
_____	☐	☐	☐	Guitar	☐	☐	☐
_____	☐	☐	☐	First Aid	☐	☐	☐
				_____	☐	☐	☐
				_____	☐	☐	☐

Comments _____

_____

Figure 12-8. Recreation interest checklist form.

Checklist. This instrument merely lists items that are checked in terms of frequency of occurrence when compared to a standard criterion. Checklists are easy to develop and administer.

Attitude scales. There are three major types of scales in use for collecting data on attitudes including the Likert scale (summation), equal appearing intervals (Thurstone) and, the cumulative scale (Guttman). Of these three, the Likert scale is the most popular. The respondent is asked to indicate a degree of agreement or disagreement to a series of statements. The value to a response involves a five-point scale: strongly agree (SA) (5), agree (A) (4), undecided (U) (3), disagree (D) (2), strongly disagree (SD) (1). When using negatively stated items, reverse the scoring.

A more specialized attitude measurement is the semantic differential developed by Osgood (1967). The technique measures the meaning of an object to a person by establishing bipolar adjective pairs (good-bad) and a rating scale for the respondent to select a position. These adjectives may evaluate nature (good-bad), indicate strength or potency (strong-weak), or reveal motion or action (fast-slow).

Sociogram. This instrument is used to evaluate the nature of the structure within a group by demonstrating interactions or relationships among group members. Use of the sociogram helps evaluate group cohesiveness, communication patterns, compatible subunits, and emergent leaders. Its use is not feasible with groups over twenty people.

Behavior observation. This data collection method does not involve participant response; it focuses on participant behavior. The observations are planned and designed to record selected behavior to determine whether a correlation exists between specified in performance objectives and the behavior being observed. The effectiveness of this particular method is dependent upon proper training in how to observe and record behavior.

Case studies. Case studies are in-depth investigations, which reveal more information than a cursory observation or review. Sources of information for a case study include rating

NCS Trans-Optic E 05-8457:3

CODES I	CODES II	INSTRUCTIONS:
A B C D E F G H I	J K L M N	

EXER-FIT AEROBIC RHYTHM EVAL.

Darken the appropriate circle:
Code 1, Column A-Freshman=0, Sophomore=1,
Junior=2, Senior=3, Graduate=4, Faculty/
Staff=5, Public=6
Code 1, Column B - Male=0, Female=1
Code 1, Column C - Session A=0, Session B=1
Session C=2, Session D=3, Session E=4,
Session F=5, Session G=6, Session H=7,
Session I=8, Session J=9
Responses-Strongly Agree=1, Agree=2, Unde-
cided=3, Disagree=4, Strongly Disagree=5,
No basis for responses =6.

GENERAL OPINION SURVEY FORM
BUREAU OF EVALUATIVE STUDIES AND TESTING
INDIANA UNIVERSITY, BLOOMINGTON, IN. 47405

1. The leader is prepared for each session.
2. The leader provides a cheerful, encouraging environment for the participant.
3. The leader is open to suggestions and criticism.
4. The leader clearly answers participant's questions concerning the session.
5. The session has been enjoyable and beneficial to me.
6. The initial presentation concerning pulse rates was clear and easy to follow.
7. This leader would be highly recommended by me to others.
8. The leader took proper action if an injury or accident occured.
9. The music and routines were well-suited for one another.
10. The music can be clearly heard during each session.
11. My participation in the program is based on my desire for a fun recreational activity.
12. The facility is adequate for the number of people in the session.
13. I would be willing to pay for an additional day each week in order to attend three times per week, instead of two.
14. This program would be recommended by me to others.
15. I take part in the I.U. Fit fitness testing program.
16. Please circle all that apply to you:
    I learned about the program
    a. from a friend
    b. from the ads in the IDS
    c. from radio announcements
    d. from flyers in my dorm
    e. from flyers in my sorority/fraternity
    f. from flyers around the HPER buidling
17. Please provide any written comments you may have below:

Thanks for your time.

Figure 12-9. Example of a Likert attitude scale.

forms, anecdotal records, attitude scales, observations, interviews, and tests. Although case studies are often time-consuming, they may signal a difficulty requiring further evaluation or pinpoint an elusive problem area.

CLUB SPORT STAFF
OPINION SURVEY

Please circle the number closest to the word that best represents your opinion to the following statement:

"I feel the club sport staff are _____ ."

Accepting	6	5	4	3	2	1	Rejecting
Satisfying	6	5	4	3	2	1	Frustrating
Enthusiastic	6	5	4	3	2	1	Unenthusiastic
Productive	6	5	4	3	2	1	Nonproductive
Warm	6	5	4	3	2	1	Cold
Cooperative	6	5	4	3	2	1	Uncooperative
Supportive	6	5	4	3	2	1	Hostile
Interesting	6	5	4	3	2	1	Boring
Successful	6	5	4	3	2	1	Unsuccessful

Figure 12-10. Example of semantic differential scale.

PERFORMANCE OBSERVATION SHEET

X = Able to perform before instruction
0 = Unable to perform before instruction
1 = Unable to perform after instruction
* = Able to perform after instruction

	Forehand	Backhand	Lob	Volley	Cross-Court	Approach Shot	Overhead	Footwork	Service
1. Rin Curtis	*	*	*	*	*	*	*	*	1
2. John Seibert	*	*	*	*	*	*	*	*	*
3. Don Erdman	*	*	*	*	*	*	1	1	*
4. Steve Kintigh	X	*	*	*	*	*	X	*	*
5. Bill Kolstad	*	1	*	*	*	*	*	*	1
6. Steve Wolter	*	*	*	*	*	*	*	*	*
7. Kathy Bunn	*	*	*	*	*	*	*	*	1
8. Connie Elliott	*	*	*	*	*	1	1	1	*
9. Bob Albert	1	1	1	1	1	1	1	1	1
10. John Harper	*	*	*	*	*	*	*	*	*
11. Jan Moldstadt	*	*	*	*	*	*	*	*	*

Figure 12-11. Example of behavior observation method.

EVALUATION THROUGH OPERATIONAL FORMS

Daily operational forms, records and reports have provided the traditional basis for determining success in a given area of responsibility. Programmers often use them to measure success in terms of quantity: attendance figures, frequency of participation, maximum use of facilities, percentage of participants returning and number of events, yet statistics may not indicate quality. People may participate when no other acceptable alternatives exist—does that indicate provision of a quality service?

In addition, total reliance upon quantitative measurements as the basis for deciding whether or not to provide an activity ignores sports that, by their nature, draw limited numbers. These sports still meet the needs and interests of individuals who would not otherwise participate. Consequently, we present the types of forms, records and reports commonly used within recreational sport, their function in evaluation, and methods of data collection.

Records and reports. Records and reports exist to give an account of operations to administrators or a constituency, demonstrate compliance with laws, policies and procedures, establish accountability and protect against lawsuits, provide information for decision-making, serve as a basis for evaluation. This last item is the focus of our discussion.

The types of records and reports utilized by the programmer comprise the following categories:

—Program records—document participation, results, facility and equipment use. These records may be completed at the conclusion of a sport or program, or on a seasonal or annual basis.
—Personnel records—identify volunteers and employees, service records, time cards, and attendance.
—Utilization records—document attendance, participation, use patterns, constituency groups.
—Operational records—document accidents and injuries, maintenance needs, discipline problems, inventory of equipment and supplies, fee collection and deposits.

Of these categories, the programmer deals most frequently with utilization and program records, consequently, we present an overview of those records commonly used as instruments of evaluation within each category.

Utilization records. The types of data that reflect utilization include:

1. Number of entries/enrollments/memberships—Such data is often collected to be sure adequate resources are available to accommodate potential participants, to compare with previous totals or those of another activity, to complete preparations for scheduling, and to determine drop-out incidence prior to participation. In the event of high drop-out rates, an investigation of contributing factors may be needed.

2. Number of participants—This figure differs from the number of entries because it indicates those who actually participate at least once. The findings are useful as a basis for comparison with future participation statistics.

3. Number of participations—This figure represents the total number of times a participant engages in the sport or program under evaluation. If the number of participants in a sport is consistently high among the entered participant population, the events are successful. If there is a low percentage of participants in comparison to the total number possible, the success of the event is questionable. In some instances, as informal sport participation, it may not be possible to determine the actual number of individuals participating or the number of participations per individual during a given time period. Instead, the data may merely reflect the collective number of participants occuring at a given time. This information is still useful for comparative purposes and determining use or growth patterns.

4. Number of sessions/contests scheduled, forfeited, postponed, completed—This statistic is used to identify growth within a sport, program, or use of a facility. If the rate of forfeits and the number of postponements are high, an investigation of contributing factors is warranted.

5. Hours of facility availability—Such data describe the history of facility availability for scheduled or unscheduled purposes. When past and present availability comparisons are made, the programmer may reveal changing use patterns and evolving participant interests.

6. Staff-participant/staff-facility ratios—Information expressing these relationships is useful for comparison with requirements and for cost analysis and personnel allocation decisions.

Rarely are variables common or consistent enough from agency to agency or setting to setting to permit standardization of forms or procedures for collection of data—nor is such standardization always desirable. Data collection methods should be appropriate, simple to implement and the results easy to interpret. In some agencies, computer systems greatly facilitate tabulation and analysis of data. Programs analyzing participation statistics may correlate individual participants with frequency of facility use or examine total facility use on a daily, weekly, monthly, seasonal or annual basis. Since most agencies still use manual tabulation of data, our examples of data collection methods reflect that orientation.

Head count sheets, occupancy or reservation sheets, result forms, or sales records are the most common tools used to collect data on facility use.

Head counts. Within an informal sport program, head count and reservation sheets are common tools for obtaining participation statistics. Head count forms for individual facilities often receive tallies at set intervals during the day. They may represent total participation as in Figure 12-12, individual participation as in Figure 12-13, or participation by user classification as in Figure 12-14. Daily head counts are often transferred to forms such as Figure 12-15 that show monthly use.

Occupancy/reservation sheets. A common form used in such commercial settings as racquetball, tennis, or bowling facilities, is the occupancy report or reservation sheet. These forms indicate use levels at specific facility sites taken on an hourly basis and tabulated for daily, weekly, monthly, seasonal, and annual reports. Figure 12-16 illustrates a weekly

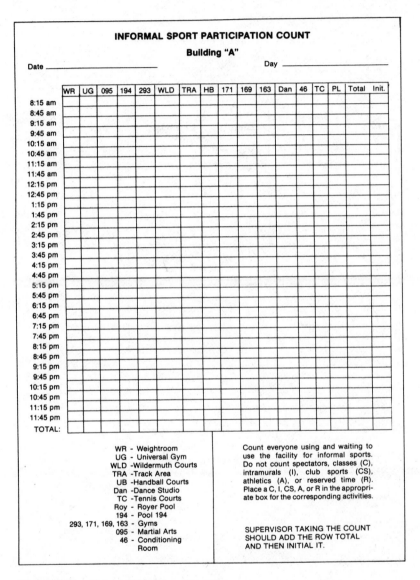

Figure 12-12. Total participation count form.

occupancy report for a racquetball facility developed from daily reservation sheets. Court time is recorded in 60 minute or 30 minute time slots. Results may pinpoint a day or time of consistent use—high or low.

TABLE SPORT ROOM

Facility _____

Date _____ Shift _____

Name	Time Entering	Time Leaving	User Code
1.			
2.			
3.			
4.			
5.			
6.			
7.			
8.			
9.			
10.			
11.			
12.			
13.			
14.			
15.			
16.			
17.			
18.			
19.			
20.			
21.			
22.			
23.			
24.			
25.			

User Code:
M = Member
G = Guest

Figure 12-13. Individual participation count form.

Result forms. Whenever contests occur, the results—win, loss, forfeit, score—are recorded. Score sheets indicate the number of times each person participates over the course of the tournament or season, or the total number of participants from a target group involved in the tournament.

INFORMAL SPORT USER BREAKDOWN/SPOT CHECK

Use For: (Circle)
Weightroom
17th St. Fieldhouse
NFL Fields & Tennis
Woodlawn & Tennis   Date _____
HB, RB Squash Courts
Royer Pool
Pool 194

Time	Student	Faculty	Staff	Family	Alumni	Public	Supervisor Name
8-9 AM							
9-10 AM							
10-11 AM							
11-Noon							
12-1 PM							
1-2 PM							
2-3 PM							
3-4 PM							
4-5 PM							
5-6 PM							
6-7 PM							
7-8 PM							
8-9 PM							
9-10 PM							
10-11 PM							
11-12 PM							
TOTALS							

Figure 12-14. User classification participation form.

Sales records. Any sport activity or program which assesses fees and charges uses sales records to record transactions. By analyzing sales, a programmer may determine use patterns. This method is particularly useful for single activity facilities selling daily passes or permits. In settings where a pass or permit allows multiple use, determine general use patterns by comparing sale of passes or permits on a weekly, monthly, seasonal, or annual basis.

Program records. At the conclusion of any sport activity or program, it is customary to prepare a summary report. A report may combine a narrative review of operational procedures and recommendations with a numerical summary. Examples of summary reports are provided in Figures 12-17, 12-18, and 12-19. The information provided in these reports are

TENNIS COURTS

Facility _____   Month _____ Year _____

Day Date	1	2	3	4	5	6	7	8	9	10	11	12	13	14	15	16	17	18	19	20	21	22	23	24	25	26	27	28	29	30	31	Tot.	Avg.
6:15																																	
6:45																																	
7:15																																	
7:45																																	
8:15																																	
8:45																																	
9:15																																	
9:45																																	
10:15																																	
10:45																																	
11:15																																	
11:45																																	
12:15																																	
12:45																																	
1:15																																	
1:45																																	
2:15																																	
2:45																																	
3:15																																	
3:45																																	
4:15																																	
4:45																																	
5:15																																	
5:45																																	
6:15																																	
6:45																																	
7:15																																	
7:45																																	
8:15																																	
8:45																																	
9:15																																	
9:45																																	
10:15																																	
10:45																																	
11:15																																	
11:45																																	
TOTAL																																	
Average																																	

Figure 12-15. Monthly facility participation form.

the basis upon which annual reports are developed for a particular program division. These reports are also instrumental in implementing similar programs in the future.

Evaluation results. The usefulness of data lies in proper interpretation and application. Once the data are analyzed, document the results thoroughly and include your recommendations for improvements or further analysis to aid future planning efforts. Review the report with an immediate supervisor to help avoid misinterpretation and obtain feedback regarding the recommendations.

WEEKLY COURT OCCUPANCY SUMMARY

Facility _____Tennis courts_____

Week ending Sunday _____

Time	Mon	Tues	Wed	Thurs	Fri	Sat	Sun	Week Days Total	Week Nights Total	Week End Days Total	Week End Nights Total	Actual Week Usage Total	% Usage Week Days	% Usage Week Nights	% Usage Week End Days	% Usage Week End Nights	Total % Usage
6:00 am	—	1½	—	½	3½	1	—	5½		1		6½	11%		5%		9%
7:00 am	—	—	—	2	—	—	—	2		—		2	4%		0%		3%
8:00 am	1	—	—	—	1	½	3	2		3½		5½	4%		18%		8%
9:00 am	1	4	3	—	—	2	1	8		3		11	16%		15%		16%
10:00 am	1	4	1	2	1	2½	—	9		2½		11½	18%		13%		16%
11:00 am	3	1	4	1	4	4	2	13		6		19	26%		30%		27%
12:00 N	—	—	1	2½	3	5	1	6½		6		12½	13%		30%		18%
1:00 pm	3	—	6	1	3	3	3	13		6		19	26%		30%		27%
2:00 pm	—	2	2	2	5	1	1	11		2		13	22%		10%		19%
3:00 pm	4	2	1½	2	4	4	½	13½		4½		18	27%		23%		26%
4:00 pm	8	3	4½	5½	4	½	—	25		½		25½	50%		3%		36%
5:00 pm	2½	3	2	1	2	2	2		10½		4	14½		21%		20%	21%
6:00 pm	4	3½	5½	8½	4	1	2		25½		3	28½		51%		15%	41%
7:00 pm	5	7	1	9½	4½	4	2		27		6	33		54%		30%	47%
8:00 pm	5½	9	6	8	5	2	5		33½		7	40½		67%		35%	58%
9:00 pm	3	5	1	5½	6	3	5½		20½		8½	29		41%		43%	41%
10:00 pm	4	—	5½	1½	3½	—	2½		14½		2½	17		29%		13%	24%
Week Days	21	17½	23	18½	28½			A. 108½									
Week Nights	24	27½	21	34	25				B. 131½								
Weekend Days						23½	11½			C. 35							
Weekend Nights						12	19				D. 31						
Total Usage	45	45	44	52½	53½	35½	30½					E. 306					
% Usage Week Days	19%	16%	21%	17%	26%								F. 20%				
% Usage Week Nights	37%	42%	32%	52%	38%									G. 44%			
% Usage Week-End Days						21%	10%								H. 16%		
% Usage Week-End Nights						20%	32%									I. 26%	
% Occ. TOTAL	26%	26%	25%	30%	31%	21%	18%	TOTAL COURT HOURS									J. 26%

Figure 12-16. Weekly court occupancy summary.

CONCLUSION

Programmers often just go through the motions of planning and evaluation. Those who combine the technical knowledge

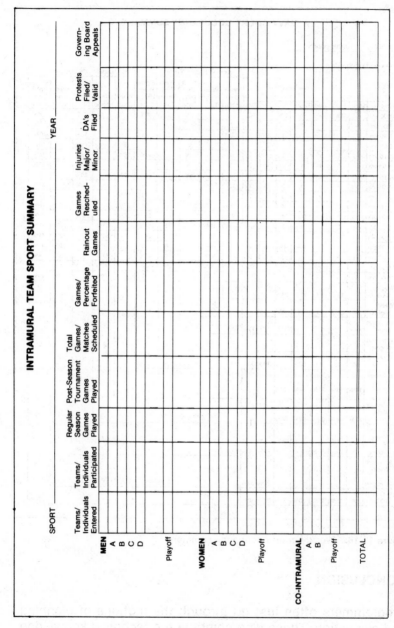

Figure 12-17.   Intramural team sport summary form.

INTRAMURAL TEAM SPORTS SUMMARY REPORT

Event _____ Date _____

Regular Season:
Format _____
Date Started _____ Date Ended _____

Post-Season:
Format _____
Date Started _____ Date Ended _____

Budget:

BUDGETED FOR:	EXPENDED FOR:
Officiating _____	Officiating _____
Supervision _____	Supervision _____
Other Labor _____	Other Labor _____
Equipment _____	Equipment _____
Publicity/Promo. _____	Publicity/Promo. _____
Awards _____	Awards _____
Duplicating _____	Duplicating _____
Office Supplies _____	Office Supplies _____
Miscellaneous _____	Miscellaneous _____
TOTAL _____	TOTAL _____

Notes:

Figure 12-18. Intramural team sports summary report form.

of these tools with an understanding of why and how they are used, are able to provide meaningful experiences for participants and personnel within the resource capabilities of the setting. Successful management begins with understanding the needs of the constituency and continues with selecting appropriate forms of involvement, implementing them efficiently, evaluating the outcomes properly and applying the findings to future endeavors.

```
┌─────────────────────────────────────────────────────────────────────┐
│                  INTRAMURAL INDIVIDUAL/DUAL SPORTS                    │
│                         SUMMARY REPORT.                              │
│                                                                      │
│   Event _____   Dates _____  │
│                                                                      │
│   STRUCTURE:                                                         │
│   ___ Single Elimination   ___ Timed Competition   ___ Other, Specify ___ │
│   ___ Double Elimination   ___ Single Elimination w/Consolation      │
│                                                                      │
│   ENTRIES:                       Team/Individual        % Change     │
│    Number of entries          _____      _____ │
│    Number of contestants                                            │
│      (i.e., scratches from com.,                                    │
│      etc.)                    _____      _____ │
│    Number of defaults         _____      _____ │
│    Number of forfeits         _____      _____ │
│    Number of contests/matches _____      _____ │
│   Conflicting events and comments: _____ │
│   _____ │
│   _____ │
│                                                                      │
│   INJURIES:                                             % Change     │
│    Number of injuries:        _____      _____ │
│    Number of injuries treated: _____                      │
│    Transported injuries:                                            │
│      Ambulance               _____                       │
│      Police                  _____                       │
│      Private vehicle         _____                       │
│      Other, specify          _____                       │
│   Comments: _____ │
│   _____ │
│   _____ │
│                                                                      │
│   PROTESTS:                                                          │
│    Number of protests: _____                                 │
│   Basis: _____ │
│                                                                      │
│   EQUIPMENT:                                                         │
│    1. _____                                       │
└─────────────────────────────────────────────────────────────────────┘
```

Figure 12-19. Intramural individual/dual sports summary report form.

BIBLIOGRAPHY

Bannon, J.J. *Leisure Resources: Its Comprehensive Planning.* Englewood Cliffs, New Jersey: Prentice-Hall, Inc. 1976.

Bliss, E.C. *Getting Things Done.* New York: Bantam Books, 1976.

Baumgartner, T.A. and Jackson, A.S. *Measurement for Evalua-*

tion in Physical Education. Boston: Houghton Mifflin Co., 1975.

Bloom, B.S., Hastings, J.T. and Madaus, G.J. *Handbook on Formative and Summative Evaluation of Student Learning.* New York: McGraw-Hill Book Co., 1971.

Cartwright, C.A. and Cartwright, G.P. *Developing Observation Skills.* New York: McGraw-Hill Book Co., 1974.

Edginton, C.R., Compton, D.M. and Hanson, C.J. *Recreation and Leisure Programming: A Guide For The Professional.* Philadelphia: Saunders College/ Holt, Rinehart, and Winston, 1980.

Farrell, P. and Lundegren, H.M. *The Process of Recreation Programming Theory and Technique.* New York: John Wiley & Sons, 1978.

Graham, P.J. and Klar, L.R. Jr. *Planning and Delivering Leisure Services.* Dubuque, Iowa: William C. Brown Company Publishers, 1979.

Kerlinger, F.N. *Foundations of Behavioral Research.* New York: Holt, Rinehart, and Winston, 1973.

Kraus, R.G. and Bates, J.J. *Recreation Leadership and Supervision: Guidelines for Professional Development.* Philadelphia: W.B. Saunders Company, 1975.

Lopez, F.M. *Evaluating Employee Performance.* Chicago: Public Personnel Association, 1968.

Oppenheim, A.N. *Questionnaire Design and Attitude Measurement.* New York: Basic Books, Inc., 1966.

Osgood, C.E., Suci, G.J. and Tannenbaum, P.H. *The Measurement of Meaning.* Urbana: The University of Illinois Press, 1957.

Russell, R.V. *Planning Programs in Recreation.* St. Louis: The C.V. Mosby Company, 1982.

Sax, G. *Principles of Education Measurement and Evaluation.* Belmont, California: Wadsworth Publishing Company, 1974.

Shaw, M.E. and Wright, J.M. *Scales for the Measurement of Attitudes.* New York: McGraw-Hill Book Co., 1967.

Suchman, E.A. *Evaluative Research.* New York: Russell Sage Foundation, 1967.

Theobald, W.F. *Evaluation of Recreation and Park Programs.* New York: John Wiley & Sons, 1979.

Van der Smissen, B. *Evaluation and Self-Study of Public Recreation and Park Agencies.* Arlington, Virginia: National Recreation and Park Association, 1972.

CHAPTER 13

PUBLIC RELATIONS

Cutlip and Center (1971, p. 4) define public relations as "the planned effort to influence opinion through socially responsible and acceptable performance, based on mutually satisfactory two way communication".

How can one establish positive public relations? The challenge begins with a commitment to serving participant needs and interests. Gather as much pertinent information as possible about the public to be served, including demographic information, availability, proximity, socio-economic level, educational attainment, customs, values, needs and interests. Apply this knowledge to create programs that satisfy participant needs and interests. What we provide various publics, and how we present it, determines how they will respond to it.

Efforts undertaken to establish goodwill with various publics have specific objectives in mind. Typical functions of public relations are:

1. To keep the public informed of opportunities.

2. To justify and interpret goals, objectives, policies and procedures.

3. To modify negative impressions or attitudes and correct misunderstandings.

4. To foster appreciation of the benefits of participation.

5. To encourage and motivate involvement by participants and volunteers.

6. To stimulate interaction and input.

7. To focus attention on a given topic, program, need or service.

8. To help attract and retain participants and employees to a setting.

9. To orient personnel to the philosophy and expectations of the agency.

Obtaining the goodwill of the public requires a comprehensive plan. The programmer is responsible for implementing the plan through such tools as volunteers, interagency cooperation, personnel, facilities, programming, and publicity and promotion.

USE OF VOLUNTEERS

Volunteers often help plan, organize, conduct, and evaluate programs out of necessity. They serve an important functional purpose, and may acquire an extensive knowledge of program operations, problems, concerns, needs, strengths, and weaknesses. Consequently, provide genuine support, proper training and adequate recognition for volunteers to reinforce their commitment, understanding and productivity.

INTERAGENCY COOPERATION

Rarely is a single agency involved in providing recreational sport. Consequently, all staff must understand what others provide to avoid unnecessary duplication or conflict of effort. The spirit of cooperation leads to resolution of problems and strengthens ties that may result in joint projects, shared resources, personnel referrals and other pursuits that enhance and expand opportunities for participation.

PERSONNEL

Every person associated with the recreational sport program has the potential to affect public attitudes. A programmer and his or her subordinates are in constant contact with participants. He or she should seek to engage those capable of contributing to a positive image. The following list, suggested by Graham and Klar (1979, p. 211), illustrate what kinds of individual attributes contribute to a positive public image. We need people who:

1. are courteous to other individuals at all times

2. are easily accessible to participants

3. maintain an open mind and are willing to listen to various opinions

4. follow-up on all details

5. keep employees and participants informed of all aspects of the program

6. avoid becoming embroiled in controversy

7. are willing to mediate disputes and do so fairly

8. view situations in an optimistic manner

9. maintain a high level of visibility through participation in a variety of organizations and functions.

Most individuals require specific orientation and training before they can apply the preceding attributes with consistency. Other measures require only practice and an occasional reminder, reflecting a personal approach to interaction and including the following orientations:

1. Conveying a genuine interest and willingness to be of service.

2. Addressing people by name whenever possible.

3. Maintaining a pleasant demeanor.

Not all responsibility for contributing to positive relations rests with personnel at the operational level. Administrative staff must adequately select, train, place and monitor personnel. As problems arise, competent administrative action contributes to morale and good will. Finally, administrative staff are responsible for hiring personnel capable of providing the support services necessary to meet demand. An agency with a limited, inefficient staff will be overextended, leading to a deterioration of positive relations.

FACILITIES

One's first impression of a program often arises from the appearance and state of facilities. The positive image created by sufficient facility quantity and quality stimulates participant interest. When they are adequate, clean, well-maintained, and properly supervised, favorable public opinion results.

PROGRAM

Efforts directed toward public relations must include strategies for providing programs that are appropriate, relevant, and capable of satisfying a broad spectrum of needs and interests. Each program should provide realistic, "hassle-free" policies and procedures, adequate supplies and equipment, safety and accident prevention measures, appropriate behavior controls, quality leadership, reinforcement and recognition systems, and efficient, reliable operations.

PUBLIC AND PROFESSIONAL SERVICE

Numerous opportunities exist within all settings for the programmer and other staff to engage in service work as consultants, speakers, technicians, organizers, committee members, and advisors. Involvement in service and professional functions is an invaluable learning experience, providing opportunity for interaction with diverse publics. Dependable attention to public service establishes the programmer as a valuable member of the community.

PUBLICITY-PROMOTION

The foundation of an agency's public relations effort is the publicity and promotion function.

Publicity involves the creation of advertisements, news and information designed to attract public attention through the mass media: newspapers, magazines, radio and television. Promotion is a process used to advance, recommend or endorse a program offering. It involves "selling" a program to potential participants.

As you prepare for publicity and promotion tasks consider these reminders:

1. Publicity does not sell a program by itself.

2. Publicity and promotion require constant effort involving the entire recreational sport staff.

3. Timing is extremely important! Expedient release of information affects your results—attendance, participation, input.

4. Post-event program publicity and promotion elicits participant goodwill, enhancing the probability of success for future events.

Writing Style. All publicity or promotional material should reflect a functional writing style. Effective writing permits the reader to grasp the message quickly and accurately. One of the best ways to assure comprehension is to use common words that participants can understand: "the English language has about a half-million words. The average college graduate knows and uses about 15,000. About 2,000 make up most of our conversations" (Joseph, 1960, p. 43.).

Gunning (1968) suggests ten principles to help guide the writer.

1. Keep sentences short.

2. Prefer the simple to the complex.

3. Use familiar words.

4. Avoid unnecessary words.

5. Put action into your verbs.

6. Write as you talk.

7. Use terms your reader can picture.

8. Tie in with the reader's experience.

9. Make full use of variety.

10. Write to express, not impress.

Elements of publicity and promotion. Various avenues exist to convey information to participants. For the purposes of this manual, we organize the main avenues under four categories: mass media, print media, visual aids and other promotional techniques.

MASS MEDIA

News Releases

A news release is a formal channel for distributing information to the news media. A concern for accuracy and brevity influences content and style.

Writing the release. The typical news release style uses the inverted pyramid form. The most important or interesting details appear in the first tier and comprise the "lead" or the first two paragraphs of the release. The lead answers five important questions:

1. *Who:* Who was involved in the event; individual or group names, addresses, organization involved, titles of positions.

2. *What:* What happened. The purpose of the recreational sport event.

3. *Where:* Where the event took place.

4. *When:* When the event occurred.

From this draft, paragraphs or tiers are written to cover each detail in descending order of importance as the article continues. Figure 13-1 is an example of the inverted pyramid.

Steps in the construction of the lead. The following are general steps for constructing an effective lead:

1. Confirm your facts.

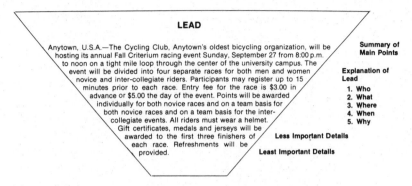

Figure 13-1. Inverted pyramid.

2. Develop a list of the key points of the news event.

3. Spell names correctly.

4. Provide addresses where possible.

5. Organize the information for the lead in your mind.

6. Write a rough draft of one or two paragraphs.

7. Use simple, easy to understand words.

8. Be specific as possible.

9. Revise and edit the lead before submitting for release.

Format of a news release. Figure 13-2 illustrates how a news release is prepared and submitted to the media.

Newspaper

One of the most venerable vehicles for publicity and promotion is the newspaper: "publicity in newspapers, day in and day out; 52 weeks a year, forms the foundation of most informational programs. Reading the newspaper is as much a part of the influential American's daily habit as eating and sleeping. The influence of the press is still great" (Cutlip, 1978, p. 357).

The newspaper provides the programmer with an opportunity to reach the widest audience, on a daily or weekly basis, for the lowest cost. Since sports are one of the most popular subjects in a newspaper, ask your editor to include your releases in the sports section.

NEWS RELEASE

DATE

NAME
ORGANIZATION
STREET ADDRESS
CITY, STATE, ZIP CODE
PHONE

FOR IMMEDIATE RELEASE

Adhere to the following guidelines in preparing and placing news releases. The lead or topic sentence should be a brief introductory statement answering the questions of who, what, where, when and why. This lead statement should be written so that if it is the only part of the release published, the reader will be aware of the essential points of the story.

Other guidelines are:

TYPING:

1. Use 8½ in. by 11 in. white bond paper.

2. Typing should be clear, double or triple spaced and typed on one side of the paper only.

3. Indent first word of each paragraph five spaces.

4. Begin news copy three inches from top of paper.

5. Type the word "-MORE-" at the bottom of the page if the story continues onto another page.

6. When the story ends, the symbol "#", "-30-" or the word "END" should be centered immediately below the last paragraph.

Release Guidelines

PLACEMENT ON PAGE:

On First Page:

Upper Left; type the name, address and phone number of the **author** submitting the release.

Upper Right; (1) Date the release was submitted.

(2) If there is no particular release date involved, mark your copy FOR IMMEDIATE RELEASE.

MARGINS: Use wide margins, preferably between one to two inches on each side for editing purposes.

LENGTH: Limit the release to one or two pages. Paragraphs should run five or six lines, maximum about 35 words. Do not split a paragraph from first to second page.

HEADLINES: Do not put a headline on a release. That's the editor's job.

SLUG: If the story runs more than one page, a slug or a one or two word title must be used. The slug appears in the upper left corner of each page. Also indicate the page number as shown above.

NUMERALS: In general, spell below 10, use numerals for 10 and above. However, fractions used alone are spelled: three-fourths of a mile. In reporting sport scores it is acceptable to use numbers such as: Smith's Bluejackets won 25-2.

PROOF: Always check and double check for typing errors before submitting to the news media.

ENDING: Use

-30-

or

-##-

or

END

2-2-2-2

Figure 13-2. Sample news release.

Ground Rules. Before approaching a newspaper, familiarize yourself with general press policy, procedure and orientation.

1. Learn what types of newspapers exist in your community—national, weekly, daily and shopping guide.

   a. Visit each newspaper and introduce yourself to the publisher.
   b. Make an appointment with the city editor, sports editor, and picture editor and other appropriate representatives.
   c. Convince these individuals of the importance of your sports program to the community. Determine their needs and wants and how you can satisfy them.
   d. Leave a business card so that you may be reached to answer questions.
   e. Ask about the newspaper's readership. Show you will attempt to gear your releases for that particular clientele.
   f. After meeting with representatives from each of the newspapers, organize a file on the people you need to contact concerning deadlines, writing style, circulation and other pertinent information. This will eliminate guesswork.

2. Know the deadline for copy and photograph submission. A newspaper wants news while it is still fresh. As a general rule of thumb, an evening newspaper's deadline is around noon, while the morning edition is midnight.

3. Avoid sending the same release to more than one person or department in the same newspaper. This only causes confusion.

4. Make sure your releases are worth printing. Stagger the number you submit to increase the chance for publication. Concise, well-edited releases have a better chance for publication when an editor's work is significantly decreased.

5. Don't expect all of your releases to be printed in the newspaper. Show appreciation for those that are.

6. Learn how to handle an interview. The following are guidelines to consider:

   a. Know the subject of the interview.
   b. Anticipate controversial or difficult questions.
   c. Be honest and direct in answering questions.
   d. If you don't know an answer to a question, say so and make an offer to contact or refer the question to the appropriate individual.
   e. Keep the interview as friendly as possible even under tense situations.
   f. Avoid any off-the-record remarks unless you know and trust the interviewer. If you cannot release specific information, explain that it is not for public record and politely reserve the right not to answer. Be sure to answer questions that are public information and/or not against company policy.
   g. Exhibit dress and manners of a professional nature.

Types of coverage. There are a number of ways to obtain coverage in print and each has a particular use. Knowledge of which avenue to use for a given situation is essential.

1. *General information.* Develop material to keep the reader informed about current or upcoming events. You may emphasize special events, entry deadlines, tournament results, club sport events, feature stories on players/officials/games of the week, or a preview for a new program.

2. *Advertising.* Regardless of whether the organization is profit or nonprofit, advertising is a valuable promotional tool. Placement is critical. The most read pages of a newspaper in order are: front page, comics, sports and want ads.

3. *Editorials and letters to the editor.* Generally speaking, editorials are not written by the agency unless they are solicited. Encourage a newspaper staff to

REC SPORTS REPORT

Volume 1   Issue 6

Participants Recognized Through Awards

by Anne Phillips

The rewards gained through participating in a recreational sport are often as many and diversified as the participants themselves. But whether it's the thrill of victory or just the fun of sport that attracts you to I.U.'s recreational sports program, there is a special awards system to honor its outstanding participants.

Sponsored by the Student Recreational Sports Association (SRSA), the award certificates are given at an honor reception held each spring. The actual nomination process, however, begins months earlier.

Nomination forms are distributed among all areas of recreational sport programs for recognitions such as Club and Intramural Male/Female Athlete of the Year, Employee of the Year, Intramural Officials of the Year, and so on.

These nominations usually come from fellow participants or leaders within a program area and must be turned in to a selections committee of students and staff who then make the final decisions. Judgement of each recognition award is based upon a set of written criteria considerations for the particular award being given. Demonstrations of positive attitude, leadership skills, fair play, regular attendance and enthusiasm are some such considerations given to each nomination.

While the awards are considered a great honor by those who receive them, they are not intended to be extremely competitive. They are simply one way of saying "thank you" to those of you that choose to be involved.

Our "Roving Photographer" found this member of the Faculty/Staff Mixed Doubles Bowling League at the IMU lanes Sunday night. She is entitled to a Free I.U. Fit T-shirt upon presentation of this photo in HPER 290.

SRSA Award Winners

Intramural Sports:		Supervisor of the Year	Keith Milling
Manager of the Year		Official of the Year (female)	Evelyn Butler
Cream	John Nadelka	Official of the Year (male)	Jim Ferree
Crimson	Brian Hooker	Club Sports	
Sorority	Sheryl Stewart	Male Athlete	Robert Craft
Independent (Female)	Sally Derengoski	Female Athlete	Amy Krahl
Independent (Male)	Jack Edmiston	Outstanding Representative	Carl Lamb
Residence Hall	Brian Cook	Outstanding Senior	Jim Moser
All Campus	Jack Edmiston	Most Improved Club	Cycling
Athlete of the Year		Informal Sports	
Cream	Randy McNutt	Employee of the Year	Ed Carroll
Crimson	Bill Foy	I.U. Fit	Reyne Rus
Sorority	Nancy Pugliese	Chairperson of the Year	Beth Coleman
Independent	Sally Derengoski	SRSA Honor	Joel Widdows "JLW",
Residence Hall (female)	Vyrgynya Johnson		WTTS Radio
Residence Hall (male)	Walter Begley	Medallion Awards	Steve Adams,
All Campus (female)	Linda Angell		Residence Halls Association
All Campus (Male)	Bill Foy		

meetings

Handball Team Captains/Participants Meeting
Wednesday, Sept. 30, 7:00 p.m., Woodburn Auditorium 101
Table Tennis Team Participants Meeting
Wednesday, Sept. 30, 8:00 p.m., Woodburn Auditorium 101
Residence Hall Rec Sports Programming Meeting
Thursday, Oct. 1, 6:30 p.m., HPER 290 Conference Room
"Spirit of Sport" All-Nighter Committee Meetings
Each Monday at 7:00 p.m. in HPER 290 Conference Room. All interested persons are welcome!

INTRAMURAL DEADLINES

Miniature Golf

entry deadlines: Friday, October 2 at 4 pm
meet is Saturday, October 10
from 9 am to 12 noon

Wrestling

entry deadline: Wednesday, October 7 at 4 pm
mandatory meeting: Sunday, October 11
7 pm in Ballantine 013

announcements

The new 1981-'82 Sport Club Federation Executive Officers are:

President	Dave Filer
Vice President	Jan Steck
Secretary	Jeff Moster
Treasurer	John Apathy
Assistant	Alex Zai
Advisor	Lee Esckilsen

A Stress Management Clinic will be offered Tuesday, Oct. 6, from 6:30-7:30 p.m. at IMU Room 300B. Greg Griffith of the Student Health Center's Counseling and Psychological Services (CAPS) will discuss various topics related to stress and how to cope with them in everyday life. Admission is free for all I.U. Fit members and $1.00 at the door for non-members.

Recreational Sports Information Numbers

337-8788

Intramural Sports

- Daily Game Schedules
- Postponements
- Cancellations
- Announcements

337-8809

Informal Sports

- Facility Hours • Gym
- Weightroom • Pools, etc

*for other information call 337-2371
or stop by HPER 290*

Congratulations to all who participated in the Intramural Golf Meet held on the I.U. course last weekend. Mark Flannagan, Allan Balding, Greg Riddle, Tony Wood and Duane Schaefer give their Wendy's team smile after overcoming the Sigma Chi team for first place. Al Balding emerged the top male player and Karen O'Neal finished the top female contender of the meet.

photography by Tim Olney
a paid advertisement

Figure 13-3.   Example of a recreational sports page in a local newspaper.

Figure 13-4. Example of a recreational sports advertisement.

provide insight to a special interest or controversial topic. Whenever a negative perspective is expressed, request an opportunity to respond as soon as possible to minimize unfavorable opinion. On occasion, an agency may prepare a letter to the editor to express appreciation for the efforts of various individuals or groups.

4. *Complaints.* Complaints often serve as a warning of a problem area. Hopefully, they never surface in the newspaper. Unresolved complaints result in negative public sentiment. Prompt resolution of complaints by phone or letter promotes goodwill. The use of a newspaper column to address questions and complaints on a regular basis provides an effective public relations tool.

5. *Submitting pictures to a newspaper.* A sports action photograph is an effective complement to a newspaper article. Pictures draw attention and encourage the reading of an accompanying article. Figure 13-5 is an example of a good sports action picture. Submit photographs in 5 inch by 7 inch or 8 inch by 10 inch black and white glossy formats whenever possible. Check to see whether your picture is more effective in a horizontal or vertical format.

Do not assume that the newspaper can identify your photograph. *Tape* a label to the *back* of each photo indicating:
   a. Individual submitting picture
      Title or position
      Organization
   b. Photo caption of individual or group pictured
      Name(s)
      Title
      Organization, if any
      Event
      Date of Event

If you would like to have your picture returned after use indicate "Return to . . ." with your name and address. Without such notice, editors assume that they may keep the pictures

Courtesy: John Terhune.

Figure 13-5.   Example of an action sport photograph.

for their file or for disposal. File your negative so that the paper may dispose with the photograph as it wishes.

If you need a photographer at an event, request such coverage on your news release form. Call a day in advance of the event to remind the editor. Also, all should be ready for the photographer's arrival. Identify the individual(s) you would like to have photographed by name and title. Provide printed background information that the photographer can take back to the paper.

Use of the newspaper as a vehicle for public exposure also has limitations: "the average reader reads only a portion of his daily newspaper . . . thus it is a mistake to assume that publicity printed is publicity received. Basic though newspapers are, they cannot carry the information task alone" (Cutlip, 1978, p. 359).

Another drawback of the newspaper concerns its production schedule. Newspapers operate on a deadline, which "leads to many inaccuracies and fragmented, superficial coverage—a fact of life that the programmer must cope with" (Cutlip, 1978, p. 359).

Radio and Television

Radio and television, like the newspaper, are effective in reaching a large audience.

Broadcasting requirements. When preparing a broadcast message, eliminate long, complicated sentences and stick to a simple vocabulary of ordinary, everyday speech that all can understand. Contraction of words is also acceptable. The eye is used to seeing "is not", but the ear is tuned to "isn't".

Since broadcast messages are perishable, make every effort to ensure that the audience will recall the message. Mention the most important element of your message, the title of the sports event, for example—at least three to four times during a one minute announcement.

Broadcast possibilities. The range and scope of a broadcast message are greater than other avenues afford since radio and television audiences are so extensive. Many programmers shy away from broadcast opportunities because of cost, yet free air time is feasible in more situations than one would imagine. The following are examples of opportunities for broadcasting sports information:

1. *Interview.* Conducted between two or more individuals concerning opinions, viewpoints and overall reactions to an aspect of a program, the interview may highlight program procedures, sports information or

specific issues of interest. It is best to prepare a script in advance and schedule a rehearsal.

2. *Panel discussions or symposiums.* Panel discussions or symposiums offer a forum on specific concerns involving the organization, conduct or needs of the recreational sport program.

3. *News story.* Announcements and news stories about sports activities may occur prior or following an event. They may include speculation as to the value and expected outcome of the event.

4. *Public service announcements.* A common way to obtain free usage of air time, PSA's are similar to commercials in that they are designed to sell a product. These announcements usually provide time slots of 15, 30 or 60 second duration to make the presentation, idea, concept or program. Consequently, the message conveys only essential information.

5. *Sports talk show.* This format is a popular one in which participants or staff have opportunities to elaborate particular interests or job responsibilities. Casual in nature, talk shows often use a question and answer structure.

6. *Paid advertising.* There are two basic types of commercials: standard and production. The *standard* commercial involves a straightforward narration of an announcement while a *production* commercial often includes music or sound effects to set a mood. The length of either commercial depends on the budget and the message you wish to convey.

7. *Radio and Television Appearances.* A public appearance is more personalized than previous methods and requires different preparation. A few simple things to remember are:

    a. Bring along supporting material. If you are appearing on radio, bring an appropriate tape. Visual aids enhance television appearances.
    b. Ask the interviewer or host in advance what topics will be covered.

    c. Direct your comments to the TV interviewer. You
      may want to speak directly to the camera on occa-
      sion.
    d. Use natural hand expressions when speaking.
    e. Use make-up provided by the TV studio. Avoid
      wearing distracting clothes or jewelry.

Media Relations

Recommend the same type of reading as used for Radio and
Television.

Reporters appreciate sources who are cooperative and professional. Basic hints when communicating with the press include the following reminders (adapted from Newson, 1976,
p. 228):

- Listen and remember.
- Do not use technical jargon.
- Smile when answering questions.
- Speak in 30 second quotes. Longer answers are seldom
  used.
- A simple "yes" or "no" may keep you from being
  quoted.
- Lose your temper in front of a reporter and find a spot on
  the six o'clock news.
- Never tell a lie. A reporter doesn't forget.
- Preface remarks are taboo.
- Represent your organization when appearing on radio or
  TV, not your personal opinion.
- Keep up with current events.
- Know more about your subject than a reporter does.
- Don't say "no comment"; it makes you sound guilty.
- Don't speak "off the record" to a reporter.
- Have a positive message to deliver.
- Know why you were asked to appear. The days of being
  invited on television just to "chew the fat" are over.
- Dress conservatively. No flashy colors or short sleeves.
- Do your homework.
- Question your position. Play the "devil's advocate" and
  force yourself to justify your point of view.

- Keep your position simple enough to be understood by the average tenth-grade student.
- While in a television or radio studio, assume every microphone and camera is live. Don't do anything you wouldn't do in church.
- Do not leave the set until the program is over.
- Edit your message before you deliver it.

PRINT MATERIAL

The mass media facilitates promotion of recreational sport opportunities to the general public. Print material, on the other hand, is designed to reach a targeted readership. Popular formats include: handbooks, brochures, pamphlets, and newsletters. Recreational sport use of print material has increased tremendously in recent years through advances in printing technology.

Handbooks

The handbook is an accepted format for the distribution of orientation material for a recreational sport program. Develop a handbook design that appeals to your prospective reader, based on the following parameters:

1. *Size.* Purpose often dictates size. If you are interested in being distinctive or flamboyant, consider a large magazine format. If you are more practical, use a pocket or standard (8½" × 11") dimension.

2. *Length.* Keep length to a minimum. The more that appears in print, the less gets read.

3. *Color.* Color, particularly on the cover, attracts attention.

4. *Illustration.* Cartoons or photographs add appeal and cost.

5. *Type.* The typeface style should be easy to read.

6. *Content.* Remember that a handbook is a collection of information designed to attract, encourage and motivate participation in the program. The following is an adapted version of a list of elements from Means (1973, p. 362) that may be included in a handbook.

—Action photographs
—Awards and recognition
—Bulletin Board
—Calendar of events
—Club sports information
—Cover
—Employment opportunities
—Entry instructions
—Equipment
—Events and programs
—Facility hours and scheduling
—Fees, forfeits, protest procedures
—First aid and injury information
—General information
—General sport rules and regulations
—Greetings from agency officials
—Health examination policy
—Independent organizations
—Instructional sports
—Insurance information
—League play-off regulations
—Locker and towel regulations
—Officials, supervisors, managers
—Organization of the program
—Participation statistics
—Point system and scoring records
—Postponements
—Practice opportunities
—Program champions from previous year
—Regulations
—Rental equipment policies
—Special events
—Staff introduction
—Swimming permits
—Units of competition

Brochures and Pamphlets.

Brochures and pamphlets are versatile tools. A brochure is generally smaller and more concise than a pamphlet. It covers between four to twelve pages in length whereas the pamphlet may contain two to four times the copy.

The values of brochures and pamphlets are numerous. For example:

Figure 13-6. Example of a handbook cover.

1. *Exclusivity of subject.* The entire message you wish to convey is presented free of the distractions common to newspapers and other media. You can concentrate on one message without having to compete with unrelated stories or pictures.

2. *Timing and distribution.* This is your publication, and you determine the schedule and method of distribution—mail, hand delivery, or display.

3. *Budget.* Brochures and pamphlets are often the least expensive ways to communicate a message.

Newsletters.

With the diversity in recreational sport personnel and participants, a newsletter serves a valuable communications function.

NEWSLETTERS

VOLUME_____, ISSUE_____   DATE _____

THE NEWSLETTER is a technique used to keep all participants aware of the organization's activities. These activities may range from individual recognition to participation highlights and special announcements. The constituency may consist of current team members, past participants and alumni.

IT SHOULD BE printed on the organization's 8½ in. by 11 in. letterhead paper and limited to a single sheet. Cost of a newsletter should be kept to a minimum since it is issued weekly or monthly.

WRITING THE NEWSLETTER. Don't bother with fancy headlines. The title "Newsletter" in capital letters is sufficient. Stay with a very informal and brief format.

KEEP IN MIND that a newsletter is not designed to flow with dialogue like a letter. It is bits and pieces of business news that is informative to the participants.

THE BEST FORMAT is a series of separate short paragraphs which should include no more than four or five sentences. Each paragraph opens with a capitalized heading or the first few words in upper case. The gossip column in a newspaper is an example of good writing style for newsletters.

REMEMBER, NEWSLETTERS are a direct means of communicating and promoting the recreational sport organization in a brief, concise and positive way.

Figure 13-7. Newsletter format.

It allows versatility and diversity in content, length and design from issue to issue and is inexpensive to mass produce. The newsletter easily addresses a target group and complements other promotion-publicity methods. (See Figure 13-7)

Calendars.

Calendars are excellent promotional tools that may publicize weekly, monthly or yearly recreational sport events by listing entry deadlines, rules, regulations, jobs, leadership opportunities and facility availability. They may appear on desk blotters, wall posters, or pocket calendar form.

Sport information sheets.

Such notices usually accompany each entry form or facilities schedule and contain pertinent information necessary for participation: entry fees, entry deadlines, date and location of orientation meeting, schedule distribution or rules interpretation meetings, tournament format, and days, dates and location for participation.

Memoranda.

The departmental or internal update memorandum is written primarily for staff, employees and key volunteer leaders. It provides an opportunity for the agency to inform those who know the organization best—the staff. Figure 13-8 illustrates a model update publication.

Visual presentations

Are useful, necessary tools to promote recreational sports opportunities. When preparing visual aids, use the following steps:

1. *Decide upon a subject.* The most important thing to consider is the relationship of a visual concept to the sport or subject. Focus on conveying one principal thought, idea or theme to avoid confusion.

2. *Develop a caption.* A good caption entices the viewer to pursue a subject presentation further. The wording should be simple and direct to stimulate interest and attention.

3. *Gather the material.* Content should be concerned with (a) illustrating the idea, (photographs, drawings, cartoons, illustrations or actual objects), (b) attracting attention, (colored materials or three-dimensional devices) and (c) equipment for attaching the material to a permanent fixture.

4. *Plan the placement of the visual.* Accomplish the placement of a visual in such a manner as to be attractive and interesting to the viewer's eye.

⌒ OFFICIAL BUSINESS

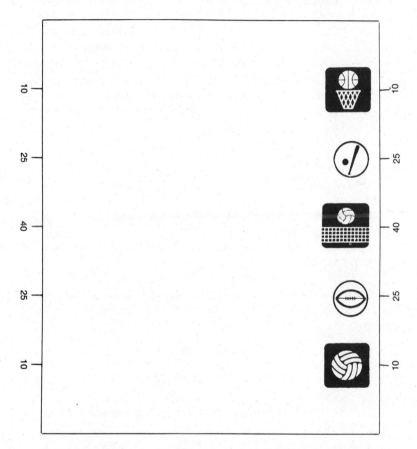

Figure 13-8. Example of an intramural sport official's update publication.

5. *Select the lettering.* Lettering can make or break a visual. A simple letter style is the easiest to read. Captions or labels should be large enough to be visible from a distance.

6. *Don't expect miracles.* Visual aids do not guarantee effective promotion and publicity. Unless properly constructed, visuals are distracting, cumbersome and wasteful.

Bulletin Boards.

A bulletin board is a visual way of reminding potential participants of program offerings. Consider it a continuous updated newspaper and place it wherever participants regularly pass by or congregate. Since a bulletin board may be portable or permanent, it may be put in numerous locations: outdoor sports complexes, gymnasiums, office lobbies, hallways and locker rooms. Set the board in a glass covered case that can be locked when it is necessary to prevent tampering.

The merit and effectiveness of the bulletin board may be enhanced by following these simple guidelines:

Simplicity: Simplify shapes, lines, space and color in order to present a readable board.

Unity: Emphasize a basic line of direction throughout the board.

Emphasis: To focus attention on an important item, set it apart by using space, color or texture.

Balance: Balance invites a quick and thorough inspection by the participant.

Supplies for Bulletin Boards: Maintain a sharp, fresh appearance by promptly replacing worn or damaged supplies. Materials frequently used in the preparation of bulletin boards include:

Background Materials:

Cork	Wall paper
Linoleum	Carpet remnants
Cloth	Corrugated cardboard
Blotters	Colored cardboard
Brown wrapping paper	Fabric remnants
Gift wrapping paper	Map paper
Crepe paper	Newspaper
Grass cloth	Wood
Screening	Plastic
Foil	Shelf paper
Colored paper	Felt

Line Materials:

Pliable wire	Rick Rack
String	Ribbons

Yarn or wool   Adhesive tape
Rope   Paper strips
Colored tape

Fastening Materials and Devices:

Cellulose tape   Thumb tacks (push pins)
Loops of tape   Bulletin board wax
Map tacks   Straight pins

Lettering:

Newspaper headlines   Cardboard
Magazine ads   Cork
Large numbers from   Linoleum
  calendars   Foil
Felt   Bright scraps of magazines
Construction paper   Carpet remnants
Map paper   Stencils
Newspaper copy   Corrugated cardboard
Colored paper   Felt pen or bottle ink
Gummed Letters   Rubber stamps
Crayons or Chalk

3-D Lettering:

Yarn   Colored string
Manila Rope   Electric cords
Clothesline   Metal house numbers
Wire   Plastic numbers and letters
Sticks-driftwood   Alphabet blocks
Colored thumbtacks   Beads
Upholstery tacks   Pipe cleaners
Cellophane straws

DO'S OF THE BULLETIN BOARD

1. Use the bulletin board to promote a single theme.

2. Use large scale drawings and captions.

3. Use a colored background for mounting displays or material.

4. Keep work neat, attractive and orderly.

5. Present material in unique, unusual, and humorous ways.

6. Add emphasis to the bulletin board by using projecting materials.

7. Plan and sketch a display before constructing it on the board.

8. Always keep material current.

9. Attract attention to the display by highlighting the more important words or phrases.

10. Balance the placement of material on the board. Leave more margin at the bottom than at sides and top.

11. Hide any mechanical parts used in operating the display.

12. Vary the color scheme.

13. If the board includes posted information (rules and regulations), change it often before it becomes "dogeared" or tattered.

14. If the board becomes broken, immediately repair it. Damaged boards encourage vandalism.

DON'TS OF THE BULLETIN BOARD

1. Don't clutter the bulletin board with unnecessary information.

2. Don't leave displays up too long. Two or three weeks is maximum.

3. Don't use the space wastefully by posting unrelated materials.

4. Don't use excessive printed matter. A picture is worth a thousand words.

5. Don't use vertical lettering—it's difficult to read.

6. Don't use frilly "curly-cue" lettering.

7. Don't make the board too fancy.

Posters.

The purpose of the poster, like the bulletin board, is to remind the participant. Present an idea but do not attempt to explain or convince.

Standard poster size is 14 by 22 inches. For tacking or taping to a wall, paper material is sufficient. For free-standing or outdoor use, use heavy weight poster board.

Poster design consists of three basic elements: slogan, illustration and group name. Do not include more than these three elements into a poster. Focus on one of these elements to attract attention.

Color selection is important to poster design since it aids the legibility of the printed message. Use unusual or contrasting color combinations. Keep typography clear and simple.

Posters have approximately five seconds to communicate 10 or 12 words and a picture. The best formula to guarantee success is logical order, bold letters, attention-getting colors and a simple illustration. Posters need not be a work of art.

Flyers.

A flyer is an inexpensive promotional piece having mass distribution. It is usually printed on a single, pastel-colored sheet of paper. Its format consists of a central theme with simple layout, color and design. Figure 13-9 illustrates an example of a flyer.

Among numerous ways to display or distribute flyers are:

—bulletin boards
—team captains' or managers' meetings
—departmental mailboxes
—sport facilities
—locker rooms
—Chambers of Commerce
—mail
—schools
—grocery stores
—clubs
—businesses
—sporting goods stores

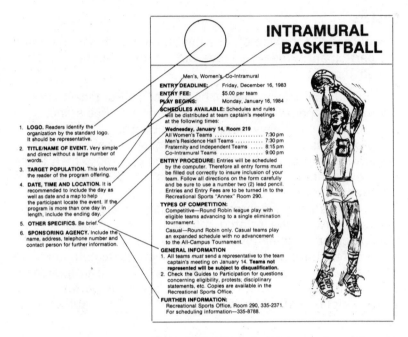

Figure 13-9. Example of intramural sport flyer.

Exhibits and Displays.

An exhibit is usually three-dimensional and used for a particular period of time while a display is two-dimensional and considered a permanent part of the environment. Both seek to achieve the same results, which involve:

1. *Attracting attention.* If the content of the exhibit or display does not "jump" at the passing public, it will fail.

2. *Creating involvement.* Once you have gained attention the display must somehow encourage and stimulate the individual to participate.

3. *Distributing information.* Concentrate on communicating the most important information. Remember, you have an individual's attention for a short period of time.

4. *Promoting goodwill.* The viewer should receive something free by spending a few moments at the display or exhibit. For example, a Frisbee Club might promote its activity by giving away frisbees.

The following guidelines apply to the set-up of any display or exhibit. (Adapted from Baeckler, 1978, page 60.)

- Plan in advance. Determine the best location and reserve it early.
- Know your material and develop one theme.
- Keep it simple. Don't try to cover a lot of details.
- Use illustrations. Variety and vibrancy of colors mean a livelier display.
- If your display involves a booth, always make sure that a knowledgeable individual is accessible to give accurate information.
- Never use items you cannot afford to lose.
- Aim your material at diverse age groups.
- Distribute as much information as possible through free samples, discount coupons, posters and pamphlets.

Logos.

The use of logos provides a visual identity that establishes continuity from one program offering to the next within the same organization. A symbol should identify the organization in every promotional format available to the programmer. A logo is an attention-getter. It should appear on such items as:

flyers	bulletin boards	handbooks
press releases	brochures	calendars
posters	bookmarks	T-shirts
entrance signs	slide presentations	uniforms
vehicles		

The design of the logo is critical. Most professional printers provide design assistance in this area.

SLIDE PRESENTATIONS

Slide presentations offer versatility in design content and focus which may be easily altered to accommodate changes in emphasis or audience. When constructing a presentation, begin by selecting a theme. This establishes the purpose of the presentation and dictates the type of slides needed to convey the message.

A slide presentation often uses approximately 80-140 slides running 20-30 minutes in length (Graham and Klar, 1979, p. 200). If it runs any longer than this, audience interest tends to decline.

Although slide presentations need not include narration, they are much more effective with it. For an effective script, the content should be simple and concise. Rehearse your presentation to synchronize the slides with the narration. Cues on your script should indicate when to advance each slide.

Slide presentations traditionally involved the use of one projector. Now they commonly involve multiple projectors with automatic cueing devices for activating the slide advance. Another recent development is the slide-tape presentation, used in conjunction with a prerecorded narrative track. The slide advance may be activated by a hand-held unit or controlled by a signal on the tape. This feature is particularly useful for conventions, exhibits, offices or other settings experiencing a constant traffic flow or where it is not practical to have a narrator present.

OPEN HOUSE

An open house event seeks to attract large numbers of prospective participants to the premises of the sport facility. A tour of the facility combined with an oral presentation of the program is the most important feature of this event.

The following is an adapted version of a checklist developed by Richard Darrow (1979, pp. 680–683) for staging a successful open house.

Setting the Date and Time

1. Check the schedule of other events to avoid conflict.
2. Choose the least busy day of the week.
3. Consider a school holiday when the entire family may attend.
4. Allow ample time for registration, tours and refreshments.
5. Set an alternate date in case of bad weather.
6. Select and announce date well in advance.

Budget Considerations

1. Attendance estimate.
2. Refreshments, supplies and decoration.
3. Printing signs and displays.
4. Payroll.

Facilities

1. Reception area and tour designations.
2. Parking.
3. Housecleaning.
4. Equipment function.
5. Registration set-up.
6. Refreshment tables.
7. Information signs and arrows.
8. P.A. system for announcements and music.
9. Display of sport equipment.
10. Badges for employees.

Facility Tours

1. Brief welcome.
2. Continuous slide presentation.
3. Map or directory.
4. Tour guide duties.
5. Rest break.
6. Question and answer period.
7. Concluding remarks.

Refreshments

1. Quick service items.
2. Ample supplies.

3. Table arrangments and decoration.

4. Waste containers.

5. Attractive area.

Printed Material

1. Program of event.

2. Name tags.

3. Map of facility.

4. Registration form.

5. Literature.

6. Application for employment.

7. Sports entry forms.

8. Information sheet.

Publicity

1. Advance press invitations.

2. Newspaper, radio, TV announcement.

3. Photographer.

4. Sport program display.

Follow-up

1. Worker recognition.

2. Guest's comments and suggestions.

3. Evaluation.

TELEPHONE

The telephone is not a promotional tool, yet positive impressions made during phone conversations are beneficial. Telephones serve several purposes: (1) solicitation, (2) announcements, and (3) message distribution.

Solicitation. Because the telephone is immediate and efficient it overcomes many problems encountered in using printed materials. Participants and personnel often rely on the telephone to obtain information regarding the program or their responsibilities.

Announcements. When people want to know such information as facility hours, club sport events, daily intramural sport schedules and cancellations, a recorded message is an ideal way to disseminate this information. Messages may be recorded on tapes in advance and updated as required. Used after regular office hours, this mechanism eliminates participant frustration by providing a consistent source of reliable information.

Messages. The telephone provides the easiest, simplest and most economical method for messages regarding program changes, rescheduling of tournament contests, reminders of meeting dates and times, and distributing any other general information.

Here are some helpful hints for effective use of the telephone:

Before Calling. . .

1. Answer the questions "Is the telephone the best way to handle the message?" and "Is this the best time to call?".

2. Be in a positive frame of mind.

3. Gather material before you place a call.

4. Plan your thoughts and write down what you need to say.

Placing a Call. . .

1. Be certain of the number you want.

2. Dial carefully—know how to dial for internal, local and long distance calls.

3. Address the individual you are calling by name. Identify yourself by name, title and agency.

4. Keep conversations brief and to the point. If the conversation requires a lengthy discussion, demonstrate courtesy by asking if the individual has the time.

5. Speak in a calm and polite tone of voice.

6. Leave a concise message if your contact is absent.

7. End all calls courteously and replace the receiver gently.

Answering a Call. . .

1. Answer promptly—before the second or third ring, if possible.

2. Answer the phone yourself.

3. Identify yourself.

4. Note essential details of your conversation.

5. If you need to leave your desk during a phone conversation, always put the caller on hold. Never allow a caller to hear office conversation.

6. Always say goodbye when completing a call.

WORD OF MOUTH (GRAPEVINE)

This informal avenue of communication is one of the least controllable but most effective. A programmer stimulates word of mouth by providing a quality program. When people enjoy themselves, they recommend an activity to others. Unfortunately, the grapevine often embellishes the truth. If information is inaccurate or harmful, issue a statement citing the full facts on the situation to squelch gossip.

NOVELTY ITEMS

There are a variety of other methods for program publicity and promotion purposes that are not widely used. We classify these as novelty items because of their innovative nature. Novelty items may include:

—bus advertisement   —video tape
—balloons   —cartoons
—bumper stickers   —airplane advertising
—flags   and skywriting
—banners   —uniforms
—buttons   —maps

—postage meter imprints	—window decals
—billboards	—rubber stamps
—imprinted clothing	—display racks
—pencils	—keychains
—pocket calendars	—desk blotters

Whatever means you choose, follow good taste, judgement and simplicity.

CONCLUSION

Effective public relations requires an understanding of the needs of the public, the process of communication and the vehicles of promotion and publicity. The degree of community participation, support and goodwill depends upon our ability to create a message, select a medium and choose a time to reach a desired audience for reasonable cost and effort.

REFERENCES

Baeckler, V.V. *PR for Pennies.* Hopewell, New Jersey: Sources Publishing, 1978.

Cutlip, S.M., and Center, A.H. *Effective Public Relations.* Englewood Cliffs, New Jersey: Prentice-Hall, Inc., 1971.

Cutlip, S.M., and Center, A.H. *Efffective Public Relations.* Englewood Cliffs, New Jersey: Prentice-Hall, Inc., 1978.

Darrow, R. *The Dartnell Public Relations Handbook* Chicago: Dartnell Corp., 1979.

Graham, P.J. and Klar, L.R., Jr. *Planning and Delivering Leisure Services.* Dubuque, Iowa: William C. Brown Company Publishers, 1979.

Gunning, R. *The Techniques of Clear Writing.* New York: McGraw-Hill Book Co., 1968.

Joseph, A.M. "How to Write Better," *Management Methods Magazine.* November, 1960, p. 43.

Means, L.E. *Intramurals: Their Organization and Administration.* Englewood Cliffs, New Jersey: Prentice-Hall, Inc., 1973.

Newson, D. *This is PR.* Belmont, California: Wadsworth Publishing Co., Inc., 1981.

CHAPTER 14

RECOGNITION

Recognition is a social expression for acknowledging accomplishment. In today's competitive society we recognize
and reinforce those who aspire to succeed. We also condition
people from childhood to expect recognition when their goals
are met. As an example, consider the preschooler who
receives a treat for accurately reciting the A-B-C's or, the first
grader who is rewarded with money by Mom and Dad for bring-
ing home a report card filled with A's.

Consequently, we perceive recognition as a way to satisfy
our ego and bolster self-esteem. While we satisfy physiological (food and shelter), safety (security), and social needs
(acceptance and affiliation) on a daily basis, we experience
sporadic ego gratification. Although this need provides a rationale for the inclusion of a recognition system within recreational sport, recognition itself remains a controversial aspect
of programming.

Exceptional performance and achievement in sport is
customarily recognized through some form of tangible award.

Historically, problems have arisen within athletic sport concerning this aspect of recognition. Whenever one agency gave awards to participants, another agency would attempt to outdo it. This kind of rivalry continued until the cost of awards became prohibitive and the tangible reward of victories and trophies became more important than the intangible desire to participate for enjoyment.

The shift in the focus of participation from enjoyment to accomplishment and victory has been gradual. Part of the responsibility for this change rested with programmers who recruited the best athletes to a program regardless of consequences. Another contributing factor was a lack of understanding regarding the effect of awards upon participant attitudes and expectations.

The controversy over recognition has carried over into recreational sport. Although recognition remains largely associated with athletic achievement and supremacy, the programmer is in a position to broaden its scope and application by acknowledging the efforts of participants, employees, and volunteers. Recognizing those who excel or reach a goal maintains interest and involvement while an overemphasis on outcome or excellence discourages them. Since a concentration on results honors only the few who are capable of top performances, this conveys an attitude that anything short of excellence is unworthy of recognition. Limited opportunities for recognition foster disinterest, apathy, resentment, hostility and low self-esteem. When the system acknowledges involvement, effort, improvement, accomplishment, and contribution, it encourages participation, reinforces program control, promotes goodwill, and aids participant development.

Incentive. Inquiry into why people participate in sport events reveals useful information to the programmer. Alderman and Wood (1976) found that participation in sport gives a person an opportunity to establish close personal relationships with others, achieve excellence, receive recognition for success and gain status, prestige, and social approval. When the recognition system is designed to satisfy these needs, it stimulates involvement.

Motivation. Some people who participate in recreational sports are reluctant to continue due to such perceived or real deterrents as effort, sweat, commitment of time, stress and or skill level. Maintaining participant interest is a challenge for the programmer. How does one encourage participation in a beneficial activity that may not give immediate pleasure, but may result in discomfort? How does a programmer motivate those who have a fear of failure?

The keys to increasing motivation lie in minimizing obstacles and satisfying individual needs, interests, and expectations of participation

Control. A quality recognition system strengthens program control, especially within club and intramural sports, by reinforcing desirable behavior, improvement in performance, and contribution to the program. When recognition is provided through point systems, media, personal gestures, and awards in conjunction with a quality governance system, such control problems as physical abuse, verbal abuse and the use of ineligible participants are mitigated.

Public Relations. Recognition, as a symbol of both individual and social achievement, enhances the agency's image with the participant and the public by attracting interest and providing opportunities for publicity.

When participants leave the sport environment with a good feeling, they readily recall and relate both the experience and the recognition they received. A system of recognition also provides an opportunity to express special appreciation to individuals who make important contributions to the program, like the merchant who works non-stop to have a printed program of events ready for an opening ceremony, or the active supporter who donates the budget for a specific event.

A word of warning about recognition and public relations: avoid using recognition as a means for generating publicity. Establish guidelines and purposes for whom, when and how it is used.

Participant Development. A recognition system that reinforces desirable and deters disruptive behavior serves as a valuable learning laboratory for participants, employees, and volunteers. Edginton, Compton and Hanson (1980, p. 114) note:

"The learning process is not complete without consideration of the factors of motivation and performance. Learning, will not take place in the absence of a motivator; and even after learning has occurred the learning will not be applied for 'performed' without sufficient motivation."

Consequently, the recognition system must acknowledge and encourage individual accomplishments, improvements, and contributions to motivate learning and involvement. When criteria and guidelines for recognition are realistic, fair and equitable, individuals know what is required or expected.

TYPES OF RECOGNITION

The methods or techniques available for bestowing recognition include awards, point systems, media coverage and personalized delivery. When selecting types of recognition consider the needs and characteristics of your clientele. For example, age is a factor. Recognition is not as significant to most children as it is to an older participant who places a social value on it.

Awards

Many agencies use awards as the primary components of their recognition system since they cater to participants desiring evidence of individual merit. Many professionals in the field, however, are opposed to their use, contending that participation should not be contingent upon the presence of such tangible incentives as awards. Figure 14-1 summarizes the advantages and disadvantages of awards.

AWARDS

Advantages	Disadvantages
1. Recognizes achievement in a tangible way.	1. Emphasizes the award rather than inherent values of sport participation.
2. Serves as incentive for participation.	2. Involves more expense.
3. Provides an excellent public relations tool.	3. Stresses winning, promoting increased intensity of competition.
4. Fosters esprit de corps.	4. Recognizes a few highly skilled individuals or teams rather than a majority of participants.
5. Represents a way to recognize accomplishments in all program divisions—informal, intramural, and club sports.	5. Represents artificial incentives.

Figure 14-1. Recreational sport awards.

The nature and value of an award should correspond to the degree of accomplishment it represents. An award can be a meaningful momento or symbol of accomplishment regardless of its monetary value. However, when the cost and attention associated with an award is out of proportion to the significance of the performance or accomplishment, individuals may develop unrealistic expectations toward participation and the recognition process. Once awards are given out indiscriminately, they lose their value.

Many objects are used as awards within the recreational sport program. They range in size, shape, cost, construction, and purpose. Among the most common ones are trophies, medals, medallions, plaques, clothing, certificates, ribbons and accessories.

Trophies. These awards are fashioned from wood, metal or plastic and consist of three parts: the base, the body and a figurine that represents a specific event or accomplishment. Customarily, engraved plates attached to either the base or body of the trophy specify the event, the date and the recipient. Trophies may be awarded on a permanent or rotating basis depending upon the budget and philosophy of the setting.

Medals. Medals, ideal for individual and meet events, may be used as a platter, paper weight, wall hanging or as decoration on clothing. As with trophies, they permit the use of interchangable sport figures. A color code usually indicates first-place (gold), second-place (silver), and third-place (bronze).

Medallions. Similar in appearance to medals, medallions are machine engraved and may include a custom design such as the agency's own logo or a sport motif. Depending upon weight, medallions may be suitable as part of a dish, paperweight, keychain or charm.

Plaques. Plaques are ideal awards due to their durability and potential for engraving. Multiple plates are also available for the addition of names to permanent plaques.

T-Shirts. T-shirts are popular, especially among youth and young adults. The T-shirt may serve as a walking advertisement to identify the agency and specific event. Disadvantages in their use include the expense incurred when distributed to large number of people, the space required to maintain stock in various sizes and the expense and time required to handle special orders.

Certificates. Paper certificates represent the most simple and economical form of award because they can be designed in advance and printed in bulk. Certificates customarily include the agency's name and logo, a blank line for the recipient's name, a brief description of the purpose of the award and a blank line for the signature of the program director or other authorized staff member. A genuine signature of the staff member provides a personal touch.

Ribbons. Ribbons of various size and color are available in large quantities and may be purchased prior to the start of the sports program. Custom-made ribbons often include the agency's name, event, and location. Traditional colors, representing place of finish are: blue (first-place), red (second-place), and white (third-place).

Rosettes. Rosettes provide a more expensive and "classier" look than ribbons because of their ruffled perimeter.

Gift Certificates. Gift certificates redeemable for items at a pro shop, sporting goods store or a local merchant represent another form of award. These awards do not supply identification with the agency or specific accomplishment.

Desk Items. Desk items are formal awards often given for adult program recognition: paperweights, calendars, pen and pencil sets and holders, desk sets, ashtrays, envelope openers, name plates, mugs and clocks.

Apparel and Accessories. Other items suitable as awards include: jackets, blazers, sweaters, jerseys, sun visors, caps, cuff links, tie clasps, belt buckles, charm bracelets, pendants, blankets, patches, lapel pins, emblems, keychains, and team pictures. Each requires a system for maintaining an accurate inventory and adequate stock.

Point Systems

Point systems have had a traditional association with intramural sport programs. However, more and more agencies are finding additional applications for them in such programming areas as fitness, club and informal sports. The basic purpose of a point system is to stimulate interest and maintain participation by awarding a certain number of points to individuals or teams that participate in designated sport activities or events. Additional points may be allocated for achievement. At the conclusion of an event, the point tally may be used in two ways: charting individual improvements in performance or ranking all the participants for comparison. Point systems, like awards, have their advantages and disadvantages.

POINT SYSTEMS

Advantages	Disadvantages
1. Encourages participation.	1. Represents an artificial incentive system for participation.
2. Stimulates interest in an event that continues for an extended period of time.	2. Encourages forced participation just to receive points for the team or group.
3. Reorganizes both participation and performance.	3. Eliminates some activities because they can not be quantified to fit into a point system.
4. Increases attendance.	4. Discourages participation if the focus is too much on excellence rather than participation.
5. Provides a standard system for determining recognition.	
6. Encourages individuals to participate in a wide range of activities in which otherwise they might have hesitated to participate in.	5. Discourages participation if the classification system for involvement is not equitable.
7. Stimulates goal-directed behavior which motivates individuals to strive for improvement.	6. Necessitates that record-keeping is time consuming and a burden for office staff.
8. Fosters esprit de corps.	7. Encourages possible unsportsmanlike or unethical conduct to earn more points.
9. Provides a way in which individuals may measure their own ability or achievement with past performance or the performance of others.	8. Creates unnecessary pressure to excel.

Figure 14-2. Point system.

Point systems are seldom similar because of the diversity of program offerings and philosophy. Here are some suggestions to consider when designing a point system:

1. Encourage involvement by a large number of people. Take into account differences in age, ability, and interests to develop a suitable classification system for involvement.

2. Encourage participation in diverse activities to enhance the potential for participant development.

3. Establish realistic standards of accomplishment and communicate them to all potential participants.

4. Maintain a simple point distribution process for ease of interpretation and recording. Use a small point spread when allocating points to maintain involvement by as many persons as possible over a long period of time.

5. Recognize and allocate points on the basis of participation and effort in addition to achievement and winning.

6. Guard against allocating more points for activities requiring specialized skills.

7. Recognize components of desirable behavior as well as performance.

8. Maintain up-to-date records and communicate results regularly.

In addition to these general suggestions, specific operational factors to consider when developing a point system include purpose, classification system, and point distribution.

Purpose. The programmer must determine the purpose for the point system. Will the system be used to encourage participation, maintain interest, reward achievement in performance, reinforce behavior, or serve as criteria for an awards system? Is it designed for one event or for a number of events throughout a specified time span? Will the point system be used by individuals or groups? Without a clear explanation of its purpose, a point system is ineffective.

Classification. In order to assign equitable point values, group together similar events and activities when possible. Classifications could be based on:

Sport area—team sports, individual sports, dual sports, meet sports, club sports and fitness.

Skill level—advanced, intermediate, novice, and others.

Special focus—major sports, minor sports, special events, and specific goals.

Extent of involvement—number of teams entered, number of individual participants required, number of games or matches required, length and type of tournament design (round robin, single elimination, challenge).

Degree of difficulty—physical skill, knowledge, endurance and conditioning.

Demographic background—age, sex, height, weight, size and unit of participation.

After choosing your classifications, keep the point value distribution equitable in terms of performance standards. Even though some events are given higher priority and greater emphasis because of the higher point distribution assigned to them, the programmer should reassure the participants that all recreational sport activities receive equal treatment in terms of programming considerations.

Point value designation. The distribution of points should be simple. Keep the total sum of the actual point scale as low as possible even though participants enjoy accumulating a large point total. The less the amount, the easier the computation of points and recordkeeping.

Distribute points on a descending high to low order with top placement given the highest amount of points and so forth. If the system is designed to encourage participation, give points to all individuals and teams that enter. However, monitor those who enter events for the sole purpose of accumulating entry points without intending to participate. Failure to attend a scheduled activity is unacceptable and the programmer should take whatever measures are necessary to discourage such behavior. If the point system is designed to recognize performance, award bonus or advancement points for winning a contest or surpassing a designated goal. The following sections describe two methods of point distribution.

Fitness point systems serve as both a motivational tool for involvement and a way of keeping track of participant performance during sport and exercise activities.

It is important that participants set realistic goals. Goals of 500, 1,000, 1,500, or 2,000 points are common in a fitness point system. Regular participation in diverse fitness activities is necessary in order to achieve maximum benefits from the point system. As a way to encourage regular participation, bonus points are allocated as follows:

Participation Days

Per Week	Point Value
one day	1
two days	2
three days	3
four days	4
five days	6
six days	8
seven days	10

Cooper (1980) provides specific point values for sport activities according to intensity and duration. His charts also indicate how to allocate points for attendance at such events as lectures, clinics, or workshops.

Intramural sport points provide another example of point distribution used to stimulate interest and participation and recognize performance outcome. Under this system, entry points are awarded to every team or person that participates while points are subtracted for those that forfeit. Additional points are awarded for place of finish. The following examples illustrate the point distribution for a basketball tournament involving a 5-team round robin league, followed by an all-league single elimination tournament.

Entry Points
A-section . . . 60 points

League Points
1st place . . . 75 points
2nd place . . . 60 points
3rd place . . . 45 points
4th place . . . 30 points
5th place . . . 10 points

Tournament Points
1st place . . . 35 points
2nd place . . . 30 points
3rd - 4th . . . 25 points
5th - 8th . . . 15 points

As long as point systems remain relatively simple, they offer equal opportunity for all to succeed, reward participation for its own sake and motivate interest in the program.

While awards and point systems are the most commonly utilized forms of recognition, there are several other types appropriate for use. Among these are media and personal approaches.

Media

The sports programmer customarily recognizes participants through such mass media as newspapers, television and radio. Recipients enjoy the public attention afforded by media recognition while the agency also benefits from such exposure. The newspaper has been the most consistently accessible vehicle recognizing achievement and expressing appreciation to both participants and staff. Formats for newspaper recognition include:

—Group pictures of championship teams
—Box scores
—Feature articles
—News stories
—Advertisements congratulating award winners
—Leaders of the month
—Participants of the month
—Interviews with participants
—Event coverage
—Statistics

Many opportunities to promote recognition exist in the field of broadcasting if the programmer uses a little creativity and imagination. Suggested formats include:

—Videotapes of events for replay
—Public service announcements recognizing individual contributors
—Personal interviews at sport events
—Coverage featuring a special event or performance
—Special interest series which recognize a unique contribution or idea
—Live coverage of a sport event

Although the technical aspects of radio and television may seem intimidating, sports directors are very interested in local coverage and newsworthy human interest stories.

Other media for recognition include bulletin boards, billboards, flyers, posters, newsletters, and even letters of congratulation to a participant for exceptional performance.

PERSONALIZED APPROACH

An overlooked yet effective form of recognition to extend to all participants, employees and volunteers, is the personal approach. The traditional recognition system acknowledges performance *outcome* to the neglect of performance output. For example, the softball player who hits three long fly balls that fall short of a home run gets little recognition. While the performance (batting stance, swing, eye contact, follow-through) is excellent, the outcome is insufficient to merit recognition. A recognition system must somehow take effort into consideration. A simple handshake, smile, thank-you, word of commendation or pat on the back may be all the reinforcement people need. These gestures require little effort but still promote goodwill. Intangible reinforcement that recognizes individual effort may do as much—if not more—to motivate individuals than tangible awards.

CRITERIA FOR RECOGNITION

Criteria for recognition are needed prior to the selection of recipients. When formal or structured recognition presentations are involved, the criteria should follow an established policy set forth in the agency's administrative manual. When possible, develop uniform criteria regardless of sport program area. Examples of recognition criteria to use with different target groups follow.

    A. *Recreational Sport Employee*

       1. Outstanding work performance

       2. Reliability

       3. Communication skills (written and oral)

       4. Conflict resolution skills

       5. Grooming

      6. Volunteer service

      7. Successful employment evaluations

  B. *Recreational Sport Volunteer*

      1. Ability to promote participation

      2. Enthusiasm

      3. Contributions

      4. Cooperation

      5. Dependability

      6. Competency

      7. Attendance

      8. Grooming

  C. *Recreational Sport Participant*

      1. Degree of participation in team sports, lifetime sports, meet events, club sports.

      2. Above average sport skill as demonstrated by individual success in the sport or sports.

      3. Positive attitude for sportsmanship, citizenship, fair play and honesty.

      4. Leadership contributions to group or team.

      5. Effort to improve group or team morale.

      6. Compliance with established rules and regulations.

      7. Ability to promote participation and sportsmanship.

After defining the award criteria, choose a panel of judges to select the deserving recipients. The judging process must be conducted in a professional manner to preserve credibility.

RECOGNITION PRESENTATIONS

Recognition presentations usually follow the conclusion of an activity or occur later in conjuction with a formal presentation, reception or banquet. Proponents of the first approach contend that the excitement level is at its highest immediately following an event, and recognition received then is more meaningful and significant to the recipient. On the other hand, recognition for individual outstanding achievement, unusual service and other significant awards are appropriate for special ceremonies distinct from an activity. Although the thrill of an achievement may have waned, the opportunity for the recipient to relive the experience with teammates, relatives, peers and other participants in the program is a rewarding one. Examples of such ceremonies include a seasonal or year-end party, recognition banquet, an annual sports dinner and a reception.

Regardless of when or how recognition is given, plan your presentations carefully. Make certain that the presentor is knowledgable about the purpose of the recognition. Whenever possible, select someone who has a positive rapport with the recipient or someone who witnessed the performance or event for which the recognition is being given. Keep the actual presentation brief and concise. Recipients and audience alike have little patience for long, drawn-out speeches or delays in the ceremonies.

Formal ceremonies, receptions or banquets require time and effort to assure that they will run smoothly. Approach these events from the same perspective as sport programs in terms of the effort needed to plan, organize, conduct, and evaluate them. It makes little sense to develop a sound recognition concept only to have the presentation aspect fail.

CONCLUSION

Our recognition recommendations by no means represent an exhaustive list of all techniques and strategies. They merely provide the programmer with a perspective from which to formulate creative ideas for an effective recognition system in a recreational sport environment. When we provide recognition for the efforts, contributions and accomplishments of participants and personnel we reinforce their involvement and promote goodwill toward our programs.

REFERENCES

Alderman, R. B. and Wood, N. L. "An Analysis of Incentive

Motivation in Young Canadian Athletes," *Canadian Journal of Sport Sciences.* 1976, Vol. 1.

Atkinson, J. W. *An Introduction to Motivation.* Princeton, New Jersey: Van Nostrand, 1964.

Cooper, K. H. *The Aerobics Way.* New York: Bantam Books, Inc.,1980.

Deci, E. L. "Effect of Externally Mediated Rewards on Intrinsic Motivation," *Journal of Personality and Sound Psychology.* 1971, Vol. 18, pp. 105–115.

Deci, E. L. *Intrinsic Motivation.* New York: Plenum Press, 1975.

Edginton, C. R., Compton, D. M. and Hanson C. J. *Recreation and Leisure Programming: A Guide for the Professional.* Philadelphia: Saunders College/Holt, Rinehart, and Winston, 1980.

Gerou, N. *Complete Guide to Administering the Intramural Program.* West Nyack, New York: Parker Publishing Co., Inc., 1976.

Harris, D. V. *Involvement in Sport: A Somatopsychic Rationale for Physical Activity.* Philadelphia: Lea and Febiger, 1973.

Hyatt, R. W. *Intramural Sport: Organization and Administration.* Saint Louis: C. V. Mosby Co., 1977.

Kleindienst, V. K. *The Recreational Sports Program: Schools. . . Colleges. . .Communities.* Englewood Cliffs; New Jersey: Prentice-Hall, Inc., 1978.

Leavitt, N. M. and Price, H. D. *Intramural and Recreational Sports for High School and College,* 2nd edition. New York: The Ronald Press, 1958.

Lepper, M. R. and Greene, D. *The Bitter Costs of Reward: New Perspectives on the Psychology of Human Motivation.* New York: John Wiley and Sons, 1978.

Means, L. E. *Intramurals: Their Organization and Administration,* 2nd edition. Englewood Cliffs; New Jersey: Prentice Hall, Inc., 1973.

Mueller, P. and Resnik, J. W. *Intramural-Recreational Sports: Programming and Administration,* 5th edition. New York: John Wiley and Sons, 1979.

Rokoz, F. M. *Structured Intramurals.* Philadelphia: W. B. Saunders, 1975.

Webster's New Collegiate Dictionary. Springfield, Massachusetts: G. and C. Merriam Co., 1959.

INDEX

DATE DUE
DATE DE RETOUR

FEB 1 8 1987			
MAR 2 4 1987			
FEB 2 9 1988			

LOWE-MARTIN No. 1137